Early Mississippi Records

Volume #4

Washington County

- 1860-1912 -

Compiled by:
Katherine Clements Branton
and Alice Wade

Southern Historical Press, inc.
Greenville, South Carolina

This volume was reproduced
from a personal copy located in
the Publishers private library

Please direct all correspondence and book orders to:
SOUTHERN HISTORICAL PRESS, Inc.
1071 Park West Blvd.
Greenville, SC   29611

Originally printed Leland, MS 1986
ISBN #978-1-63914-326-9
Printed in the United States of America

EARLY MISSISSIPPI RECORDS
WASHINGTON COUNTY

The time period of 1866-1875 was a troubled one for the conquered South. The State of Mississippi had suffered severe devastation in Gen.Grant's determined quest for supremacy on the Mighty Mississippi. Washington County,bordering on this River, had been under Federal rule since late 1862, and the County seat,Greenville, was burned in the Spring of 1863. After the fall of Vicksburg in July 1864, Federal troops moved en masse into the area. It was estimated that of the 10,000 occupying troops, 8000 were negroes.

The official Government was in the hands of the Reconstruction forces. While there is no indication in the court records covering this time that blacks were in control of the local offices, this was the pattern in other areas. Many former slaves held official positions, having had no training for these jobs. The State Legislature was faced with passing laws that would give the local whites and blacks protection from scalawags and do-gooders, yet still pass the scrutney of the Government Officials.

The financial outlook of the landowner was desperate and the countryside was innundated with blacks who had won their freedom and didn't know what to do with it. To magnify their problems, the crop years of 1866-1867 were disastrous. In 1866 it rained from early July until late fall; the army worm arrived in early August and ate everything in sight. Property mortgaged for the crop year 1866 had to be refinanced in order to produce another disaster in 1867, when flood waters were on the Delta as late as June. Again the army worm arrived in August to consume what little had been planted.

Foreclosures were frequent. Even some "Counting Houses" went bankrupt. Being broke was no longer a disgrace, but the common denominator of a desperate populace. Extreme measures were used to cause delay in order for the planters to raise more funds before the land and equipment passsed into the hands of the Bankers from New York,New Orleans,Kentucky,etc.

An influx of illiterate farms workers fruther clogged the already groggy economy. The Packets, or loose papers,in the Chancery Clerk's Office deal mainly with the local landowners who entered the 1860s in debt, and who never had a chance after that to fully redeem their land. Many of them resorted to the Equity Court,for protection. (K.B.)

EARLY MISSISSIPPI RECORDS
WASHINGTON COUNTY - VOL.4

TABLE OF CONTENTS

TITLE PAGE - WASHINGTON CO.----------------------------------i
TABLE OF CONTENTS--ii
GLOSSARY OF LEGAL TERMS & ABBREVIATIONS-------------------iii
DR.OFFUTTS LETTER---iiii,v
CHANCERY COURT RECORDS -(1866 - 1872)--------------------1 - 44
PROBATE PACKETS -(1871 - 1884) ---------------------------45 -116
EXCERPTS FROM "THE STOCKWELL PAPERS"(1890-1906) ---------117-137
WILL BOOK "2" (1894-1913)-------------------------------138-168
NATURALIZATION BOOK (1891-1906)----------------------------169
SOMMERS FUNERAL HOME RECORDS-(1892-1895)--------- ------170-172
GUARDIANSHIP BOOK "1"(1873 - 1913)---------------------173-185

CEMETERY RECORDS:
    GREENFIELD -Lake Washington-Pictures--------------------186
    MT.CARMEL - MAUD BRYAN PARK-----------------------------201
    ERWIN, LAMMERMOOR, COLDSPRINGS,COUNTY PAUPERS,-------202
    LINDEN, KEYSTONE, GREENVILLE GOLF COURSE---------------203
    MONTGOMERY FAMILY -AUBURN PLT., ------------------------204
    FERGUSON FAMILY,MOUND CEM.At STONEVILLE ---------------204
    YELLOW-FEVER CEMETERY----------------------------------205
    McKEONE FAMILY-- 206
    LOUGHBOROUGH PLT.,WILKERSON FAMILY --------------------207
    METCALFE FAMILY,PETERS-PETTIT FAMILY-------------------208
    LELAND-STONEVILLE--------------------------------------210
    LOCUST, MULBERRY PLT.----------------------------------220
    PAXTON FAMILY, ARCOLA BAPTIST CHURCHYARD--------------221
    ALDRIDGE-ROBERTSHAW PLOT-G'VILLE CEM.,----------------222
    RIVES FAMILY --222
    ARCOLA CEMETERY,---------------------------------------223
    WINGFIELD FAMILY---------------------------------------226
    HOLLANDALE CITY-------------------------- -------------227
    ALEXANDER-DREW-BAREFIELD FAMILY -----------------------235
    CLETONIA---236
    ALDRIDGE FAMILY-ESTILL, -------------------------------237
    SMITH FAMILY-ARCOLA/CASEY FAMILY-HOLLANDALE/DUPUY-MURPHY-238
    HUDDLESTON/ESTILL FAMILY/COLLIER FAMILY--------------239
    INDEX---240 - 257

WASHINGTON CO., MS.
GLOSSARY OF TERMS USED IN THE FOLLOWING SECTIONS OF CHANCERY COURT RECORDS AS TAKEN FROM THE POCKET DICTIONARY OF LEGAL WORDS BY JOHN J. KASAIAN, EDITED BY DOUGLES B.OLIVER,J.D.- A layman's guide to legalese.

ABSTRACT: The essence or summary
AFFIDAVIT: A written statment witnessed by an authorized officer of the court and made under oath.
ATTACHMENT: The lawful seizure (of property) by the court during a lawsuit in order to secure the property until controversy is resolved, so that the plaintiff can have recourse against it. If the defendant lives outside the state or territory where the court has jurisdiction, his property within jurisdiction of the court will be seized, and if he does not appear in court, the court gives the authority to dispose of the property to the plaintiff.
CHATTEL: A piece of property other than land or a building; personal property, including an animal.
COMPLAINANT: A party who files a complaint.
CONVEYANCE: The transference of title or property (usually real property) from one party to another.
CROSS COMPLAINT:(Bill of) A counter claim; a charge or claim by a defendant agst. the plaintiff.
DECREE: An announcement of a court's decision and the legal remedy to correct the situation.
DEED OF TRUST: (D/T) Definition taken from The Reshaping of Plantation Society by Michael Wayne-P.78: A Deed of Trust is identical to a mortgage, with the exception that the property in question is deeded to a third party for a nominal sum rather that to the lender. Should the debt not be paid, the third party is empowered to sell the property at public auction and give proceeds from the sale to the lender.
DEMUR: A formal objection
DEPOSITION: Sworn testimony, in writing, taken from a witness outside the courtroom.
EQUITY: A form of justice that is based on what is fair and just, as opposed to strict adherence to the written law.
FEMME SOLE: An unmarried female.
FEMME COVERT: A married female.
FIERI FACIAS: A court order commanding a Sheriff to seize the property of a debtor in order to pay off a debt.
GUARDIAN: A person appointed by the court to care for and manage the affairs of someone who is considered unable to take care of his own affairs.
GUARDIAN *ad litem*: A guardian appointed by the court to represent an infant and to defend him or her, or to bring an action in court in the infant's behalf.
INJUNCTION: An order by a judge commanding that a person perform or refrain from performing certain acts. Example: A court order forbiding the construction ... until zoning law is clarified.
INSOLVENT: A person without the means to pay his debts.
INSTRUMENT: A formal legal document such as a deed or bond
INTESTATE: Dying without leaving a valid will.
LIEN: A claim upon, or a right to retain possession of, property of another as security for some debt owed by the person to whom the property belongs.
QUIT CLAIM: The name given an agreement by which one party gives whatever rights he had in property to another.
SEQUESTER: (2) To place property that is under dispute into the hands of a third party to hold until the question of ownership is settled.
SURETY: A person who agrees to be responsible for the obligations of another should those obligations not be met.
TESTATORS: Someone who make or has made a will.

ABBREVIATIONS: ADM.-Administration or Administrator//ADM./Bd.-Administrators Bond.// DECD.- deceased//Est.-Estate//GRDN.-Guardian//GRDNP.-Guardianship//GRDNP./Bd.-Guardianship Bond.//L/A-Letters of Adm.//PET.-Petition//W.O.W.-Woodmen of The World.

Letter written to RUFUS KING, Cincinnati, Ohio.
BY DR. ZACK OFFUTT, Bolivar Co., Ms.
May 10th 1865

Dear sir;

    Your letter of the 5th of Mar. has reached me I suppose entirely by accident, being picked up by the river and sent me. We have no means of corresponding and you are entirely mistaken about cotton being got out easily. Maj. Hunt is the only man who saved any of consequence from the torch and he got it out with the greatest hazard through the protection of a gun boat and is the only man within my knowledge in this vicinity that can pay a cent.
    I will say that at commencement of this War, I owned a property estimated at $300,000 - that in '61, I raised 1000 bales of Cotton and all expense paid on it by previous crop. That every bale was burned by C.S. Government or incendiaries, that the crop of '62, some 200 bales, shared same fate, except a few bales left for family use, and 10 bales of that was taken by the U.S. Government, not by any order, but was turned over to it, as I learn, from Col. commanding expedition. In Apr. 1863, all the colored people (every one) was removed from my Plantation and every place in the neighborhood, with all my stock, teams, and many tools. The Col. commanding the expedition said these people were free and it was his duty to assist them to their freedom and protect them in it. That his orders were to remove them to Govt. Plantations near Military posts and get or put all the men into the army - to take everything that would be useful to the Govt. and destroy the rest. I was under arrest on board of one of the transports and when released at late hour of dark night found myself reduced to the suit I had on. I asked him if my treatment was not unusual and if there was any thing personal against me. He said No., but to the contrary. He had heard me spoken of as opposed to Seccession and a <u>Gentleman.</u> I am here with a few incumbered women who are lazy (and trifling men - 2 or 3 of them) who has been permitted to return, contending for a subsistance rather than be a pauper refugee.
    I write this with no disposition to complain of the acts of the government. I propose that I will convey back these lands to you - I have in no way incumbered them. I cleared as soon as I had purchased them all the arable land, leaving 200 ac. for fire wood and lumber, leaving the rail timber for 1st fencing. I was offered in the spring of '60, $19,000 for this 280 acres near by. $10,000 cash & 9 at 9 months. The offer was renewed in paper of my neighbors spring '61, for money loaned. I certaintly do not owe the $600 note which you recollect is conditional, and I had institued sale to compromise the Loan better(?).

I am broken down in fortune health and spirits and entirely unable to conjecture the influence of emancipation on the value of this country. You are better posted for that. I live as a hermit.

I should be glad to settle this matter during my life, which I am admonished will be short. One place every building is burned and all stabling crops-corn, forage of another, and no machinery around. If I were young I would make the effort to start over again, but old and broken down in health - will be content to make a living. But cant see how I am to do even that. I should like to hear from you again, but do not know how to advise you to address me.

Very Respectfully,
Z.C.OFFUTT

[Note: Dr.Offutt had bought some land in 1859, and given a series of notes for it. One became due in 1862, and apparently this is his answer to a request for payment. Later, his son Geo.W.Offutt, the exector of his father's estate, said his father had told him the title to sd.land was faulty, and he would forfeit his $3000 already paid out, and let the land in question go back. DR.OFFUTT was born 1807 probably in Scott Co.,Ky. and had been in Wash.Co.and then Bolivar Co. very early, by 1845. He borrowed money from his father-in-law, and three brothers to buy the Plantation Utopia. He married MARY ELIZABETH FORD, before coming to Miss. dau.of BENJAMIN B.FORD, who had presented his dau.with several slaves to take to their new homestead in Miss. Later Benjamin Ford also sent many of his own slaves to the Plantation in Miss. to be worked by Dr.Offutt.
At the time of the writing of this letter to Lawyer King,(1865) Dr.Offutt was 58 yrs. old, and living in Bolivar Co.,Ms. on a plantation called Glenora. He died in Jan. 1872. In a deposition, taken for a Chancery Court case #540 styled JANE DAND, CATHARINE MUNDELL vs GEO.W.OFFUTT, Exect.of Est.of Dr.ZACK OFFUTT, decd., the son, George W.Offutt states that at the time Gen. Sherman was trying to get through to Vicksburg, they had been warned of his coming, and he,George,had taken some of his father's papers and valuables, placed them in a tin box and had buried them in a cornfield. A negro named Watt Lewis dug them up, burned the papers and kept the money. Later they found the top of the box at Watt's house and he admitted the theft. This left their business affairs in even more of a tangle. K.B.]

WASH.CO.PKT.GLEANINGS
CHANCERY COURT RECORDS

Pkt.#155:WM.P.SANDERS,ROBT.P.HUNT. surviving partners vs WM.F.SMITH & THOMAS B. LEE,et al.:Original Bill filed 12 Sept.1866 by WARD SANDERS & HUNT (Robt.J.Ward now decd)as Complainants of New Orleans CHAS.G. McHATTON,JAS.A.McHATTON and his WIFE ELIZA; ROBT.M.LASHLEY;WM.F. SMITH - all of Wash.Co.,Ms and THOS.B.LEE,CORNELIUS FELLOWS,DANL.P. LOGAN,THOMPSON GREENFIELD all of New Orleans - the last named partners in the firm FELLOWS & CO. and JOS.CABBOT AND HENRY SENTER under the firm name of COBOT & SENTER (sic) - all defendants.Complts.state that defdt.Smith owes $45,000 in 7 notes beginning 1859 -made out to the McHattons in N.O. They understand that Jas.A.McHatton has left this country and resides outside the limits of the U.S. - leaving no funds.CHAS. McHatton owns a plantation in Wash.Co.,Ms.,now being leased and under the management of Robt.M.Lashley,an agent of Cabbot & Senter who have rented sd.plt. Chas.G.McHatton bought the plt.from Arnold Lashley in 1859 who has since decd. and whose sole heir and representative is ROBT.M. Lashley. The plantation lies in T15N,R8W - @1000 ac.//COMPLTS. had received a WRIT of ATTACHMENT in Circuit Ct.in 1861, after which the McHattons and Lashley conveyed a D/T to Smith and Lee as Trustees for FELLOWS & CO. Complts.claim this D/T was never filed,and is therefore not valid,and even though Smith and Lee have advertised the property for sale, Complts.seek an INJUNCTION to stop sale.//PKT.contains many doc.;Ones of interest - SUMMONS to deftds.12 Sept.1866 delivered in person to CHAS.G.MCHATTON, but a copy for ROBT.M.LASHLEY was left at his usual place of residence with Miss LOUISA GAYDEN ,he being absent.// INJUNCTION filed Nov.Term 1866//Deftds.file PROTESTS,with Mrs.Eliza McHatton and Chas.G.McHatton signing in Parish of Baton Rouge,La.

Pkt.#156:FARLEY,JUREY & CO. vs L.L.&S.P.TAYLOR
Orig.Bill for foreclosure filed 20 Sept.1866 by Complainants Harry W. Farley,Louis C.Jurey,Jno.T.Caldwell - merchants of New Orleans trading under the firm name of FARLEY,JUREY & CO. show that Littleton L.and Susan P.Taylor of Wash.Co. have made a mortgage to Robt.W.Durfey at the Counter of the Citizen Bank of La. for $35,000. Some of the notes were paid. Land mortgd.was SE1/4,Sec.29,NE1/4,Sec.32,T19N,R7W + L.1,3,5,Sec.5 & L.6 of Sec.6,T18N,R7W +E1/2,Sec.31,W1/2 SE1/4,Sec.32,T19N,R7W - 1300 ac. The Taylors answer,saying it is true they owe money on the land,and foreclosure is eminent. Sale is ordered for Jan.10,1867,&bought by Lewis (sic) C.Jurey for $26,000.

WASH.CO.PKT.GLEANINGS
CHANCERY COURT RECORDS

Pkt.#157:JOHN A.SCOTT vs WM.LITTLE,et al:Orig.Bill missing from PKT. Mortg.to JOHN A.SCOTT dated 20Jan.1859,made out from WM.LITTLE, BENJAMIN LITTLE,MONTGOMERY LITTLE,.//This suit filed 28 Sept.1866, when Scott states that he sold land in T18N,R8W in Wash.Co. to the Littles,for which they signed notes - now due - on 1178 acs. //Summons made out 1 Oct.1866,shows that the Sheriff of Wash.Co.Wm.G.Yerger,tried to serve the Littles and found that Montgomery and Benjamin Little are now dec. and that Wm.Little is a nonresident of Ms.Wm.Little of Shelby- ville,Tn.answers stating:They bought the land,but that both Benjamin and Montgomery have died intestate,unmarried,and without children,leaving brothers and sisters as follows,with Post Office as shown Mar.1867:
   WM.LITTLE, of Shelbyville,Tn.one of the orig.3 who bought the land.
   JOHN LITTLE - Wash.Co.,Ark.Fayetteville
   SAML.LITTLE - Lincoln Co.,Tn.
   EMILY LITTLE and her husb.ALFRED LITTLE - Shelbyville,Tn.Bedford Co.
   PATSY CHICLE and her husb.ALFRED CHICLE   "   "   "   "
   ELIZABETH TAYLOR - Also Shelbyville
   REBECCA DAVIS and her husb.Jos.Davis - somewhere in Ill.
No heirs appeared in court 20 Nov.1867,so the lands were sold toWm. Nugent for $1800 - land in T19N,R8W + T18N,R8W ,after having been previouly sold to Julius Varien for $250,and sale canceled when John Scott and Wm.Little protested the low price.

Pkt.159:S.P.BAILEY & WIFE vs GRANT A.BOWEN
SARAH A.E.BAILEY,late SARAH A.E.GRIFFITH and wife of RICHARD GRIFFITH now decd.has remarried to S.P.BAILEY,who exhibited the Orig.Bill against BOWEN,defendant.Orig.Bill filed Nov.Term1866 shows that as the widow of RICH.GRIFFITH,SARAH owned a tract of land in her own right -
  W1/2 SEC.8,all of SEC.9,L.1 in SEC.11;N1/2 SEC.12,T18N,R8W @1402 ac. Sarah avers that her previous husband,Griffith,now decd.,entered a con- tract with Grant A.Bowen on 7 Nov.1856 in Jackson,Ms. to sell him the above described land, and that Bowen has fallen behind in the payments. Bowen has been in possession of place,since purchase date.//Bowen asks permission to continue payments.//Case was appealed to High Court of Appeals - Case #11622.//Pkt. contains DEED - from BENJAMIN WHITFIELD and his wife LUCY E.of Hinds Co.,Ms."for love and affection to our daughter Sarah A.E.Griffith,wife, of Richard Griffith" ofHds.Co. Description matches that above. Both Rich.and Sarah A.E. sign 13 Feb.1856.

WASH.CO.PKT GLEANINGS
CHANCERY COURT RECORDS

PKT.#161:D.KELLY, a citizen of New Orleans vs JAMES T.ANDREWS
ALEXANDER D.KELLY shows in orig.bill that on 13 Apr.1859,he sold to
Andrews,then and now a resident of Ala,the following parcel of land in
Wash.Co.:SE1/4,SEC.8;SW1/4,SEC.9,T18N,R6W - W1/2 of S1/2 Sec.4;
  E1/2,Sec.8;W1/2of W1/2,Sec.9;E1/2&SW1/4,Sec.21,T17N,R6W
1360 ac.Seeks payment through the court.//Summons to Andrews,Nov.1866
sent to Montgomery Co.,Ala.

PKT.#162:Z.C.McGINTY vs TECUMSEH F.ROYALL,et al
Orig.Bill filed 17 Oct.1866 by ZYLPHIA C.McGINTY a resident of Ms.,Complt.
vs T.F.ROYALL,O.WINN,E.S.WINN,NATHL.G.NYE, and unknown heirs of
JEFFERSON J.HUGHS,decd. - Defdts. Complt.states that a mortgage was
made in Yazoo City 11 Dec.1858, on the following land in Wash.Co.:
  S1/2,Sec.15,N1/2 Sec.22,T16N,R3W - 640 ac.
1st payment went to J.J.HUGHS,the 2nd to N.G.NYE. HUGHS,who has since
died, endorsed his note over to McGINTY,who doesn't know whether any of
the other notes have been paid,but knows that his has not.//SUMMONS for
ROYALL,delivered to Warren Co.,Ms.to his wife Mrs.E.B.ROYALL - 27 Oct.
1866//Pkt.contains orig.mortg.(1858) showing Royall living in Yazoo Co.,
EMELINE S.WINN - wife of ORASAMUS WINN both of Yaz.Co.,Ms.//NYE
ANSWERS 13 May 1867,stating that McGinty is living in Jeff.Co.;Royall in
Warren Co.;Winns in Wash.Co. NYE files a CROSS BILL//14 Apr.1868 - the
Adms.of Z.C.McGINTY,who has died intestate,are ROBT.F.McGINTY and OSCAR
McGINTY who pursue the case.//SUMMONS Apr.1868-WINNS found in Wash.
Co.,ROYALL not found in Warren//Nov.1869,ROYALL sells his interest to the
WINNS and they state that they are aware of the lein on the property.//A
Commissioner is appointed by the court to decide the best way to settle
the matter; its report:
  To R.F.& OSCAR McGINTY,Adm.of Z.C.McGINTY----$3233.26
  To N.G.NYE   6,477.74
              Total owed $9,711.00
WINN ordered to pay or sell//May term 1870 - N.G.NYE bought 2/3rd
interest,W.R.TRIGG bought 1/3rd int.//Final decree - Aug.1870

PKT.#163:THOMAS REED vs S.MYRA SMITH,et al
Orig.Bill filed 23 Oct,1866 by THOS.REED,Complt.of Jeff.Co.,shows that
ABRAM SMITH,now decd.,but lately of Wash.Co.,mortgd.a piece of property
on 15 Dec.1860 to the late firm of HUGHS HYKESTER & CO.Desc.of sd.
property, - All of Sec.30,W1/2 Sec.29,Fract.of Sec.23,L.3,4 of Frac.Sec.24,
T19N,R9W - 1300 acs.Complt.names the heirs of ABRAM SMITH,decd. as -
S.MYRA SMITH his widow;EVELINA SMITH - a minor under 21;ALFRED

WASH.CO.PKT GLEANINGS
CHANCERY COURT RECORDS

C.SMITH;WM.L.NUGENT;ELEANOR NUGENT; AND ABRAM F.SMITH - the last 3 (Alfred,Eleanor,Abram)being under 21,all res.of Wash.Co.REED seeks foreclosure.//Pkt.contains the orig.mortg.and copies of the notes.//On Dec.22, 1866,the Defdts.seek a delay,stating that there has been no Adm. appointed for the SMITH Est.//May Term 1867,EVELINA has married E.J.COMSTOCK,and he is appt.Grd.to minors ABRAM,JR..and ELEANOR NUGENT,and is appt.the Adm.to SMITH's Est.//9 Nov.1868 land is sold for $15000 to THOS.REED.

PKT.#164:RICHARD S.DRONE,of Hds.Co. vs JACOB S.YERGER,of Wash.Co.
(Case appeared before JUDGE JACOB S.YERGER,presiding Judge of Chancery Court of Wash.Co.)Orig.Bill filed 26 Oct.1866,DRONE,Complt.states that he held 2 promissory notes made to W.S.JONES or bearer - dated 9 Feb.1859 @8%.made by J.S.YERGER .JONES has sold out his interest - DRONE is sole holder by 1866. In 1860 the bearer of the notes was STEWART FISK,who filed suit to collect them,then endorsed sd.notes over to DRONE. All pro.-ceedings concerning this case have been lost in Wash.Co., and the principal and interest are now due.//Pkt.contains orig.mortg.signed in Vicksburg (1859) by J.S.YERGER,W.YERGER,JAMES RUCKS.//DECREE - Dec.18,1871 - "Ordered by the court this case be dismissed for want of prosecution."

PKT.#165;HARVEY W.WALTER & FRIDONIA WALTER,his wife - Marshall Co.Ms. vs JOHN T.COURTNEY,surviving Partner - Wash.Co.
Orig.Bill filed 6 Nov.1866 - Walter,Complt.states that on 13 Sept.1859,he sold to the defendant - COURTNEY and E.A.WALLIS,now decd.,who were partners @205 ac.in Tunica Co. + land in Coahoma Co. - sale price was $106,750,of which some was pd.in cash,with remaining $90,000 in (10) promissory notes due ea.yr.beginning1861.Security on the notes was signed by J.S.YERGER and W.E.DANIEL. The orig.mortg.shows that the sale was for land,improvements on it,+ slaves. The note due 1863 was paid in Confederate currency .During the War,everything was destroyed with nothing left of mortgd.property but the land.//A DEMURRER,filed by the Attorney for the Defendant,states that the heirs at law of E.A.WALLIS should have been made partners to suit,and that since the slaves have all been emancipated, the amount that has been paid covers the cost of the land.//Motion to override the Demurrer//AMENDED BILL filed Nov.22,1867 shows:WALLIS decd.insolvent,and no Adm.has been appointed for his estate..Heirs at law of E.A.WALLIS are listed as:MARIAN M.WALLIS - Salerno Landing,Ark.
    WILLIAM A.WALLIS;JOHN A.WALLIS;SARAH S.DANIELS over 21 yrs.
    JULIA A.MORRIS,MARY THOMPSON,ERMELINE THOMPSON,minors
    ANTHONY MORRIS - Philadelphia,Pa.   (more)

WASH.CO.PKT GLEANINGS
CHANCERY COURT RECORDS

PKT.#165:WALTER vs COURTNEY,cont.
All from Wash.Co.,Ms.unless otherwise stated.//Commissioners Report 6
May 1868 shows SUMMONS delivered to SARAH S.DANIELS,JULIA A.MORRIS
in person in Wash.Co.and the one earmarked for W.A.WALLACE and John
Wallis given to SARAH S.DANIELS at usual place of abode.//Oct.1868
shows MARION M.WALLIS's address is Moro Bayou,Ark. and ANTHONY MORRIS
is living in Pine Bluff,Ark.//23 Feb.1871 - death of SARAH E.DANIELS,
leaving as her surviving heirs - LEE DANIELS,WADE DANIELS,FRANKLIN
DANIELS - minors under 21.//May 1871 the DANIEL children's address is
Little Rock,Ark.;Marion is back in Salerno Landing,Ark.,Tony is back in
Philadelphia.//Apr.1872 - suit still active - no final decree given here.

PKT.#166:LEROY P. PERCY VS W.P.PERCY,et al
Orig.Bill filed 6 Nov.1866 by LEROY P.PERCY,Complt.,shows that on 1Feb.
1859, he sold to J.WALKER PERCY and WM.A.PERCY all his interest in a
plantation called "THE PERCY PLACE",+ slaves. For payment,Wm.A. and
J.Walker gave a series of promissory notes. Leroy also states that in the
original mortg.,part of the land description was omitted. - L.1,2,5,6 OF
S.27,T18N,R7W and all the parties involved intended it to be included.
Furthermore the notes have not been paid,and since making out the mortg.
J.WALKER PERCY has died - leaving a widow FANNY E.PERCY and 1 child
MARIA W.PERCY. In his will,J.Walker appointed his wife,Fanny E.exctx.and
Grdn.of minor child Maria,but now Maria is over 18.In May 1859,Fanny
E.gave a relinquishment of dower rights to Leroy P. for her share of the
property. Complt.asks that the defendants in this case be listed as WM.A.
PERCY,as surviving partner,with FANNY E.&MARIA.PERCY//ANSWER: of
WM.A.PERCY who states that he paid $2800 interest on the notes in 1860 +
another $500 in 1865. He also states that he is a resident of Wash.Co.,a
married man with a family,and if sale of the land in question is forced,he
is entitled to 240 ac.of land exempted for homestead.(Note:HOMESTEAD
ACT PASSED BY LEGISLATURE IN 1866)//Commissioner's report,filed by
Haycraft,shows amt.owed $50,815.74 -Nov.1866//Pkt.contains a copy of
the Will of J.WALKER PERCY - written 29 July 1864 in which he names his
wife FANNY E. and dau.MARIA, and brothers LEROY P.PERCY,WM.A.PERCY//
ANSWER of FANNY E.PERCY,widow of J.WALKER PERCY,decd.,who admits to
all things as set out in orig.bill,but states that her residence is on said
land,and as head of a household she claims exemption allotted by law if
land is forced into sale.Filed 13 Nov.1866.Sworn before Justice of the
Peace R.H.HOWARD,of Cooper Co.,Mo. Land desc.of "THE PERCY PLACE":

WASH.CO.PKT GLEANINGS
CHANCERY COURT RECORDS

PKT.#166:PERCY vs PERCY
   S1/2 of Sec.22;all of part N1/2 of Sec.22 lying S of the line of R.L.
   DIXON;L.2,3,4,6,Sec.23;L.3 Sec.26 + S1/2 of N1/2 Sec.21;S1/2 of
   NE1/4 Sec.20, all in T18N,R7W
Land sold at public auction 15 Apr.1867 and bought by LEROY P.PERCY for $16,000.
(Note:From "LANTERNS ON THE LEVEE" BY WILL A.PERCY - [b.1885/d.1942 - Grandson and namesake of the Wm.A.PERCY named in suit above]:The author speaks in reference to the hard times facing the southern families after the War."By the time of the surrender,Uncle Walker had died,Uncle Lee (Leroy) had been stricken with paralysis and when Fafar(gr.father Wm.A.Percy) the youngest and soldier of the three,returned,it was to a diminished and penniless household of which he found himself the head and the breadwinner....(he rode his horse to Greenville) and hung out a shingle announcing to the bankrupt countryside that W.A.PERCY had opened offices for the practice of law." Unquote. In the Will of LEROY P.PERCY - Probated Wash.Co.1882, he leaves everything to his surviving brother,WM.A.PERCY.)

PKT.#168:JAMES A.KING vs CHARLES VERNON & JOSEPH TINKOR
Orig.Bill filed 16 Nov.1866:KING, the Complt.,states that on 1 June1866,the defendants - VERNON and TINKOR - leased 'SMITHFIELD PLT.'to grow cotton. VERNON was resident and managing partner,and Tinkor resided in Vicksburg. KING claims that VERNON told him he had the aurthority to act for the partnership,and entered an agreement in writing in order to cultivate 102 ac.of MRS.HALSEY'S Plt.in Wash.Co. adjoining "Smithfield Plt.",KING was to supply labor for "Smithfield" + $500,while VERNON supplied tools,equip., etc. - sharing the proceeds. That fall VERNON sold out his interest in the agreement to TINKOR for $5000.KING states that TINKOR is ginning the cotton and shipping it out of Wash.Co.,out of the jurisdiction of this court, and he claims that 50 bales of the cotton are his. KING seeks an injunction to stop the sale of the crops,until the matter is settled.//Pkt.contains copies of lease notes made out to CHAS.H.SMITH and JOS.TINKER for rent of 21ac.on MRS.HALSEY'S "RIVER PLACE",1866,signed by D.D.JACKSON// INJUNCTION prohibited the removal of any crops - KING posted bond.//AFF-IDAVIT of BEN ROACH who states that he had a verbal agreement withCHAS VERNON,made on 1 Oct.1865 concerning "Smithfield Plt." and 135 ac.of his home place in Wash.Co.//AFFIDAVIT of DR.D.D.JACKSON,agt.oF MRS.ANN D. HALSEY,gives details of lease to land below Greenville. He further states that VERNON came to see him at the residence of his(Jackson's)Mother - MRS.HALSEY,and VERNON said he had turned everything over to TINKER.

WASH.CO.PKT.GLEANINGS
CHANCERY COURT RECORDS

PKT.#169:ABAT & GENERIS vs A.J.PHELPS & MARY B.PHELPS,his wife - residents of Ky. Orig.Bill filed 17 Nov.1866,by Complts. Joseph Rens Abat and Louis G.Generis who state that MARY B. is sole heir of Estate of her father HENRY W.VICK,late of Wash.Co.,who decd.intestate;MARY B. is also the sole heir of her Mother MRS.SARAH VICK,who has also died. MRS.VICK was possessed of a large landed Est.in Wash.Co.,Ms.+ a large personal Est. that she had conveyed in 1850 in trust to her husband,Henry W.Vick to be used for the benefit of their children - HENRY VICK,GEORGE VICK,ANNE VICK,MARY B.VICK,now PHELPS. In order to run the Plantations,HENRY W. VICK drew a note in New Orleans on 23 Jan.1861 for $2284.71,for which he gave a mortgage. All the children are dead now,but MARY B. They all died intestate,unmarried,and leaving no issue,and no Administrator has been appointed for their Estates. ABAT & GENERIS want an Adm.ofsd.Ests.apptd. and the matter of the debt satisfied.//SUBPOENA:delivered to Dr.Phelps at Nitta Yuma delivered in person - Jan.1867.// SUMMER of 1867 an AFFIDAVIT signed by THOMAS W.COLESCOTT,M.D.,a practicing Physcian ofLouisville,Ky,who states that due to yellow fever in Memphis and Vicksburg,he felt MR.& MRS.PHELPS could not come to Greenville until "a very decided change takes place in the temperature,bringing killing frosts"(which would be)@25 Oct.1867.//A.J.PHELPS answers from Louisville,Ky.verifying Dr.COLESCOTT's statement.Further states,that the merchandise that ABAT & GENERIS are seeking payment for was partially for HENRY W'S personal use.Seeks a continuance.//Nov.1868 - case dismissed.Death of JOSEPH RENO ABAT proven.

PKT.#170:JOHN R.BLANCHARD vs E.P.BYRNE :Orig.Bill filed 22 Dec.1866, BLANCHARD,Complt.,states that on 2 Apr.1866 he entered partnership with EDWARD P.BYRNE,defdt., in a Wharfboat named "Glendale",valued at $6,000 to be located at Greenville,Ms.1/2of proceeds were to go to Byrne who was to pay1/2 of the costs.If BYRNE defaulted,his1/2 was to revert to BLANCARD. Original cost of the hull and alterations to outfit the Wharfboat for merchandising,etc.+ expenses for bringing same from Louisville,Ky + Insurance came to $6,550. The "Glendale" was also supposed to serve as a hotel,which entailed additional expense.BLANCHARD claimed his partner developed an overbearing and domineering spirit and it increased....heaping abuse on your orator and threatening his life. He further accused BYRNE of keeping a separate and secret set of books for the business. BLANCHARD seeks dissolution of partnership and demands that the private books be brought before the court.//INJUNCTION :preventing BYRNE from conducting further business //DECREE to turn everything over to JONAS PIERCE,as receiver appointed by the court,to decide what to do.//

WASH.CO.PKT.GLEANINGS
CHANCERY COURT RECORDS

PKT.#171:EDWARD T.& WM.W.WORTHINGTON,JR.of Wash.Co.,Ms. vs ALEXANDER C.CAPERTON,ROBERT MINISTER of Wash.Co. and ROBERT McGREGOR & -------- McGREGOR res.of Memphis,Tn. the last 2 under the firm name of ROBT.McGREGOR & CO. Orig.Bill filed Dec.Term1866 by WORTHINGTONS,Complts.,who state that they own land in Wash.Co. on the Miss.River known as "The Maryland Plantation":
   L.3,4,5,6,7,8 Sec.2; 147 ac.in L.1,2 Sec.1; 56 ac.of Sec.2;
   Lot1,Sec.18;all in T14N,R9W + L.4,5 Sec.25;T15N,R9W
The WORTHINGTON Brothers leased this land to CAPERTON and MCGREGOR & CO. - Jan.1866 to Jan.1867 -for $10,000 rent - 1/2 up front and the other 1/2 to be paid Jan.1867+stock,etc. MINISTER was the agent for CAPERTON. The defendants paid $5,000 and took possession.The WORTHINGTON's claim that the leasees removed everything out of the state except @40 mules and some horses.The Complts.seek a restraining order before the defts.remove the rest of the stock.//So granted.//Pkt.contains a D/T showing CAPERTON resided in Tunica Co.,Ms.1866.

PKT.#173:RICHARD TEN BROECK and his wife PATSY D.,THOMAS J.KENNEDY and wife KATE M.;MARY MARTIN ANDERSON vs JOHN T.COURTNEY;Orig.Bill filed Feb.Term 1867,with MARY MARTIN ANDERSON suing by her Guardian and best friend W.GEORGE ANDERSON + other named Comlpts.who state that on 8 Dec.1843,J.L.MARTIN,Executor of Last Will and Testament of JOHN F.ANDERSON,decd.,sold the following tract of land lying on Deer Creek in Wash..Co.Ms.NW 1/4 Sec.7,T18N,R8W - 160 ac.@$12 per ac.for$1920,for which COURTNEY,defdt.,gave 4 promissory notes - 2 of which are still due.Complts.further state that J.L.MARTIN has "long since decd."and the entire estate of JOHN F.ANDERSON,decd.,was administered except for these 2 (unpaid) notes. The sole heirs of JOHN F.ANDERSON are your orator(Rich. Ten Broeck),PATSY D.BROECK,KATE M.KENNEDY and MARY M.ANDERSON.// ANSWER of COURTNEY,claiming the title is cloudy.//COURT orders COURT-NEY to pay up or sell.//Pkt.contains original Deed from JOHN L.MARTIN of Jeff.Co.,Ky,Exect.of Est.of JOHN F.ANDERSON,decd.,who sells land in question to COURTNEY,then of Bolivar Co.,Ms.-dated 8 DEC.1843 //Comm.Report by HAYCRAFT states that COURTNEY now owes $2004.60, 20 Nov.1867// Sale ordered//JANE E.COURTNEY bought it Jan.1868 for $1817.

PKT.#175:OLIVER T.MORGAN of Wash.Co. vs
WM.WARREN,Adm.;WM.L.NUGENT,Trustee,et al
Orig.Bill filed 2 Mar.1867.The defendants are listed asWM.WARREN,Adm. with Will attached of JOHN T.WARREN,decd.;PHIL WARREN,resident of

WASH.CO.PKT.GLEANINGS
CHANCERY COURT RECORDS

PKT.#175:MORGAN vs WARREN,et al,cont.
Illinois;AGNES WARREN,res.of Ark.;and WM.L.NUGENT,surviving Trustee; ANDREW CARSON,Shrf.of Wash.Co.,Ms.and Adm.of all the worldy goods,etc.of JOHN F.WARREN,late of ----Co.of Ark.MORGAN,Complt.,states that on 15 Nov.1860,he bought the following land lying in Wash.Co.,Ms.from JOHN F.WARREN.(since decd.):

    400 ac.in Sec.27,adjoining Sec.24,known as "The Percy Tract",leaving 240 ac.of Sec.27 to SAML.WORTHINGTON + 40 ac. being so much of Sec.21as lies in front of sd.Sec.27: L.2,3, Sec.25;E1/2 of L.1,Sec.20; 40 ac. in a triangle out of SW Corner of Sec.20; L.1,2,3, Sec.19 - all in T15N,R9W

The sale price was $63,000,for which MORGAN gave prom.notes,putting up the above land + personal property. He later signed a D/T withWM.L.NUGENT and ABRAM F.SMITH,now decd., as Trustees,should he(MORGAN) default on payments. Then JOHN F.WARREN died in Ark.,his place of residence,leaving surviving him,his widow,AGNES F.WARREN,one of the forenamed defdts.but no children.ANDREW CARSON was the Adm.for the Wash.Co.,Ms.partof the Est.of JOHN F.WARREN.The Will of JOHN F.WARREN,appointed WM.WARREN Executor,and MORGAN wants the Court to make Wm.WARREN produce sd. Will,claiming same will show that WARREN never had in his possession but 1 of the prom.notes signed by MORGAN - the last and 4th for $18,600,due 1 Jan.1864. MORGAN said he has pd.the rest and that JOHN F.WARREN had endorsed the 4th note to the Bank of La. MORGAN said he had pd.it off in N.O. when it came due.MORGAN continues his plea,by stating that he then took all 4 paid notes and placed them in a private drawer at his residence in Wash.Co.,and during his absence from home a "Military force commanded by Gen.ELLET appeared and entered the residence of your orator,wickedly and feloniously removed said documents".At best Morgan hoped the thief would destroy sd.notes,upon finding them worthless to him(the thief) but some how WM.WARREN wound up with them,and MORGAN suspects that he paid a sum of money for them. Wm.WARREN then delivered sd.notes to Trustee WM.L.NUGENT,who has since advertised sd.land for sale 4 Mar.1867. Morgan further claims that WM.WARREN's position on the notes is that they were paid in Confederate Treasury Notes,and were therefore invalid. WM.WARREN and PHIL WARREN are nephews of the decd.- JOHN F.WARREN. MORGAN asks the Court to compel Wm.WARREN to show how he got sd.notes,how much he pd.for them,and that the defdts.be restrained from any proceedings in this matter until it is settled.//ANSWER of WM.L.NUGENT,Trustee,filed 23 Mar. 1867,who states that at the time of JOHN F.WARREN's death in Apr.1863, WARREN was the holder of all the notes,that they were not pd.in Conf.Trea. Notes or of any other kind; that MORGAN rented out the land in question for 1864, to '67 for $10,000 per yr.and the WARREN heirs want an accounting.

WASH.CO.PKT.GLEANINGS
CHANCERY COURT RECORDS

PKT.#175:MORGAN vs WARREN,cont.//ANSWER of WM.WARREN,Exect. of Est. of JOHN F.WARREN,decd.-filed 29 Apr.1867-states that at one time,JOHN F..WARREN held all of sd.notes,but at the time of his death,he held only 1, and that MORGANS claim of "theft" was ridiculous!//There is no Will of JOHN F.WARREN in Pkt.,- Inventory is included.//NUGENTS Answer becomes a CROSS BILL//On 23 Nov.1867,MORGAN did not answer to CROSS BILL and the INJUNCTION was dissolved.(Note:Impossible to tell whether name is JOHN I or F WARREN. The Will of JOHN F.WARREN is found in PROBATE PKT. #174 and abst.in EARLY MISSISSIPPI RECORDS-WASH.CO.-Vol.III -p.149)

PKT.#177:JAMES S.GUIGNARD,Adm. vs THOMAS SHELBY
(Note:Most of the documents are missing from this folder.)Orig.Bill missing.DECREE 22 Nov.1867 orders sale of property//DEED 17 Jan.1868 - W.A.HAYCRAFT,Comm.of Chancery Court of Wash.Co.,Ms. and JAMES S. GUIGNARD,Adm.of Est.of JOHN A.SCOTT,decd. Land in a dispute between SHELBY and GUIGNARD is sold at public auction for $250 to GUIGNARD: NE1/4 and E1/4 of NW 1/4 S.33,T19N,R8W// In Nov.1868,the same land was sold to heirs of JOHN A.SCOTT,decd.-SARAH E.SCOTT,FANNIE SCOTT, CAROLINE GIBBS for $2,000 which they turned over to JOHN A.MILLER.

PKT.#179:ALFRED B.CARTER vs C.A.BROWN and C.H.TUPPER
Orig.Bill filed May Term 1867:CARTER,Complt., a resident of Va. vs Defdts.BROWN of Ark.,and TUPPER of Wash.Co.,Ms. CARTER states that on 21 Sept.1860,he owned land in Wash.Co.,Ms.:
   1 L.located on NE1/4 of Sec.5;W1/2 of E1/2 of Sec.4 @220 ac.
   + 1 L.lying adjacent in NW1/4 of Sec.4 - @145 ac.:all in T19N,R7W
CARTER sold sd.land to TUPPER and BROWN for $2624,keeping a lein .Notes have never been paid.//Also Original DEED conveyed by ALFRED B.CARTER and his wife ELIZABETH H. of Fauquier Co.,Va. to C.H.TUPPER and C.A.BROWN, a res.ofNapoleon,Ark.//Land sold to A.B.CARTER 22 Feb.1871

PKT.#180:WM.MASON WORTHINGTON,res.of Wash.Co.,Ms.vs DEAN ADAMS & GAFF,et al Orig.Bill filed 22 Mar.1867 by WORTHINGTON,Exect.of WILL of SAMUEL WORTHINGTON,decd. ,Complt.,vs THOMPSON DEAN,JOHN D.ADAMS, THOMAS GAFF - merchants and partners in DEAN ADAMS & GAFF of N.O. - Wm.M. WORTHINGTON states that he is the son of SAML.WORTHINGTON,who died Nov.1866 while on a business trip to Washington D.C. In Feb.1866, Samuel had gone to New Orleans and borrowed $10,000 with additional funds to be advanced during the crop season - not to exceed $8,933. Wm.M.feels that Samuel was charged an exhorbitant amt.of interest,but Saml.went on and made a D/T to THOS.H.HUNT,a Trustee ,with the PLT.

WASH.CO.PKT.GLEANINGS
CHANCERY COURT RECORDS

PKT.#180:WORTHINGTON vs DEAN ADAMS GAFF,cont.//"REDLEAF" as collateral.In the WILL of SAML.,Wm.M.was named Exect.,but the said WILL has not been probated because the witnesses are all non-residents of Wash.Co.,Ms.and 2 are from out of State,and he has been unable to collect assets belonging to his father's Est.or pay his debts. Wm.M.further states that his father - SAMUEL- had anticipated making 500 bales of cotton that yr.,but actually made only 23*, and then he died without leaving any means within reach of your orator to pay off the debts. But DEAN ADAMS & GAFF refuse to allow a delay and insist on selling the mortgd.property. WM.M. seeks an INJUNCTION in EQUITY Court to stop foreclosure measures until the WILL of SAML. is probated.//PKT. contains D/T from SAML.and AMANDA (his wife)WORTHINGTON to DEAN ADAMS & GAFF-filed Wash.Co.22 Mar.1867 with THOS.H.HUNT as Trustee - Land description for "REDLEAF PLT.":
    S1/2 Sec.32;NE1/4 Sec.31;both in T17N,R7W@480 ac.+S1/2 Sec.37,
    T17N,R8W - 320 ac.+S1/2 and NW1/4 Sec.28,T17N,R8W - 480ac.
INJUNCTION allowed and WM.M.posts bond May 1867//PKT. contains WILL of SAML.WORTHINGTON(Abst.EMR VOL.I,p.93) filed 22 Mar.1867,Wash.Co.,Ms. names wife AMANDA,now residing on"Willowby Plt."and child. WM.MASON, MARY G.,AMANDA,SAML.MASON WORTHINGTON.*(Note:There was a complete crop failure in all of Miss.for the year 1866 and 1867 was nearly as bad. In 1866 it started raining in July and continued all fall,with the army worms moving in and destroying everything in sight. The following May 1867,when the financial plight of all farmers,bankrupted by the War, was in fearful jepodardy,the flood stayed on the Miss.Delta land until early summer. Again the invasion of army worms,and foreclosures were eminent.Saml.Worthington was 76 yrs.old at the time of his death.)

PKT.181:<u>JACOB BARKER,Exect. of Est.of ELIZABETH BARKER,decd. vs R.L.SIMS;CHARLES SIMS;W.R.SIMS;JOHN H.SIMS;ROBT.B.SIMS - Heirs at law of WM.R.SIMS,decd. & ELIZABETH SIMS widow of sd.WM.R.SIMS;MOSES PHARIS,Shrf.of Wilkerson Co.,Ms.Adm.of Est.of sd.WM.R.SIMS - all of whom are res.of Wilk.Co.+ JOHN P.DILLINGHAM,A.C.HOLT citizens of N.O. + SAML.TAYLOR,A.G.PAXTON - cit.of Wash.Co.,Ms.;R.G.SIMS,WM.E.SIMS and ELIZABETH A.SIMS - heirs at law of JOHN H.SIMS,decd.;with WM.E.SIMS being Adm.to Est.of JOHN H.SIMS;+ G.G.SIMS,LEANOR SIMS,NANCY SIMS- heirs at law of CHAS.SIMS,decd.and PHILADELPHIA SIMS - widow and Adm. of CHAS.SIMS,decd. R.G. and G.G.SIMS are res.of Wash.Co.</u>
Orig.Bill filed by BARKER,filed 31 Mar.1869, states that his wife ELIZABETH died 1863,testate.In Jan.1855,before her death, she sold an undivided 1/3rd interest in 6,321 ac.called "Sligo Plt." in Wash.Co.,Ms. - located in T17N,R7W - to 3 SIMS brothers - WM.R,JOHN H.,CHARLES(except

WASH.CO.PKT.GLEANINGS
CHANCERY COURT RECORDS

PKT.#181:BARKER vs SIMS,et al://a portion sold to MRS.LOUISA N.YOUNG - @81ac.)-In 1857,ELIZABETH sold another undivided 1/3rd to A.C.HOLT(who filed a CROSS BILL).Complt.states that the 3 SIMS Bros.are all dead,leaving heirs,but BARKER says their ests.are all insolvent. HOLT says he has pd.for his 1/3rd int.//From other documents in Pkt. - the SIMS had sold off portions of sd.Plt to ANDREW PAXTON in 1858;some to DILLINGHAM in 1859 - "the Black Bayou Tract";WM.R.SIMS DEEDS all of his part to WM.E.SIMS in 1865//Pkt.contains orig.Bill of Sale from MISTRESS ELIZABETH HAZARD wife of JACOB BARKER,of New Orleans to WM.R.SIMS//EDWARD BARKER presented the mortg.note to the Bank in N.O.,but no funds existed to pay same.//COMM.reports defdts.owe $6,508.75-sale ordered-20 May,1869.

PKT.#183:WM.E.SMITH vs V.F.P.ALEXANDER,Adm. & A.B.CARSON
Orig.Bill filed 1 Apr.1867 by SMITH of Wash.Co.,Ms.,Complt.,stating that V.F.P. is the Adm.of Est.of AMOS ALEXANDER,decd. from whom SMITH borrowed $3000 in 1856,and still owes.SMITH claims he has pd.//

PKT.#186A:BIRKHEAD & HOFFMAN vs F.G.WALCOTT,et al
(Note:Very fat Pkt.with many documents missing)Case heard before Judge J.S.YERGER: Orig.Bill filed 20 Mar.1867 by Complts.JOHN H.BIRKHEAD and CHARLES HOFFMAN,citizens of the State of Maryland,who show that on 18 Jan.1866,T.G.WALCOTT,a cit.of Wash.Co.,Ms.,applied for (crop)loan,claiming to hold a 7 yr.lease on 200 ac.of cleared land,belonging to NELSON T. WARREN,a cit.of Warren Co.,Ms. The loan was for $15,000 in return for 225 bales of cotton - to be delivered at certain designated points on Ms.River at specific times.WALCOTT mortg.his lease,his equipment + stock,+ 1 note signed by NELSON T.WARREN . The mortg.was supposedly filed as required by law,and properly recorded in Wash.Co. and a copy mailed to the Complts. The Complts.never received their copy,presuming it to be lost in the mails. The Complts.state that the mortg.should have included a conveyance clause which Clerk of Wash.Co. omitted in recording the sd.document. They then charge WALCOTT with "flagrant fradulent acts" and accuse him of shipping 100 bales of cotton to New Orleans,but never putting same in the account of BIRKHEAD & HOFFMAN. They also charge that WALCOTT entered into a conspiracy with NELSON T.WARREN and B.C.WALCOTT,T.G.'S wife,to defraud Complts.by releasing WARREN from orig.lease and then placing all equip., etc.in T.G.'s wife's name. Complts.state that WARREN and WALCOTT were "near relatives".Also named as defendant is DR.GREENLEE who bought some of the stock in question. Complts.then proceed to try to show that all assets of MRS. BETTIE C.WALCOTT were actually her husbands'. (more)

WASH.CO.PKT.GLEANINGS
CHANCERY COURT RECORDS

PKT.#186:BIRKHEAD& HOFFMAN /WALCOTT,cont.ANSWER of T.G.WALCOTT, filed 14 May 1867. He denies applying for loan,stating that the Complts. approached him at his residence on Deer Creek 18 Jan.1866 and offered to lend him money for crops on land owned by NELSON T.WARREN in return for 225 bales of cotton. Respondent agreed,executing a mortg. The anticipated price of cotton for fall of 1867 was @40¢ per lb.At that price the Complts. would more than double their money.WALCOTT further vows that the mortg. was prepared by the Complts.and their solicitors and if there was an omission in reference to the crop being part of it,it was their fault and not his. WALCOTT charges that the Complts. delayed payments at crucial times..i.e. Once WALCOTT went to Ga. to procure labor,and had to abandon his plans because the money had not been deposited.The money came so late that WALCOTT insisted that BIRKHEAD go to Ga. to get the labor,"which he never did entirely" bring only 20 hands. WALCOTT denies that any part of the crop was mortg. Upon inspection of the crop in Nov.1866,BIRKHEAD could see it would fall short of anticipated amount,and they then agreed WALCOTT should sell whatever he could to liquidate his debt.He then proceeded to sell 100 bales of cotton + other things.WALCOTT also stated that in the meantime his wife BETTIE C.(HARRIS) WALCOTTdied.//14 July 1867 WALCOTT seeks dismissal//INTERROGATION of Witnesses for the Defense (Judge C.C.SHACKLEFORD is now Judge of 3rd Dist.,Judge J.S. YERGER having decd.14 July 1867 in Warren Co.,Ms.)ANSWER of N.T.WARREN who states "he knows nothing of this matter."//ANSWER of A.G.PAXTON who reported that T.G.WALCOTT operated a plantation in Floyd,Carroll P., La.in 1861. That WALCOTT is seeking to separate his Est.from that of his wife,now decd. PAXTON stated that WALCOTT left La.in 1865.//DEPOSITION: by GEORGE W. VAUGHN - May 1868,who states that he was a partner of MRS. Walcott's in purchase & sale of goods(in Plantation Commissary)beginning 27 Mar.1867. He has no knowledge of where she got the funds to back him.All his arrangements were made with Mr.WALCOTT.//DEPOSITION of THOS. H.HILL-May Term 1868-taken at the office of DIXON & PERCY in Greenville 24 Apr.1866 Hill says he knew of $15000 loan and of the sale of one of the mules.Testyfying as to the financial means of WALCOTT,HILL states that:"Walcott came to my neighborhood (on Deer Creek near present Hollandale)to the best of my recollection,bringing with him 3 mules and 3 horses - one of these claimed by his little son as given him by a soldier."That horse died, and another horse died last winter". R.P.HARRIS of Warren Co.,Ms.gave a negro man to MISTRESS'WALCOTT. When WALCOTT came to Deer Creek after the War,I heard him say the negro had been sold and proceeds of the sale
(more)

WASH.CO.PKT.GLEANINGS
CHANCERY COURT RECORDS

PKT.#186A,cont.BIRKHEAD vs WALCOTT:
invested in cotton. MRS.WALCOTT came to Deer Creek the following June and corroborated this - all before the transaction with BIRKHEAD. HILL stated that WALCOTT also had a gold note. In 1866 WALCOTT only made between 90 and 140 bales of cotton, and this was their only source for money. "I (HILL) live a quarter mile from them,was intimate with them and WARREN." I heard WALCOTT tell WARREN the mortg.would not stand up in court. Apparently BIRKHEAD had succeeded in getting a court order to stop sale of the crop,etc.,for HILL said,that after the INJUNCTION,13 more bales were shipped out by A.B.GLOVER (Agent of WALCOTT's) under different labels,down Deer Creek, on the Steamboat "Bierce".//Under CROSS EXAMINATION,HILL stated that the gold note was MRS.WALCOTT'S, that at one time @1857 or 8,she owned 6 negroes + a small tract of land from her father's Est. HILL also said he heard WALCOTT say he never intended paying the note due BIRKHEAD & HOFFMAN.(See next PKT.)

PKT.186B: BIRKHEAD & HOFFMAN VS T.G.WALCOTT,et al
(NOTE: This is a continuance of the Pkt.186A above.) Additional defendants are named as NELSON T.WARREN and his wife SARAH LUCINDA; T.G.WALCOTT and wife BETTIE C.;THOMAS H.HILL and wife -----; and THOMAS HILL'S son,unnamed. Land description of mortg. prop.:
    E1/2 of NE1/4 S.30;S1/2 of N1/2;SE1/4 & E1/2 of SW1/4 S.19,T16,R6W
    SE1/4 & S1/2 of NE1/4 and S1/2 of E1/2 of NW1/4 of S.24,T16N,R7W
DEED from WARREN to MRS.WALCOTT - 16 Feb.1867 - WARRENS sign in Noxubee Co.//CROSS EXAMINATION of A.G.PAXTON: shows that BETTIE C.and T.G.WALCOTT were married 1857,that she owned 10 slaves - 3 workers and the others children. In 1858,BETTIE C. and T.G. moved to LA. In 1860, her Uncle,Major R.P.HARRIS,gave her a negro blacksmith called WESTON. The slaves were used to make brick and raise cotton. In 1864,T.G. sold WESTON for $5000,partly paid in Confederate money and part in cotton at 25¢ per lb. T.G. continued to speculate in cotton in 1865 and until they moved to Ms. He invested in her name,so she would have a separate Est. Filed 2 Dec.1867.//DEPOSITION of T.A.ANDERSON and JOHN L.CHEATHAM of Floyd, La. show that they knew WALCOTT ran a brick kiln in 1860,and that he left many debts when he removed to Ms.in 1865. Some of the brick was sold after T.G. went to the Army. T.G. removed his family to Morehouse,La. during the War.Filed 30 Mar.1868.//When MRS.WALCOTT received a Bill of Sale for the store (on Plt.) from WARREN,she agreed to give comfortable quarters to freedwoman HARRIET ARCHER.//Pkt.includes correspondence - T.G.WALCOTT to BIRKHEAD & HOFFMAN - 24 SEPT.1866   (more)

WASH.CO.PKT.GLEANINGS
CHANCERY COURT RECORDS

PKT.186B;cont.BIRKHEAD,et al vs WALCOTT,et al: *"It has been raining for 1 month, the swamps have become impassable, Deer Creek and the Bogue have been rising very much...crops much damaged by rains. One week ago the army worms made their appearance and have now nearly completed or rather finished the cotton crop of this season...Much sickness among my hands...Cholera very bad on the River near Eggs Point...about 100 deaths reported for Wash.Co....All our people are very much discouraged and many a man will lose his last stake this year...Nelson (Warren) has spent all his money and he is drinking all the time and is rarely ever sober..."* (signed)T.G.WALCOTT//

DEPOSITION taken Baltimore,Md.-30 Apr.1868-of WM.GILMORE HOFFMAN (Elder brother.of CHARLES HOFFMAN and 1st cousin of JOHN BIRKHEAD,who made the orig.loan to WALCOTT) age 41,resident of Baltimore,Md.;Member of Baltimore Stock Board;who stated that his bro.CHARLES was in Europe, and he (WM.G.) became concerned about the loan to WALCOTT, and came to Deer Creek to check on it. "WALCOTT's general tone and bearing impressed me very unfavorably". After staying the night at WALCOTT's res.,he left and went to Greenville and instigated this suit.//DEPOSITION of MARY HARRIS, taken before HERBERT W.HILL,Justice of the Peace of Warren Co.-30 Apr. 1868: Mary states that she is the widow of ROBERT P.HARRIS...that BETTIE got slaves from her father's estate and "my husband" gave her WESTON // DEPO.of SALLIE B.HARRIS,Warren Co.-no new infor.//DEPO.of HENRY F.COOK of Vicksburg-no new infor.//Court suggests that a compromise be made.// FINAL DECREE - May 1869 - The land was divided into 3 shares:

    The Husband and 3 minor ch.of BETTIE C.WALCOTT - 1 share
    NELSON T.WARREN ------------------------------ 1 share
    BIRKHEAD & HOFFMAN ---------------------------- 1 share

(Note:I have included a full account of this case as it showed the life and hard times of the era. The personal correspondence reflected the abject misery of the planters and the equal misery of the financial backers,as they tried to pry money out of a bankrupt countryside. The contents of this Packet are not used as an editorial comment on a family,but rather as an example of the desperate struggle to stay afloat one more year. K.B.)

MARRIAGE RECORDS - WARREN CO.,MS.
THOS.H.HILL to JENNETTE C.V.WALCOTT 30 Sept.1847
THEODORE G.WALCOTT to BETTIE C.HARRIS 26 May 1858

WASH.CO.PKT.GLEANINGS
CHANCERY COURT RECORDS

PKT.187: TUFTS & COLLEY et al of New York City vs MORRIS ASH and A.D.GOODS: Orig.Bill filed May Term 1867, by Complts. S.E.SPROULDS, J.B.MEEKER, J.B.HOOVER, S.R.LONE, P.C.CALHOUN, ROWLAND B.LACEY, HENRY T.SHELTON - partners in firm SPROULDS MEEKER & CO. of New York City and WM.L.NUGENT for the use of W.R.TRIGG of Wash.Co., Ms.who state that MORRIS ASH, defendant, late a citizen and merchant in Greenville, Ms."but more recently residing in State of N.Y.", borrowed $2832.55 on 6 Aug.1860 + additional notes. TUFTS & COLLEY, also of N.Y. had some of the notes. The Complts.further state that in 1864 MORRIS ASH declared himself insolvent. His assests went on the block - 26 Oct.1865, worth about $89,000. They were bought by ISAAC PERRY, THEODORE PHILLIPSON, and E.FORBUSH for a nominal sum of @$800 through an asignee-RINO BEREL. The Complts. claim fraud.//PKT.contains a "true account of all the creditors" of MORRIS ASH + a full Inventory of his Estate.(Note:Everybody in Wash.Co.is on ASH's list of debtors!)//PKT.also contains a draft of A.ASH on MICHAEL ASH of Palestine,Tx.15 Aug.1861, and another one to EDWIN E.MORRIS-Jan.1,1862// ANSWER of MORRIS ASH, in which he shows that he left the South in the fall of 1863 to escape the Confederate Confiscation Laws, and the disordered condition of the country. His home in Greenville had been destroyed by the Federal Army, and he was unable to maintain his family and educate his children under the prevailing conditions. He removed to N.Y., where he filed for bankruptcy.//PKT.contains the answer of each defdt., no additional information.//Final decree - CASE DISMISSED.

PKT.188: ANN MATTHEWS of New Orleans, Complt. vs THOMAS KERSHAW, ANN D.MONTAGUE, ROSE SARAH TURNBULL and her husband CHARLES R.TURNBULL, RICHARD C.KERSHAW, JOHN PARIS C.KERSHAW, GEORGE T.KERSHAW, the last 3 minors under 21 -Defendants. Orig.Bill filed 6 Apr.1867 by Complt.MATTHEWS, states that THOS.KERSHAW and his "then wife"-MARY JANE KERSHAW executed a mortgage on 20 May 1854 on @1600 ac. -1/2 S.8;S.9;S.10;T14N,R9W. They gave 5 notes totaling $30,000. MARY JANE had bought the sd.land at a sale resulting from a suit filed by JOHN P.CUNNINGHAM, Adm.vs THOS.KERSHAW[notes attached]Complt. says the notes are unpaid, no one has qualified as Adm.of the Estate of MARY JANE KERSHAW, who is now deceased, and the above named defdts.are her heirs at law, and are now in possession of the land. She seeks payment or sale of land.//PKT.contains original mortg., showing MARY JANE & THOS.KERSHAW were residents of Pass Christian, Ms.in 1854, and MRS. Matthews a res.of S.C.//SUBPOENAS announcing the proposed sale of

(more)

WASH.CO.PKT.GLEANINGS
CHANCERY COURT RECORDS

PKT.188;MATTHEWS VS KERSHAWS,cont.
the land in question was delivered to all defdts.in Wash.Co.Apr.1867 with exception of CHAS. & ROSA TURNBULL,"who were not found in my county"//SUBPOENA delivered to home of TURNBULLS,Sept.1867,accepted by ANDREW TURNBULL,a member of the family.//None of the defdts appeared at the hearing.Sale was ordered 18 Jan.1868.WM.YERGER,Agent and Atty.for MRS. MATTHEWS bought the land for $30,000.

PKT.#191:<u>B.M.LEE of S.C.Complt. vs THOS.KERSHAW, ANNIE de MONTAGUE,RICHARD C.KERSHAW,JOHN PARIS C.KERSHAW,GEO.TRENHOLM KERSHAW - res.of Wash.Co.,Ms. and ROSE SARAH TURNBULL and her husband CHARLES F.TURNBULL,res.of Issa.Co.,Ms. as Defdts.</u>
Orig.Bill filed May Term 1867,stating that on 2 Mar.1852 MARY JANE KERSHAW,decd.,"the then wife" of THOS.KERSHAW,was legal owner of a certain Plantation in Wash.Co.,Ms.Lots5,6,7,8,Sec.8;Sec.9,Sec.10;T14N;R9W as her separate property.MARY JANE and her husband THOS. gave a D/T to her brother JOHN PARIS CUNNINGHAM for the above described property + more. (NOTE:CUNNINGHAM was trustee to protect MARY JANE'S interest,as married females could not own property in their own righ-it automatically reverted to their husbands) CUNNINGHAM died and afterwards MARY JANE died on 8 Jan.1857. She left her husband surviving her,not having appointed another Trustee before her death.B.M.LEE filed a suit agst.THOS.KERSHAW (Case #1860 Circuit Ct.) for $519.77,and won it. In Oct. there was a writ of FIERRI FACIAS - a court order commanding the Sheriff to seize property in order to pay off debt - . At the sale B.M.LEE became purchaser of all rights and interests of THOS.KERSHAW to the above desc.land + other land not desc. The children of MARY JANE KERSHAW,named as defdts above, claim they are the only heirs to the property of JOHN P.CUNNINGHAM and of their Mother.They further state that another dau.(named for her mother) MARY JANE has since decd.[NOTE:The other described land was in Harrison Co.,Ms,known as the residence of MRS.KERSHAW,containing 225 ft.fronting on the Gulf of Mexico and extending back @13 arpents, + slaves.)

PKT.#192:<u>HEWITT,NORTON & CO. of New Orleans vs ELIZABETH A.and GEORGE R.FALL of Wash.Co.,Ms.:</u> Orig.Bill filed 22 Apr.1867,showing that on 31 Dec.1860,the FALL'S mortgaged property for $6400 to the Counting House of WRIGHT & ALLEN of N.O. who made notes payable to THOS.B.WARFIELD,who in turn endorsed them to HEWITT NORTON & CO. The land was @160 ac.lying NE1/4,S.24,T17N,R7W.//Sale ordered by court. // WM.G.YERGER,Atty and Agent of Complts.bought it for $320.

WASH.CO.PKT.GLEANINGS
CHANCERY COURT RECORDS

PKT.#193:PHILLIP WIGERT & FRANCIS K.HUNT,Exec.of Est.of JOHN H.HANNA,decd.   vs   JUNIUS JOHNSON,EDWARD P.JOHNSON,FITZWILLIAM LONSDALE and his wife NANNIE J.LONSDALE - late NANNIE J.JOHNSON, BETTIE IRWIN a minor under 21: all residents of Wash.Co.,Ms.Orig.Bill filed 22 Apr.1867 by Complts.who state that on 27 July1852,EDWARD P. JOHNSON,now decd.,and his wife BETSY M.JOHNSON,borrowed $37,500 from JOHN H.HANNA + interest,for which JOHNSON gave a series of notes. The land mortgaged was Sec.17 and Sec.14;Lots 3,4,5,6, Sec.3;Sec.15 - all in T16N,R8W - @1850 ac.+ 59 negroes. EDW.P.JOHNSON paid the interest and some thousands on the principal,and time was extended on the rest under new terms. Edw.P.died leaving 3 children - JUNIUS L.JOHNSON, EDWARD P.JOHNSON,JR. and NANNIE J.LONSDALE. Also 1 grandchild - BETSY IRWIN. No Adm.has been appointed for EDW.P.'S Est.,and JUNIUS L.JOHNSON is in residence on the land. In 1861,JOHN H.HANNA died at his res.in Franklin Co.,Ky.;testate;appointing Complts.as his executors. They have qualified,Will has been probated,and the notes signed by EDW.P.JOHNSON were included in the Inventory of HANNA'S Est. They seek payment or sale of prop.//COMMISSIONER declares debt now at $50,000//Sold to MARY HANNA for $12,000 on 20 Apr.1869//(Note:Pkt.states that the WILL of JOHN H. HANNA was filed for Probate in Wash.Co.,Ms.but there is no rec.of it in WILL BKS. or this PKT.).

PKT.#194:WM.M.LEE vs E.G.COOK: Original Bill filed 22 Apr.1867,by LEE, stating that in Mar.1859,COOK mortgaged "AVA PLANTATION" -
   Lot 5,6,Sec.13; L.5,Sec.14;L.4,Sec.23;SE1/4 Sec.15,T18N,R5W
612 ac.+ stock,equipment,etc.COOK signed notes payable to WM.P.MELLEN and wife of Adams Co.,Ms. who in turn,endorsed sd.notes and delivered the last one to LEE.// 18 Nov.1867,SUBPOENA for E.G.COOK left with his son.// On 28 Sept.,1868,the same land was sold to LEE for $2000.//Included in this Pkt. is a QUIT CLAIM DEED from WM.L.NUGENT,Agent for JNO.R.KING,to ANNIE KING (numbered #1387).In this DEED,NUGENT gives ANNIE KING all his rights to the 612 ac.described above.DEED dated 17 Oct.1870-Recorded D.Bk."Y",p.623//On a small piece of paper,marked DO NOT RECORD - is a Conveyance of Sec.14,T18,R5W to JNO.R.(B?)KING and remanded to MRS. MARGARET GILLESPIE. 240 ac.to KING,including allbuildings,improvements, etc.//(NOTE:T18N,R5W is now in Sunflower Co.)

THE HANDY BOOK FOR GENEALOGISTS:
WASHINGTON CO.,MS was formed 1827 from WARREN & YAZOO
SUNFLOWER CO.WAS FORMED 1844 from BOLIVAR (and Wash.)
ISSAQUENA CO. was formed 1844 from WASH.(and Warren)
SHARKEY CO. was formed 1876 from WARREN,WASH.,ISSAQUENA.

WASH.CO.PKT.GLEANINGS
CHANCERY COURT RECORDS

PKT.#194 1/2:M.L.& L.E.REESE - vs WM.YERGER,et al: Orig.Bill filed 24 Apr.1867 by MARIA LOUISA REESE and LAURA ELIZABETH REESE of Williamson Co.,Tn. - being the children and heirs at law of W.B.REESE,decd. and the Bank of Kentucky at Louisville,Complts. vs WM.YERGER and wife MALVINA H.;MARY M.RUCKS widow of ARTHUR RUCKS,decd.;AMANDA RUCKS, JAMES RUCKS,GRANT B.RUCKS,SALLY RUCKS - all minor children of the aforementioned ARTHUR RUCKS,decd;MARIA L.YERGER,late RUCKS;JAMES T.RUCKS;HENRY RUCKS;ALEXANDER YERGER and wife ELIZABETH B.;WM.S. YERGER and wife HENRIETTA;FRANK VALLIANT and wife MARIAN;L.T.RUCKS children and divisees of JAMES RUCKS,decd.;and JAMES T.RUCKS,HENRY RUCKS,and FRANK VALLIANT - exect.of WILL of the said JAMES T.RUCKS, decd.;and ROBERT W.SCOTT of Franklin Co.,Ky.Defdts.Original Bill states that in July 1851,W.B.REESE and his wife Henrietta;ORLANDO BROWN and said Defdt.ROBT.W.SCOTT,each by separate DEED,conveyed to JAMES RUCKS a fee simple title to an undivided 1/5th interest in the tract of land in Wash.Co.,Ms known as "THE BROWN PLACE" + 1/5th of the mules,ect. The land was acquired by REESE,BROWN,and SCOTT by their intermarriage with children and heirs of DR.PRESTON W.BROWN and his wife ELIZABETH. JAMES RUCKS,who also married one of the BROWN daughters,was seeking to swap 'THE BROWN PLACE' for land on Deer Creek in T18N,R7W, and took out a mortg.on sd.place. Complts. state that W.B.REESE has died,leaving the 2 girls - MARIA LOUISA and LAURA ELIZABETH + 2 sons - JOHN W. and W.B. REESE,JR. JOHN W.REESE is the Adm.for his father's Est. The Complts.then claim that JAMES RUCKS paid all notes up until 1861,1862.They seek payment//FINAL DECREE May Term 1868---DEFDTS. owe $10,000 and sale of land ordered.//CROSS BILLS filed//Judge found in favor of the Complts.and ALEXANDER YERGER and LT.RUCKS appealed to the HIGHCOURT OF ERROR & APPEAL 13 Jan.1870//Pkt.also includes Grdnp.papers naming L.B.VALLIANT Grdn.ad litem of the minor children of ARTHUR RUCKS -AMANDA,JAMES, GRANT B.,and SALLIE RUCKS.L.B.VALLIANT also seeks the Grdnp.of minor heirs of HENRY RUCKS,decd.-ARTHUR,BENJAMIN N,SAML.T.RUCKS. The widow of the sd.HENRY RUCKS,decd.,is SARAH JANE RUCKS.

PKT.#202:WM.F.SMITH vs JOHN A.MILLER,et al:Orig.Bill filed 1 June 1867 in which SMITH,Complt.,states that in 5 Feb.1859 he mortgd.some property and gave a D/T to WM.HARDEMAN,Hinds Co., with certain stipulations..ie before selling sd.property,either the land or negroes,HARDEMAN must give 60 days notice of time and place of sale in New Orleans and Vicksburg newspapers. Should HARDEMAN die or refuse to act,then the Trusteeship reverts to the Sheriff of Wash.Co.,Ms. JOHN A.MILLER holds one of the

WASH.CO.PKT.GLEANINGS
CHANCERY COURT RECORDS

PKT.#202:SMITH vs MILLER,et al:cont.
(mortg.)notes, and has started foreclosure measures. SMITH seeks an INJUNCTION to stop sale.//Pkt.contains a copy of D/T with land desc.:
    Sec.1;Sec.2;Sec.11.T16N,R7W - Sec.6;Sec.7;T16N,R6W
    E1/2 Sec.35;SE1/4 Sec.26;SW1/4 Sec.31;W1/2 of SW1/4 SEC.30
    W1/2 of NW1/4 Sec.30;W1/2 Sec.9;SW1/4 Sec.10;W1/2 of SW1/4
    Sec.10 - All in T17N,R7W - 4,640 ac. on which SMITH resided 1859
Mortg.for $100,000 + 10% interest.//In notice of sale,1 June 1867,A.B. CARSON,Sheriff,stated that WM.HARDEMAN had decd.//No other doc.

PKT.#204:JOHN A.MILLER vs EUGENIA P.BERTINATTI,et al:
Orig.Bill filed 15 June 1867 : MILLER,Complt.,a resident of Wash.Co.,Ms names the defendants as EUGENIA P.BERTINATTI and her husband JOS.BERTINATTI;PHILLIP ROTCHFORD & SHEPHERD BROWN - surviving partners in firm of ROTCHFORD BROWN & CO.,merchants;CORNELIUS FELLOWS,DANIEL P.LOGAN & THOMPSON GREENFIELD,merchants trading in firm FELLOWS & CO.in New Orleans($9,783 + Int);E.P.TYREE and any other unknown persons interested in Est.of the sd.EUGENIA,as creditors. MILLER contends that EUGENIA owns a tract of land in Wash.Co. - in T14N,R9W @1750 ac.,but it is hopelessly in debt. Unless the existing court order for the sale of sd.porperty is stopped,no one will regain a portion of their money. MILLER seeks an order for the court to rent out sd.land,and repay the debts that way. EUGENIA also owns an undivided 1/2 of 838 ac.in T14N,R9W + crops,mules,ect. EUGENIA's address is Washington City (D.C) or Constantinople,Turkey,where her husb.is Minister to the King of Italy. The debts were incurred before she married BERTINATTI,when she was a widow of COUNCIL BASS,decd.//A CROSS BILL has suggested that there was a conspiracy between EUGENIA,ELLA,and TYREE to defraud creditors// DEPOSITIONS for the Defdt. follow:J.J.MHOON,taken 2 Nov.1867 "I am 47 yrs.old,a res.of Memphis."Knows that MISS ELLA BASS,the dau.of EUGENIA, leased a Plantation on the River to GEN.W.B.BATE,the partner of E.P.TYREE who acted as overseer of the sd.place.MHOON does not for one minute believe the GEN.would lend himself to any fraudulant scheme.When questioned about the relationship between MHOON,EUGENIA,TYREE, - MHOON states he is distantly related to EUGENIA and TYREE and friendly to all. He doesn't know the age or place of birth of ELLA BASS. TYREE has married a cousin of EUGENIA's.// JAMES H.BATE - age 26 yrs.,a res.of Memphis,a Commission Merchant. He states the name of the Plantation in question was "GREEN GROVE" on the Riverside. JAMES is a cousin of EUGENIA's,and E.P.TYREE is his brother-in-law.He continues by saying that ELLA BASS is the dau.of

WASH.CO.PKT.GLEANINGS
CHANCERY COURT RECORDS

PKT.#204:MILLER vs EUGENIA P.BERTINATTI,et al: (cont:) EUGENIA's,@ 21 yrs.old,born Tn.,"I think". and that ELLA married at the end of the War.. Taken 2 Nov.1867.//Both parties in the preceeding DEPOSITIONS make a firm statement that they do not believe the parties concerned entered into "a secret agreement".//ATTACHMENT by CARSON,SHRF.(#1621)//ANSWER ofE.P.TYREE,Nov.1867,who denies being an Agent of EUGENIA's, states that in the fall of 1865,he and WM.B.BATE,a resident of Nashville,Tn.leased land for 3 yrs. from HENRY C.BATE,an Agent of sd.EUGENIA .The sd. place was known as THE BASS & MURPHY Place. At the time EUGENIA was living in Washington City, and EMIDICUS MURPHY,who owned the plantation with her,had died and his heirs had never appeared to take over any part of the land. Then in 1867,TYREE and BATE leased RIVERSIDE PLANTATION from ELLA BASS-sometimes called GREEN GROVE PLT.He denies any conspiracy// By Nov.Term1867,other creditors file claims:BEN HARDAWAY of Warren Co. Ms.: WM.FRAZIER KELLY ,by his Agent A.D.KELLY debt owed since Jan.1861 - New Orleans:A.B.CARSON of Wash.Co.//INJUNCTION was lifted as far as the cotton crop was concerned, and TYREE may ship and sell it in order to pay the rent,now due.//In Nov.1870- Case DISMISSED without prejudice//

PKT.#205:<u>ANN B.FINLAY,Adm. vs G.S.MOSBY:</u>
BILL OF DISCOVERY,filed 8 July 1867,ANN B.,the Adm.of the Est.of DR.JOHN L.FINLAY,decd. and his widow,has found 3 open accounts in favor of said Est. bearing date 1 Jan.1861 and against G.S.MOSBY in favor of the FINLAY EST.$11,360 debt,with only $1,019 having been pd. Note was made when ELIZA G.MOSBY,the wife of G..S.MOSBY was alive. ELIZA died 1862,owning 'LOUGHBOROUGH PLT.' which G.S.MOSBY controlled as her agent and was the sole witness of the debt due. (for medicines,drugs,medical care,etc.for ELIZA and her children and slaves) A suit #1596 is pending in Circuit Court,and G.S.MOSBY is in "very delicate and infirm health" and is about to leave this state for Virginia.//ANSWER by MOSBY,who admits that all the above is true//SUPB.delivered 9 July 1867// (Note:'LOUGHBOROUGH PLT.' was heavily in debt.ELIZA MOSBY had converted all her money into Confederate Treasury Notes,which of course were worthless after the War. ELIZA GLOVER (BURKS)MOSBY b1830/d.18 Sept.1862/dau.of SAML.BURKS and his 2nd w.ELIZA GLOVER of Jeff.Co.,Ky.:From MONTGOMERY PAPERS)

PKT.#206:<u>SAMUEL T.TAYLOR,resident of Wash.Co.,Justice of the Peace vs ANDREW B.CARSON,Shrf.& Tax Collector of same:</u>
Orig.Bill filed 22 July 1867(NOTE:This is similiar to the present day (1985)"Class Action Suit";in this case an individual challenges the legality

WASH.CO.PKT.GLEANINGS
CHANCERY COURT RECORDS

PKT.#206:TAYLOR vs CARSON,Shrf.(cont.)of the 200% County Tax,levied on the basis of the State Tax,+200% Courthouse Tax on top of that for building a new Ct.house,Jail and other Public buildings in Wash.Co.The town site of Greenville was moved to BLANTONIA Plt.and the money supplied by the new taxes was to replace the public buildings destroyed by Federal Forces when they burned the town of "Old"Greenville-Spring 1863.See PKT.#208, #209 below) TAYLOR,Complt.,states that CARSON,Defdt.,under the guise of Sheriff, has siezed 10 of his mules to discharge $1028 due for the alledged State,County and Courthouse Taxes.Said Taxes were levied on:

```
     1 Buggy   --- Value $50-----------$   .25
     200 bales of cotton-at $1 ea.------200.00
     1 horse-------------------------    1.00
     7 dogs @50¢ ea.-----------------    3.50
     Poll Tax on self----------------    1.00
              Total Amt.of State Tax$205.75
     County Tax @200% ---------------411.50
     Courthouse Tax @200%             411.50
              Total Taxes Due     $1028.75
```

TAYLOR said he had no knowledge of Taxes levied by the Board of Police at its Oct.Term,and the cotton Tax was assesed under an Act.of the State Legislature (Reconstruction Government)approved 5 Dec.1865 entitled 'AN ACT TO RAISE A REVENUE TO DEFRAY THE EXPENSE OF GOVERNMENT OF THE STATE OF MISS.' TAYLOR says the 200 bales of cotton so assessed was raised,sold and shipped prior to Legislative Act in 1865,so can not be so assessed (retroactive). In addition,$1 per bale has been levied on next yrs.cotton crop and personality. He has no means to pay this exhoribitant tax at this time,and must have use of the mules to make a crop. TAYLOR seeks an INJUNCTION - 29 June 1867 - to stop seizure.//SUBPOENA sworn out by SAML.TAYLOR,T.J.FOSTER,ED.T.TAYLOR to restrain CARSON from collecting.//INJUNCTION set in motion.

PKT.#208:THOMAS H.HILL vs A.B.CARSON,Sheriff: Filed 26 Aug.1867 HILLstates that CARSON is selling 2 of his mules for taxes (See Pkt.#206 above)//Judge R.L.DIXON allows INJUNCTION//No other doc.

PKT.209:WM.H.LEE vs A.B.CARSON,Shrf. (Same type suit as #206,#208) LEE seeks INJUNCTION on sale of 3 of his mules//So allowed.

PKT.#207:(Note:Taken out of order,so that #206,#208,#209 could be in consecutive line.)

WASH.CO.PKT.GLEANINGS
CHANCERY COURT RECORDS

PKT.#207:ANN POINDEXTER vs HENRY T.LONSDALE,A.FOSTER ELLOITT of La.,and FITZWILLIAM LONSDALE of Wash.Co.,Ms.,and WM.YERGER of Hds.Co.,Ms. Orig.Bill filed 19 Aug.1867 by Ann P.,Complt.,who states that her late husband George Poindexter,died in 1853 in Hds.Co.,Ms.(Note:former Gov.of Ms.)leaving a WILL,naming ANN P. as his Extrx. He left her all of his worldly goods and she is now in possession of same. In 1853 WM.YERGER mortgd.502 ac.of land lying in Wash.Co.,making a series of 6 notes. YERGER then gave a D/T to CASWELL R.CLIFTON. In 1855,YERGER bought 320 ac.in Wash.Co.from CHAS.L.ROBARDS,adjoining the forementioned land. YERGER then sold all of sd.land,822 ac, to H.T.LONSDALE and ELLIOTT,who promised to pay off the remainder of notes + int. ANN P.gave them an extension on principal,but she insists that the interest be paid. She believes that FITZWILLIAM LONSDALE is now in possession of the land,having been put there by his father - HENRY T.LONSDALE.She further states that the slaves named in the mortg.have been freed,and CASWELL CLIFTON is dead. ANN P. seeks relief in EQUITY COURT.//PKT.containsd DEED from ANDREW FOSTER ELLIOTT and wife MARIE ANTIONETTE ODILE to HENRY T.LONSDALE - all of New Orleans.dated 26 Jan.1856 for land on Deer Creek as described:
  L.1,2,4,5,6,Sec.35;L.8,Sec.34;W1/2 Sec.36,all in T18N,R7W
Also DEED from YERGER to ELLIOTT and LONSDALE - 1855//Also D/T YERGER to CLIFTON and POINDEXTER 1853//Commissioners report $22,068.41 now due - Nov.1868//Sale ordered.//Sold 17 Apr.1871

PKT.#211:THOMAS B.WARFIELD vs SAML.T.TAYLOR:Before Circuit Ct.Judge of 3rd Judicial Dist.,C.C.SHACKLEFORD. Orig.Bill filed 25 Oct.1867 by WARFIELD,Complt.,who shows that on 17 Dec.1860 he and his wife ALICE D.WARFIELD sold land to SAML.T.TAYLOR of Tipton Co.,Tn. desc.as:
  E1/2 Sec.13;E1/2 & E1/2 of NW1/4 of Sec.12;E1/2 Sec.1,T17N,R7W
  W1/2 of NW1/4,W1/2 of SW1/4 Sec.6,T17N,R6W --1200 ac.
WARFIELD seeks payment or sale of prop.//Amt.owed $8,040.//Sale ordered for 20 July 1868.

PKT.#212:E.MARQUEZA & CO. vs CHRISTOPHER GILLESPIE,DR.J.S.ROBINSON Orig.Bill filed 26 Oct.1867 by MARQUESA, who was lately a merchant in New Orleans. He states that on 7 June 1860,he recovered a judgement in Circuit Court of Sunflower Co.,Ms.against GILLESPIE,Defdt. It was returned,GILLESPIE being hopelessly insolvent,his only asset being 1 note drawn by P.M.WALKER in favor of sd.GILLESPIE for $9560. MARQUESA claims that GILLESPIE endorsed sd.note over to DR.ROBINSON to keep from

WASH.CO.PKT.GLEANINGS
CHANCERY COURT RECORDS

PKT.#212 MARQUESA VS GILLESPIE,(cont.)paying the debt owed Complt. P.M.WALKER has died,and M.H.WALKER is his Admx.and has left Ms. for good. MARQUESA seeks attachment of all phases of sd. note..ANSWER of ROBINSON:note is payment for an old debt owed him.//Attachment allowed.

PKT.#213:TOOF PHILLIPS & CO. vs WETHERBEE & PHILLIPS:Orig.Bill filed 28 Oct.1867 by Complts.JOHN S.TOOF,CHAS.PHILLIPS and ----MAHAN,merchants in Memphis,who state that JAS.W.PHILLIPS and D.J.WETHERBEE rent a Plt.from MARIA LOU YERGER and MARY H.YERGER. TOOF PHILLIPS & CO. furnished (crop loan)the rentors for $3345,and seek a lien on crop. MARIA LOU and MARY H. claim they should have prior right to same.//Seizure order of stock,etc.28 Oct.1867//Final decree Nov.1867- Complts.case dismissed.

PKT.#214:PLANTERS BANK OF TN. vs HARVEY LATHAM and his wife LUCY ANN of Warren Co.,Ms. and THOS.H.MARTIN,JR.a res.of Louisville,Ky. Orig.Bill filed 28 Oct.1867 by Complts.,who state that on 27 Aug.1856,they sold land in Wash.Co.,Ms.by their Agent WM.HARDEMAN who has since died, to HARVEY LATHAM - 2094 ac. In 1865 LATHAM sold part of sd.prop.to MARTIN,stating at the time he owed @$2500 on it.Land desc.:
    Sec.14;Sec.15;L.1,Sec.17;L.1,Sec.21;L.5,7,8,Sec.22;L.1,Sec.29;
    L.1,2,6,Sec.26 - all in T16N,R5W
MARTIN pays his portion in Apr.1872.

PKT.#215:GIVEN WATTS & CO. of New Orleans vs W.M.MERRIWEATHER,MATT F.JOHNSON: Orig.Bill filed 19 Nov.1867,by Complts who state that on 14 Apr.1866,they loaned the Defdts.$8,000 on 23 mules,5 horses,wagons,carts,harness,plows,+ crop to be raised. Debt is unpaid. In 1867,MERRIWEATHER applied for further advances,which they agreed to do . He now owes $20,000.MERRIWEATHER gave a D/T to MATT F.JOHNSON on more equipment + stock. In 1866, MERRIWEATHER failed to make a "fair crop" and made little or nothing in 1867.//Commissioners report that MERRIWEATHER owes $23,605.//Court orders seizure. (NOTE:There was a complete crop failure for the entire Ms.Delta in the years 1866,1867. The money lenders had little choice but to let the farmers try to work out their debts. Some foreclosed,but the value of the land had fallen to match the rest of the hard times. The future for this area looked very bleak.)

PKT.#216:C.R.ESTILL vs WM.GANT:Orig.Bill filed 30 Nov.1867.Complt.ESTILL states that on 1 Mar.1867,he sold GANT 5 mules for $750,which were to be

WASHINGTON CO.,MS.
CHANCERY COURT RECORDS

PKT.#216:C.R.ESTILL vs WM.GANT:(cont.) worked on Plantation "Glen Mary", the property of JOHN R.WOODBURN. GANT farmed 90 ac.on "Glen Mary",and gave a lien on his crop which was filed for record as required by an Act entitled AN ACT FOR THE ENCOURAGEMENT OF AGRICULTURE (NOTE:brainstorm of the Reconstruction Govern.)and sd.loan was approved 18 Feb.1867. The Plt."Glen Mary " was occupied by DAVID B.BELL and when CARSON,Shrf. went to confiscate sd.crop,he found it to be stored,unginned. CARSON then deputized BELL to keep the cotton in his control,but "unavoidably" it was burned. ESTILL wants payment or the mules back.//C.R.ESTILL appoints J.H.ESTILL his Agent - 1865//FINAL DECREE - 28 Nov.1870 - sale ordered.

PKT.#217:E.B.KIMBALL, W.C.KIMBALL as "E.B.KIMBALL",merchant of New Orleans vs HARRY YERGER,Grdn.of MAGGIE,MALVINA,HARVEY MILLER - minor heirs at law of HARVEY MILLER,decd.;HARRY YERGER and his wife SALLIE,late YERGER. Orig.Bill filed 30 Nov.1867 by Complts.who state that HARRY YERGER and SALLIE MILLER were married 1866,SALLIE being an heir of HARVEY MILLER,DECD. HARRY YERGER then took out Grdnp.papers on minor sisters and brother of SALLIE'S. With the consent of HARVEY MILLER'S Adm.EDW.P.JOHNSON, he took possession of sd.MILLER'S Est. HARRY YERGER then sought a crop furnish for 1867,and borrowed $5000 in New Orleans. Acting in his capacity as Grdn.for the minors and Agent for wife Sallie, he then mortgd.equipment,stock,etc.on "STELLA PLT.",lying in Wash.Co.,Ms. (NOTE:Chattel Loan) Complts.seek attachment to prevent HARRY from selling the current crop,before KIMBALL gets pd.//PKT.contains Letters of GRDNP.mentioned above//Also mortg.//Bill from KIMBALL & CO.//Bond for ATTACHMENT signed by E.B.KIMBALL, W.C.KIMBALL, BETTY McHATTON , W.P. HALL.//Writ OF SEQUESTRATION May Term 1868(See Glossary)//A list of creditors,hurt by Writ of Seq.file motion to cancel same - signed RICHARD COLEMAN,HARRISON TAYLOR,RICHARD CLARK,ROBT.GIVENS,NED CHINN , BEVERLY TUCKER,ALLEN BRISCOE,GREEN THOMPSON,JOHN McCANE,HENRY RANDELS,HEZEKIAH BRISCOE,MANLUIS THOMPSON,LEWIS HAWKINS,MINOR JACKSON,TERRILL CHINN,WM.THOMPSON,WHITFIELD HENRYDEN,LEWIS CLARK, SIMON JEFFERSON,GILBERT SWAN,MAT COLEMAN,MOSES COLEMAN,AMOS BROWN,SANFORD TAYLOR,WM.HERRON,MILLY BROWN,EMILY BRISCOE,GREEN TINSON,NICK HAWKINS,WM.McCUTCHIN,IRENE FLETCHER,BYRD SMITH,DAVE CHINN,BOB FLETCHER,JUNIUS HUGHES,BEDFORD BANKS,CHARLEY PRESTON, JAMES BAKER,AMANDA WILLIAMS,HESKY BRISCOE,REUBEN TAYLOR,REUBEN JOHNSON,MARIA JEFFERSON,RANDEL JEFFERSON - all res.of Wash.Co.who state that part of the goods and Chattel belong to them.11 May 1868//Court ordered the Complts.to file an amended Bill//FINAL DECREE filed 1 May 1872 - Complts.are entitled to relief,but not at the expense of other creditors, HARRY YERGER filed for BANKRUPTCY..Complts.case dismissed.

WASHINGTON CO.,MS.
CHANCERY COURT RECORDS

PKT.#219:RICHARD D.SHIPP,ERNEST BURGESS,(BOURGES ?)JEREMIAH WILSON,WM.SHIPP,Merchants of New Orleans in Firm SHIP BURGESS & CO. vs ROBT.H.CARTER of Wash.Co.,Ms.;ROBT.H.CARTER as Adm.of Est.of ALFRED G.CARTER,Decd.;ROBT.H.CARTER,as Adm.of Est.of A.GRAYSON CARTER,decd. Orig.Bill filed Dec.Term 1867:Complts.state that ROBT.H.CARTER made a crop loan in 1867 for "WOODSTOCK PLT.",the property of ALFRED G.CARTER decd.,for $7,768 for which he gave a mortg.Complts.also state that A. GRAYSON CARTER,now decd.,did,in his lifetime make a similar arrangement for cultivating "SOLONA PLT."for 1867."SOLONA PLT." is also the prop.of the sd.ALFRED G.CARTER,decd. Complts.further show that ROBT.H.CARTER and A.GRAYSON CARTER were two of the sons of the sd.ALFRED G.CARTER, decd. who left as heirs 6 children. ROBT.H. is also heir at law of his brother A.GRAYSON CARTER,decd. SHIPP BURGESS & CO. appoint HORACE H.MILLER of Vicksburg P/A 14 Dec.1867//No answer of Defdt. in Pkt.//(NOTE:the 6 children of ALFRED G.CARTER and his wife ELIZABETH L.CARTER were as follows:ROBERT HILL,MARY E. - called MITTIE,ELEANOR S.,WILL,ANN B.who marr.WM.F.RANDOLPH,A.GRAYSON named in suit above. Taken from Cens.1850- Wash.Co.;Cens.1870 Wash.Co.;Death notices from G'ville Times;Wash.Co.Pkts.#420,#219)

PKT.#220:SAML.H.KENNEDY & CO. of New Orleans vs W.F.RANDOLPH: Chattel Mortg.Orig.Bill filed 23 Dec.1867,showing Complts.are SAML.H. KENNEDY,JULIUS VARIEN,PAUL E.MORTIMER,Merchants of N.O. vs W.H. RANDOLH,F.R.WINDSOR,DAVID WINDSOR,W.A.WALLIS,Defdts. Complts.show that RANDOLPH applied for crop loan for 1867 for "ALDOMAR PLT." lying in Wash.Co.,Ms. Collateral was mules and implements + crops. RANDOLPH and F.R.WINDSOR owed KENNEDY & CO. for a previous loan. Complts. had heard that RANDOLPH and WINDSOR had sold the mules to DAVID WINDSOR who resides in Alexandria,Va.and who proposed shipping them there.Complts. seek an INJUNCTION to prevent DAVID from removing same. Complts.also claim RANDOLPH has sold some of the property to WALLIS,and they seek to prevent WALLIS from paying directly to RANDOLPH.//ANSWER of RANDOLPH and F.R.WINSDOR:"Aldomar Plt."belonged to E.J.FLOURNOY,Exectx.of Est.of V.M.FLOURNOY,decd.,and her claims(for rent) must come first under owner and tenant laws.//FINAL DECREE - filed 4 Feb.1874 -in favor of Complts.// SUPREME COURT MANDATE:D.A.WINDSOR,et al vs S.H.KENNEDY #1440-filed 12 Feb.1877-shows decree ofFeb.1874 reversed and Complts.Bill dismised.//PKT.also contains several documents on the part of ex-Shrf.CARSON to turn over all monies collected by him in this case,or show that he had turned over same to his successor.

WASHINGTON CO., MS.
CHANCERY COURT RECORDS

PKT.#221:(HENRY F.)GIVEN,WATTS & CO.of New Orleans vs JOSEPH C.JONES, THOS.G.JOHNS,ARCHIE BAUGH,res.of Wash.Co.,Ms.: Orig.Bill filed 2 Jan.1868 by Complts. who show that JOHNS and BAUGH rented a tract of land lying in Wash.Co. called "PERU PLT." from JOSEPH C.JONES who was the receiver in a suit styled H.PARISH,et al vs H.CARPENTER,et al-sd.suit pending in Claib. Co.,Ms. JOHNS & BAUGH cultivated "Peru Plt." in 1866 and GIVEN WATTS & CO. furnished them after receiving a CHATTEL Mortg. Then JOHNS,BAUGH and JONES entered a partnership.JONES & BAUGH are owners of 1/2 of sd.Plt. Complts.seek INJUNCTION to stop the sale of any Chattels//FINAL DECREE - INJUNCTION dissolved.//In Feb.1868, GIVEN,WATTS,& CO. file bankruptcy.

PKT.#222:GUSTAVE GREENWOOD vs LAWSON ROUSE,JAS.P.FERGUSON of Wash.Co.:Orig.Bill filed 9 Jan.1868 by GREENWOOD,who states that in 1867 he formed a verbal partnership with ROUSE in the general receiving and shipping business,commission merchants and dry goods business at Maryland Landing in Wash.Co. They leased a piece of property on the (Ms.)River with exclusive right of way through "MARYLAND PLT.",which was adjacent to sd.land,for time period of 1867 through Feb.1868.Suddenly,on 1 Nov.1867 GREENWOOD claims he was prevented from participating in any of the business by the above named Defdts.,and furthermore ROUSE seized the books and accounts,goods,etc.and without even consulting him,turned everything over to JAS.P.FERGUSON and the MOTT BROS. of Issa.Co.GREENWOOD seeks an INJUNCTION until an accounting can be made by the Court.// INJUNCTION Bond $2000.//ANSWER of D.W.MOTT & Bro.by D.W.MOTT,one of the family,who says that GREENWOOD lived at Leota Landing about 150 yds. away from Maryland Landing,and was never barred from the premises.So far as they knew he had never bothered to come and ask for the books,for they were always in the store,available to him.//DECREE - 15 May 1869, Case dismissed as Complt.GREENWOOD has made no effort to pursue case.

PKT.#224:C.R.ESTILL vs GIVEN WATTS & CO. of N.O. and ANN D.HALSEY of Wash.Co.,Ms.:Orig.Bill filed 23 July 1868,shows ANN D.HALSEY borrowed $460 on 26 Mar 1867 (ChattelMortg.) from C.R.ESTILL. Previously she had mortg.her Plt. at the head of Fish Lake for $12,000 to GIVEN WATTS & CO.:
    Sec.17;L.3,4 Sec.11:S1/2 Sec.12;S1/2 Sec.13,T18N,R8W
+ the crop of 1867.(When there was a crop failure for that yr.)GIVEN WATTS & CO. loaned her $10,000 more in 1867. GIVEN WATTS & CO.failed (filed Bankruptcy) 29 Feb.1868,and ESTILL charges that their successors GIVEN BROWN & CO.are trying to attach Mrs.Halsey's crop to settle their debt at the expense of his.//GIVEN BROWN state that there was no real

WASHINGTON CO., MS.
CHANCERY COURT RECORDS

PKT.#224:ESTILL vs GIVEN WATTS & CO.,et al (cont.)
effort on the part of Mrs.HALSEY to prepare the mortgd.crop for sale.//
ANSWER of MRS.HALSEY - 9 May 1868:There was a delay in ginning the cotton in question because there was no gin on the Fish Lake Plt..The cotton had to be hauled to "the home place" to be ginned after 1/4 was removed as payment to negroes who raised it.(Note:She was operating under the "sharecropping"system,developed after the slaves were freed. The War had stripped the landowners of any cash they may have had,so a system of paid wages was out of the question. The Freedmen had no cash to lease land,so the two groups entered a compromise situation. The landowner provided the land, most of the equipment,seed,a homestead, extra land for a garden spot and money or credit to live on for a year. The "tenant" furnished the labor and at the end of the crop year,they split the proceeds according to a prearranged agreement.On MRS.HALSEY's place,the sharecroppers cut was 1/4. After deducting the tenants' various expenses from the final total,there was seldom any money left,but both groups were eating,and more or less taking care of each other.). INJUNCTION Bond signed by C.R.ESTILL;JOHN H.ESTILL,Agent and son of C.R.;JAMES STONE; W.N.HOOD - $5000//Commissioners Report shows that MRS.HALSEY owed $1797,17//Included in Pkt.is a letter from W.A.PERCY,Atty.for GIVEN WATTS &CO. and for GIVEN BROWN - dated 20 Nov.1868 - in which Mr.Percy states that GIVEN WATTS & CO. never indicated to him that they would file for Bankruptcy//FINAL DECREE - May 1869 - ESTILL to keep 1/2 of money from sale of cotton and the other 1/2 goes to MRS.HALSEY.

FROM THE NATCHEZ DISTRICT 1860 - 1880 by MICHAEL WAYNE(1983) In the Chapter entitled "THE RESHAPING OF A SOCIETY",Mr.Wayne discusses the dreadful agricultural failures of 1866,1867 + the humiliating influx of outsiders grabbing for the spoils of War. He continues by saying,quote,"By the time 1868 arrived,few Yankee lessees were left in the district. Of necessity almost all former slaveowners were operating their own plantations or renting to freedmen. In light of the experiences of the previous two seasons,there was widespread pessimism. And then -as if Providence had summoned the armyworms soley to drive the outlanders from the region - things took a turn for the better. Cotton prices rose again and,more important,yields increased dramatically..By October (1868)Will D.Gale was able to write from Sartartia in the Delta. '*The condition of the country is vastly improved since last winter.*'"

WASHINGTON CO., MS.
CHANCERY COURT RECORDS
RANDOM SELECTIONS

[NOTE: The next court cases deal, basically, with foreclosures and forfeitures of farm land and equipment. Unless the case had genealogical information, it was not abstracted. SEE VOL.I of this series for an index to the remaining Packets. K.B.]

PKT.#229: GIVEN WATTS & CO. (of New Orleans)vs THOMAS H.JOHNS, et al: Filed Feb.8,1868. Defendants are THOMAS H.JOHNS, ARCHIE BAUGH of Wash.Co.,Ms. and JOSEPH C.JOHNS of Jeff.Co.,Ms. Suit is over the non-payment of a $40,000 crop loan on "Peru" and "Lake Island Plts."

PKT.#223:JUREY & HARRIS vs ROBERT H.HORD, ET AL
FILED:20 MAY 1868:Complainants were L.C.JUREY and J.L.HARRIS,merchs.of N.O. with deftdts.ROBERT H.HORD,Adm.of Est.of JAMES B.JACKSON, decd. and late husband of MARY J.HORD,and 2 minor children of JACKSON's - ANDREW AND LIZZIE. Orig./B. shows that JAMES B.JACKSON owned a plantation, 'Coldsprings' in Wash.Co., at the time of his death, which was completely destroyed during the war...fences burned, slaves emancipated, stock depleted,etc.MARY J.JACKSON,widow,was married to ROBERT H.HORD 2 Dec.1858, and he assumed the Adm.of Jackson's est. Creditors state that HORD owns no property of his own.//Pkt. includes a copy of a bill for $50 for tuition for Andrew JACKSON at St.Mary's College, Ky.// Case was appealed to the Miss.Supreme Court (Case #12137) 23 Jan.1872.// In PKT.#379:MOTHER COLUMBA CARROLL vs ROBERT H.HORD, the Mother superior of Nazareth Academy in Ky.is suing for the money owed for the education of LIZZIE JACKSON for 1866,1867 - $800. Description of 'Coldsprings Plt.':W.1/2 of W.1/2 & E.1/2 of N.W.1/4, Sec.30,T19N.,R7W: E.1/2 of L.6, Sec.23; S.1/2 of Sec.24; L.1,2,3,4,& part of 7, Sec.25; L.5,6,7, and E.1/2 of Sec.26 all in T19N,R8W. containing 1299 ac.//An instrument filed July 23,1872, "suggests" the death of ROBERT H.HORD, and states that LIZZIE JACKSON has intermarried with CHARLES PARTEE.

PKT. #1730:ROBERT CLARKE VS LYMAN G.ALDRICH,et al:Filed May 1868: CLARKE accuses LYMAN G. and wife,the former BETTY A.WILSON,** of trespassing,and seeks damages of $1600. Included in this pkt.is a personal letter written to Col.ROBERT CLARKE,from 'London Plt.',Feb.28,1867 by L.G.ALDRICH, in which he states that he regrets that he has no (cash) money at this time to pay his debt to Col.Clarke,but that he intends to pay as soon as he is able. Bill in question is dated Nov.29,1861, Natchez, for equipment-$858 to MRS.BETTIE A.WILSON. [NOTE: BETTY ANN BUCKNER, dau./ of DR.THOMAS BUCKNER, marr.1st THOMAS W.WILSON,who decd.21 Apr.1861]

WASHINGTON CO.,MS.
CHANCERY COURT RECORDS
RANDOM SELECTIONS

PKT.#235: JOHN T.FOOTE, of N.J. vs. HARVEY MILLER's Heirs at law. Filed 4 Apr.1868: Orig./Bill- FOOTE states that on 30 July 1855 HARVEY MILLER bought land from GEORGE W.WARD, a resident of La.,but now living in Ky. MILLER decd.around 1858, and exects. of his est. were his widow BETTY and E.P.JOHNSON. He also names the 5 children of Miller, decd. as :BETTY,since dead;SALLY marr.to HAL YERGER; MAGGIE; MALVINA, and HARVEY. JOHNSON as exect.of est.of MILLER, made out a note to WARD for debts owed by Est., and WARD,in turn,endorsed same over to JOHN T. FOOTE. Because of business complications, FOOTE adds the names of the BULLETS,SMITH and WARDS as defts.+E.J.COMSTOCK, as Grdn.to minor ch.of MILLER.//Court decreed that they owed FOOTE $19,000. Land sold for debt and FOOTE bought it for $5,000.

PKT.#248:S.F.WHITE of Wash.Co.,Ms.vs GORDON G.SIMS,et al.
S.F.WHITE has entered a contract of partnership with GORDON G.SIMS in the latter part of 1865 for farming in 1866, on a portion of 'Sligo Plt.' WHITE's part was 1/4th of the money,equipment,etc.and he was to do all employing, farming,and act as manager of place. GORDON G. furnished 3/4th of everything and was to sell the crops. WHITE is unhappy about the division of the partnership's chattels,and accuses GORDON G. and R.G.SIMS of mortgaging some of the stock to other persons-such as JOHN H.NELSON,A.J.PAXTON, JUREY & HARRIS.

PKT.#256:E.J.BOWERS vs N.C.ORRICK and wife,et al:Filed Apr.30, 1868: <u>Orig./Bill</u>:by Complt.EATON J.BOWERS of Madison Co.,Ms. vs NICHOLAS C.ORRICK and his wife MARY ORRICK of Mad.Co. and ANDREW G.SEMMES, address unknown.EATON shows that JOHN R.SEMMES decd.1864, a resident of Wash.Co.,Ms.,leaving as heirs MRS.LUCY SEMMES, his widow,since decd.; MARY ORRICK and her husband N.C.ORRICK,the latter claiming the right of his wife; and ANDREW G.SEMMES whose residence is unknown to orator. JOHN R.SEMMES owned: Secs.13 & 14 in T17N,R6W-@1200 ac.recorded in Deed Bk."R"Wash.Co.,P.325,326.[**Note**: From Bourbon to the Sunflw.River] LUCY SEMMES decd.1867,having never claimed dower rights and the land remains undivided between MARY and her husband, and ANDREW G. In May 1866,ORRICK petitions for L/A on Est.of Mr.and Mrs.Semmes, and receives it. E.J.BOWERS claims that SEMMES owed him $240 + 10% int. since Jan. 1861, and entered suit in the Circuit Ct.in Mad.Co. Judgement awarded BOWERS $401. When he moved to collect same from the sd.estate, the sheriff of Wash.Co.,A.B.CARSON returned the subpoena,stating there

WASHINGTON CO.,MS.
CHANCERY COURT RECORDS
RANDOM SELECTIONS

were no goods,possessions,chattel "in my county" belonging to J.R.SEMMES. IN 1868:GEORGE MOORMAN, Sherf.of Mad.Co.,states that JOHN R.SEMMES had no property in Mad.Co.// BOWERS claims that JOHN R.SEMMES owned 1200 unemcumbered acrs. in Wash.Co. in 1868.//Document shows the original debt was made to THOMAS T.LITTLE, who passed the note on to BOWERS.// One of the documents shows that the Shrf.of Mad.Co.in 1867 was JOHN T.SEMMES.//Complts case was dismissed.

PKT.#251: E.W.JACK & E.H.PORTER vs WADE HAMPTON &JNO.D.COBB
Orig./B.says that on 1 Dec.1859,COBB sold to HAMPTON the following lands: All of sec.5; N.W.1/4 of Sec.8 - both in T.14N.,R7W. + all of Sec.32; S.1/2 and N.W.1/4 of Sec.29; L.2 in Sec.30 - T.15N.,R7W + L.5 in Sec.24 - T.15N.,R8W. $10,431 to be pd.in 3 notes. The 1st note was paid in 1860. The 2nd payment, due 1861 was pd.by note, which COBB turned over to JACK. The 3rd note was turned over to PORTER.//Subp.28 Apr.1868 left with WADE HAMPTON,SR.//Subp. 2 Nov.1868 left with E.E.ROOT// S.W. FERGUSON is asignee in the Bkrpty of WADE HAMPTON - 27 Jan.1871.

PKT.#263:THOMAS H.HOOD vs WM.N.HOOD,et al- Filed May 23,1868. Complt.THOMAS H.HOOD files Orig./B.stating that his late father owned a large plantation with one SIDNEY R.SMITH. After his father's death,THOS.'s mother,MARY A.HOOD, filed for a division of the estate and a sale of HOOD'S portion. There were 3 children-THOS.H.,WM.N.,and LIZZIE. His mother chose to take a child's share .[note: she had a choice between a child's share and her dower share which would have given her a larger portion of the est.] Sister LIZZIE intermarried with W.R.FLEMING and has since decd.leaving a dau,MARY H.FLEMING, as her only child. When the plantation was put up for sale, WM.N.HOOD bought the sd.plt.for $100,000, of which $25,000 was THOS.H.'s part as his inheritance. THOS.H. was a minor at the time, and did not need the money, so he accepted WM.N.'s note for his share, with his mother signing the note as surety. W.R.FLEMING was Thos.H.'s Grdn. Then MRS.HOOD died in Ky. and W.R.FLEMING was the Adm.of her est.in Ky.,where he resides. In 1861, WM.N.HOOD gave a D/T to R.L.DIXON to secure a separate estate for his wife CLARA H.HOOD, from whom he had borrowed sums of money. THOS.H.HOOD feels that he is due much more from the estate of his mother who acted as surety on Wm.N.'s notes. Thos.H.is not yet 21, but the State of Ky, where he resides, has waived "this disability", and recorgnizes him as an adult capable of attending to his own affairs.// INDENTURE:Dated 29 May 1861: Contract entered into at the time of their

WASHINGTON CO.,MS.
CHANCERY COURT RECORDS
RANDOM SELECTIONS

marriage between WM.N.HOOD and his wife CLARA HICKMAN, shows that she is entitled to inherit from her father,WM.HICKMAN of Bourbon Co.,Ky and also from her brother,DAVID HICKMAN. This inheritance has been partially received from her grdn. in Ky.,JOHN H.SHACKLEFORD + a part received through ROBERT DAVIS and converted to her own use,@$7000. Included in the D/T from WM.N.HOOD and R.L.DIXON,Trustee were slaves and land on Deer Creek,Wash.Co.,Ms.known as the 'SMITH & HOOD Plt.',described by WM.N. as having been from his father and mother's estates,"or by purchase by him".//Nov.Term 1868:Comm.reports that WM.N.HOOD owes THOMAS HOWARD HOOD $437,579.65//Nov.18,1868: Bankruptcy of WM.N.HOOD "suggested".

PKT.#363:DAN WILLIAMS * VS S.T.TAYLOR, et al Filed:July 2,1870
Original/Bill:DAN WILLIAMS states that he bought 80 ac.of land up for sale because of delinquent Levee Taxes due $62. The land - W. 1/2 of S.E. 1/4 of Sec.10, T17N,R7W - belonged to SAMUEL T.TAYLOR and wife JANE TAYLOR. The land holdings of Saml.and Jane Taylor in the 1860's was 2644 ac.,more or less,lying in T17N,R7W and called 'SALLY' and'KILLARNEY PLTS.'
    S.W. 1/4 & W. 1/2 of S.E. 1/4 of Sec.2; E. 1/2 Sec.10; E. 1/2 & S.W. 1/4 of Sec.11; E.1/2 & E. 1/2 of N.W. 1/4 Sec.12; E. 1/2 & S.W. 1/4 & W. 1/2 of the N.W. 1/4 of Sec.13; All of Sec.14
SAMUEL T.TAYLOR didn't appear for the court hearing on the delinquent taxes Aug.1870 - he was living at that time in Memphis,Tn. according to a subpoena issued for the hearing.
*[Note: DAN WILLIAMS decd.1902 in Mississippi City.]

PKT.#364:JONES S.HAMLITON vs J.H.& W.A.P.DILLINGHAM :Filed Nov. 22,1870. Pkt.contains a copy of a document showing that on Sept.1869, J.L.CARTER, asignee of Bankruptcy of one JONES S.HAMILTON, put up land for sale, and that JONES S.HAMILTON bought it back at the City Hall in Jackson,Ms. 6 Sept.1869 for $50-5000 ac.in Wash.Co.,Ms. desc.as follows: Sec.19,and Sec.30; W.1/2 and N.E. 1/4 of Sec.31-T17N,R7W + E.1/2 Sec.29; E.1/2 Sec.30; N.E.1/4 Sec.38-T17N.,R8W; N.W.1/4 Sec.32; N.W.1/4 Sec.33; W.1/2 Sec.29; W.1/2 Sec.20 - T17N, R7W.// DEPOSITION: of JONES S.HAMILTON taken in open court (Wash.Co.)on 22 Nov.1870 in which he says that he owned a store in Woodville,Ms.,Wilkinson Co. and J.P.DILLINGHAM approached him in Oct.'1864 to buy 1 undivided 1/2 interest in some land in Wash.Co.,paying $25,000. Of this amount,$10,000 was paid. Land was previously owned by the SIMS. JONES S. stated that he talked to DR.W.R.

WASHINGTON CO.,MS.
CHANCERY COURT RECORDS
RANDOM SELECTIONS

SIMS about the character of the land,etc. DILLINGHAM told JONES S. that he(DILLINGHAM) was the sole owner and the title was clear. At this same time MR.ELDER,the brother-in-law of J.P.DILLINGHAM was doing business in Woodville, and he,JONES S., saw him regularly. No one mentioned the D/T J.P.DILLINGHAM had made out to his cousin,W.A.P.DILLINGHAM, until 1865, when JONES S. was contacted by WM.L.NUGENT,a lawyer from Wash.Co. When asked about the D/T, JOHN P.DILLINGHAM professed ignorance of such and said he would get it straight when his cousin came to Ms.in the fall from Maine. JONES S. avows that W.A.P.DILLINGHAM served in the Union Army at Natchez and he and J.P.were in contact at that time. There follows a chronicle of swapping documents, missing signing documents because of steamboat schedules,etc.that borders on the slap-stick// Others involved in the final business arrangements were ALFRED C.HOLT and DAN WILLIAMS.

PKT.#376:WM.SCOTT of Wash.Co.,Ms.vs PARMELIA EMELINE SCOTT Filed 16 Aug.1870. DIVORCE: WM.SCOTT says they were marr. Philips Co., Ark.14 yrs.ago. 3 children: WILLIAM,age 8,and JAMES-4, and ALICE,age 2. They moved from Bolivar Co.,Ms.to Wash.Co.in 1867.PARMELIA has a dau., age 14, by another husband, and WM.SCOTT accuses them of trying to kill him with a brick,a club and then an ax.[Note: Divorce was not easy to come by. Grounds were either extreme Cruelty or Adultery.]

PKT.#377:J.B.M.LAWSON vs E.A.LAWSON . Filed 16 Aug.1870;DIVORCE: J.B.M. states that on 1 Sept.1847 in Lancaster Co.,Va., he and ELIZABETH O.BANACK were marr. by ---JONES a Method.minister. They had children- LUCY, who died young,OSCAR now a res.of Mo.and age @20, and WILLIE-7 yrs. They have lived in Ms.18 yrs.//DIVORCE granted and alimony set at $15 per month,to start June 1,1871.

PKT.#440:EVERMAN & CO.vs. W.N.JOHNSON: Filed 12 May 1871.Chattel Loan to JOHNSON for work on MRS.A.C.WEST's plt.on Deer Creek. EVERMAN claims debt never paid. 4 bales of cotton were seized at G.W.THOMAS's gin by the Sheriff, who placed them in the hands of HARRY PETERS,ginman,for safe keeping, until the suit could be settled. //DEPOSITION of G.W.THOMAS, of Canton,(Ms.) who states that he is 31 yrs.old,an agent for MRS.A.C.WEST, and said he sold the cotton in question to pay the rent due. Shrf.L.T.WEBBER is accused of letting the 4 bales of cotton get away and WEBBER appeals to the Supreme Court of Ms..

WASHINGTON CO.,MS.
CHANCERY COURT RECORDS
RANDOM SELECTIONS

PKT.#445:WELLS,BUCKNER,&ROBB vs JEROME CROSS: Orig./B.filed by Complts.J.A.WELLS,D.M.BUCKNER,J.H.ROBB merchants at Auburn Landing,Ms. who agreed on 12 Mar.1870 to furnish JEROME CROSS for not over $150 for cultivation of part of 'Morehead Plt.'(Chattel Loan) 32 ac.,owned by heirs of C.I.MERCHANT.//Summons to deftds.returned, not executed,19 Sept.1871// Summons delivered to JEROME 8 July 1872.

PKT.#448:JEFFERSON DAVIS,et al Exect. vs MARY M.RUCKS,et al Filed June 10,1871: The Complts. were JEFFERSON DAVIS, of Memphis; J.H.D.BOWMAR of Vicksburg,Ms.;HUGH R.DAVIS of Wilk.Co.,Ms.;JAS.D.SMITH a res.of La. as Exects.of Last Will and Testament of JOSEPH E.DAVIS,decd. vs MARY RUCKS wife of ARTHUR RUCKS,decd.;AMANDA RUCKS,JAMES RUCKS, GRANT RUCKS,SARAH RUCKS-minor heirs of whom MARY RUCKS is the natural Grdn.and the Adm.of her husband's Est.-all residents of WAsh. Co. + JAMES T.(or F) RUCKS and wife SARAH res.of Friars Point,Ms.Coahoma Co., ORIG/BILL JOS.E.DAVIS, a res.of Warren Co.,Ms.decd.1870,testate.His WILL has been probated,L/A allowed. Adms. show that on 1 June 1859,JOS.E. DAVIS and his wife ELIZA, sold to ARTHUR and JAMES RUCKS, partners in planting, a tract of land in Wash.Co.:Sec.1 and Sec.12,T18N, R7W + E.1/2 SEc.9;E.1/2 Sec.17; E.1/2 of S.W.1/4 SEc.20-T18N, R6W@1900 ac.[Note: JAMES later sold S.W.1/4 of Sec.12 for Levee taxes.] Scheldule of payments follows.(DBk."R"pgs.552-554 Wash.Co.) ARTHUR RUCKS decd.1860, intestate. In 1868 JAMES RUCKS,surviving partner,filed for Bankruptcy, with GEORGE R.ALCORN appointed as his asignee. The Adms.further show that when JAMES was forced to sell a portion of the land for taxes, it was bought by WM.YERGER,who in turn sold it to SARAH B.RUCKS,JAMES's wife. They claim that this piece is in the hands of JAMES RUCKS and his brother L.T.RUCKS// FINAL DECREE:MARY M. and heirs of ARTHUR RUCKS,decd. are ordered to pay $48,345 in 10 days.//PKT. also contains **WILL OF JOSEPH EMORY DAVIS**: of Warren Co.,Ms., WRITTEN-18 Mar.1869-"I am 85 yrs.old" Filed Wash.Co.,Ms.10 June 1871. He names:
2 gr.children:JOS.D.MITCHELL and MARY ELIZABETH MITCHELL
Dau:FLORIDA LAUGHLIN to get "Diamond Place"in Warr.Co. @1200 ac.and at
    her death it reverts to JOS.D.MITCHELL. Should JOS.D.MITCHELL die
    before FLORIDA,then the place goes to "my nephew" JOS.E.DAVIS-son of
    HUGH R.DAVIS of Wilk.Co.,Ms.
Dau:CAROLINE LEONARD-land in Mad.P.La.@1100 ac.to be sold and she is to
    get $1000 a yr.for life.
The estate should realize $300,000 from the sale of 'Hurricane Plt.' and

WASHINGTON CO.,MS.
CHANCERY COURT RECORDS
RANDOM SELECTIONS

'Brierfield Plt.' below Vicksburg, to BENJ.T.MONTGOMERY,WM.THORNTON
MONTGOMERY,ISAIAH MONTGOMERY, payable in 1876.
Exects. are to set aside *100,000 for gr.dau.MARY ELIZABETH MITCHELL and
$50,000 to gr.son JOS.D.MITCHELL
To:MARGARET DAVIS,JEFFERSON DAVIS,WILLIAM DAVIS,VARINA DAVIS-
    children of my brother JEFFERSON DAVIS- $20,000 each.
Requests his Exects. to sell land near Grand Gulf in Claib.Co.,Ms.
States that he has sold land in Wash.Co.,Ms to ARTHUR AND JAMES RUCKS,
whose notes for $42,000 I hold. + lands on Cash River,White River,in
Monroe Co.,Jackson Co., and Woodruff Co.,Ark. @12000 ac. + a small tract of
318 ac.on Wash Lake in Warr.Co.
Sisters:ANNA SMITH,AMANDA BRADFORD,LUCINDA STAMPS
Neice:LUCY BOYLE
Neices:LUCY MITCHELL,MARY M.DAVIS-daus.of my nephew ISAAC STAMPS
To:MRS.MARTHA HARRIS
Nephews:J.DAVIS BRODHEAD,JOS.E.DAVIS,JOS.DAVIS SMITH,ROBERT
        ANDERSON,ALEX T.MITCHELL
Faithful Servant:JACK RAILEY
Exect.:brother JEFF DAVIS of Warren Co.,Ms.;J.H.D.BOWMAR of Vicksburg;
HUGH R.DAVIS of Wilk.Co.,Ms.;JOS.D.SMITH of La.,to serve without security.
Wit"B.R.THOMAS,J.A.KLEIN,GEO.M.KLEIN
Presented for Probate in Warren Co.,Ms. 10 Mar.1871. Recorded Will
Bk."B",p.11-13
Pkt. also contains copy of Deed from JOS.E.DAVIS and wife ELIZA DAVIS to
ARTHUR RUCKS of Wash.Co. and JAMES T. RUCKS of Hinds Co.

PKT.*452:JOHN ALLEN vs ELLEN JOHNSON and WM.H.JOHNSON,her
husband, and BETTY SHELBY and her husband THOMAS SHELBY.
Filed:July 13,1871: Orig./Bill JOHN ALLEN states that he was hired in 1870
by WM.H.JOHNSON and THOMAS SHELBY as an agent and overseer on "SALLY'
and 'KILLARNEY PLTS.' S.E.1/4 of Sec.11; E.1/2 of S.W.1/4 of Sec.11;
S.W.1/4 & W.1/2 of N.W.1/4 of Sec.12; W.1/2 of Sec.13; and all of Sec.14,
in T.17 N.,R7W. and N.W.1/4 of Sec.7 in T17,R6W. On Feb.4,1871, settlement
day came for the previous year,and he submitted his bill for $959. THOMAS
SHELBY gave him 2 drafts on JOHNSON & SHELBY for $450 each on the Com-
mercial House of JOS.HAY & CO. in N.O. At the time of the maturity of
these sd.notes, WM.H.JOHNSON was connected to Jos.Hay & Co., and he and
his wife ELLEN were living in N.O. ALLEN claims neither note was ever
paid,for when they were offered for payment they were turned down for

WASHINGTON CO.,MS.
CHANCERY COURT RECORDS
RANDOM SELECTIONS

lack of funds on part of JOHNSON & SHELBY.// In Dec. the Bill was dismissed, and ALLEN filed for an appeal to the Miss. Supreme court.on Nov.5, 1873. Commissioner CALDWELL McGRATH reported ALLEN's claim was valid,and with interest,JOHNSON & SHELBY now owed ALLEN $1113.57, and ordered the deftds.to pay. THOMAS SHELBY'S name was dropped from the final decree. PKT.#502:JOS.HAY & CO. vs JOHNSON & SHELBY deals with the the same property,and the same people. This Pkt.contains a copy of the DEED from MARTHA J.JONES and her husband T.N.JONES to ELLEN JOHNSON and BETTIE SHELBY,dated 22 Mar.1870-and shows that ELLEN and BETTIE paid $40,000 for 'SALLY' and 'KILLARNEY PLTS.' on Deer Creek, formerly the property of SAMUEL T.TAYLOR.(Same descrption as above) In additon, the JONES quit claim any interest they may have in E.1/2 of S.E.1/4 of Sec.10,T17N,R7W.adjacent to and heretofore included as part of sd.plts. Filed July 11,1872.Name of sd.Plts - 'SALLY'and 'KILLARNEY'was now changed to "ISOLA PLT.'// In the Orig./bill of Jos.Hays & Co.the following facts emerge: ELLEN and WM.H.JOHNSON have moved to Ark.by 1872. After the purchase of the two Plts.,now called 'ISOLA', BETTIE and THOMAS SHELBY moved on sd.plt.,he as manager and agent for his wife. They did their ginning at 'Magenta Plt.'// In his ANSWER to Orig./Bill,Filed 26 Aug.1874, JOHNSON claims that he was employed by HAYS & CO. as business manager,with the understanding that,as such,his salary was to be used to cover the cost of supplying 'ISOLA PLT.'. In the meantime,HAYS & CO. were forced to go out of business, and it was taken over by E.E.NORTON. JOHNSON claims the books were no longer available to him, and he dosen't know how much is owed by 'ISOLA' or how much is owed to him, nor how much had been applied to 'ISOLA'// ANSWER of BETTIE SHELBY-filed 27 Aug.1872, who states that her husband,THOMAS,is now decd.and claims complete ignorance of the whole affair. She said that her husband had handled all the affairs. He had been very ill, and had gone to Hot Springs, Ark.for his health. He has since died.// In Nov.1872 the Bill of Complts. was dismissed. It was appealed to the Ms.Supreme Ct. and the decision was reversed. 9 Feb.1874.

PKT.#453:WALLACE & CO. vs AMELIUS C.WEST,et al
Orig./bill filed 10 Aug.1871 in which Complts. DAVID WALLACE, JAMES WALLACE and GEORGE G.WILDER, merchts.in N.O. claim that AMELIUS and CARRIE WEST, as Adm's. of the Est.of GEORGE W.VAUGHAN, owe them $270. AMELIUS and CARRIE are living in St.Louis.[Note: CARRIE was the widow of GEO.VAUGHAN]

WASHINGTON CO.,MS.
CHANCERY COURT RECORDS
RANDOM SELECTIONS

PKT.#408:N.W.WILSON, et al vs C.S.STONE, et al: Filed 28 Jan. 1871 O/B:shows that N.W.WILSON of Boone Co.,Mo. is the father of THOMPSON WILSON of same county, and LOUISA WILKINSON,wife of A.G.WILKINSON, of Washington,D.C.-sole heirs of JAMES S.WILSON,late of Wash.Co.,Ms.Complts. vs CALEB S.STONE, Exectr.of Last Will and Testament of said JAMES S. WILSON,decd. and KATE STONE,OWEN STONE all of Boone Co.,Mo. and JOS.W. STONE,W.W.STONE,DAVID L.STONE and W.A.EVERMAN and JAMES S.WALKER, the last 2 being surviving partners in EVERMAN & WILSON, merchants in G'ville,Ms. as Defendants.The following facts concerning the WILL of JAMES S.WILSON,decd..emerge:N.W.WILSON was the father of JAMES S. WILSON by a previous marriage, and JAMES S.WILSON was the 1/2 brother to FRANKLIN and LOUISA. JAMES S. decd.in Boone Co.,Mo.leaving a WILL,his father claims is not valid. All property was in Greenville,Ms.and was extensive-interest in a wharehouse, lot and a stock of goods.//COPY OF WILL OF JAMES S.WILSON :[Not recorded in Will Bk.in Wash.Co.,Ms.] Written 17 Aug.1870-Names his cousin DR.JAMES WALKER of Greenville,Ms. who has shown great kindness and attention to me. Requests that the business be split up, and his share sold. His beloved Uncle CALEB S.STONE to be exect. and to keep all his possessions in trust for CALEB S.STONE'S 5 children-KATE,OWEN, W.W., JOSIAH, DAVID L.STONE. Wit:H.B.LONSDALE, JOHN MACHER [sp.varies] WILL proven Columbia,Boone Co.,Mo.26 Sept.1870. // **ANSWER:** of W.W. and JOSHIAH W.STONE-June 8,1871: They state that they are 1st cousin of JAMES S.WILSON,decd. and their father CALEB S. STONE is JAMES's maternal Uncle. JAMES S. lived with the Stone family on and off for sometime. JAMES's mother died when he was very young. She was the sister of CALEB S.STONE and JAMES was her only child. JAMES's father, N.W.WILSON married a 2nd time, and JAMES was very unhappy due to this marriage.// ANSWER: OF KATE, CALEB S.,DAVID L.and OWEN STONE- July 20, 1871. [Note: In this document it becomes apparent that CALEB S. STONE'S sister married N.W. WILSON and CALEB S.STONE's wife was the sister of N.W. WILSON. The children KATE,W.W.,DAVID, OWEN,JOSHIAH were <u>double</u> 1st cousins to JAMES WILSON. The given names of the mother, step- mother, and Aunt are never used.]// DEPOSITION: JOHN MACHER(wit.to WILL)-age 51, resident of Columbia, Mo., a farmer. He states that JAMES S.WILSON sent for him Aug.1870. At the time JAMES was lying ill at his Uncle CALEB S.STONES. JAMES asked JOHN to write down his WILL. JAMES S. WILSON died 8 or 9 days after the said WILL was written, at the home of his Uncle CALEB'S, of consumption. He,JOHN MACHER,was a 1st cousin to CALEB STONE'S wife. JOHN took his notes to the law office of SQUIRE TURNER,JR.,

WASHINGTON CO., MS.
CHANCERY COURT RECORDS
RANDOM SELECTIONS

who wrote the WILL, and JOHN returned with it the next day for JAMES to examine it. He did and signed it before the 2 aforementioned witnesses.// DEPOSITION; JULIA ANN CURRY, age 55, ex-slave, lives with SQUIRE TURNER,JR. in Columbia. I am a cook. I've known JAMES S.WILSON ever since he was born on 30 Aug.1837 in Columbia,Mo. I belonged to his mother when she married N.W.WILSON and was a servant in the family of Mr. WILSON until 5 Jan.1865. I was JAMES'S principle nurse during his infancy and childhood. I first knew MR.WILSON in 1837,and have known JAMES'S step-mother since she was a girl. In Spring of 1839, N.W.WILSON moved his wife and son to the country to live with his mother's family, while he went east, and while he was gone, JAMES's mother died. In Spring of 1841, N.W. WILSON marr.again. In spring of 1842, N.W.WILSON then moved his family away from his mother's. James thought highly of his father,but never got along with his step-mother. He loved his UNCLE CALEB, and died at his house Aug.24,1870. My dau.SALLY ANN waited on him. Asked if there was any relationship between CALEB S.STONE and his lawyer SQUIRE TURNER,JR. who wrote out the WILL, JULIA ANN said SQ.TURNER,JR.'S mother and CALEB S.STONE were double 1st cousins,and MRS.TURNER is also related to CALEB, her father being CALEB'S 1st cousin. The children all played together when little.// DEPOSITION : HENRY B. LONSDALE [wit.to WILL] age 39,live Columbia,Mo.,a merchant-tailor. He swears that JAMES was of sound mind when signing WILL. LONSDALE had once been a business partner of CALEB S.STONE. //DEPOSITION: of JOHN A.WOODSON -age 28, resident of Wash. Co., Ms., a Planter. Have known JAMES S.WILSON all my life. JAMES Served in the First Delaware during the War,the same company as his Uncle CALEB -they messed together,he thought highly of him. JAMES boarded with JOSHIAH STONE in Greenville,Ms.(his cousin) He loved his father, but had no use for his step-mother or her children. I saw him one week before he died at CALEB S.STONES. //INJUNCTION: The WILSONs succeed in getting an injunction to stop the sale of JAMES's interest in EVERMAN & CO.Bond was $5000. **FINAL DECREE:** In favor of defendants.

PKT.266: R.T.CARRICO vs ROBERT H.LOWREY and DAVID HOLLIS: Filed 22 Sept.1868: O/B shows that CARRICO bought land lying in Wash.Co., Ms. in 1864 from LOWREY. LOWREY had bought it from HOLLIS, and the title is not clear.//July-1864:ASHLEY CO.,ARK, LOWREY to CARRICO of Franklin P.,La. n 1/2 Sec.4,T19N,R10W - 320 ac. $10,000 to be paid in 4% Confed. bonds. A penciled note on back: "*LOWREY lives in Texas*". HOLLIS also a non-resident. DEED issued through the court. 18 Nov.1868.

WASHINGTON CO.,MS.
CHANCERY COURT RECORDS
RANDOM SELECTIONS

PKT.284:MARY W.RIVES and her husband O.C.RIVES vs JOHN DE
SOUTER: Filed 18 Nov.1868: JOHN DeSOUTER, a carpenter, files suit (a
mechanics Lien) to recover the money spent remodeling a house for O.C.
RIVES. DeSOUTER states that the agreement was for him to move a house
belonging to RIVES from its place in Black Bayou, to a lot on Deer Creek.
(Near present Arcola) During the construction of sd.house, he and his
workers lived with the RIVES. But DeSOUTER claims that RIVES didn't pay
him in full, and he asks that the court force the sale of sd.house to get
him his money.//MARY RIVES states that the house is sitting on her
private property, and is not subject to debts of her husband.and seeks an
injunction to stop DeSOUTER and the Sheriff from selling same. Land she
bought on Feb.25,1866 in her own right-200 ac.SW Corner Sec.36,T17N,
R7W,Wash.Co.Ms. O.C.RIVES'S land is S 1/2 and the N.--1/4 of Sec.33 and
the SW 1/4 SEc.34,and SW 1/4 of Sec.36, all in T17N,R7W.//Mary received
an injunction after appearing before Justice of the Peace SAML.T.TAYLOR.
Bond for $800 co-signed by GUSTIN W.THOMAS,WILSON BELL,D.D.JACKSON
and wit.by H.R.WEST,M.R.SANDERS.//Court decreed that DeSOUTER was
entitled to $405, and the injunction was dissolved.

PKT.*318 1/2:CLARINDA G.MARTIN vs MRS.WILTON WILLS
(sometimes spelled WELLS) Filed 14 Oct.1869: PARTITION of LAND
CLARINDA G.MARTIN,widow of JOHN MARTIN,decd.;HENRY MARTIN; ELLEN
ROGERS,ANDREW ROGERS,WILLIE ROGERS,minors under 21,suing by their
father and next friend WM.O.ROGERS as Complts. vs MRS.WILLIE WILLS,
widow of WM.S.WILLS; WM.S.WILLS(JR.),MINNIE LEE WILLS,SALLIE WILLS-
last 3 named minors under 21. O/B:CLARINDA states that long before
1848 her late husband and father of your orators owned land with WM.S.
WILLS in Wash.Co.,Ms. called RECLUSE PLT.-2443 ac.undivided moity.
    SW 1/4 and W 1/2 of SE 1/4 of Sec.5 - S 1/2 of Sec.6 -
    E 1/2 of E 1/2 of Sec.7 - All of Sec.8 - W 1/2 of SW 1/4 of Sec.9 -
    All of Sec.17 - E 1/2 and S 1/2 of NW 1/4 Sec.20 - all in T16N,R4W
    [Land lying east of Sunflower river,above Hyw.12]
JOHN MARTIN died in 1848, leaving his widow CLARINDA and 9 children:3
daus.and 6 sons. 1 son and 1 dau.died shortly after his death,never having
married. Since then a dau.CLARINDA, 3 sons - JOHN, DWIGHT,and HOWARD
have all died,none having marr. Of the 3 remaining, GEORGE MARTIN gave
her,his mother, his rights to sd.land; MARY MARTIN married with WM.O.
ROGERS and died leaving the 3 children named above-ELLEN,ANDREW,
WILLIE ROGERS, minors; and HENRY MARTIN. In 1867 WM.S.WILLS died,

WASHINGTON CO.,MS.
CHANCERY COURT RECORDS
RANDOM SELECTIONS

leaving his widow WILLIE A. and 3 minor children-WM.S.,MINNIE LEE,SALLIE. The MARTINS and the WILLS seek partition of lands they hold jointly.// DEED of conveyance shows the land to lie on East and West of Cold Lake and S.W.Ferguson was appoinmed Commissioner to divide the land.// DEPOSITION of WILLIE WILLS taken Nov.8,1869, shows that she married WM. WILLS in Jackson,Ms. and he died 1867,leaving 3 ch. Wm.S.age 8,Minnie Lee-6,Sallie-3,sole heirs of Dr.W.S.WILLS.

PKT.#415:JAMES STONE, et ux vs AMANDA WORTHINGTON, et al
O/B states that JAMES STONE and his wife MARY (WORTHINGTON) STONE vs AMANDA WORTHINGTON,WM.W.WORTHINGTON,AMANDA W.BUCKNER, and her husband DAVIS BUCKNER, SAML.W.WORTHINGTON - both Complts and Deftdts. are the heirs at law of SAML.W.WORTHINGTON,decd. JAMES STONE is buying back a piece of land that had been lost for taxes,and found the land description was incorrect -Seeks clarification.

PKT.#347:JOHN W.HEATH vs MARGARET V.TAMPLIN :Filed Apr.8,1870:
O/B shows that HEATH a resident of Wash.co.,Ms. had bought on 25 Oct.1869, fromZACHARIAH TAMPLIN. late of sd.Co.,decd., 400 ac.of land known as the DOUGLASS and MCHATTON tract.
 Secs.11,12 and N 1/2 of Sec.14, T15N,R8W
DEED (of intent?) was signed by ZACHARIAH and MARGARET V.TAMPLIN, and then Zachariah fell ill before the final papers could be filed, leaving a widow and minor children, intestate.//Nov.28,1870:ANSWER: of JOHN KIRKLAND TAMPLIN, MARY LOU,OLIVIA,EUGENIA-minor heirs of Z.TAMPLIN who were appointed a Grd.Ad litem-JOHN FAWN.//SUBPOENA for MARGARET V.TAMPLIN left with her brother, HUDSON TAYLOR 26 Apr.1870.// AMENDED BILL: names children of ZACHARIAH TAMPLIN as PRICILLA COBER, a married dau., and the 4 minors named above.//PKT. contains a receipt signed by Z.TAMPLIN at Leota Landing 25 Oct.1869 from JOOHN W.HEATH.//DEPOSITION of L.B.VALLIANT, attorney,who made out the deed and delivered it to Zack.and stated he decd.before it was notatized.//H.A. TAYLOR,age 31,resident of Wash.Co.,Ms.a farmer,brother of the widow MARGARET V.TAMPLIN,went with ZACK to sign the Deed, but the Magistrte was absent, and Zack took sick and died before it could be signed.

PROBATE PKT.#342: * EST.OF H.R.WEST,decd., A.C.WEST, et al:Filed Aug.24,1868: Pet.for L/A.by AMELIUS C.WEST,HECTOR R.WEST,E.WINSTON WEST shows that their father,H.R.WEST, decd.-----, along with LIZZIE M.

WASHINGTON CO., MS.
CHANCERY COURT RECORDS
RANDOM SELECTIONS

and SALLIE B.WEST, daus.(unmarried minors) and his widow-V.O.WEST. H.W.WEST decd.,intestate, leaving the following land, 1720 ac.

    SW 1/4 & W 1/2 OF W 1/2 OF SE 1/4 SEC.20//   T15N
    W 1/2 & W 1/2 OF W 1/2 OF NE 1/4   " 29- All of SEC.30   R6W
    SE 1/4 of SEC.22//L.6,7 SEC.25//L.1,2,5,6 SEC.35   T15N, R7W

The heirs seek partition of property. They show that the widow, V.O.WEST, lost her interest as a result of a judgement against her in Wash.Co.Circuit Court, which sd.interest was bought by WM.A.HAYCRAFT, who in turn conveyed it to your petitioners by DEED 10 July 1867.// Written on cover in pencil *"Dismissed at the cost of petitioners"* .//E.J.COMSTOCK was appointed Grdn.ad litem for the minor girls - Oct.27,1868// COMMISSIONERS appointed to divide the Est.:THOS.H.HILL,A.D.ALDRIDGE,JULIUS THOMPSON,J.W.WINGFIELD, A.CHEW, Oct.1868//JUNE 28,1869, LIZZIE WEST has married WM.T.**BARNARD and SALLY is still a minor. COMMISSIONERS are changed to F.J.MOSS,DAVID FRILEY,JULIUS THOMPSON,JOHN BAREFIELD, GEO.R.FARMER.**[NOTE: LIZZIE MAURY WEST married WM.BAILEY BARNARD, not his father,WM.T., on 17 Dec.1868.Marr.Bk."A"p.101; Wash.Co.,Ms.]

PKT.#434:MARIA L. and her husband C.E.MORGAN, heirs of R.T. ARCHER,decd. vs A.B.CARSON :Filed Apr.20,1871: MARIA and C.E.MORGAN are from Wash.co.,Ms. as Complts. vs MRS.----ARCHER,widow of R.T. ARCHER, decd.;ABRAM,MARY,JENNIE,R.T.ARCHER,JR, ELIZABETH PERCY and her husband ----PERCY of Copiah Co.,Ms.; and ANNIE IRVIN and ---IRVIN,her husb. of Henrico Co.,Va.(Richmond)- all heirs at law of RICHARD T.ARCHER, decd. and unknown heirs of HORACE CARPENTER,decd.,residence unknown. O/B concerns land sold for taxes: On 23 Apr.1867,Shrf.CARSON of Wash. Co.,Ms. sold,for delinquent levee taxes,land owned by sd.R.T.ARCHER, now decd., and HORACE CARPENTER,also now decd..Land was:

    S.1/2 of Sec.27,W 1/2 of Sec.29,N 1/2 Sec.31,L.7 Sec.33,All of Sec.28,
    W 1/2 of Sec.30,All of Sec.32: lying in T17N,R8W - @2643 ac.;

On 7 Jan.1870, sd.land was struck off to MARIA L.MORGAN, Recorded DBk. "X"p.214,215,Wash.Co. The time for redemption has expired, and MARIA seeks title // Court warded her a clear title, May 1871.

PKT.#556: EST.MARSHALL BURDETTE -R.BURDETTE Adm. Filed Dec.2, 1878. Pet.for L/A by RICHARD BURDETTE,shows that MARSHALL decd. in Wash.Co.,Ms.1 (Nov.?)1878 at his residence,leaving a small personal est. @$1500;the crop on the place is mortgd.; he had no wife or children,"I am his only brother and next of kin". Bd.$2000

WASHINGTON CO.,MS.
CHANCERY COURT RECORDS
RANDOM SELECTIONS

PKT.#289:JULIA R.WORDEN vs GEORGE WORDEN - Divorce Case. O/B. filed by JULIA's father H.B.PUTNAM vs her husband GEORGE who is a non-resident of Ms. Facts about the family: JULIA and her family, consisting of her mother, and others, lived in Wayne Co.,Mich. Her father,H.R.PUTNAM,was away as a member of the National Army, in the South. On Apr.16,1865,JULIA (age 14) eloped with GEORGE(age @21) agst. her mother's wishes. They lived with her family for a few mos. then he left and went to Ill. In late 1865, Mr.Putnam moved his family to Wash.Co.,Ms. Julia joined them there in Mar.1866, and her dau., of whom she seeks custody, was b.there in late Mar.// DEPOSITIONS: (1) HIRAM B. PUTNAM;father of JULIA;age 50;merch; res. G'ville,Ms.;lived in Ill.before moving to Mich.(2)MRS.ELIZABETH A.PUTNAM:mother of JULIA; age 45;wife of HIRAM;res. G'ville;lived Belleville, Mich.(3)CHARLES PUTNAM;age 21; farmer;res.G'ville;bro.of JULIA's;"I was in the army when they marr."// DECREE granted May 1869.

PKT.#521:RACHEL DAWSEY vs JOHN DAWSEY : Divorce-Dec.9,1872; Rachel claims both are of Wash.Co.,Ms.,married Oct.1856 in sd.co. Seeks alimony.DEPOSITION: John states thay had both been former slaves, and never were legally marr.//Divorce granted-no alimony.

PKT.#526:SUSAN ADDISON vs CALEB ADDISON : Divorce-Filed Dec.17, 1872// They were marr.1865 or 66 by one THOMAS SAMPSON .

PKT.#538:ELIZA KEONE vs EMMA EASTIN,et al: Filed Jan.20,1873 ELIZA of Wash.Co.,Ms.in O/B. shows that she bought land from Y.J.COMPTON on 23 Jan.1869. Y.J.COMPTON decd.leaving EMMA EASTIN as his sole heir. C.C.EASTIN is EMMA's husband,and they live Fresno,Calif. ELIZA seeks clarification of Title.// DECREE in favor of ELIZA KEONE.

PKT.#482: JOHN S.& AMELIA E.PENRICE vs W.B.WHEATLEY: O/B missing. AGREEMENT: 2 JAN.1871,between AMELIA and her husband JOHN S. PENRICE and EMMA N.WHEATLEY- a lot,bought by the Penrice's,L#10, Court - house Add.on which the Planters Exchange Hotel now (1871)stands worth $12,500// DEPOSITION:(1) W.M.SAUNDERS; Taken Apr.1872;age 55;Bkkpr. at the "Penrice House";res.G'ville; Heard a conversation between JOHN S. and W.B. in the barroom of the Penrice House sometime last Dec.in which WHEATLY stated that he had sold to MRS.PENRICE all his property in G'ville except for his wife's furniture.(2)WM.WHEATLY;age 35;Hotel keeper.

PKT.#414:H.L.BUCKNER (OF NEW ORLEANS)& H.L.BAKER (of Wash.Co.,Ms.) vs NANCY WILLIAMS , widow and mother of HENRY J.,THOS.J,J.B.,M.A.-a

WASHINGTON CO., MS.
CHANCERY COURT RECORDS
RANDOM SELECTIONS

minor, and J.C.WILLIAMS-a minor,all of Wash.Co.,Ms., and heirs at law of J.C.WILLIAMS,decd. O/B. filed Feb.14,1871,by BUCKNER & BAKER, claims that J.C.WILLIAMS,now decd.,died owing a debt incured on Oak Hill Plt.'
    S 1/2 of Sec.3; portions of SW 1/4 of Sec.2,all in T15N,R8W
    W 1/2 of SE 1/4 & E 1/2 of SW 1/4+ 10 ac. along E side of W 1/2 of
    Southern 1/4 of Sec.33,T16N,R8W - @561 ac.
DEPOSITION: HENRY J.WILLIAMS;age 22;res.Oak Hill Plt in Wash.Co.; farmer;states that his father,J.C.WILLIAMS now decd.,bought Oak Hill Plt.from Mr.Buckner in 1869. HENRY is the Adm.for his father's estate,and said his father had told him just before his death that he had not paid the last 2 notes//SALE of land advertised.

PKT.*576 :SALLIE B.WEST vs B.CAHN,et al: Filed Dec.10,1873
O/B/. SALLIE WEST,OF WASH.CO. vs MAHALA SCOTT and B.CAHN,who is Adm.of estate of F.J.MOSS. SALLIE is Femme Sole and so is MAHALA,who was in partnership with MOSS on Apr.1873, living on and in the cultivation of land lying in Sec.7,8, T15N.R6W @250 ac. belonging to MAHALA. SALLIE loaned furnish money. MOSS decd.26 Oct.1873,at which time MAHALA (falsely,Sallie claimed)to be MOSS's widow. B.CAHN was also a creditor.//

PKT.*518:NAPOLEON JOURDAN vs LYDIA JOURDAN ; Divorce-filed 20 Nov.1872;both of Wash.Co.,Ms., married 6 yrs. ago in sd.county.

PKT.*500:TIMOTHY M.SHANAHAN vs MARGARET ROACH,et al-Filed 10 July 1872. O/B. filed by TIMOTHY SHANNAHAN;ANN SHANNAHAN-widow of DANL.M.SHANNAHAN,decd.;MARY;FANNY ELLA; and TIMOTHY BARTHOLOMEW DANIEL SHANNAHAN, the last 3 being minor heirs of Danl.,decd. vs MARGARET ROACH, widow and exectx.of Est.of BENJAMIN ROACH,decd.TIMOTHY is seeking clarification of Title to L.1,2 Block 8,Central Ave. Roach's WILL is recd. in Adams Co.,Ms.// DEPOSITIONS:Taken 24 Oct.1872(1) MRS. ANN SHANNAHAN,widow of Danl.and mother of the other deftds.states that Danl. decd.16 Oct.1871. Their ch.were ages: MARY-5 on Nov.5 next;FANNIE E. -3 on 24 Aug.last;TBD- 5 mos. They have continued living in house with TIMOTHY..(2)TIMOTHY SHANNAHAN: age 58 next Nov.; living G'ville,brother of DAN'Ldecd.//ANSWER of M. ROACH:shows that BENJAMIN decd.24 Jan. 1870.

PKT.*459:JOSEPH HART,et al vs MARY A.HINES,et al:filed 22 Aug. 1871-O/B. by JOSEPH HART,W.C.HART,J.H.HART,partners in Jos.Hart & Sons of Bardstown,Ky. vs MARY A.HINES,widow now residing in St.Louis, Mo.; THOMAS HINES, JOHN & HOWEL HINDS,heirs at law of HOWEL HINES,decd. and

WASHINGTON CO.,MS.
CHANCERY COURT RECORDS
RANDOM SELECTIONS

S.W.FERGUSON,Adm.of his Est. The HINDS Family owned PLUM RIDGE PLT.in Wash.Co.,and when HOWEL decd.he owed money on it. The widow claims homestead exemption of 243 ac.on Rattlesnake Bayou-W 1/2 SW 1/4 Sec. 22, T18N,R8W. Complts.state HOWEL decd.1868,insolvent,and no family occupies homestead,therefore it no longer qualifies as an exemption.They want it seized for the debt.//AMENDED BILL; JOHN & HOWEL are minors, and live with their mother in St.Louis.The complts.seek a Grdn.appointed for them.//DEPOSITIONS; Taken Oct.26,1872 (1)THOMAS HINDS; His father died 13 May 1868, and THOMAS has lived in homestead ever since then until Feb.1872//(2)MARY A.HINDS: She and their 2 minor sons moved to Mo.for her health, and to educate the 2 boys. She expects to return to Plum Ridge Plt. and that THOMAS,HOWEL's son,lived there until 1872. She rents the land out,and that is her sole source for income. Questions why the Complts.waited 3 yrs to bring up indebtedness.//INTERROGATIONS: (1)JOSEPH HART; at his residence in Bardstown,Ky,Nelson Co. on 29 May 1873.Age 61 on 3 Nov.1872,saddler and trader of horse and mules. A "lot" of mules went to HOWEL HIND's place in Wash.Co.,Ms and some to his place in Jeff.Co.,Ms. In 1867 or 68 I was in G'ville and met with Mr.Hinds, and he invited me to go to his home. I did and spent the night there. We discussed the debt,and he sd.it was just and sent his son,THOMAS to a local man named BROWN whom he had loaned money to to see if he would pay up so HINDS could pay me. Thomas returned saying he could not find the man. Later HINDs said BROWN was killed, and he would never get his money. In 69 or 70 I saw him again at his brother in laws-Dr.Frank COLEMAN// DEPOSITION Filed Feb.18,1874:(1)WILHELMUS B.CONGER;Complts.witness; age 46,living N.O.Cotton factor//(2)J.C.SLAUGHTER: 22 JAN.1874 Vicksburg;age 32, salesman, //Final decree sale of the small portion of land left after the Homestead Exemption was removed.

PKT.#498: W.E.HUNT vs WM.W.ROBINSON ,Adm.-Filed July 8,1872. ROBINSON is Exect.of est.of IKE ROBINSON,decd.of Bolivar Co.,Ms. W.E.HUNT and WMA.HAYCRAFT were securites on the Adm.bond for Wm.W., and HUNT wants release. Hunt filed his plea from Frnaklin Co.,Ky.July 1872 and is released.

PKT.498: (Probate PKT.) EST.THOMAS H.HILL - S.W.FERGUSON,County Adm. files for L/A. Feb.11,1875. Appraisal of est.by DAVID FRILEY,JAMES C.ESTILL,J.A.MORSON, MANSFIELD WILMOT,THOMAS M.WILLIAMS-same date. THOMAS H.HILL decd.1872,intestate,small est.consisting of farm equipment. His widow, MOLLIE,is living in Petersburg,Va.and has requested that FERGUSON act as Adm. Their children are THEODORE W.,THOMAS H. HILL.

WASH.CO.,MS.PKT.GLEANINGS
PROBATE RECORDS - 1871/1884

PKT.#404: JESSE L.CARTER,minor/J.W.WINPEGLER,Adm.
Hon.E.STAFFORD,CHANCERY DIST.#15,CHANCELOR OF GREENVILLE,MS.
Pkt.contains: Guardianship Bond listing Estates of MARY J.WINPEGLER,KATY F.COLLUM(both names marked out) & JESSE L.CARTER,minors-at-law of JOHN(marked out) JESSE(written in)H.BAREFIELD,decd.JOHN W.WINPEGLER seeks Grdn.Bd.with GEORGE R.FARMER as surety. JOHN W.WINPEGLER is appointed Grdn.to JESSE L.CARTER, minor child of CROCKETT and SARAH CARTER,both decd. GRDN.BD.-$2,000.Apr.Term1871//On 26 Oct.1872,JNO. W.WINPEGLER filed his annual account stating that the Letters of Grdnp. were issued 19 Apr.1871 when JESSE L.CARTER was 9 yrs.old. That JOHN W.rented out JESSE's property and used the money for JESSE's support @$100 per yr.for 6 yrs. JESSE's first Grdn.was MARY J.BAREFIELD,and she had supported sd.JESSE for yrs.1863 to 1866. MARY J.BAREFIELD and JOHN W.WINPEGLER married and JOHN W. paid MARY J.$300 to cover the yrs.she had supported JESSE. INVENTORY offered,and JOHN W. further states he paid lawyers fees and taxes.//JOHN W.filed a/c for yrs.1872,1874//Document filed 21 Aug.1882 by "next best friend"ELBERT COLLUM for JESSE,in which JESSE states he was made an orphan in 1863 and MARY JANE BAREFIELD took charge of him. She intermarried with JNO.W.WINPEGLER in 1866. JESSE has 64 acres of land on Deer Creek in Sec.4,Sec.5,T15N,R6W in Wash. Co. - 30 ac.tillable. JOHN W.leased out the land from 1866 to 1871. In 1872 JOHN W. was made legal grdn.Since 1874,JOHN W.has made no further annl. a/c. JESSE further states that JOHN W. received $240 per yr.in 1879,1880, 1881 for rent on sd.land and applied this money to his (John W.'s) own account. JOHN W. has rented the same land for yr.1882 to THOMAS GRAVES for $240. JESSE will arrive at his majority on 17 Jan.1883 and seeks his estate and moneys - about $1500,but has reason to believe that JOHN W. is insolvent. So JESSE wants to prevent JOHN W. from collecting the rent for 1883.//30 Mar.1883:JESSE objects to final a/c submitted by JOHN W., which left $92.36 out of $240 rent money. JESSE claims that his expenses were highly exaggerated,and that the expense of the trip to Fla.erroneous since JOHN W. had promised to pay all expenses himself,and JESSE says "he didn't even want to go". Final a/c contains bills paid for schooling at Staunton,Va.to H.L.HOOVER.//1883:JOHN W.WINPEGLER ordered to pay JESSE L.CARTER $200.

PKT.#405:MARY ALICE VAN ALLEN,minor vs D.M.SHANNAHAN,Grdn.
PET.FOR GRDNP.filed 8 May 1871,for ALICE MARY VAN ALLEN by D.M. SHANNAHAN,a citizen of Greenville,Ms.who states that MARY ALICE is @13 yrs.old,res.of Wash.Co.,an orphan,no kin or remote kin near. She wished to

WASH.CO.,MS.PKT.GLEANINGS
PROBATE RECORDS - 1871/1884

PKT.#405:VAN ALLEN,minor,cont.
enter the family of SHANNAHAN's as his ward. She is heir to a small Est.of property from her grandfather's Est.in Ohio (State of)the particulars of, he doesn't know,but believes it is an annuity of @$600. She has lived with him and his family for some time.// Surety for Grdn.Bd.signed by TIMOTHY SHANNAHAN,DANL.SHANNAHAN - $1800.//No other doc.in Pkt.

PKT.#406:F.G.WINGFIELD,decd.R.G.SIMS,Adm.
Adm.Bd.$2,000 with Surety by C.W.LEWIS,L.GADDIS filed 8 May 1871.// PET. for Letters\Adm.filed by R.G.SIMS,states that F.G.WINGFIELD decd.6 Mar. 1871 leaving F.G.SIMS-wife of the petitioner,W.J.WINFIELD,A.P.WINGFIELD, BOWDRE WINGFIELD,FRANK WINGFIELD,ANNA WINGFIELD,WALTER WINGFIELD all minors under 18,except the first 3 who waive all right to Adm.Est. The decd.left no provisions in his WILL for an Adm. R.G.SIMS is also appointed GRDN.of the minor heirs.//R.G.Sims seeks dismissal of GRDN.May 1874 - so Ordered.//Inv. - F.G.WINGFIELD,the decd.owned "Sligo Plt."on Deer Creek,but it was heavily mortgd.(See WINGFIELD CEMETERY,this Vol.)

PKT.#407:EST.OF RICHARD R.BEASLEY,decd.- SAML.FERGUSON,Adm.
Copy of WILL of R.R.BEASLEY,decd.presented by M.E.BEASLEY,Exectx.1 May 1872:Proof of WILL same date,same Exectx.who qualifies by law of Prince Geo.Co.,Va. **WILL OF R.R.BEASLEY** (copy falling apart) Will names: Wife:MARTHA E.-to get slaves LENORA and REBECCA + many other slaves; R.R.relinquishes any claim to any real or personal Est.of his wife's that she may get from her father or any other relation. At the death of MARTHA E., the sd.named slaves to go to his children and the ch.of his decd.children. "Plantation Puddledock"to be kept intact until son RICHARD gets to be 21 yrs.of age,unless MARTHA E. marries first-then MARTHA E.inherits nothing and the children split it all. R.R.requests that the exect.purchase stocks of States of Va.,N.C. & the U.S.of A.and use the interest to support and educate the family.Asks that $10,000 be invested at 6%int.to be paid to wife if she should remarry. He names four dau.-MARY ALICE,ROSA ANNA,MARTHA E., AMANDA who each get 1 portion,with the stipulation that they use only the int.,and when they die the principal is to go to their children. R.R. further states that he has money and debts due him in La.and Ala. Exect.-friends ROBERT R.JONES of Brunswick Co.,Va.and WM.C.RAWLINGS of Prince Geo.Co., Va.WILL written 1Jan1851-Filed 13 Nov1862,Prince Geo.Co.,Va.//CODICILE #1:17 Jan.1851:Wife,MARTHA E. to get all household furnishings + carriage etc.//CODICILE#2:23 Jan.1854:R.R.changes provision concerning "Puddle- duck"Now wants it to be held intact until son JOHN COLLIER reaches (more)

WASH.CO.,MS.PKT.GLEANINGS
PROBATE RECORDS - 1871/1884

PKT.#407:EST.BEASLEY,cont.
21 and R.R.,JR.and JOHN COLLIER will split it.//By 24 Jan.1859,R.R. has 3 more children than in 1851-MINERVA J.,JOHN COLLIER,SUSAN SCRIBELLA(?) who are to get equal proportions with the 5 named earlier in WILL. R.R. requests that the "Plt.Diamond Grove"in Brunswick Co.,Va.be sold.//WITNESSES to handwriting: WM.C.RAWLINGS,ROBT.R.JONES,WM.B.WESTBROOK, JAS.E.WOLFF. WM.C.RAWLINGS refused to act as Adm.and wife MARTHA E.BEASLEY qualified. Bond $400,000.//Document dated 11 Jan.1866:The Will Book in which the above Will was recorded in Pr.Geo.Co.,Va. was destroyed and a clerk made another copy,filed it 13 Aug.1868.//WILL filed Wash.Co. Ms. 24 Nov.1870,when MARTHA E.BEASLEY states that she needs an Adm.in Wash.Co.to handle debts owed to her late husband's Est.in Ms.and asks that the court appoint one, as much of her Estate has been burned,and she is without funds to travel.// 1 May 1872,SAML.FERGUSON is apptd.local Adm.

PKT.#409:SALLIE MONTGOMERY,minor-WILLIAM MONTGOMERY,Grdn.
GRDN.\BD.$3,000with J.M.MONTGOMERY and WM.L.NUGENT as surities-25 May 1871,showing SALLIE as the minor child of ELIZA A.MONTGOMERY.//Petition of ELIZA A.MONTGOMERY,filed 24 May 1871,stating that she bought an insurance policy for $3600,put it in the name of her dau.SALLIE and paid for it. She further states that since paying for sd.policy,she has lost her home because of debts of her husband WILLIAM and she was forced to buy her home back.Now she wants to redeem the policy,even though it is made out to her dau.and asks that her husband and SALLIE'S father,WILLIAM MONTGOMERY, be appointed Grdn.so the money may be collected,and applied where it is most needed.//Decree - Agreed,same date.

PKT.#410:Out side of Pkt.says her name is SARAH A.PENNY:
Inside of Pkt.name is spelled SYLVIA A.PENNY: PET.\L.\ADM.by F.BARKSDALE,surviving partner of BARKSDALE and McFARLAND,states S.A.PENNEY departed this life --day--18--,leaving a WILL with W.L.NUGENT named as Exect.and he refuses to function. 60 days has passed since the death of sd. S.A.PENNY and BARKSDALE is a creditor and asks that the County ADM.-SAM. FERGUSON be appointed. 24 May 1871. AGREED//WILL OF S.A.PENNY; (Top 3 lines rotted off)Will written 16 May 1869:"I,SYLVIA A.PENNEY of Wash. Co.,Ms." leave everything to eldest daughter ELEN S.PENNEY.//EXEC.WM.L. NUGNET of Greenville,Ms.//Wit.J.T.GREEN,WM.W.MORRIS//FILED 19 May1870.

PKT.#413:EST.OF JAMES W.THOMAS,decd.vs G.W.THOMAS,Adm.
Adm.\Bd.filed 12 July 1871 with surety by W.A.EVERMOND-$750//Pet.for

WASH.CO.,MS.PKT.GLEANINGS
PROBATE RECORDS - 1871/1884

PKT.#413:THOMAS vs THOMAS,cont.
L/Adm. G.W.THOMAS,states that JAMES W.decd.2 July1871,Wash.Co.,intestate,leaving no wife or child,or any relative in this state;owning 2 mules,3 plows,+ an int.in crop on 10 ac.+ some personal Est.Filed 12 July 1871//No heirs listed,nor relationship between JAMES and G.W. explained.

PKT.#414:EST.OF JOHN T.SWITZER,decd.- W.A.HAYCRAFT,ADM.
Pet for L\A and PET.for DOWER RIGHTS filed 22 July 1871 by HAYCRAFT stating that SWITZER decd.23 May 1871,intestate,owning a small personal Est.;leaving a widow,NANNETTE SWITZER, who waives right to sd.dower.The widow states that JOHN T.owned @$2,000 worth of mules and horses.// Bd. signed by WM.A.HAYCRAFT,NANNETTE SWITZER,JOHN H.NELSON,STEVENSON ARCHER for $2,000,22 July 1871.//Inv.16 Aug.1871//Sale of mules named Jerry,Mollie,Jake,Bloodsaw,Kittie,Jane,Nance - 1873.

PKT.#415:EST.OF DANIEL HUNSICKERL,decd. - W.R.TRIGG,Adm.
Pet.for L\A filed 7 Aug.1871,by TRIGG,who shows that Danl.decd.Feb.1871, intestate, leaving personal property-crop worth $500 or less.No relatives living within the jurisdiction of this court.//Inv.& Sale//No heirs listed.

PKT.#416:WM.HENRY JOHNSON,et al minors-HENRY J.JOHNSON, Grdn.:{One side of this document is missing}L\A and BOND filed 18 Sept. 1871 naming WM.HENRY age 20;CLAUD M. age 19;George G.17;Robt.A.is age 19;SALLIE age 11-minor heirs of SALLIE JOHNSON,decd. GRDN.BD.signed by H.J.JOHNSON,MATT JOHNSON,V.F.ERWIN.// Pet.for L\Grdnp.by H.J.JOHNSON of Wash.Co.states that he is the father of sd.minors,the issue of his former wife SALLIE GRADDY ------,sd.minor ch.---- become the owners of an Est. in ----Co.,Ky.,consisting of 1/4th interest in @250 ac.of land,and perhaps as much as $2500 in cash. The sd.minors have no legal Grdn.in Ms.,but there is a legal Grdn.in Ky. H.J.seeks to sell the property in Ky.and remove the proceeds to Ms. Filed 18 Sept.1871//Pet.granted 20 Dec.,1871// 14 Mar. 1872,the 4 children over 14 request that their father be appointed Grdn.//

PKT.#417:EST.of E.J.FARR,decd. - E.R.POOLE,Adm. Pet.for L\A filed 23 Sept.1871 shows that MRS.E.J.FARR,widow of W.B. FARR,late of Wash.Co. Ms.,decd.5 June 1871,intestate;leaving a small Est.- $450 + interest in a cotton crop,but not enough to pay the rent on the land she was leasing at $600. POOLE is a creditor,saying she owes him $1724. No near relation in this state who are willing to Adm.her Est.//VOUCHER-Bill owed by Mrs.W.B. FARR to E.R.POOLE submitted by POOLE's bookkeeper JOHN G.EUSTIS of N.O.

WASH.CO.PKT.GLEANINGS
PROBATE RECORDS - 1871/1884

PKT.#418:EST.EMELINE S.WINN,decd. - JAMES B.WINN,Adm. L\Adm. by JAS.B.WINN,who states that EMELINE S.WINN,decd.Dec.1869 at her residence in Wash.Co.,leaving a considerable real & personal Est.,i.e. land in S1/2 of S-,N--Sec.2,T16N,R10W.[Document disintegrating,very difficult to read]Surviving EMELINE is her husband O.WINN who is step-father of petitioner(JAMES B.WINN);ALONZO R.KEZER a son of sd.decd.by a former husband; CHRISTIANA ANDERSON;your petitioner;LOUELLA F.WINN,called ELLA;RICH. M.WINN. The sd.ALONZO,CHRISTIANA,LUELLA,RICHARD and Pet.JAMES B. are the children and only heirs of decd.EMELINE S.WINN,the 4 four last named are the issue of the marriage of sd.decd.and RICHARD M.WINN,also decd. The sd.land contains dwelling house,where MRS.WINN lived,outhouse, sawmill, etc.and is likely to be subject of litigation. All named heirs are of age,but RICHARD. There was no issue by EMELINE's marriage with O.WINN.Adm.approved.Filed 2 Aug.1871// On 11 Oct.1871,INV.& APPRAISAL,with the heirs asking that their brother,JAMES B.WINN be appointed Adm.and signed by A.R.KEZER,C.W.ANDERSON,ELLA F.WINN,R.M.WINN.//ADM.BD. - $2405.//12 Dec.1871:Order for SALE of personal property clouded by the fact that O.WINN had the SHERIFF OF YAZOO CO.,MS. remove 2 mules from Est.of decd.

PKT.#419:EST.OF FANNIE GRIFFIN decd. - JOHN L.GRIFFIN Adm.
PKT.contains a copy of the WILL of FANNIE GRIFFIN,as recorded in WILL BK.'1',p.393(Abst.in Vol.1 p.94,this series.)In her WILL,FANNIE asks to be buried beside her children and leaves everything to her beloved husband. WILL dated 10 Mar.1870 and filed 25 June 1870. On reverse side of WILL is an affidavit by RUVININO HILL,sister of FANNIE,dated 13 May 1870,stating that the WILL is authenic;also an affidavit by J.L.GRIFFIN,husband,Sept. 1871.//Pet.for acceptance of WILL states that FANNIE decd. 10 Mar.1870, leaving a handwritten WILL.She owned a small Est.in Wash.Co.,Ms. - a house and lot on Central Ave.in Greenville,Ms.+ furniture,etc.;no debts;and J.L.is sole heir;filed 20 Sept.1871.//DECREE-WILL accepted 24 June 1872.

PKT.#420:EST.of E.L.CARTER,decd. - R.H.CARTER,Adm. [Right half of doc.rotted off]PET.for L\A filed 7 Nov.1871 where R.M.CARTER states that MRS. ELIZABETH -----,decd.--July 1871,intestate,leaving a small personal Est.-$2300. Heirs are R.H.CARTER,W.G.CARTER,NANNIE B.RANDOLPH,ELEANOR S.CARTER all children of decd.and all over 21. Petitioner(R.M.CARTER)is nephew of decd.by marriage and the heirs asked him to apply as Adm.of Est. 7 Nov.1871//ADM.BD.is signed by WM.G.CARTER,WM.F.RANDOLPH,R.M.CARTER on 7 Nov.1871//12 Aug.1872-R.H.CARTERis SUMMONED to appear before court in Wash.Co.On reverse side,the dep.Sherf.says that R.H.CARTER (more)

WASH.CO.PKT.GLEANINGS
PROBATE RECORDS - 1871/1884

PKT.#420:EST.E.L.CARTER,cont.
not found in my county"and he gave the summons to W.G.CARTER,a bro.of R.H.CARTER,"W.G.being over 16,and at the usual residence of R.H.CARTER".// In 1874,R.H.CARTER is Adm.of EST.OF ELIZABETH L.CARTER,decd.,who owned 'Woodstock Plt.'(Note: Due to the tattered condition of this Pkt.,only these four children of ELIZABETH L.and ALFRED G.CARTER's could be identified. But from other doc.there were other ch.MITTIE,and A.GRAYSON. The use of initials R.H(ILL) for the son and R.M. for the nephew is confusing.)

PKT.#421:EST.of W.A.P.DILLINGHAM - JOSEPH W.PATTERSON,Adm.
KENNEBEE CO.,MAINE-JOS.BURTON,Clerk of Probate,7 Oct.1871.INV. of EST. of WM.A.P.DILLINGHAM,late of Sidney,Maine,decd.intestate. Promissory note dated 30 Dec.1859,Woodville,Ms.signed by JOHN P.DILLINGHAM,for $31,703 payment due Jan.1864 with interest,secured by a D/T. Adm.PATTERSON is a resident of Augusta,Me.//Adm.Bd.,Maine,$30,000,8 May 1871// Acknowledgement of Adm.documents,18 Dec.1871.//No other papers.

PKT.#422:EST.WM.H.OFFUTT - BENJAMIN A.OFFUTT,Adm.
PET.for L\A by BENJAMIN states that WM.H.decd.29 Oct.1871;intestate;a considerable Est.both real and personal in Wash.Co.,Ms.consisting of a " Plt. UTOPIA"+ crops. BENAJMIN is the brother of WM.H.,decd.//Adm.Bd.signed by BENJAMAN A.OFFUTT,Z.C.OFFUTT,W.E.HUNT 6 Nov.1871.//Inv.shows "PLT. Utopia"to have 500 ac.on which WM.H. still owed $3,480. BENJAMIN leased the sd.plt.to WM.H.TAYLOR for that sum for the yr.1872.//No heirs named.

PKT.#423:EST.HENRY C.DINGY,decd. - Adm. BOHLEN LUCAS
Pet.for L\A by LUCAS,states that DINGY decd.13 Dec.1871,intestate;possessed of real and personal Est.;and that LUCAS and DINGY were partners in a cotton farm. Lucas stated further that DINGY had no living relatives in Miss.//ADM.BD.$2,000 with sur.C.W.LEWIS,WM.H.BOLTON.//On 5 Aug.1872,In ANSWER to Adm.Pet.,a Petition for DOWER and HOMESTEAD rights was filed by DINGY's widow,MARTHA DINGY.//ANSWER to DOWER PETITION of widow DINGY,Lucas,seeking Adm.of Est.of HENRY C.DINGY,decd.,states that he had known the decd.for 10 yrs.and had never heard of MARTHA.He demanded that she prove she was legal wife and heir of sd.decd.//6 Jan.1873:DEPOSITION of E.D.CLARK of Vicksburg,Ms.who states he is an attorney,age 28. He knew MARTHA and HENRY C. and that the couple was married at Rolling Fork,(Ms.) in Issa.Co.(now Sharkey Co.)in the winter of 1855 or 1856."I remember it because it was the first wedding I ever attended. I think they lived awhile in MR.POWELL's family as man and wife."CLARKcontinues by saying that the

WASH.CO.PKT.GLEANINGS
PROBATE RECORDS - 1871/1884

PKT.#423:DINGY,DECD. cont.

couple had 2 children,and MRS.DINGY became blind and went home to her relations in Maryland."..."been neglected by her husband". He expressed surprise that the marriage was ever questioned as they were known and accepted in the most respected circles of the community.//DEPOSITION of V.S.JEFFERDS,Clk.of Court in Issa.Co.,states his age as 23 yrs.and testifies that there is a license for marriage for HENRY C.DINGY and MARTHA L.JONES and sd.Lic.was returned.(NOTE: The Minister who performed the ceremony signs the lic.and it is returned to be recorded.)There is no record there of a divorce.Statement signed by Dep.Clk E.P.TOY,3 Jan.1873-Exhibit attached shows lic.issued 10 Dec.1855,Issa.Co.,Ms.and filed 20 Dec.1855. Marr.Bk.p.53,54.Lic.return shows the marr.to have taken place 13 Dec.1855 signed by LEWIS T.DAMERON,J.P.//ANSWER of MARTHA L.DINGY-17 Jan.1873 who states that she is 37 yrs.11 mos.,16 days old. "I live with my mother about 3 miles from the town of Berlin in Worcester Co.,Md. My maiden name is JONES."..was married at house of MR.MORDECAI POWELL on Deer Creek in ISSA.CO.on 13 Dec.1855 to HENRY C.DINGY. I lived with him 2 yrs.and 5 mos. (until we came to Md.)and had 2 children,MINNIE OLIVIA who was b.1857 and is now 16,and EMMA ELLA who was b.1859 and is now 14 1/2.MARTHA states that she has "tolerable" health but is totally blind,ever since 1 mo. after the birth of her 1st child. DR.BALFOUR of Vicksburg thought a change of climate might restore her sight.//Admitted as evidence is a very chatty letter written by HENRY C.DINGY to MARTHA,dated 13 Apr.1861-Deer Creek, in which he asks if she had heard of the deaths of THOS.Y.CHANEY,COL. RUSHING,and MARY SHELBY.(Note: The widow of Thos.Y.Chaney,Sr.had marr. Mordecai Powell,and Thos.Y.Chaney,Jr.died 1861.WM.Rushing decd.between Dec.1860 and Apr.1861)Proof of Publication,7 Feb.1873, notifying MARTHA L.DINGY,widow of decd.and MINNIE OLIVER DINGY, EMMA ELLEN DINGY, minor children and heirs,non-residents of Ms.,living in Berlin,Md.//DEPOSITION of ROBERT PAXTON filed 20 Jan.1874,states that he is 29 yrs. old and a resident of Wash.Co.,knew HENRY C.DINGY,the decd., since 1864. "HENRY lived on the FALL place",but had bought a homestead in SE1/2 of Sec.24,T14N,R7W meaning to clear the land and build a house and"live on his own land." He mentioned to me he was a married man, but his wife lived in Md.and they were separated.//Suit appealed to the Ms.Supreme Court,Apr.Term 1873. LUCAS was ordered to pay the widow MARTHA $1500 + interest.

PKT.#424:EST.of LORENZO B.BURT,decd. - ADM.S.W.FERGUSON

Pet for L\A by W.L.NUGENT,who states that BURT decd.leaving a small personal Est.and there was an article of agreement between them of 1/3rd

WASH.CO.PKT.GLEANINGS
PROBATE RECORDS - 1871/1884

PKT.#424:EST.BURT,cont.
interest in and to the "Oakwood Plt."-stock,tools,etc.and that BURT is entitled to 1/3rd of proceeds.NUGENT asks that FERGUSON be appointed Adm. Filed 20 Dec.1871.//SALE of personal property 12 Feb.1872 - $10,000.//INV.contained "real" debts and "doubtful"debts.//VOUCHERS reveal that DR.L.M.BALL attended BURT Dec.6,and again on Dec.9,1871.

PKT.#425:EST.JACOB ADDISON,decd. - L.PICARD,ADM.
(PKT.IN POOR CONDITION)Adm.Bd.18 Dec.1871,$500 for Est.of JACOB ADDISON alias JACOB TURNER.//Pet.for L\A filed same day, stating that ADDISON, sometimes called TURNER,decd.,intestate,leaving no widow that PICARD is aware of,but leaving several children who are all of age and living in Wash.Co.,Ms. ADDISON decd.some 60 days before,leaving a small personal Est. PICARD is a creditor of sd.decd..Pet.granted.

PKT.#426:EST.EMMA MORGAN,minor - OLIVER T.MORGAN,Grdn.
(Pkt.disintegrating)GRDNP./BD. and OATH filed 15 Feb.1872 before OLIVER WINSLOW,Clerk.(right side of doc.gone!) Bond is $1,000//PET.filed 15 Feb.1872 to HON.E.P.HARMON by O.T.MORGAN,who states that his wife LILLY decd.--day --yr.leaving 1 heir - EMMA,a minor under 14,(age 6)and a small real estate of 240 ac.of land in Wash.Co. OLIVER T. is EMMA's father.// DECREE - so granted 15 Feb.1872.

PKT.#427:EST.OF HENRY BARLOW - S.W.FERGUSON,Adm.
Pet.of SHEPHERD BLACKBURN,Coroner,Filed 23 Feb.1872 stating that HENRY BARLOW DECD.bu violence on 19th instance,leaving a small personal Est.@$27.30 in money and some household furniture + other effects;leaving no *man* relative in this state to Adm.//APPRAISAL ordered//No other doc.

PKT.#428:EST.LYDIA MITCHELL,Orphan - MRS.CATHERINE FERGUSON,Mistress (Orig.Pet.in WILL BK."1",p.392/Vol.I of this series.)
Pet.of CATHERINE FERGUSON who states that LYDIA is an orphan,age 11,and seeks to be bound to MRS.FERGUSON as lady's maid until she is 18,and that she has been in her employ since Dec.last. Mrs.FERGUSON believes her to have no relatives in state,and her only relatives are her brothers and one sister residing in Ky. Filed 23 Feb.1872//BOND filed same day by MRS. FERGUSON, SAML.W.FERGUSON,J.I.McNEILLY for $500.MRS.FERGUSON must teach LYDIA to read,provide her with clothes,etc.//DECREE granted same day.//25 July 1872,CATHERINE FERGUSON reports to the court that LYDIA disappeared,taking all the clothing,etc.petitioner had furnished her.(more)

WASH.CO.PKT.GLEANINGS
PROBATE RECORDS - 1871/1884

PKT.#428:EST.MITCHELL,cont.
After a 10 day search,they found her in the employ of J.C.HEARD,sent after her and had her brought back,but she again disappeared on 22nd after being caught stealing. Now her whereabouts are unknown.MRS.FERGUSON seeks release from her BOND.//RELEASE GRANTED.

PKT.#429:EST.SHELTON J.HENDERSON,decd.   - JOHN HENDRICKS,Adm.
Pet.for L\A by W.H.HENDERSON,who states that SHELTON departed this life 16 Feb.1872,intestate,leaving a personal Est.of @$1,000. The Petitioner is the brother and heir at law of decd.and also a creditor. Decd.left neither wife nor children surviving him,and all the heirs and next of kin are non-residents of Ms.and do not desire to Adm.Est. W.H.asks that JOHN HEND-RICKS be appointed.//Adm.Bd.$1,000 Filed 9 Mar.1872//HENDRICKS,as Adm requests permission to sell property by private sale on 23 Apr.1872//INV. $1885.//In June 1877,W.H.HENDERSON files exception to annual report by HENDRICKS,saying that many items such as taxes had not been paid.// DEPOSITION of W.S.HENDERSON,the son of W.H.HENDERSON,who states that a suit is"under dispute". His father,who is in Mo.,has been asked to come to Ms. The HENDERSONS "suggest" that HENDRICKS has skipped the country.// 11 June 1878,S.W.FERGUSON is appointed Adm.in place of HENDRICKS,who claimed to have paid 2 notes for $1151.29 that were due. S.W.FERGUSON found out that HENDRICKS had a large sum of money due the Est.of sd.decd. and the sd.notes had not been paid.//Land description for tax purposes: Sec.6,T19N,R8W - 130 ac.+NW part of Sec.7,T19N,R8W+S1/2 of SE1/4 of Sec.27,T19N,R9W the last 2 being 90 and 80 ac.respet.//Notes ordered delivered to W.H.HENDERSON 11 June 1878.

PKT.#430:CATHERINE SMITH,et al,minors - C.B.TULLY,Grdn.
(Name sometimes spelled TILLY)Heirs of ANDREW W.SMITH-CATHARINE, ANGELA,MARGARET,and ISABEL SMITH of Wash.,D.C. TILLY Pet.for L\Grdn. stating that the SMITH sisters are sisters to his wife,all of Wash.,D.C. A.W.SMITH left a small tract of land on Deer Creek in Wash.Co.,Ms belonging now to sd.minor children,+ $600 or $700 in the hands of A.J.PAXTON - rent money. Sd.minors are living with TILLY and his wife. 25 Mar.1872.//Mar. 1872:WASH.,D.C. Grdn.Bd. signed by CHARLES B.TILLY,GEORGE W.KNOX,JOHN S.BARBOUR as sec.for CATHARINE age 18,ANGELA 13,MARGARET 11,ISABEL 9,orphans of ANDREW W. and CATHARINE SMITH,late of Wash.D.C.//Oct.1873 TILLY petitions to sell land - W1/2 of SW1/4 of Sec.30;SW1/4 & W1/2 of NW1/4,Sec.31-all in T17N,R6W 320 ac. All minors and their half sister MARY get 1/5th share. They have a relative in Ms.,an Uncle WM.F.SMITH of

WASH.CO.PKT.GLEANINGS
PROBATE RECORDS - 1871/1884

PKT.#430:SMITH,minors.cont.
Wash.Co.//5 May 1874:MARY V.TILLY seeks to have Grdnp.of CHAS.B.TILLY revoked and succeeds.//Apr.1875:The Grdnp.of ANGIE G.SMITH,MAGGIE L. SMITH,ISABEL SMITH,minor heirs at law of ANDREW W.SMITH,decd.together with their sisters MARY S.TILLY AND KATIE W.SMITH,the latter 2 of lawful age,own a small acreage of land. The minors are living with and are mainly supported by their 2 older sisters in Wash.,D.C. Their Ms.Grdn.is W.A.HAYCRAFT.//10 Aug.1876:2nd annual a/c of HAYCRAFT contains a letter written by MARY L.TULLEY,who says she is the girl's 1/2 sister.She complains of the expense of raising the girls and asks if the "place" could be sold.(HAYCRAFT had sent the rent money of $275 for 1875) MARGARET must have reached her majority by 1877,for she signs along with MARY L. TILLY The sale of the land had been suggested during the Grdnp./of CHAS.B.TILLY,but the idea had been dropped.//No other infor.

PKT.#431:EST.R.J.HORD,decd. - MARY J.HORD,Admx.
29 Mar.1872:Pet.for L\A by MARY J.HORD,who states that ROBERT H.HORD departed this life intestate on 2 Dec.1871. MARY J. is his widow. He left no Est.-real or personal-except just before his death a suit styled 'JURY & HARRIS vs the HORDS and others" was tried before the SUPREME Court of Ms. and the Defendants - HORDS,et al- had won.//Adm.Bd.same date,MARY J.HORD,with ANDREW JACKSON as sec.$250.//No other papers.(NOTE: ANDREW JACKSON was the son of MARY J.HORD by a previous marriage to JAMES B.JACKSON,late of Wash.Co.,Ms.)

PKT.#432:EST.EDWARD P.JOHNSON(JR.)decd.-JOHN W.HARROW,Adm.
13 May 1872:L\A by J.W.HARROW,who states that EDWARD P.JOHNSON departed this life 25 Apr.1872,intestate,leaving a considerable real Est.and personal Est.of $10,000. The decd.left surviving him the following heirs at law:BELLE G.JOHNSON,widow of sd.E.P.;LAURA G.JOHNSON,dau.age 5;HARROW JOHNSON,son age 6 months. The widow has asked J.W.HARROW to apply for Adm.//Adm.Bd.signed by J.W.HARROW with E.RICHARDSON sec.$10,000.//28 Oct.1872:INV.& APPRAIS. - Life Insr.Policy for $10,000. $1800 is set aside by the court for the support of the widow and ch.//27 Oct.1873:SALE of personal Property $114.75. Cotton belonging to firm of HARROW & JOHNSON partners in 'REFUGE PLT' not ready yet.//9 Apr.1874:PET of DANIEL H.REYNOLDS,a citizen of Chicot Co.,Ark.,who states that at the time of E.P.JOHNSON's death,E.P.was living in Ark.even though he died in New Orleans where he had gone to find skillful medical help. The last dwelling that E.P.had was in Chicot Co.Ark,but it was burned by the Federal Troops

WASH.CO.,MS.PKT.GLEANINGS
PROBATE COURT - 1871/1884

PKT.#432:EST.JOHNSON,cont.
and he didn't rebuild it.E.P.JOHNSON moved temporarily to Wash.Co.,Ms.with his family,where they lived with his father-in-law,FRANCIS GRIFFIN, late of sd.Co.in Ms.E.P.was the Adm.of the Est.of FRANCIS GRIFFIN (NOTE: E.P.had married GRIFFIN's dau.ISABELLA.) When applying for the Adm.of GRIFFIN's Est.,E.P. stated that he was a citizen of Chicot Co.,Ark. After the death of E.P.,REYNOLDS applied for Adm.papers on the Est.of E.P.in Chicot Co.Ark.and posted bond of $6,000 on 9 May 1872. This was before J.W. HARROW was awarded same in Ms. REYNOLDS further stated that E.P. held an undivided interest in Island 84 in the Ms.River. At the same time, REYNOLDS also assumed the Adm.of EST. of FRANCIS GRIFFIN,DECD. This ADM.BOND was for $16,000. REYNOLDS claimed that many mistakes were made in the Adm.of GRIFFIN's Est.;that J.W.HARROW has handled everything within his jurisdiction,but the Ark.portion is yet to be dealt with. REYNOLDS also seeks Grdnp. of minors-LAURA and HARROW JOHNSON. He said the Est.owes him $3,000 for services performed,so far.//18 Apr.1874:ANSWER of J.W. HARROW to claims of DANIEL H.REYNOLDS-J.W.HARROW claims that E.P. JOHNSON,decd. was a resident of Wash.Co.,Ms.and that the charges set out by REYNOLDS are exhorbitant and ridiculous.//9 May 1872:Copy of ADM.BD., Chicot Co., Ark,showing DANL.H.REYNOLDS signed with LYCURGUS R.JOHNSON as security//23 Mar.1874:REYNOLDS appealed to the SUPREME COURT of ARK.,stating that E.P.JOHNSON owed the GRIFFIN EST.$16,000 +$8,587 more.//1875: Chancery Court CITATION to ISABELLA G.JOHNSON,widow;LAURA G.JOHNSON both living in Louisville,Ky(NOTE: NO mention of Baby HARROW JOHNSON)// 3 FEB.1875:RULE to dismiss without prejudice the petition of D.H.REYNOLDS //PKT.contains many account sheets for Firm HARROW & JOHNSON.

PKT.#433:EST.E.B.HORNBICK,decd.-W.D.HULL,ADM.   Pet.for L\A presented May 1872,filed -- 1873,stating that E.B.departed this life about 15 Mar.1872,intestate,owning personal property worth @$300. He was a resident of Wash.Co.,and engaged in planting with petitioner (HULL).No heirs or representative in this state.// Adm.Bd. signed by W.D.HULL,principal,with SAML.G.WORTHINGTON,F.S.ESTERLING as sec. $600-31 May 1872.

PKT.#434:EST.ELIZA M.BUCKNER,et al-MRS.P.M.BUCKNER,GRDN:
(NOTE: Most of Pkt.missing, a single piece was tucked inside of Pkt.#460) Only document is a citation to MRS.P.M.CHAMBERS,GRDN.of minors ELIZA M.BUCKNER,MARY V.BUCKNER,KATIE C.BUCKNER,JOHN W.BUCKNER,P.C.BUCKNER. Sd.Citation was sent to Bolivar Co.,Ms.3 Jan.1875 to answer petition of H.C.GIVENS(?) to be released from Grdnp.Bd.

WASH.CO.,MS.PKT.GLEANINGS
PROBATE COURT - 1871/1884

PKT.#435:EST.OF JOHN S.SCOTT,decd. - WM.L.JACKSON,Adm.
18 July 1872:L\A by WM.L.JACKSON of New Orleans,surviving partner of SCOTT & JACKSON,who states that SCOTT departed this life 16 Apr.1872 in N.O.,intestate. JACKSON applied and received L\A in 2nd Dist.Court, N.O., La.May 1872. He believes that SCOTT owned (held mortg.)land in Wash.Co., Ms.known as 'The Sligo Plt.' Mortg.was for $12,000 with $5,000 still due.// Adm.Bd.with G.G.SIMS,S.W.FERGUSON,as sec.// Amount of Bd.torn off doc.

PKT.#438:EST.HENRY R.MERCHANT,decd. - U.MERCHANT,Adm.
30 Sept.1872:Pet.for L\A by U.MERCHANT,who states that HENRY R.decd.15 Sept.1872,intestate,possessed of small real and personal Est.@$1500. U.MERCHANT is the father of HENRY R.MERCHANT,decd.//21 Oct.1872:Pet of U.MERCHANT,stating that he had received Adm.of the Est.of his son HENRY R.,but had been advised that the sole heir is MRS.ELIZABETH JANE COOPER. U.MERCHANT surrenders his L\A,stating further that he had shipped some cotton to BROOKS NEELY & CO.in Memphis to pay debts owed by the decd., and because of the nature of the business of sd.decd.(he farmed and was mortgaged) the Est.had to be immediately managed. But upon learning that MRS.COOPER wanted to be Adm.,he resigns.Signed by ULYSES MERCHANT.// 29 Oct.1872:Pet.by ROBERT S.COOPER and wife ELIZABETH JANE COOPER, who state that on 15 Sept.1872,HENRY R.MERCHANT decd. ELIZABETH JANE is the sister of sd.decd.and sole heir. ULYSES MERCHANT has resigned and the COOPERS seek L\A //Bd.sec.by E.A.ROBB,SAML.G.WORTHINGTON.//

PKT.#439:EST.ANNIE SHELBY,et al minors-MRS.BETTIE SHELBY,G.
(Pkt.in very delicate condition)Oct.1872:Pet.for L\GRDNP.by MRS.SHELBY, who states that her husband THOMAS SHELBY has lately decd.,leaving a Life Insurance Policy for $10,000,benefiting your petitioner and her children ANNIE,AUGUSTUS N.,BETTIE,KATE B.,BAYLESS P.SHELBY. In order to collect the money from sd.Policy,MRS.SHELBY asked to be declared Grdn.

PKT.#439 1/2:EST.HANNAH BROWN,decd.-F.VALLIANT,ADM.
Pkt.found inside #437. Filed 1 Sept,1872:Pet L\A by VALLIANT who states that HANNAH decd.May1872,a collered woman,leaving 3 grandch.as her sole surviving heirs-ANDERSON HUNTER,LEWIS HUNTER,WALTER HUNTER all minors under 21. HANNAH owned a small house in Greenville, Wash.Co.,Ms. on the property of HENRY FISHER,worth $400,with the priviledge of removing sd.house at anytime.She also left $120 with a friend named VINEY CHINN + enough money with others to pay her funeral expenses and wanted the house and cash to go for the benefit of her gr.children.// So Allowed.

WASH.CO.,MS.PKT.GLEANINGS
PROBATE COURT - 1871/1884

PKT.#440:EST.KATE D.BUCKNER,decd. - S.W.FERGUSON,Adm.
17 Oct.1872:Pet.for L\A filed by J.G.BROWN,surviving partner of CUMM-
INGS,BROWN & CO.,a creditor,who states that KATE died 1872,INTESTATE(!)
owning an undivided interest in a large plantation,and BROWN requests
that the County Adm.,S.W.FERGUSON,be appointed.//Pet.of SARAH F.BUCK-
NER,asking the Court to accept the WILL of KATE D.BUCKNER,decd.for Probate,and to take the testimony of AUGUSTUS CHEW and W.B.GIDDEN as Witnesses to same.//WILL is accepted,and FERGUSON is removed as Adm. and
SARAH F.BUCKNER is granted L\A,with BOND @$1,000 - JOHN M.PARKER as
security.SARAH F. states that KATE decd.3 May 1872.//**WILL OF KATE D.
BUCKNER:** (Not recorded in Wash.Co.WILL BK."1")Written 4 Aug.1872-Filed
29 Oct.1872:KATE D. leaves a life interest of her share of 'Buckland Plt.' on
Deer Creek,Wash.Co.,Ms.to her Mother,(SARAH F.BUCKNER)+ personal property on sd.Plt. + the family residence in Claib.Co. Ms.+1/4th interest in a
tract of land in Layfayette and Hempstead Cos.Ark. + interest in town lots
in Fulton,Ark.(NOTE: SARAH (FREELAND) BUCKNER, widow of JUDGE ROBERT
H.BUCKNER,lived in Wash.Co. after the death of her husband,and later moved
her family to Claib.Co. Their children were THOS. F.;EMILY E. who married
LEWIS DeN.EVANS;SARAH ROBERTA who marr.JOHN M. PARKER; ROBT.H.,JR.;
CATHERINE D.(KATE);ELLEN F. who marr.DR.LOMAX ANDERSON.)

PKT.#441:EST.WILLIAM SUTTON,decd.: Pet.for L\A applied for by WM.H.
TERRY with ROBT.B.SCOTT as security. TERRY states that WM.SUTTON,decd.
--1872,leaving a WILL,with he and SCOTT appointed as Exects.;a large personal and real est.in Wash.Co.,Ms.and in Carroll Parish,La. Copy of WILL
inclosed,(Recorded WILL BK."1"P.393,Abst.Vol.I this series.) in which he
states that he is of Carroll P.,La.;names 2 youngest daus. EMMA WILSIE
SUTTON and SARAH ELIZA SUTTON to each get $2500.Other children CARO-
LINE S. SCOTT,VIRGINIA S.WILLIAMS,AMELIA S.TERRY,WILLIE S.MERRILL,
STEPHEN T.SUTTON. Exects.:WM.H.TERRY,ROBT.B.SCOTT. Written Vista Plt.in
presence of JOHN HARING 19 May 1872.//Recorded 9 Nov.1872 in Wash. Co.
Ms.//1 Feb.1873,R.B.SCOTT seeks permission to cultivate 'LaGrange Plt.'
Granted-SCOTT then rents out 'La Grange' to MR.NORVELL MERRILL for 1874//
4th Mon.in Apr.1875:CITATION NOTICE:to WM.H.TERRY and AMELIA TERRY;
R.B. SCOTT and w.CARRIE SCOTT;R.W.WILLIAMS and w.VIRGINIA S.WILLIAMS;
SARAH ELIZA SUTTON with her Grdn.R.B.SCOTT;Court seeks hearing to grant
permission to sell personal property of EST.of WM.SUTTON,decd.//Apr.1875
CITATION to N.MERRILL and SARAH ELLA MERRILL,his dau.,and EMMA WILSON
SUTTON by her Grdn.NORVELLE MERRILL.(SEE PROBATE PKT.#443,next page.)

WASH.CO.,MS.PKT.GLEANINGS
PROBATE COURT - 1871/1884

PKT.#442:EST.WM.L.GRAVES,decd.-ELIZA   G.GRAVES,Adm.
Pet.for L\A missing from Pkt. Adm.Bd.set at $1,000 with JOHN HENDRICKS
as security.//ELIZA A. accepted as Adm.8 Nov.1872//9 Dec.1872-INV.and
APPRAISAL by WM.E.HUNT,THOMAS SUTTON,W.L.HENDERSON.//CITATION to
ELIZA to file annual a/c for 1874,returned unexecuted "not in my county"
15 Apr.1875.

PKT.#443:EST.EMMA   WILSON SUTTON,minor:
Pet.for L\Grdnp.filed 7 Dec.1872 by NORVELL MERRILL,who states that
WM.SUTTON departed this life a few weeks ago,leaving a minor dau.,age
10,who,at the time of her father's death, was living with your petitioner
(MERRILL)and his wife who is a sister of sd.minor. Both parents are decd.
At EMMA W.'s request and the request of other relatives,MERRILL applies
for Grdnp. EMMA W. is to receive $2500 from the terms of her late father's
WILL,+ an equal share of his Est.//Grdnp.Bond co-signed by MERRILL and
JOHN H.NELSON $5,000,same date.

PKT.#444:EST HENRY H.MORRIS - S.W.FERGUSON,Adm.
Pet.for L\A filed 29 Oct.1872 by STEVENSON ARCHER,who paid MORRIS's
funeral expenses,and requests that the County Adm.S.W.FERGUSON be
appointed Adm.of sd.Est.//SALE of property 17 Jan.1874.//Note mailed
from Banking House of JOHN LONG &CO.,Carrollton,Ill.10 Aug.1874 from
L.D.MORRIS,seeking information concerning the Est.of his late brother,
HENRY H.MORRIS.

PKT.#445:EST.ALFRED   M.SMILEY,decd. - W.M.WALLACE,Adm.
4 Feb.1873:Pet.for L\A by WALLACE,who states that SMILEY departed this
life 23 Sept.1872,a citizen of Wash.Co.;intestate;leaving heirs - a wife
MARY ANN SMILEY and an infant child WM.WALLIS SMILEY.Decd.left a
personal Est.of @$1500.WALLACE is the uncle of the widow MARY ANN
SMILEY.//Adm.Bd.co-signed by WALLACE,L.WILZINSKI, G.WITKOWSKI for
$1400.(NOTE: The spelling of the Adm.'s name is WALLIS within doc.,but
signature shows WALLACE.)

PKT.#446:EST.SOLOMAN   WEISS decd.-J.E.HARRIS,Exec.(Name also
sp.WISE)Pet.L\A states that SOLOMAN decd.9 Jan.1873,leaving a WILL,
written in SOLOMAN's handwriting, appointing your petitioner,HARRIS,as
Exect. (WILL recorded WBk."1") In sd.WILL,SOLOMAN left $500 to his young-
est child and his wife IRENA WEISS. All the rest is to be divided between
heirs(unnamed).Filed 6 Feb.1873//Adm.Bd.$2000.//14 Apr.1875: (more)

WASH.CO.,MS.PKT.GLEANINGS
PROBATE COURT - 1871/1884

PKT.#446:WEISS,cont.
Lawsuits developed over debts of Est. One suit went to the Ms.SUPREME COURT. One was resolved by the death of a mule.//Apr.1876:CITATION to HARRIS, received by Mrs.HARRIS at place of abode.//8 Nov.1876 AUGUSTINE CHEW accused of seizing all stock before time for appraisal.//8 Nov.1876 JOSHUA SKINNER demands an a/c of Est.//No final solution given.

PKT.#447:EST.WM.C.BLACK,decd.-H.B.PUTNAM,Adm.
Pet.for L\A by PUTNAM,who states that BLACK died 7 Feb.1873,a single man,intestate,no relations in Ms.,owning a personal Est.of $280 + 4 bales of cotton. Your petitioner is his largest creditor.//Adm.Bd.$600,with H.A.POGGEL,J.H.WILSON signing as sur.14 Feb.1873.//VOUCHERS:by DR.V. Y.P.ALEXANDER for attending BLACK at his last illness. Money was received by MARGARET FLANNERY from ANDREW POGLE//Final a/c 28 July 1874.

PKT.#448:EST.THOMAS H.JOHNS,decd. - JOE WILCZINSKI,Adm.
21 Feb.1873:Pet.for L\A by JOE WILCZINSKI who states that JOHNS decd.11 Feb.1873,intestate,leaving a small Est.+some personal property +an unexpired lease on a plantation in Wash.Co.- to run for 2 more yrs.-all estimated @$1500.JOE was a creditor,holding a D/T for loan on mules and other stock for $1700 (Chattel Loan).JOE further states that JOHNS had no widow or relation in this state. His widow lives in Ky.and does not wish to Adm.Est. The eldest son,W.E.JOHNS, had come to Ms.from Ky. where he resides,to attend the personal affairs of his father, and sd.son requests that JOE act as Adm.//LETTER attached,written Leota Landing,18 Feb.1873:in which the eldest son(W.E.JOHNS) one of the heirs of THOMAS H.JOHNS confirms that he wishes JOE WILCZINSKI to be made Adm.// APPRAISAL by GEO.V.WARD, C.W.WOLFE,JOHNSON ERWIN,THOS.H.BERRY.//26 Feb.1873:Personal property to be sold at 'Marathon Plt.',at the dwelling house formerly owned by A.W.DUNBAR on Lake Washington.//VOUCHERS:show the body to have been returned to Lexington,Ky from Canton,Ms.where he decd. Funeral expenses $697.60-with the casket costing $135.,all paid by Adm.WILCZINSKI.

PKT.#449:EST.PRUE B.HUNT,minor - ELIZABETH E.HUNT,GRDN.
Pet.for L\A filed 8 Mar.1873 by ELIZABETH E.HUNT who states that her 2 younger sisters PRUE B.HUNT,b. 25 Nov.1854 and ALICE C. HUNT b.15 Mar. 1858, heirs at law of WM.HUNT,decd.,and over 14 yrs.seek ELIZABETH E.,as Grdn. Their inheritance includes an undivided interest in 'Montrose Plt.'in Wash.Co.,Ms. + uncollected interest in a Life Insurance Policy with St.Louis Mutual Life Ins.Co.-@$5000.//GRDNP.Bd.$5000,with W.E.HUNT as security.

WASH.CO.,MS.PKT.GLEANINGS
PROBATE COURT - 1871/1884

PKT.#450:EST.JOHN CARRIGAN,decd.- D.A.LOVE,Adm.
Pet.for L\A by LOVE,who states that CARRIGAN decd.in Wash.Co.,Ms about 26 Sept.1871;intestate,leaving a small personal est.$400. LOVE is a creditor,believes there is no kin in Ms. Filed 20 Mar.1872.//Adm.Bd.$800.

PKT.#451:EST.CAESAR HOWELL,decd.(Colored) - J.M.HOWELL,Adm.
Pet.for L\A by J.M.HOWELL,filed 5 Apr.1873,who states that CAESAR died 29 Mar.1873,intestate,leaving a small personal Est.+ 40 ac.he was cultivating on 'Otterburne Plt.'in sd. county,on a rental contract with your petitioner. No kin in Ms.,some neices and nephews in South Carolina.//SALE of personal property,bought by OLIVER WILLIAMS for $172.50,4 May 1874.

PKT.#453:EST.JAMES S.GUIGNARD,decd.
27 Mar.1873:Petition for DOWER,filed by ANNA M.GUIGNARD,written Augusta,Ga., who states that she is 49 yrs.old, relict of JAS.S.GUIGNARD, late of Columbia,S.C.,who decd.Feb.1868,intestate,leaving a small estate in Wash.Co.,Ms. Land description: part of L.2;all of L.3;Sec.2;T18N; R8W+E1/2 of W1/2 of W1/2 of Sec.33;T19N; R8W-in all 199 ac. The land is long and narrow with frontage some 300 yds.,while length and depth are about 1 mi. Partition is impossible. ANNA seeks sale. She further states that JAS. S. left 5 children:JAMES S.GUIGNARD,JR.,who lives in Columbia,S.C.,; JOHN G. GUIGNARD of Williston,S.C;WM.GUIGNARD who has since decd.,under age,unmarried,and intestate; SUSAN G.JENKINS with her husband PAUL G.JENKINS living in Washington,Ark.; EMMA S.and her husband D.GAMBUEL in Columbia, S.C.//28 Jan.1874 a DECREE in favor of division in thirds.//PRINTED notice of division in GREENVILLE TIMES 31 May 1873. Heirs ordered to appear to defend against DOWER DECREE; none did. Closed Jan.1876.(NOTE: According to 'The Touchberry Papers',ANNA M.EDWARDS,widow,was the 2nd wife of JAS.SANDERS GUIGNARD and not the mother of the 5 children named above. The Mother of the ch.was ELIZABETH RICHARDSON. 4 other ch.died young - CAROLINE FRANCES,SARAH SLAUN,LAURA,BENJAMIN. There was no issue from the marr. with ANNA.In a later doc.the Rev.PAUL G.JENKINS was living in Washington D.C.)See Pkt.#612

PKT.#454:EST.JOHN S.FISHER - ANDREW B.CARSON,Adm.
Pet.for L\A filed 9 June 1873,by B.CAHN,who states that JOHN S.decd.in Wash.Co.,Ms.on 8 Apr.1873. That he had and occupied "a mansion house"at the time of his death. He decd.intestate,no relations,CAHN was a creditor and since no relations have applied for L\A,he asks that the court appoint one.// THE court appointed CARSON.// 4 June 1873:Petition by Attorney

WASH.CO.,MS.PKT.GLEANINGS
PROBATE COURT - 1871/1884

PKT.#454:EST.JOHN S.FISHER,cont.
SAMUEL L.RAY,Agent and Atty.for GEORGE W.MITCHELL and his wife ELLEN MITCHELL. RAY states that ELLEN is the dau.of JOHN S.FISHER,who decd.7 Apr.1873,leaving a half interest in a cotton Plt.+stock,now in the hands of MRS.MARY BELLE BLACKBURN,who is the owner of the other half interest. ELLEN is the only heir of sd.JOHN S.FISHER,DECD. The MITCHELLS live in Montgomery Co.,Ms.and sent your petitioner (RAY) to Wash.Co.to see after their interest. The pet.does not care to Adm.the Est.,nor does ELLEN or GEO. being content with the Court appointed CARSON//INVENTORY 8 Sept1873// ADM.BD.signed with MRS.M.B.BLACKBURN,W.E.HUNT as surety-$4000.// SALE of personal property on the 'Erin Plt.' in Wash.Co.on Jan.19 and Jan.23 1874. A large number of mules were sold that were owned half/half with MRS. BLACKBURN.Sale held on the premises occupied by the decd.in his lifetime.

PKT.#456:EST-(blank)-BOYD,decd. - N.C.SKINNER,Adm.
Pet.for L\A. filed 12 June 1873 by SKINNER,who states that BOYD decd.1873,intestate, leaving personal property $40,no heirs or creditors other than SKINNER.

PKT.#457:EST.LOUIS NEWMAN,decd. - BURNETT NEWMAN,Adm.
Pet.for L\A. by LOUIS NEWMAN's widow,BRUSETTE(?)who states that LOUIS decd.17 June 1873 in Greenville,Ms.and had a "mansion house and known place of residence"+ personal property. As his wife she wants to Adm.Est. Filed 19 June 1873//BOND $500.

PKT.#458:EST.C.W.DUDLEY,JR. - C.W.DUDLEY,Grdn.
who Pet.for L\Grdn. for his minor son CHARLEY, stating they are citizens of Wash.Co. C.W.,JR. owns some property in this County, real estate worth $5000 + some property in Ark.the value of which is doubtful. Filed 27 June 1873// Grdnp//Bd with JOHNSON ERWIN as surety.

PKT.#459:EST.OF JACOB A.GOLDMAN,decd.-JULIUS I.LENGSFIELD, Adm.
Pet.for L.\A.is missing.//17 July 1873,Pet.for SALE of personal property + pet.for allowance for minor heirs namely BERTHA, HENRY,JULIUS, BERNARD GOLDMAN-$300 ea. In order to have the required $1200 in cash, the Adm. sold some merchandise from decd.'s store.//Adm.Bd. $2000 with J.HEIDINGSFELDER as surety.// INV.& APPRAISAL:Est.-$1400.// EXCEPTIONS to report,state that decd.did not leave a widow and feels the children's allowance exhorbitant. Filed 1 Nov.1873 by creditors J.ROSENFIELD,FRENCH & LOCKHART.//Judge agreed it was too much,and set a new amt.//Report of J.LENGSFIELD shows that store with merchandise, burned Sept.1874.

WASH.CO.,MS.PKT.GLEANINGS
PROBATE COURT - 1871/1884

PKT.#460:EST.BERTHA GOLDMAN,et al minors - J.LENGSFIELD,GRD
The signatures of BERTHA and HENRY GOLDMAN show they are over 14,and they petition the Court to appoint their Uncle J.LENGSFIELD as their Grdn., and also that he be appointed Grdn.to their brothers BERNARD and JULIUS GOLDMAN.Filed 17July 1873//Annl. a/c: A Life Insurance Policy for $2432 has supported two of the minors,HENRY and BERNARD age 16 and 12. But the interest on sd.Policy is not enough to pay their bills.Filed 8 Nov.1876.

PKT.#461:EST.FREDERICK FRANCES,decd - S.W.FERGUSON,Adm.
Pet.for L.\A.by FRANCES PARSON,filed 18 July 1873,who states that FREDERICK FRANCES decd.17 July 1873,intestate,no relatives in Miss.,his Mother being a resident of Kerry Co.,in England. He decd.owning personal property:a horse,chest of carpenter tools,trunk of clothes,1 watch-now in possession of MRS.ANNA YOUNG. PEARSON requests that FERGUSON be appointed Adm.

PKT.#462:EST.ELIZABETH ARCHER,minor - WM.H.ARCHER,Grdn. With STEVENSON ARCHER;JAMES ARCHER,JR;A.B.TRIGG as sureties.Bd.$20,000// Pet.for L\A.Filed 25 July1873 by W.H.ARCHER,father of ELIZABETH ARCHER, a minor of 2 yrs. who lives with him in Wash.Co.Ms.,with no present income but could receive the sum of $7000 due from her mother,MRS.FANNY VAN WICK ARCHER,now controlled by MRS.ARCHER's Administrator in Baltimore Md.//25 July 1873:GRDN./BD.shows ELIZABETH ARCHER to be the minor heir of FANNIE VAN WICK ARCHER,and the child of WM.H.ARCHER.//31 July 1875: WM.H.ARCHER is Grdn.of FANNIE ARCHER,minor//1878:3rd annual a/c shows ELIZABETH ARCHER living in Hinds Co.,Ms.with her father//1883:A.TAYLOR asks to be released from GRDNP.\BD. and a new bond for $10,000 set.

PKT.#463:EST.G.W.STEWART,decd. - E.F.EUBANKS,Adm.
Pet.for L.\A.,filed 15 Aug.1873,by W.J.SUMMERS,surviving partner of G.W. STEWART,decd,late of Wash.Co..SUMMERS and STEWART were in the Livery Business in Greenville,Ms. SUMMERS states that STEWART decd.14 June, 1873 owning personal property-4 buggies,steam tanks,& pump,about $1000 worth.STEWART decd.,intestate,owing $2266.Petitioner requests that E.F.EUBANKS be named ADM.// ADM./BD same date with A.M.St.CLAIR, C.H.SMITH as sureties.//EUBANKS said STEWART left no wife,or children, was never married,and owes more that his Est.can pay.

PKT.#464:EST.S.M.SLOAN,decd. - S.W.FERGUSON,Adm.
Pet.for L\A filed 18 Aug.1873 by J.R.HAMMET(scratched through)who states

WASH.CO.,MS.PKT.GLEANINGS
PROBATE COURT - 1871/1884

PKT.#464:SLOAN,cont.
that SLOAN decd.sometime in 1872,leaving no relative known to petitioner, leaving a small estate - 1 gin stand and boiler now on a Plt.known as 'The Morgan Place',owned by WORTHINGTON & HILL. Sd.decd.owed HAMMETT $300. He requested that FERGUSON be appointed Adm.//APPRAISAL:19 Aug. 1875 : by J.A.BENNETT,C.M.BEARD,CHAS.HILL,W.D.HILL,JOHN STEWART.

PKT.#465:EST.JOHN BAREFIELD,decd.-STEPHEN T.BAREFIELD,Adm.
(Note: Name also spelled BEARFIELD,BARFIELD)Pet.for L.\A.filed 11 Sept. 1872 by STEPHEN T.,who states that JOHN decd.17 Aug.1873, intestate, unmarried at the time of death,owning considerable real and personal property,no minor heirs,and STEPHEN T.is the oldest son and heir.//Adm.\Bd. for $2000 filed 16 Sept.1872 with STEPHEN T. as principal,and DAVID FRILEY,W.E.WEST,IVERY F.RATHER as sureties before J.W.COLLIER,J.P.//INV. & APPRAISAL//Oct.1873:SALE of 75 head of cattle for $1022.//1875:J.W. BAREFIELD joins STEPHEN T. as surety,when STEPHEN an J.W. are cited for contempt of court for not filing an Adm.report.//STEPHEN's ANSWER is that he sold personal property and paid off all his father's debts. He said he was farming his father's place and was very busy when the SUMMONS came,and in ignorance he had sent the annual a/c to his lawyer's office,not realizing that was not legal.Filed Oct.1875//Included in Pkt.:A document dated 25 Sept.1873:$90-Debtors of Est.of SAML.BAREFIELD,decd.to ALFRED FERGUSON for ANN FERGUSON-payment for tombstone from R.L.ROSEBROUGH of ST.Louis,to be shipped to S.T.BEARFIELD,Vicksburg in Apr.1874 with the following inscription **JOHN BEARFIELD ,born Sept.12,1812 died Aug.17,1873 Make the Perfect man ...for the end of that man is peace**.

PKT.#466:EST.SILAS GRANTHAM,decd.-MARY GRANTHAM,Adm.
6 Sept.1873,MARY pet.for L.\A.,stating she is the widow of the decd.who departed this life Feb.1873 in Wash.Co.,intestate,leaving personal estate of $175. There were children(unnamed) by her marriage with the decd.,no debts.//Adm/Bd.with JACOB ALEXANDER as sur.//INV.& APPRS. by JAMES GRANTHAM,DOCK WHITEHEAD,THOMAS BLACK,H.SCOTT, L.WEITZENFIELD-consisting of 1 brown mule @$65. The widow's allowance was set at $65.

PKT.#467:EST.F.J.MOSS,decd.-B.CAHN,Adm. with BOND @$2000.
28 Oct.1873:Pet.for L.\A. by SEELIG & CO.,creditor,who state that MOSS, late of a plantation on Deer Creek in Wash.Co.,departed this life (more)

WASH.CO.,MS.PKT.GLEANINGS
PROBATE COURT - 1871/1884

PKT.#467:MOSS,cont.
26 Oct.1873,Intestate,no near relative,but owed SEELIG & CO.a considerable amt. The company seeks to have B.COHN appointed as Adm,(he's with the CO.)// Pet.granted.//SURETY by JACOB HERSCH,M.GENSBERGER.//4 Nov.1873:Pet.of MAHALA MOSS for L.\A.stating that F.A.MOSS decd 25 Oct.1873, intestate, leaving her as widow,but no other heirs.MOSS died owning wearing apparel + half interest in the crop he was raising with her. She does not consent to Petition for L/Adm.by SEELIG & CO.

PKT.#468:EST.B.F.PENNY,decd.-AMELIA C.PENNY,Admx. 8 Nov.1873: Pet.for L.\A. by AMELIA C.PENNY,widow of B.F.PENNY,who decd.July 1873, intestate,leaving surviving him his sd.widow,and 2 children - CAROLINE and LOUISE PENNY,the eldest not being 7.//Feb.1874:Pet.by widow PENNY, stating she requests the sale of property belonging to her late husband's estate-L.8,9,10,11,Block 13,Orig.Plat of town of Greenville,Ms.upon which her residence now stands. She further states that there is more land than necessary for town lots,and she seeks permission to sell off some.There is no blood kin to plead her cause,but intimate friends W.A.HAYCRAFT,JOHN P. FINLAY,JOHN H.NELSON,now act as next best friend to the decd.'s minor ch. and agree with her that it best to sell.//26 Oct.1874: AMELIA HEXTER was high bidder on a parcel $130;another parcel sold to the Greenville Dramatic Ass.for $650 on Nov.7,1874.//2 Apr.1881:Pet.for sale of land by A.C.PENNY, Grdn. She states they still own L.8,9,10 in Block 13,+ their resident home, and now seek alley easement and sale of more land. Reason for sale, their residence needs repair.//12 Apr.1881: W.A.PERCY intimately acquainted with MRS.PENNY and her minor children,is aware of her financial problems and states that she is a school teacher and manages a scanty support of the children. He recommends sale of lots.// Granted// Apr.Term 1883: AMELIA is Grdn.to minor dau.LOUISE F.PENNY,the only child living-about 12 yrs.old. AMELIA seeks to sell lots on Main and Poplar. J.E.NEGUS agrees as next best friend.//SALE allowed.**(Note**: CARRIE PENNY decd.1882,age 16.)

PKT.#469:EST.E.J.COOPER,decd. - ROBERT S.COOPER,Exec.
ROBERT S.,filed for L.\A.8 Nov.1873,stating that his wife,E.J.(ELIZA JANE) decd.--day of--1873,leaving a WILL in her own handwriting, appointing him as exect. He is sole legatee,except for U.(ULYSES)MERCHANT,who is to receives an annuity of $250.//28 Jan.1876:ROBERT S.COOPER petitions for discharge of Adm.of his wife's Est.and also as Adm.of his wife's brother's Est. - one H.R.MERCHANT. When E.J.COOPER died,she had received $438 from her brother's est.**(NOTE**; ROBERT S.COOPER died of yellow fever 1878.)

WASH.CO.,MS.PKT.GLEANINGS
PROBATE COURT - 1871/1884

PKT.#470:EST.MARY SHANAHAN,et al - MRS.ANN SHANAHAN,Grdn.
MRS.SHANAHAN filed Pet.for Grdn.8 Nov.1873,a citizen of Greenville;the widow of DANIEL M.SHANNAHAN; the mother of MARY SHANNAHAN age 6; FANNY ELLA SHANNAHAN-4;and TIMOTHY BARTHOLEW DANIEL SHANNAHAN age 1 1/2; only heirs at law of their decd.father who owned certain real estate -a dwelling house + lots in town of Greenville, fronting on Mulberry and Central Ave. Mrs.Shannahan seeks Grdn.of said minors.//So granted// Grdn.Bd.$2000 with T.M.SHANNAHAN and PAT McKEON, as sureties.

PKT.#471:EST.EMMA MORGAN,JR.,minor - V.F.ERWIN,Grdn.
ERWIN FILES PET.FOR GRDN.13 DEC.1873,stating he is the UNCLE of EMMA MORGAN,minor,whose father has recently decd. and she has asked him to be her Grdn.EMMA owns an undivided interest in'Mount Holly Plt.'on Lake Washington,which rents for @$1000 per yr. EMMA's mother (also decd.) was the sister of your petitioner(ERWIN).//Grdn.\Bd.13 Dec.1873 awards Grdnp.to ERWIN,and shows EMMA MORGAN to be the minor heir of OLIVER T. MORGAN, decd.Bd.is $1000 with H.J.HOLLINGSWORTH as sur.//3 May 1875:Grdn.ERWIN requests permission to rent EMMA's land to MRS.EMMA MORGAN,stepmother of sd.minor,for $700.//19 Oct.1876: WM.A.HAYCRAFT receives $882 from V.F.ERWIN to pay back taxes of 1874,'75,'76 on 'Mount Holly Plt.'in Wash.Co. - 1/6th of which belongs to EMMA MORGAN,JR.. The taxes were paid in the name of JOHNSON ERWIN,and others.//1875:VOUCHER for EMMA MORGAN,JR. who attends school in Ky.,// 21 July 1875,$166.66 received by C.W.WOLFE, due from EMMA MORGAN,JR.for her 1/6th part of a judgement against Est.of MRS.M.A.DUDLEY,decd.(NOTE; MARGARET A.JOHNSON married 1st JAMES ERWIN ©1843,and they had the following children:ELIZA JULIA ERWIN;EMILY ERWIN;VICTOR FLOURNOY ERWIN;WM.ERWIN;JAMES ERWIN;JOHNSON ERWIN; LILLIE J.ERWIN who married OLIVER T. MORGAN 1861 in Wash.Co.. OLIVER T. MORGAN marr.2nd EMMA ERWIN. The 2nd marr.of MARGARET A.(JOHNSON) ERWIN was to CHAS.W.DUDLEY in 1856 and they had one child Chas.,Jr.}

PKT.#472:EST.MARY B.BUTTS,decd. -S.W.FERGUSON,Adm.
Pet/for L.\A\filed 17 Dec.1873,stating that MARY B.BUTTS decd.;intestate. Court ruled that she had died more than 6 months prior and no one had come to claim adm.rights. FERGUSON,County Adm.was appointed.//

PKT.#473:EST.CHARLES H.BELL,decd. - S.W.FERGUSON,Adm.
Pet.for L.\A.filed 9 Jan.1874 by J.L.WALKER,citizen of Wash.Co.,Ms.who states that C.H.BELL departed this life much more than 6 mos.ago;intestate; leaving personal and other property,value unknown to petitioner.(more)

WASH.CO.,MS.PKT.GLEANINGS
PROBATE COURT - 1871/1884

PKT.#473:EST.BELL,cont.
WALKER is a creditor as attending Physcian to the decd.and the Est.owes him over $200. He requests that the court appoint FERGUSON,ADM.//Final a/c states that BELL had no kin nor property in this state.Dismissed 1876.

PKT.#474:EST.W.A.(A.W.?)CLARY - W.A.EVERMAN,ADM. Pet.for L.\A. filed by EVERMAN for firm W.A.EVERMAN & CO.,merchants of Greenville,Ms. who states that CLARY decd. Oct.1873,a resident of Wash.Co.,leaving a widow C.B.CARY and 1 child, a minor (unnamed);no real estate; but left an interest in a crop of cotton + a few personal belongings mortgaged to said firm.EVERMAN states the crop won't pay off his debts and funeral expenses and applies for Adm.Bd. for $1000.//Est.closed with INV.and sale of 1 black horse and the cotton. May 1875.(See Pkt.#482)

PKT.#475:PETITION of MALINDA BUCKNER: To have her son apprenticed to DR.STEWART WHITE. Filed 30 Jan.1874. She states that she is the sole surviving parent of HENRY SHILLING BUCKNER, a minor until 8 Apr.1879.The minor consents to apprenticeship. DR.WHITE filed BOND for $500 with sur. by WM.H.BOLTON,E.ENOS.// Conditions of Apprshp.: DR.WHITE must furnish HENRY with good clothes,food,treat him humanely,give him medical treatment,teach him to read and cipher. At the end of his apprenticeship, must furnish him with 2 suits of clothing-1 to work in,1 to attend church+$50.

PKT.#476:EST.D.D.ANDERSON,decd. - A.E.ANDERSON,Adm.
Adm.Bd.of $250 with N.B.JOHNSON,J.LENGSFIELD as sureties.//Pet.for L.\A. filed 21 Mar.1874 by A.E.ANDERSON,who states that his wife,D.D.,departed this life in Greenville,intestate,owning separate property worth $65. She owed some debts + funeral expenses.

PKT.#477:EST.THOMAS SHELBY,decd. - BETTIE SHELBY,Adm.
Pet.for L.\A. by BETTIE,filed 27 Mar.1874,stating she is the relict and widow of the decd.who died 9 Sept.1872 in Wash.Co.,Ms.,intestate,leaving a small Est.consisting of some Notes and Accounts.// Adm.\Bd.$500 with H.B.THEOBALD as surety.

PKT.#478:EST.F.Y.ULAN,decd - S.W.FERGUSON,Adm. 6 Apr.1874: Pet. for L.\A. by GRAFTON BAKER,Atty. for WM.COTTON,creditor,who states that UHLAN decd.in the State of Ill.more than a year ago,intestate,leaving goods and chattels in Miss. BAKER, asks that FERGUSON be appointed Adm.// Court granted permission.

WASH.CO.,MS.PKT.GLEANINGS
PROBATE COURT - 1871/1884

LOOSE PAPER,NO PKT.Number: EST.T.H.HILL VOUCHER:to MRS.MOLLIE HILL in Petersburg,Va. June 1877. Adm. of HILL's Est.is S.W.FERGUSON.

PKT.#479:EST.JOHN BELL,JR,decd.-J.ALLEN ROSS,Adm. who Pet.for L.\A. stating that BELL decd.at Leota Landing,Wash.Co.,Ms.on 17 Mar.1874; intestate; leaving 1 horse, 2mules, 3 head of cattle, 9 hogs + household furnishings;no heirs. ROSS is a creditor. Filed 13 Apr.1874.//APPRAISAL by JOSEPH TAYLOR,TROY PRICE,DANIEL WATERS,HENRY GARNER.Bond.-$40.

PKT.#480:EST.WILLIE ROBINSON,minor - D.C.MONTGOMERY,Grdn.
with J.M.MONTGOMERY as surety.Grdn.\Bd.$100,filed 5 May 1874.//In Pet. for L.\Grdn.,D.C.states that he now has in his care WILLIE ROBINSON minor heir of W.W.ROBINSON,decd.late of Bolivar co.,Ms. WILLIE is 3 yrs.old. His father, W.W.,left an Insurance Policy with "Carolina Insurance Co.' of Memphis,Tn. and the sd.Co. is now liquidating. They owe WILLIE $2000 and D.C. hopes to recover at least part of it.//31 May 1876: Grdn. D.C.MONTGOMERY seeks discharge saying little WILLIE ROBINSON decd.1874, while living with the MONTGOMERY's,leaving a watch valued at $100. At the time of the minor's death, he was 4 yrs.old, and D.C.MONTGOMERY had been supporting him at his own expense.//1876: Document signed by J.H.SHARP and SALLIE H. SHARP, who sign as one of the heirs of WILLIE ROBINSON, decd.minor, allowing the discharge of guardianship by MONTGOMERY.//1 July1876:Document signed at Riverton,Miss. by J.H.YOUNG,CAROLINE C.YOUNG,J.V. HARRIS -agreeing to dismissal of D.C.MONTGOMERY as Grdn.//6 June 1877:The above 3 documents attached to D.C.MONTGOMERY's final plea for discharge.

PKT.#481:EST.BURRELL ARMSTRONG,decd. - M.WEISS,Adm.
Pet.for L.\A.22 July 1874 by SARAH ARMSTRONG,wife of the late BURRRELL decd.of Wash.Co., stating that BURRELL decd.18 July 1874,and asks that Mr. WEISS be appointed Adm.as her husband was sharecropping with him.// APPRAISAL 3 Feb.1875 by AARON COLE,D.D.TAYLOR,MARTIN ANDERSON for $700. There were 15 bales of cotton.//8 Nov.1876: Pet.for discharge by WEISS states that ARMSTRONG's wife and heirs at law are all of full age, and are to divide what is left after the decd.'s debts.

PKT.#482:EST.THOMAS S.MORGAN,decd. -
ALBERT C.and MARY L.MORGAN,both minors over 14,petition for their Mother MARY M.L.MORGAN to be their Grdn. Grdn.\Bd.set at $500;27 July 1874. They state that they are the heirs of THOMAS S.MORGAN,decd.late of Copiah CO., Ms.//3 Nov.1874:Pet.for compromise by widow of THOS.S.MORGAN,decd.and

WASH.CO.,MS.PKT.GLEANINGS
PROBATE COURT - 1871/1884

PKT.#482:MORGAN,cont.
Mother of said minors,MARY M.L.MORGAN,who states that the Adm.of the Est.of THOS.S.MORGAN in Copiah Co.,Ms.wasWM.M.HALEY,who sold a parcel of land located in Copiah Co.,to J.DENNIS GRANBERRY. Description of sd.land: L.1,Square 27, Town of Hazelhurst in SW1/4 of SW 1/4 of Sec.3;T10;R8E. Petitioner, MARY M.L.MORGAN, further shows that she and the other heirs of sd.THOMAS S. MORGAN,decd.,brought a suit agst. GRANBERRY in Circuit Court of Copiah Co. The other heirs are named :ALLETRIS(?)E.BROWN and her husband JOHN T. BROWN; KATE B.CLARY and her husband A.W.CLARY,since decd.; ROBERT P. MORGAN;ALBERT C.MORGAN and MARY L.MORGAN.// Pet.for compromise granted. (See pkt.#474)

PKT.#483:EST.JOHN FAWN,decd. - CHAS.E.FAWN,Adm.
10 July 1874:Adm./Bd.,$2000,Yazoo CO.,Ms. JENNIE J.FAWN,widow of JOHN FAWN,decd.,relinquishes the Adm.of her husband's est.in favor of CHARLES E.FAWN.//Order confirming this.//No other doc.

PKT.#484:EST.SARAH SMITH,decd. - JAMES NIXON,Adm.
JAMES NIXON applies for L.\A. and for Grdn.\Bond,21 Sept.1874. Bd.$600 with T.G.WALCOTT,WM.E.RURY as sureties. In Pet.for Grdnp.,JAMES H.NIXON states that JACK SMITH of Wash.Co.,Ms. departed this life 14 Sept. 1874; intestate;leaving a small estate; a widow(SARAH) and 1 child. On 19 Sept. 1874,the widow,SARAH O.SMITH,decd.;leaving the estate of her husband; and the child,who is now 2 months old. Sd.child has no Christian name, and is in the care of your petitioner (NIXON),who is the brother of SARAH O. SMITH,decd.and therefore the Uncle of the infant. On her death bed,SARAH gave the infant to JAMES and he seeks Grdnp.+ Adm.of Estates.

PKT.#485:C.P.LEE and MARY LIVINGSTON LEE,minors,-H.P.LEE,Grdn.
21 Sept.1874: Pet.of CLARENCE PERCY LEE, son of EMMA KNIGHT LEE,who decd. 20 June 1873, and also the son of WM.H.LEE who decd.17 Sept.1873, states that both parents died intestate and he has no natural guardian. He asks that his half brother,HARRY PERCY LEE be appointed his Grdn.and asks that S.W.FERGUSON be appointed Adm.of the two estates.//Sept.1874:Grdn. BD.$3000 with JOHN M.LEE,W.A.PERCY as sureties.//4 Feb.1876:Grdn.& Adm. S.W.FERGUSON rents dwelling house on Main St.,Greenville and land on Deer Creek,both in Wash.co.,Ms. In his grdnp.report at the same time,FERGUSON names the other minor,MARY L.LEE.See next Pkt.(NOTE: EMMA KNIGHT was the 2nd wife of WM.HENRY LEE. By his 1st wife,ELEANOR PERCY WARE he had HARRY P.,NATHANIEL W.,JOHN M.,and CATHERINE S.who marr.S.W.FERGUSON.)

WASH.CO.,MS.PKT.GLEANINGS
PROBATE COURT - 1871/1884

PKT.#486 A:EST.M.L.LEE,minor - GEN.S.W.FERGUSON,Adm. Pkt.contains many VOUCHERS for MARY LIVINGSTON LEE: on 6 Mar.1878, Bill from Prins Fairmont College,Fairmont.Tn.;BOARD for CLARENCE P.LEE at Oxford Ms.23 Feb.1878 signed by LEWIS T.FITZHUGH for $33; To MRS. TEAT for sewing.; To DR.S.M.BALL for perscription; Tuition to MRS.LOUISE GRAY in 1877; Merchandise from C.M.WILLIAMS & Co.in Greenville.; To Sheriff for Taxes.; JIMMIE E.BROWN $3 for music lessions for MARY; To SOL BRILL for clothes for CLARENCE.//Among the merchants named in Greenville- SOL BRILL dry goods on Mulberry St.; J.SKALLER also on Mulberry; WEISS & GOLDSTEIN - fancy dry goods,Wash.Ave.;GEO.F.ARCHER-Stationer & Bookseller;A.B.FINLAY & Co.-Drugstore;'THE MAYOR'-fancy goods; DR.B.S.BYRNES -Dentist;to Steamers - "KATE DICKSON","J.M.WHITE" in 1880's.//6th annual a/c by Adm.and Grdn.FERGUSON,filed 23 Apr.1881,lists taxes paid on all of L.17,Reserved Addition in Greenville - value $1875,and on N part N1/2, Sec.34,T18N,R7W - 198 ac.Value $1980. **PKT.#486 B:EST.M.L.LEE& C.P. LEE** contains many more vouchers,but no additional genealogical information. See Pkt.#485.

PKT.#487:Est.A.J.SMITH,decd.-S.W.FERGUSON,Adm.
24 Sept.1874:Adm.Bd.posted for $2000,with surety by DAVID FRILEY, J.T. RATHER.// Pet. for L.\Adm. by J.T.SMITH,the father of A.J.SMITH, decd. and D.L.SMITH, the brother of sd. decd., citizens of Wash.Co.,Ms. T.J.SMITH and D.L.SMITH state that A.J.SMITH decd.14 Sept.1874;intestate;leaving no widow or personal representatives except your petitioners; but sd. decd. had made a verbal request that C.C CAMERON of Wash.Co. should have the care of his child, an infant of 2 months (named ANDREW JACKSON SMITH) + his estate. J.T. & D.L. ask that the request be honored,and C.C.CAMERON be declared Adm.and Grdn.//So ordered 2 Oct.1874// Dec.1874: BILL from C.J.NIXON for 3 months board for A.J.SMITH and wife-$60, for keeping and nursing the child for 2 weeks + other things -$130//Mar.1876: Petition of FRILEY and RATHER,in which they state that CAMERON had "entered a fray" with one HOAG in 1876, and slew HOAG and has since fled, leaving the Estate of A.J. SMITH,decd.,in MRS.CAMERON's hands. FRILEY and RATHER,who signed as sureties on the Adm.Bd.,are afraid that MRS.CAMERON may try to join her husband, and leave the estate unattended. They seek relief from sd.Bond.//23 Mar.1876: C.C.CAMERON has fled the country,being a fugitive from Justice, and leaving the SMITH Estate unattended, accounts unsettled,leaving the estate in the hands of MRS.CAMERON,wife of sd.Adm. Court revokes Adm.of C.C.CAMERON, and sends legal notice to MRS.CAMERON that if she wants to continue as Adm.of the A.J.SMITH Est.,she must post (cont.)

WASH.CO.,MS.PKT.GLEANINGS
PROBATE COURT - 1871/1884

PKT.*487:SMITH,cont.
bond of $2000. If she fails to appear, Court will appoint a new Adm.//
Aug.1876: Adm.is S.W.FERGUSON.(NOTE: Not a clue as to what happened to little ANDREW JACKSON SMITH.)

PKT.*488:EST.C.F.MEISNER,decd — LOUISA MEISNER,ADM. who filed for L.\A. 6 Oct.1874,stating that CHARLES F.MEISNER decd.30 Oct.1874 at his residence in Greenville;intestate;leaving as his heirs your petitioner (LOUISA) who is the widow of the decd.; + 5 children,all minors-CHARLES F.; HENRY W.; JOHN N.; WM.B.; FREDERICK LEWIS MEISNER. The decd. CHAS.F. owned a dry goods store + household furniture.//Adm.\Bd.$2000 with JOHN HABICHT,D.FLOURNOY HUNT,G.W.ELLIOTT as sureties.//Widow seeks permission to sell some of the goods.Granted.//VOUCHER 23 Dec.1873 a bill for a tombstone from R.L.ROSEBROUGH & SONS of St.Louis for "a tombstone 2 feet high",inscription — *MARY HELENA DAU.of C.F.and LOUISA MEISNER/b.June 11,1871/d.Nov.2,1872* -cost $25;// 1874; Tax receipt for L.4,5;Block 9;Addition T.C.,Greenville,Ms.;property valued at $5000.//Bill for HENRY W.,6 Mar.1877 for $267 to University of Sewanee, Sewanee,Tn.: (NOTE: From OLD GREENVILLE CEMETERY RECORDS,by Payne: CHAS.F.MEISNER 1821-1874;LOUISA MEISNER 1839-1915;MARY HELENA 1871-1872;CHARLIE MEISNER 1857-1878;JOHN NICHOLAS MEISNER 1865-1896;WM.B.MEISNER 1868-1906;ELECTA FISHER HANCOCK 1839-1917)

PKT.*489:EST.C.F.MEISNER,et al,minors — LOUISA MEISNER,Grdn.
L.\Grdn.filed 1874,by LOUISA MEISNER,who states that her husband, the above named CHAS.F.MEISNER,decd.30 Oct.1874,when C.F.,JR. was about 14 yrs.old;Henry W.12;John N.9;Wm.B.6;Fred Lewis 3 mos.//The children were allowed $1000.//One of the expenses-undated- of C.F.MEISNER,SR.'s estate, was the cost of a tombstone for *C.FELL MEISNER.*

PKT.*490:EST.VIRGINIA O.WEST,decd.-A.C.WEST,Adm.
who filed for L.\A.26 Sept.1874,stating that VIRGINIA O.WEST was the Mother of your petitioner(A.C.),who died Dec.1869 and no Adm.has ever been granted. The sd.decd.left several heirs of her body and died possessed of divers and sundry goods,notes,accounts. A suit was filed for $2000 before her death, and is soon to be settled. The decd.'s husband "having long since died."// Est.still open 1876. No further mention of Suit,or heirs. (Note: In DEED Bk."T",p.200;Abst.in Vol.III of this series:AMELIUS C.,HECTOR R.,E.WINSTON,LIZZIE M.,SALLIE R.WEST receive QUIT CLAIM for land)

WASH.CO.,MS.PKT.GLEANINGS
PROBATE COURT - 1871/1884

PKT.#491:PERSONS and EST.OF E.J.A. & G.WILLIAMS,minors - JOHN WILLIAMS,GRDN. L.\Grdn.granted to EMMA J.A. and G.WILLIAMS's father - JOHN WILLIAMS,15 Dec.1874.

PKT.#493;EST.THOMAS L.BROWN,decd. - R.M.BROWN,JR.Adm.
R.M.BROWN,JR. files 7 Jan.1875,for L.\A.,stating that THOMAS L. died 7 Jan. 1875,a citizen of Wash.Co.;intestate;leaving a small estate; surviving him, a widow MRS MARY BROWN who has relinquished her Adm.rights. Your petitioner is the brother of the decd.

PKT.#494:EST.ROBERT TAYLOR,decd.-MARCUS LANDAU,Adm. :
who filed Petition for L.\A.on 26 Jan.1875, stating that ROBT.TAYLOR decd. 23 Jan.1875,leaving a small estate-some clothes,etc. LANDAU is a creditor and seeks Adm. after the widow relinquished her rights.//Adm.\Bd. $500 with R.H.BRENTLEAGER,M.GENSBERGER as sureties.//Petition by widow EASTER TAYLOR, requesting that MARCUS LANDAU be appointed Adm. Wit: WM.N.WEILES, POLDO TAYLOR. 26 Jan.1875.

PKT.#495:EST.K.KIMBROUGH,decd.-S.W.FERGUSON,Adm.
1 Feb.1875:Petition for L.\A. by WADE HAMPTON,JR. who states that K.KIMBROUGH departed this life 15 Dec.1874;intestate;leaving no heirs in this State. The decd.'s mother lives Sun(?)Peachtree,Alabama River,Ala. When KIMBROUGH died,he was an employee of HAMPTON's at a salary of $700 per yr. HAMPTON asks that an Adm.be appointed to distribute balance of salary and to settle various claims against the estate.//$485 due Est.+ sale of horse for $560.04.//S.W.FERGUSON appointed Adm.//VOUCHER:filed 1 Apr.1875 by DR.W.G.ALLEN,Physcian,Greenfield,Ms. for $85 for services rendered on Dec.4 to Dec.14,1874.

PKT.#496:EST.EMMA LEE,decd. - S.W.FERGUSON,Adm. who filed Pet. for L.\A.,stating that EMMA LEE, wife of W.H.LEE, also decd., departed this life June 1873;intestate;leaving 2 minor children - CLARENCE P.and MARY L.LEE as her survivors. Her husband, W.H.LEE,decd. Sept.1874; intestate; leaving no property//In 1874 L.\Grdnp.was applied for minors by S.W. FERGUSON,who explained that MRS.EMMA LEE decd.leaving a house and lot in Greenville.//DEED for the lot,dated 30 May 1870,from HARRIET B.THEOBALD to EMMA LEE for $230 in cash + note for $470-L.17,Reserved Addition,measuring 99 ft.fronting on Main St.by 330 ft.deep.Deed recorded DBK.C^2,p.625, 627.//Included in Pkt.is a petition by J.& J.I.LENGSFIELD against the(cont.)

WASH.CO.,MS.PKT.GLEANINGS
PROBATE COURT - 1871/1884

PKT.#496;LEE,cont. Est.of EMMA LEE and her husband W.H.LEE, stating that the LENGSFIELD'S owned a store and the LEES owed them an unpaid bill for building supplies-$256. The LENGSFIELDs further claim that W.H. LEE signed a note due on Mar.14,1872, which the LEES failed to pay, and the LENGSFIELD'S filed suit in Circuit Court,saying that W.H.LEE decd.insolvent and MRS.LEE only had the lot in town. They seek amount of the debt + 6%. Filed 6 Nov.1876.They then petition to have L.17 sold to satisfy the debt// DEMURRER filed by S.W.FERGUSON,who denies that W.H.LEE was insolvent, rather that he had an income that supported his family in ease and affluance,that the money alledgedly owed is not the sole responsibility of the Est.of EMMA LEE. FERGUSON further stated that when W.H.LEE decd.he was receiving one third of rents from a 600 ac. plantation on Deer Creek in Wash.Co.,Ms.-$2000 or $2500 per yr.by DEED/Trust for W.H.LEE from H.P. LEE and J.M.LEEwith W.A.PERCY as Trustee, dated 11 Nov.1867- D.Bk."Y" p.631. FERGUSON further states that when EMMA married W.H., she was not in possession of a separate property, nor did she ever acquire such. The Plt.in Sec.33,T18N,R7W, which formerly belonged to W.H.LEE, was sold to E.J. COMSTOCK by decree of foreclosure. Your respondent(FERGUSON) bid in the name of said EMMA LEE for $50 given her by W.H. and the commissioner gave EMMA the DEED 10 May 1869-recorded in D.BK.C^2 p.227, showing that this tract consists of wild land. She sold it to J.M.LEE for $500. EMMA had a house built upon the aforementioned L.17 in Greenville,with material furnished by builder N.B.JOHNSON, who was paid in part by W.H.LEE and after his death,paid in full by J.M.LEE. No building material was ever bought from LENGSFIELD. After MRS.LEE decd.,the LENGSFIELDS tried to press a compromise against the so-called debt,but W.H.LEE refused to pay the unjust amount,and the LENGSFIELDS never pressed again until after the death of W.H.LEE The house was the homestead of the LEES and as such was exempt for $2000. The lot is worth only a fraction of the $2000.//

PKT.#497:EST.WM.R.TULLIDGE,decd.   - FANNIE C.TULLIDGE,Adm.
FANNIE C.TULLAGE,filed petition for L.\A.1 Feb.1875, stating that WM.R. TULLIDGE decd.14 Nov.1874; that she is his widow; that he owned divers goods and chattels;he decd.intestate;owning 5 shares of Wharfboat Association stock of $50,which has been attached by creditors. FANNIE seeks compromise of 2 shares of stock for debt owed to W.H.BOLTON.//Agreed.

PKT.#499:EST.BARNEY ROBINSON,decd.-JANE ROBINSON,Adm.
Note to COL.BOLTON,Clk.,from GEORGE V.WARD,Leota,Ms.,20 Feb.1875:He volunteers to sign bond for Adm.of MRS.JANE ROBINSON's husband's Est.

WASH.CO.,MS.PKT.GLEANINGS
PROBATE COURT - 1871/1884

PKT.#500:EST.FRANK JOHNSON,decd - NORVELLE JOHNSON,Adm. who filed Petition for L.\A. on 20 Mar.1875,with Bond of $100. He states that FRANK decd.11 Feb.1875 in this County;intestate;leaving no estate except a gold watch and chain worth @$100; heirs at law were 4 sisters and 2 brothers-NANCY JOHNSON, SARAH FREEMAN, EDNA FREEMAN, MARIA WEED, WASHINGTON JOHNSON, and your petitioner,NORVELLE. The watch is now in the possession of BENJAMIN SHIRLEY,who won't deliver it up. NORVELLE states that he paid the funeral expenses and wants to Adm.the estate.

PKT.#501:Person of EMANUEL KIER,minor-MATILDA ARMSTRONG, Grdn. who files for L\G.on 26 Mar.1875,stating she has cared for EMANUEL since infancy,he is her grandson aged 15 yrs.,the mother of said minor died 1 yr.ago,leaving no estate.//Attached:AFFIDAVIT by EMANUEL,asking that his gr.mother be his legal grdn.//Bd.$100,with NORVELLE JOHNSON as sur.

PKT.#502:Minor Heirs of THOMAS W.WILSON-BETTIE A.ALDRICH, Guardian; who files Petition for L.\G. 6 May 1875,naming minors MARY W.WILSON,BETTIE B.WILSON,ANNIE E.WILSON who are the daus.of THOMAS W.WILSON,decd. and Petitioner(BETTIE A. ALDRICH) by a previous marriage. The 3 minors have a small personal estate and income from their father's estate. BETTIE A. is also prosecuting a claim against the United States Government and must have the Guardianship papers to prosecute this claim before the Southern Claims Commission.//Grdn.\Bd.$3000,with surety by DAVIS BUCKNER, A.B.CARSON, W.R.TRIGG.//

PKT.#503:EST.PHIL T.BUCKNER,minor - J.H.ROBB,Grdn. Petition for a Grdn.,filed 29 May 1875 by PHILLIP BUCKNER,a resident of Wash.Co.,over 15 and under the age of 21,states that his father-THOMAS H. BUCKNER decd.5 NOV.1871;leaving a WILL.Surviving heirs were his widow LOUISA BUCKNER, and DAVIS BUCKNER,JAMES H.BUCKNER,MATTIE B.ROBB,JESSIE BUCKNER, and your petitioner(PHIL). LOUISA and DAVIS were named exect. in the Will,but no provision was made for a guardian for the minor children. PHIL chooses his brother inlaw-J.H.ROBB,a resident of Wash.Co. Wit:J.T.GUCHINGSFELDER, E.ENOS,J.STEINER.//Grdn.\Bd.set at $2500 with surety by E.A.ROBB,J.SMITH.

PKT.#505:EST.MRS.H.J.LOGAN,decd.- CHARLES H.PLATT,Adm. who files a Petition for L.\A.stating that he and his sister MRS.AMELIA BIGELOW are the surviving heirs of MRS.H.J.LOGAN,who decd.3 Aug.1874. No Adm.has been appointed for MRS.LOGAN's Est. She decd.intestate;leaving no indebtedness;with certain assets of Notes which won't be paid until (more)

WASH.CO.,MS.PKT.GLEANINGS
PROBATE COURT - 1871/1884

PKT.#505:EST.LOGAN,cont: an Adm.has been appointed by the Court.// Another petition for L\Adm.was filed by R.W.THOMAS,July Term 1875,with J.LENGSFIELD as surety on Bond of $700.//INV. & APPRAISAL 20 July 1875 showed a part payment,dated 1 July 1873, on a lot of 1 ac.to be laid off by C.P.HUNTINGTON, and signed 'M.S.MORGAN by C.E.MORGAN,Agent'.The appraisal was done by H.B.PUTNAM,G.W.ELLIOTT,JAS.F.CHESNEY on 25 July 1875 - $350.// On 31 July 1875, the Adm.Bond was raised to $500 and CHAS.H. PLATT was the principal with A.P.KEESECKER as surety. An order by the Court giving "new" Adrn. CHAS.PLATT permission to act , and signed by GRAFTON BAKER,Commissioner in Chancery.//5 Dec.1876,PLATT states he has been unable to find any estate other than the sd.lot.

PKT.#506:EST.SAMPSON HAMPTON,decd.-MARCUS LANDAU,ADM.
22 July 1875:Petition for L.\Adm.by VINEY HAMPTON,the widow of sd. decd. who waived her right to act as Adm.in favor of MR.MARCUS LANDAU of the firm of LANDAU SPINGAIN,Creditors//Pet.for L.\Adm. by LANDAU, who states that SAMPSON HAMPTON decd.in Wash.Co.20 July 1875;leaving a small estate-2 mules,wagon,15 ac.of growing cotton on "Morsewood Plt.', all of which is mortgaged to LANDAU. SAMPSON left a widow (VINEY) and 3 minor children. The widow refuses to Adm.Est.//26 July 1875 a CITATION for MARCUS LANDAU to report for annual a/c of Est., delivered to J.LANDAU, brother of MARCUS.

PKT.#507:EST.JESSE BUCKNER,minor-DAVIS BUCKNER,Grdn.
5 Aug.1875,JESSE asks that DAVIS BUCKNER be appointed her Grdn.,further stating that she is the minor heir at law of THOMAS H.BUCKNER,decd.of Wash.Co.,and over the age of 14. This note was attached to Pet.for L.\ Grdn. filed same day by DAVIS BUCKNER,who states that he is JESSE's brother.// Adm.\Bd.$2500.

PKT.#508:EST.M.A.BECK,decd.-J.G.BECK,Adm. with BOND $1000,surety by W.A.HAYCRAFT,C.W.SIMS,JOHN H.NELSON.//13 Sept.1875, Petition for L.\Adm. by J.G.BECK, who states that his wife MARY A. BECK decd.15 July 1875,a resident of Wash.Co.;intestate;a small personal est.; leaving 4 children and your petitioner(J.G.)as surviving heirs.//INVENTORY & APPRAISAL,JULY 1876, by HUDSON TAYLOR, ROBERT MARTIN, GEORGE BROWN, C.E. MORGAN, SAM BROWN estimated at $1749,giving the children an allowance of $250. Inv.shows that MARY A. owned a Mill and Millshed. [Note: Stockwell Papers show that CORA MAY BECK decd.18 July 1877-age 7;DAVIS BUCKNER BECK decd. 28 Nov.1884-age 10]

WASH.CO.,MS.PKT.GLEANINGS
PROBATE COURT - 1871/1884

PKT.#509:EST.JOHN DAVIES,decd.Testator - A.J.PAXTON,Exect.
Pkt.contains a copy of the WILL of JOHN DAVIES,in which he names his
wife, ELIZABETH DAVIES,who resides in HOLLAND PATENT,Oneida Co.,N.Y.
She is to have everything after payment of his debts to the exclusion of
his son EVAN DAVIES. Executor:A.J.PAXTON: WILL written 3 Nov.1875 and
witnessed by J.W.BUCKLEY,C.BROWN,GEORGE ROGERS.//Filed Wash.Co.,Ms. 22
Nov.1875//Attached to WILL are affidavits by the witnesses to the authenticity of said WILL.// No other document.

PKT.#510:EST.GERONIMA L.FINN,minor heir of R.R.FINN,decd. -
J.L.GRIFFIN,Grdn. who files a petition for L.\Grdn.referring to a petition
(Not included in this Pkt.)by the minor GERONIMA,who states that she is
due @$10,000 consisting of a judgement in her favor for $5000,obtained in
the City of Vicksburg. $2000 in money due her,and $3000 commissions all
collectable in Vicksburg,as she is the sole heir of her late father ROBERT
R.FINN,by the Est.of one JOSEPH PATLO. GERONIMA desires a Grdn.in order
to collect her inheritance. She is 18 yrs.old and chooses Dr.J.L.GRIFFIN to
perform without BOND. 6 Dec.1875.

PKT.#511:EST.MARY E.PRITCHARD,decd.-K.FLOYD,Adm. Petition for
L.\Adm. filed 15 Dec.1875 by J.A.TILLMAN,of Wash. Co.,Ms.who states that
MARY E.PRITCHARD,who decd.10 June 1875,was the widow of WM.PRITC-
ARD. She decd.intestate;left a small estate;and TILLMAN is a creditor. He
asks that FLOYD be appointed Adm.//Adm.\Bd.$300 with TILLMAN as surety.

PKT.#512:REBECCA R.SATTERFIELD,decd.-W.E.SATTERFIELD,Adm.
Petition for L.\Adm.filed 31 Dec.1875 by W.E.SATTERFIELD who states that
his wife REBECCA decd.16 Nov.1875;resident of Wash.Co.;intestate;leaving
3 children-MILLING MARION SATTERFIELD age 6,EARL TALIFERO SATTER-
FIELD age 4,VINES JOHN SATTERFIELD age 1,"the fruit of her marriage with
your petitioner."(W.E.);no real estate;but left an Insurance Policy worth
$2500. Minors must have a Guardian,and the Est.an Adm.in order to collect
on sd.policy.//Surety on Bd.-T.G.WALCOTT,DAVID FRILEY,//Previous surety
-C.W.SIMS,C.W.LEWIS (NOTE:see pkt.#654)

PKT.#513:EST.GEORGE JACKSON,decd.-FANNY SCHOFIELD,Adm.
Petition for L.\Adm. by FANNY dated 1 June 1876,who states that in 1854
she was united in the bonds of matrimony to GEORGE JACKSON,now decd.
At that time,she and George were both slaves of STEPHEN BAREFIELD,also
now decd. She continued to live with GEORGE as wife until 1867,(cont.)

WASH.CO.,MS.PKT.GLEANINGS
PROBATE COURT - 1871/1884

PKT.#513:JACKSON,cont.
when he deserted her and he lived in unlawful cohabitation with one MINEY RICHARDSON until his death in May 1873. MINEY has all of GEORGE's possessions,both real and personal including 20 ac.of land in Wash.Co.+ 20 head of cattle,some stock of hogs + 1 mare and 1 mule. The sole heir at law of GEORGE JACKSON is a son named GEORGE WILLIAM JACKSON,the fruit of his marriage with your petitioner (FANNY).//INVENTORY & APPRAISAL by SAM BAREFIELD,MARION BAREFIELD,P.M.ALEXANDER,E.P.COLLUM,J.W.WINPEGLER.// No other document.

PKT.#514:M.L.PETERS,decd.-HARRIET H.PETERS,Exect.
Pkt.included the WILL of DR.PETERS,(Abst.in Vol.II of this series,recorded in WILL BK."1") Land description of "The Peters Place",shows it to be a tract of land lying between Linden Plt.on the North and Ashland Plt.on the South. L.6,7,8;Sec.2; L.1,2,Sec.3 all in T16N,R8W: WILL names wife HARRIET H. and children JULIA H.,MOLLIE G.,BETTIE T.,MINNIE PETERS.// 1st CODICIL:Dr.Peters has sold the Peters Place to DR.JAMES M.SMITH.// Pet.for L.\Adm. by widow HARRIET H.,inwhich she states that MATTHEW L.PETERS decd.Wash.Co.;intestate;leaving surviving him a widow,and children named above.Filed 17 Jan.1876.

PKT.#516:EST.STEPHEN T.BAREFIELD,decd.-P.M.ALEXANDER,Adm.
Petition for L.\Adm. by FANNIE A BAREFIELD,a citizen of Wash.Co.,who states that her husband, STEPHEN T. decd.4 Dec.1875 at his residence in Wash.Co.;intestate;leaving a widow-your petitioner-and 1 minor child. There are debts due from the Estate to different persons,and the decd.left personal as well as real property. FANNIE waives Adm.rights in favor of P.M.ALEXANDER,a creditor.//Adm.\Bd.$500,with SAML.BAREFIELD,IVEY T.RATHER as sureties.

PKT.#517:EST.THOMAS KENNEDY,decd. - A.B.CARSON,Adm. Letter written on small lined paper-signed by GERTRUDE KENNEDY: Winterville, (Ms.) a request that the Adm.of the Est.of THOMAS KENNEDY be allowed to herself or A.B.CARSON. She further states that she is ill and cannot travel to town for several days. THOMAS owned a personal estate of 1 mule,1 plow,2 pair gear,7 bales of cotton in the seed,25 bu.of corn. Witnessed by A.B.CARSON,GREEN McCUTCHEON. Filed 23 Feb.1876.//Pet.for L.\Adm. by A.B.CARSON who states that KENNEDY decd.owning a small estate,leaving a widow and a large family of children. Attached to this petition is the note quoted above.//Adm.\Bd.$500 with W.A.HAYCRAFT as surety,filed 23(cont.)

WASH.CO.,MS.PKT.GLEANINGS
PROBATE COURT - 1871/1884

PKT.#517:KENNEDY,cont.
Feb.1876.//VOUCHERS: MRS.M.B.CARSON files a bill for ginning costs; to PLEASANT FRACTION for hauling cotton to gin;Bill from Dr.D.C.MONTGOMERY for "TOM's last illness" on Dec.23,1875-$9; COFFIN-$25 to N.B.JOHNSON & CO.'//INV.& APPRAISAL by J.M.MONTGOMERY,THOS.J.SUTTON,BEN DAVIS, WM. GOODSMAN-10 Aug.1876-Est.worth $280.09.Filed 5 Dec.1876.//Written in pencil on the outside flap of the packet cover:'GERTRUDE KENNEDY,mother; minors-LIZZIE,TOM,LUCY ANN,JIM KENNEDY.'

PKT.#518:EST.BRASWELL HOGUE,decd.-BELLE HOGUE,Adm.& Grdn.
(Name sometimes spelled BASIL or BOSWELL HOGUE.)BELLE HOGUE files petition for L.\Adm.& Grdn.,stating that her late husband,BRASWELL,decd.7 Mar.1876, intestate;leaving as his surviviors your petitioner and 1 infant child - BRASWELL JOSEPHINE age 6 mos. as his sole heirs at law. HOGUE owned an undivided interest in @140 ac.of land + a personal estate of 4 horses,12 head cattle,35 hogs,400 bu.corn,4 bales of cotton.BELLE requests that P.H.MALONE,WM.FIELDING,J.T.SMITH (W.B.BARWICK scratched through) J.A.SHRADER with E.COLLUM be appointed to appraise the est.//Adm.\Bd. sureties-W.E.SATTERFIELD,W.A.CLEATON-$2000.FILED 23 MAY 1876.//Inv.& Appraisal May 1876.//28 Nov.1876:Petition to sell personal property.//22 Apr.1878:Pet.by W.E.SATTERFIELD seeking release from the Adm.Bond he co-signed in 1876 for $1000 on Est.of HOGUE,because he has been told and so believes that the Admx.(BELLE) is an ignorant, illiterate person of no business capacity,and is not competent to manage sd.Est.//ANSWER of BELLE HOGUE to CITATION,May 1878:She states that she has no objection to releasing W.E.SATTERFIELD from Bond,and will replace him with J.C.ESTILL and J.A.TILLMAN.(SEE PKT.#522)

PKT.#519:EST.PHILLIP BOIS: Lunatic- A jury of "12 discreet persons" listened to DR.D.C.MONTGOMERY state the man was incoherent, not remembering anything about himself. He was sent to Lunatic Asylum in Jackson,Ms. 21Jan.,1876.

PKT.#520:EST.KEZIAH NEWMAN,: Lunatic-June 1876:Petition by MARTIN NEWMAN who states that his wife KEZIAH is of unsound mind and dangerous to herself and others. Same procedure as in Pkt.#519.

PKT.#521:EST.N.B.JOHNSON,decd.-J.Y.JOHNSON,Adm. who petitions for L.\Adm.,showing that NICHOLAS B.JOHNSON,late of Wash.Co.,Ms.,decd.5 Sept.1875;intestate;owning a third interest in firm of N.B.JOHNSON & CO.

WASH.CO.,MS.PKT.GLEANINGS
PROBATE COURT - 1871/1884

PKT.#521:JOHNSON,cont. which said firm owns various lots and buildings in Greenville,Ms.+ half interest in 2 plantations-'Forkland and Onward Plts.'in Wash.Co. [NOTE: 'Forkland and Onward' are now(1985) in Sharkey Co.] + @$10,000 in personal property. Your petitioner (J.Y.JOHNSON)is the brother and next of kin to N.B.JOHNSON,decd.,except for his widow, ELIZABETH J.JOHNSON, and 4 children,MADISON WHITNEY JOHNSON and 3 minors THOMAS BENJAMIN, FREDERICK WM.,and JOSEPH JOHNSON. The brother,J.Y., asks that the Estate be appraised by W.A.HAYCRAFT,JOHN W.WARD, WM.J. MANLY.//Attached to the petition for L.\Adm. is a waiver signed by the widow and eldest son MADISON WHITNEY JOHNSON, asking that J.Y.serve as Adm.//Adm.\Bd.for $3500,with surety by JOHN MANIFOLD,JULIUS M.LANDAU filed 2 Oct.1876.//14 Nov.1876-Appraisers set aside $1500 for the 1st years allowance for widow and children.//28 Nov.1878:Petition by J.Y. JOHNSON who states that he has served as Adm.of the property belonging to the estate of his decd. brother N.B.JOHNSON. J.Y shows that he and his sd. brother were part of the firm of N.B.JOHNSON & CO. along with JOHN MANIFOLD. J.Y. sold out his interest to JOHN MANIFOLD and left the state. MANIFOLD took over as Adm.of NICHOLAS's Est.until he (JOHN) decd.in the "late epidemic"(Yellow Fever - 1878). J.Y states that he never had any of the property belonging to his late brother,NICHOLAS. He asks that the court appoint a common Adm. for the estates of NICHOLAS B.JOHNSON, decd.and that of JOHN MANIFOLD,decd.,at the 2 widow's request. J.Y. relinquishes his Adm.// 30 Nov.1878: Court appoints S.W.FERGUSON as Adm.with S.McNEELY, W.A.EVERMAN, W.A.PERCY as sureties on Bond of $3000.[Note: Listed in THE STOCKWELL PAPERS as victims of yellow fever - <u>1878; *JOHN MANIFOLD SEPT.25.//MADISON WHITNEY JOHNSON-son of N.B.JOHNSON.-4 Oct.// FREDERICK WILLIAM JOHNSON,son of N.B.JOHNSON: -12 Oct.// THOMAS BENJAMIN JOHNSON son of N.B.JOHNSON -15 Oct.*]

PKT.#522:BRASWELL JOSEPHINE HOGUE,minor - BELLE HOGUE,Grdn.
On outside of Pkt.the number has been changed from #519 to #522. (Name also spelled BOSWELL.) Grdnp.Bond $2000 with BELLE HOGUE,Mother of sd. minor,as principal and W.E.SATTERFIELD,T.G.WALCOTT as sureties .3 July 1876. See Pkt.#518 above.//Additional information not given in Pkt.#518 shows that BRASWELL HOGUE,father of said minor, decd. owning land in Effingham,Ill.- S1/2,L.#7,#8,#9,#16;Sec.16;T6;R4E of 3 P.M. On 28 Nov. 1876, BELLE seeks permission from the court to sell the sd.land to support and educate her child,a minor ward.//So Granted.//4 Aug.1876:Letter from Law Office of WOOD BROS.(VIRGIL and BENSON WOOD), Effingham,Ill. giving MRS.HOGUE instructions in order to sell her ward's property in Ill.

WASH.CO.,MS.PKT.GLEANINGS
PROBATE COURT 1871-1884

PKT.#523:EST.J.G.SWANSON,decd.-PETER   RABONI,Adm.
PETER States that SWANSON died in Greenville,Sept.1876,"in my house",
after a malignant desease.Peter said that he cared for SWANSON,and the
estate owes him fees worth $50. The decd.held a small balance in the bank
in Vicksburg-@$150. Filed 6 Oct.1876//Court awarded him $40.

PKT.#524:WILL OF ANN JACKSON,decd. (Not recorded in Will Bk."1")
WILL names:2 daus.SALLIE ROBINSON and BELLE WASHINGTON -1/6th ea.:
2 sons HENRY JACKSON,LEWIS JACKSON-minors-1/3rd ea. Estate to be
sold and then divided. Exec.THOS.B.WARFIELD is also to act as Grdn.to the 2
minor children.WILL written 5 July 1876-Filed 6 Nov.1876.Wit:DR.S.R.DUNN,
D.C.BROOKS,//28 Nov.1876, T.B.WARFIELD applied for L.\Grdnp.and L.\Exec.
BOND $1000 with CARNEAL WARFIELD AND JONTE EQUEN as sureties.

PKT.#525:EST.S.F.WHITE,decd.-S.W.FERGUSON,Adm.
Only 1 paper in Pkt. Adm.\Bond Filed 11 dec.1876,no amount shown.

PKT.#526:EST H.H.ELLIOTT,decd.-G.W.ELLIOTT,Adm.
G.W.ELLIOTT files Petition for L.\Adm.12 Feb.1877,stating that his brother,
H.H.ELLIOTT decd.31 Jan.1877,intestate,in the town of Greenville;leaving a
widow and no children. The home and property of sd.decd.-some few goods
in Greenville @$300-was in Wash.Co.,and the widow waives rights of Adm.
and asked G.W. to apply. G.W.states that he is of full age, a resident of
Wash.Co.//INV.& APPRAISAL show that H.H. owned a "shop".//Adm.Bd. $500
with SAML.ELLIOTT and FRANK VALLIANT as sureties (Note: G.W.ELLIOTT
and his wife both decd. in Fall 1878-yellow fever.)

PKT.#527:EST.NANNIE   M.GLATHERY,minor-W.T.GLATHERY,Grdn.
Petition for L.\Grdnp.by W.T.GLATHERY,shows that he is the father of
NANNIE,minor heir at law of ELLA W.GLATHERY-late wife of your petitioner
(W.T.),who decd.possessed of both real and personal property-Estate lying
in La. She had no est.in Ms.//Grdn.\BOND $3500,with surety by NANCY
JAMES, A.J.CROW Filed 12 Feb.1877.//No other documents.

PKT.#528:EST.WM.H.HARRISON,decd.-W.A.HAYCRAFT   who files
Petition for L.\Adm.7 Apr.1877,stating that W.H.HARRISON,late a citizen of
Wash.Co.,Ms.decd. before daylight 2 Mar.1877; leaving a noncupative WILL
asking HAYCRAFT to take charge of everything he had. Statement was
made during his last illness, at his home in Greenville,in presence of Rev.
DUNCAN GREEN and MADISON JONES. "We put his wishes in writing (cont.)

WASH.CO.,MS.PKT.GLEANINGS
PROBATE COURT 1871-1884

PKT.#528:HARRISON,cont.:   6 days after his death,and witnessed it."
They do not believe that HARRISON's widow or next of kin reside in Ms.
The decd.left a small personal estate @$300.// Copy of WILL shows that
the decd.WM.H.HARRISON asked HAYCRAFT to attend to everything and if
there was anything left over,to send it to his family.

PKT.#531:HARRY ADELL, Lunatic,who was found on Williams Bayou. He
had previously been in Ala.when he had a similar "spell",now living on the
Sinsabagh portion of the HAYCRAFT plantation. ADELL was violent after
having been turned down for a church membership,and attacked a man who
shot him with a pistol. Paper signed by DR.C.W.STONE,M.D. June 8,1877.

PKT.#532:EST.RICHARD SAUNDERS,minor-RICHARD GREEN,grdn.
Petition for L.\Grdn.by GREEN,who states that he now has under his care an
infant child,one RICHARD SAUNDERS,age @4 yrs.-the child of THOMAS and
CHARITY SAUNDERS, both now decd. The petitioner is the brother of
CHARITY,decd.,who left the infant in his care at her death. CHARITY also
left a mule and a cow,now belonging to sd.infant.//BOND $100,with
T.B.WARFIELD as surety.

PKT.#533:EST.E.P.McDOWELL,decd.-S.W.FERGUSON,Adm.
Petition of HAMILTON McDOWELL, SARAH BURKE, widow and MARY HAYS,
widow, shows that E.P.McDOWELL decd.14 Sept.1877 at Burlington, N.J.;
intestate; no heirs in Ms. but your petitioner (HAMILTON) and one other
sister whose residence is unknown. The decd.left property consisting of
Lots in Greenville,Ms.(Wash.Co.);no personal property. The heirs ask that
S.W.FERGUSON be appointed Adm. Filed 27 Oct. 1877.// On 23 Nov.1877:
Letter headed-Baltimore,Md.-from N.RUFUS GILL,Atty.who states that he
had received $100 to pay for E.P.McDOWELL's funeral and was sorry to hear
that S.W.FERGUSON had been ill.//VOUCHERS;21 Feb.1880-acknowledge-
ment of check for $100.50 from S.W.FERGUSON,Adm.to A.FLANDERS,Atty.for
MRS.McKEEPY-dau.(or dower ?)of HAMILTON McDOWELL,decd.//2nd annual
a/c 26 Apr.1880:lists the following payments to heirs:A.FLANDERS -$100:
N.RUFUS GILL for a/c of MARY HAYS,SARAH BURKE,MRS.BEATTY-$301.50,pd.
at Baltimore. Annual a/c state that the estate is tied up in a suit with the
Levee Board.

PKT.#534:EST.WM.F.SMITH,decd.-JAMES D.SMITH,Adm.
Petition of JAMES D.SMITH and E.L.SMITH,citizens and residents of Wash.Co.,
state that W.F.SMITH,the father of your petitioners,decd.at his residence

WASH.CO.,MS.PKT.GLEANINGS
PROBATE COURT 1871-1884

PKT.#534:SMITH,cont. in said county on 3 Nov.instant;leaving your petitioners (JAMES D. and E.L.SMITH)and CLARK SMITH a resident of Yazoo City,Ms.; JOSEPH SMITH,a minor residing in Lima,Ohio; MARGIE ARCHER a married resident of Cincinnati,Ohio;MATTIE,a minor resident of Cincinnati; and WM.SMITH a resident of Lima,Ohio. WM.F.SMITH decd.intestate;leaving a small personal property consisting of 32 mules and 8 wagons, + a portion of a crop of cotton all under mortgage to JOHN CHAFFE & SONS, Commissioners of New Orleans. The petitioners believe the crop will barely pay off debts of Estate. There was also a Life Ins.Policy for $12,000.//INV.& APPRAISAL shows $1187 worth of stock.//Copy of Indenture between WM.F. SMITH of the 1st part,WALTER L.CAMPBELL of Ms. of 2nd part,B.M.CAMPBELL of Va. of 3rd.part. Entered into in New Orleans 10 July 1871. The mortg. covers a plantation in Wash.Co.,Ms. known as "The Home Place"-2940 ac. described as follows: Sec.1,2,11;T16N;R6(or 7?) - 1920 ac.(note: now known as Tralake Plt.) W1/2 of Sec.6;T16N;R6W-320 ac.: E1/2 of Sec.32;T17N;R7W-320 ac.:SE1/4,Sec.26;T17N;R7W-160 ac.:1 undivided interest in 1/2 of Sec.7;T16N.;R6W-220 ac. Inv.& Appr. filed 22 Nov.1877// Adm.\Bd.$4000 with JAMES C.ESTILL,E.L.SMITH as surety.

PKT.#535 1/4:EST.F.X.SCHMAHOLZ,decd.-S.W.FERGUSON,Adm.
DEPOSITIONS: by DR.J.S.WALKER of Greenville,Ms.who attended F.X.during his last illness in conjunction with DR.S.M.BALL: by DR.V.F.P.ALEXANDER,of Greenville,who stated that F.X.decd.3 Jan.1878: by MRS.LOUISE SCHMAHOLZ, widow of F.X.,decd. She is of German Nation and unable to speak English. She used L.CAFFALL as interperter,and said that her late husband was ill from Sept,1877 until his death-Jan.1878.// DR.S.M.BALL,Greenville, attended F.X.until he had to go to Woodstock. He asked Dr.WALKER to take over for him when he left. When he(Ball) returned,F.X.had discharged DR.WALKER and employed DR.ALEXANDER. Filed 8 June 1878.

PKT.#536:EST.GABRIEL WILLIAMSON,decd.-JACOB WILLIAMSON, Exect. Adm.\Bd.$500. Written in pencil on outside of CITATION to "distributees"were the following names and amounts...12 Aug.1878:

    BETSY WILLIAMSON----$32.17
    BRITTON THOMAS------$64.35 (minor under 21)Guardian Ad Litem
    CHARLOTTE AUSTIN----$32.17 (minor under 21)appointed to THOMAS
    TEMPY LAWSON--------$16.08   W.WARREN
    GABRIEL LAWSON------$16.08
    JACOB WILLIAMSON----$32.17
            Total $193.02 (cont.)

WASH.CO.,MS.PKT.GLEANINGS
PROBATE COURT 1871-1884

PKT.#536:WILLIAMSON,cont.   WILL OF GABRIEL WILLIAMSON,of Wash.Co. (written in purple ink,fading badly)Exhibit "A" names: BETSY WILLIAMSON my wife (marked through); JACOB WILLIAMSON (marked through); JANE LAWSON's children to get a child's part; BRITTON THOMAS to get a double share;JACOB WILLIAMSON to get a child's part;BETSY WILLIAMSON-a child's part;CHARLOTTE WILLIAMSON-child's part. If BETSY WILLIAMSON is decd., her part comes back to "my children". WIT: ANN D.HALSEY, REE B.HALL, HATTIE JACKSON. Will filed 17 Jan.1878. Exect.is son JACOB.//Attached to WILL is the testimony of MRS.HALSEY stating that she signed the WILL as a witness,that HATTIE JACKSON has since dec.,and asks that JACOB be appointed exec. 21 Jan.1878.//Adm.\Bd.$500,with PAUL WOODRUFF, BENJ. SAMS as sureties.//Inv.& Appraisal by D.D.JACKSON,ALLEN HARRIS,JERRY ANDERSON,ELSEY BISHOP.//1st annual a/c shows that GABRIEL was a rentor of MRS.HALSEY's.//22 Apr.1878,a division of corn and fodder of the Est.of G.WILLIAMSON,decd. by Exect.JACOB WILLIAMSON on 'Willow Cottage Plt.' Also named in a/c were HENRY JACKSON,NAT AUSTIN,JAMES LAWSON.

PKT.#537:EST.TIMOTHY   DAILEY,decd.-M.W.HUGHES,Adm.
(Name also spelled DALEY) Petition for L.\Adm.by HUGHES,who shows that DALEY decd.Nov.1877,no heirs,a certificate of deposit issued 1st Nat.Bank of Huntingdon,Penn.for $375. Filed 7 Feb.1878.//Adm.\Bd.$750 with A.J. TERNEY, W.R.HARVEY as sureties.

PKT.#538:EST.MARY   C.&J.BOWMAN   STERLING,JR.,MINORS   -J.B. STERLING,GRDN.   J.B.STERLING,a citizen of Wash.Co.,Ms.in petition for L.\Grdn, states that his 2 children named above are minors under 21,who own in their own right 8 shares of New Orleans City R.R.Stock, worth $800-each owning 4 shares. Filed 27 Feb.1878.//Grdn.\Bd.co-signed by JAMES A.V.FELTUS.//In Feb.,1878,Sterling petitions the court to allow him to sell the stock,in order to educate his children. He claims that he bought sd.stock with his own money as an investment for his children, but he needs the money,now,to properly care for them, and to keep MARY in school.//Granted Apr.1879 and stock sold for $1000.

PKT.#539:JOHN   HANWAY vs THOMAS GREANY,et al Filed 1 May 1873 (Chancery Court Pkt.,misfiled,Pkt.disintegrating) BILL OF COMPLAINT by JOHN HANWAY,who states that prior to 1 Oct.1870,THOMAS GREANY and BARTHOLOMEW HANWAY were partners in Wash.Co.,Ms.under the firm name of B.HANWAY & CO. JOHN HANWAY was an employee of that company,until the death of B.HANWAY on 1 Oct.1870...that the firm had borrowed money

WASH.CO.,MS.PKT.GLEANINGS
PROBATE COURT 1871-1884

PKT.#539:HANWAY,CONT. from JOHN-@$2594 alledgedly secured by a mortgage on L.16,Reserved Section,Greenville,3/4 of an ac.on Main St.and Walnut St.. BARTHOLOMEW's widow-MARY HANWAY and GREANY, surviving partner of sd.firm, agreed to each assume 1/2 of debt.//The RESPONDENTS to the sd.suit were listed as:THOMAS GREANY,a citizen of Indianapolis, Indiana; MARY ROBERTSHAW-the former widow;ELIZABETH JULIA HANWAY, BERTHA MARY HANWAY,ELLEN HANWAY,minor heirs of BARTHOLOMEW,decd.; and JAMES ROBERTSHAW,now the husband of sd.widow MARY. Suit filed 1 May 1873.// On 2 June 1873, a DEMURRER was filed by MARY(HANWAY) and JAMES ROBERTSHAW stating that it is not right to attach her personal property for debt of partnership since GREANY owned no part of her sd. property.//DEMURRER was sustained.//29 July 1873 JOHN HANWAY petitions for Appeal to Supreme court of Ms.(Appeal bond $200,signed by V.F.P. ALEXANDER,C.E.MORGAN.)// Nov.1873, the Chancery Court found GREANY liable for full amount of debt "as surviving partner".//Oct.1874, Grdn. Ad Litem W.H.BOLTON,Clerk, was appointed for the 3 minors BERTHA MARY, ELIZABETH JULIA, ELLEN HANWAY.//23 Jan.1875: DEPOSITION of JOHN HANWAY, age 40-50 yrs.old (No additional information)//10 Apr.1875: DEPOSITION of THOMAS GREANY,Marion Co.,Ind. who states that he is age 38,and discussed the partnership arrangements-"we all ate at the same table".Apparently there had never been any firm division between business and family life.//3 Feb.1877: L.16 in Greenville was sold by the Sheriff + some other property under dispute.

PKT.#540:G.P.WALUE-WILL,noncupative: WILL dated 23 Dec.1877,and filed 5 June 1878.//Attached to copy of Will is a note dated 26 Dec.1877, stating that the WILL was expressed by the late G.P.WALUE of 'Calla Place', Wash.Co.,Ms. on 22 Dec.1877, and again on 23 Dec.1877 in presence of J.C. ESTILL,RICHARD WALUE,MRS.L.WALUE(later called MAGGIE)-to wit:"all my property divided between my brothers and sisters and DWIGHT MARTIN and EDDIE DODSON." Note signed by T.G.WALCOTT.// Petition for L.\Adm.by GEORGE DWIGHT MARTIN,who shows that GEORGE P.WALUE decd.26 Dec.1877 and made his WILL on 23 Dec. The surviving heirs and next of kin were: -------WALUE,his mother of Canton,Ms.;MRS.E.JOYCE,sister of Canton;MRS. JENNIE EARNEST and MRS.M.NICHOLSON,sisters of Durant,Ms.;EDWIN DODSON nephew at Durant;Y.J.WALUE,brother at Vicksburg,Ms.;RICHARD E.WALUE of Wash.Co.,Ms. MARTIN further shows that the decd.owned considerable real and personal estate in Wash Co. and Madison Co.,Ms. Martin's portion is 1/7th of all est.//CITATION issued to MRS.WALUE(not to be found in "my" county-Mad.) and E.JOYCE (found her)in Mad.Co.19 June 1878.//No other doc.

WASH.CO.,MS.PKT.GLEANINGS
PROBATE COURT 1871-1884

PKT.#541:JACOB WESTBROOK,DECD.-C.L.WORTHINGTON,Adm.
(Note: file in the biggest mess! Vouchers all rolled up in big wads, stuffed in envelopes,or folded in old newsprint.) No Petition for L.\Adm.in this Pkt. only vouchers and cotton records. See Next Pkt.

PKT.#541 B;EST.JACOB WESTBROOK,decd.-CHAS.T.WORTHINGTON, Adm. WILL OF JACOB WESTBROOK: written 'Joiner Farm', Dec.4,1875. He appoints CHAS.T.WORTHINGTON as agent and Adm.to tend to his farm in Wash.Co.,Ms.which fronts on Lake Washington + all personal and real property. Everything he owns is to go to SAMUEL WESTBROOK,the son of WESTLY WESTBROOK. Requests that WORTHINGTON act as SAMUEL's Agent, until he comes of age,and that he pay off all of his debts-a note owed to H.T.BUCKNER & CO. for $10,500; a Note of HANA's in favor of JOS.MOON of St.Joseph, La.(Tensas P.) for $1500 with JOSEPH WILZINSKI holding @$600. He offers WORTHINGTON 1/2 of all clear profits made on sd.place in exchange for managing the estate. He further requested that LUCINDA SMITH and MATILDA WESTBROOK be supported by sd.plantation.//A Note written on back of WILL requests that SAML. be educated if possible. If WORTHINGTON should "have any delicacy in this matter",please turn everything over to friend JOSEPH MOON of St.Joseph,La.// Another notation on back of WILL states that by Dec.11,1876,balance due on the mortg.was $6,500. No file date// (Note: WILL not recorded in WBk."1"Wash.Co.}//PROOF OF WILL:Attesting to the authenticity of handwriting-C.T.WORTHINGTON on 17 July 1879; J.F. HARRIS on 14 July 1879.// Petition for L.\Adm.by C.T.WORTHINGTON,filed 4 Nov.1878, shows that JACOB decd.1 Nov.1878,owning considerable real and personal property;intestate (?);no heirs or next of kin to Adm.estate. C.T. is a creditor.Adm.\Bd.$10,000.//Included in this Pkt.is a copy of an earlier WILL OF JACOB WESTBROOK-written St.Joseph,La.14 Jan.1870:"I make the colored Boy WESTLY WESTBROOK,whom I acknowledge to be my son-sole and only heir...to get 1/2 of my property,a Plantation in Wash.Co., Ms.-@900 ac.on Lake Washington,Wash.Co.,Ms., called the JOYNER PLACE, bought by me from HENRY T.BUCKNER of New Orleans. Also 1/2 of stock,etc. The other 1/2 of my estate to go to ROBERT MURDOCK of Tensas Parish,St. Joseph,La. for being sole Adm." In same envelope is Original DEED to above property.// Attached is Petition for L.\EXEC.by ROBERT MURDOCK, which he withdraws upon finding out that WORTHINGTON has been appointed in Wash.Co.,and "finds him a suitable person",but seeks to have this WILL probated.Filed 5 Dec,1878.//Same date-Earlier WILL is probated.-Bond $15,000.//12 Apr. 1880:C.T.WORTHINGTON seeks discharge after the sale of personal property. The lands have been sold by W.E.HUNT,Sheriff of Wash.Co.,Ms. for

WASH.CO.,MS.PKT.GLEANINGS
PROBATE COURT 1871-1884

PKT.#541 B;WESTBROOK,cont.
default on D/T to H.T.BUCKNER.//16 Apr.1880:DECREE accepts SAML.WEST-
BROOK's claim to be the sole heir of sd.JACOB,decd. CITATION to interested
parties to appear.//16 May 1883: MATILDA WESTBROOK,Grdn.of SAMUEL
WESTBROOK signs receipt for $480 after the final settlement. Pkt.#541
C :contains more vouchers. For record of GRDN.procedures see PKT.#650.

PKT.#542:WILLIAM MARSHALL,DECD.-SARAH MARSHALL,ADM.
Petition for L.\Adm.by SARAH MARSHALL,who shows that WM.decd.2 Sept.
1878, intestate; small personal property - horses, buggy, carriage, ect.-
@$3000. Besides his widow(SARAH),Wm.left 3 other heirs:LILY MARSHALL
age 6;BELLE MARSHALL-4;FRANCES MARSHALL-2, the children of your
petitioner and the decd. Filed 7 Nov.1878.//Adm.\Bd.set at $6000 with
THEO POHL,L.CAFFALL as sureties.//7 Nov.1878-$2180 alloted to widow
and children.//Same date,C.M.JOHNSON is appointed Grdn.of minors.// Large
number of VOUCHERS.

PKT.#543:EST.B.FRANK JAMES,decd.-T.W.POWELL,Adm.
(Pkt.disintegrating) Petition for L.\Adm.filed 7 Nov.1878 by THOS.W.
POWELL,who states that B.FRANK JAMES decd.7 Oct.1878,intestate;leaving
surviving him a 1/2 sister MARTHA G.POWELL, a minor,as sole heir;he left
personal and real property. T.W.POWELL shows that he is next of kin in this
state and Grdn.to sd.minor heir MARTHA G.//Adm.\Bd.$3000 with H.L.BAKER
and F.J.CRAIG as sureties.//CITATION: 28 Nov.1879,to MATTIE G.POWELL,
minor heir and NANNETTE SWITZER,aunt of sd.minor,and ----JAMES,uncle
of sd. minor.//Annual a/c shows that MARK and S.G.WORTHINGTON rented
'Opossum Ridge Plt.'for 1878,for $500,and A.J.H.CROW rented 'Oak Ridge
Plt.' for $750. (See Pkt.#563)

PKT.#544:WM.EHLERS,decd.-L.CAFFALL,Exect.
Petition for L.\Adm.by CAFFALL,filed 11 Nov.1880,shows that EHLERS decd.
18 Sept.1878 after making a NONCUPATIVE (Verbal) WILL, which is now
presented. The decd.left his shop and its contents to DAN RUDEINGER,his
workman. The shop was the only personal property belonging to EHLERS,
except for some household goods and some notes due,and 2 policies due
from Odd Fellows Lodge and Knights of Honor,worth $4000. After payment
of his debts,he requested the remainder go to CHARLEY,AGNES,LOUISA,and
LENA CAFFALL,all minor children of your petitioner,L.CAFFALL. EHLERS and
CAFFALL were brothers-in-law,and EHLERS left no widow,or children,or
other heirs,and so willed everything to his neices and nephew.//Exect.\

WASH.CO.,MS.PKT.GLEANINGS
PROBATE COURT 1871-1884

PKT.#544;EHLERS,cont. Bd.$200 with E.A.ECKART, and JOHN HARBICHT as sureties.//Witnesses attested to WILL: E.K.STAFFORD who wrote it down,DANIEL RIEDINGER and JOHN L.PULLEN. Filed and recorded Wash.Co.,Ms. WILL BOOK "1"p.410-22 Feb.1879.(Note: Listed as victims of yellow fever, Fall 1878: *Sept.13-Willie Ehles,child; and Mrs. william Ehlers*)

PKT.#545:EST.HENRY FREUNDT,DECD.-L.CAFFALL,exect.
Petition for L.\Adm.filed 10 Nov.1878,by CAFFALL,showing HENRY FREUNDT decd.17 Sept.1878 after having made a WILL,which left all his estate,both real and personal to his Father and Mother who are residents of Prussia. He requests that CAFFALL and JOHN MANIFOLD be his exects. CAFFALL states that MANIFOLD has since decd., leaving CAFFALL as sole surviving Exect.. FREUNDT left no real estate,he was a jeweler and left considerable stock which must be appraised.// Pkt.contains copy of WILL of HENRY FREUNDT, and also several legal documents written in German (I think), and then translated into English, giving the following information about the FREUNDT FAMILY, to wit: The Father-HEINRICH FREUNDT,a coppersmith;The Mother JOHANNA FREUNDT nee HARTMAN; a sister EMILIE GOETHERT,wife of FREDERICK WILHEIM GOETHERT, a watchmaker; ERNST FREUNDT,a bro.and a coppersmith--all living in MARENWERSH;also the Power of Atty.of MARIA EMMA FREUNDT,a sister,shows her living in Weisbaden. 2 documents showing proof of heirship. ADLOPH FREUNDT, another bro.of the decd. is said to reside in St.Louis,Mo., but "is not known to this office",and a sister LOUISE decd.1875 and her infant soon after,leaving no one there. This lengthy rundown on the Family was signed- H.GERTITZ,German Consul in St.Louis, Mo.//Annual a/c shows the family split $640.

PKT.#548:EST.THOMAS P.PERRY,DECD.-ALBERT WHITEWAY,Exect.
WILL OF THOMAS P.PERRY, - written Greenville,Ms.7 Sept.1878:
To:wife and children-all property. If none survive me then everything to my brother-in-law FRANK EVANS of Canada. Appoint ALBERT WHITEWAY, formerly of England,but now of Greenville,Ms and J.H.NELSON of Greenville as Exects.// 1883 Petition for dismissal by ALBERT WHITEWAY,who states that a son, FRANK.G.PERRY is now of age, and dau.ELLEN is now ALBERT's wife. ALBERT is also the grdn.of minors THOMAS,CARRIE,SIDNEY L.PERRY.// Petition granted.//Many doc.missing.//(See next Pkt.)

PKT.#549:EST.JAMES PERRY,DECD.-vs ALBERT WHITEWAY,defdt.
14 Nov.1878,Petition for L.\Adm.by ALBERT WHITEWAY for the Estate of JAMES PERRY,decd. states that JAMES decd.11 Sept.1878; intestate;that

WASH.CO.,MS.PKT.GLEANINGS
PROBATE COURT 1871-1884

PKT.#549:PERRY,cont.
WHITEWAY has been appointed Exect.of Estate of THOMAS P.PERRY,decd.and the children of THOMAS.P.PERRY are the heirs of sd. JAMES PERRY,decd.. ALBERT SEEKS L.\ADM.//27 June 1881: Petition for discharge and final a/c,as ALBERT states it was nearly impossible to decipher the business of Mr.Perry,as his books were in a jumble,and Mr.Perry and all his family died in 1878 yellow fever epidemic.//7 Oct.1881:Petition of MARY SPENCE of Hamilton,Wentworth,Province of Ontario,Canada wife of THOMAS SPENCE of same,shows that she is the only surviving sister of JAMES PERRY,decd. late of Wash.Co.,Ms.who decd.in Greenville in 1880;intestate;leaving no widow or child,only 1 sister-your petitioner,and 1 brother THOMAS PERRY also of Greenville, who has since decd. THOMAS PERRY was a widower leaving 5 infant children,one of whom has since died. MARY contends that the Estate of brother JAMES should be shared by herself and the children of THOMAS PERRY.//A Guardian Ad Litem is appointed for the minors,because ALBERT has a conflict of interest.(Note: THOMAS P.PERRY was British Consul,stationed in Greenville,Ms.Listed as victims of Yellow Fever-Fall 1878:Sept.4.- FRED PERRY,boy and MRS.JAMES PERRY

    Sept.7 - JAMES PERRY   Sept.11 - MRS.T.P.PERRY
    Sept.18 - T.P.PERRY   Sept.23 - ------- Perry,child

PKT.#550:EST.MRS.EMMA MORGAN,decd.-V.F.ERWIN,Adm.
ERWIN files for L.\Adm.26Nov.1878,showing he is the brother of MRS.EMMA MORGAN,widow of OLIVER MORGAN,decd. That MRS.EMMA MORGAN decd.4 July 1878,intestate;leaving as her survivors J.W.ERWIN;JOHNSON ERWIN; C.W.DUDLEY,JR.; EMMA MORGAN,JR. an infant ward of the petitioner;and your petitioner(V.F.ERWIN) as sole heirs and distributees of her estate-170 ac. of cleared land,130 ac.woodland in Wash.Co.,Ms.+ personal property worth $1500. V.F.ERWIN states he was the Agent of the decd.and the other heirs asked him to act as Adm.

PKT.#551:EST.THOMAS McLEAN,decd.-PHOENIX McLEAN,Adm. who files petition for L.\Adm.14 Nov.1878,stating that his brother THOMAS,late of this County,died 15 Sept.1878 at his residence,leaving no widow or child; intestate; the brothers equal partners in real and personal property in Greenville,Ms.-2 storehouses,1 dwelling house,1workshop, hardwood, Blacksmith tools,etc.-$1000.The heirs at law are your petitioner (PHOENIX) and 4 brothers and 2 sisters who reside in Canada:JOHN,ROBERT,SAMUEL, HENRY,MRS.RANDEL,MRS.ATKINSON - all over 21.

WASH.CO.,MS.PKT.GLEANINGS
PROBATE COURT 1871-1884

PKT.#553 A:EST.JOHN MANIFOLD,decd-S.W.FERGUSON,Adm.
28 Nov.1878,a Petition for L.\Adm.was filed by MARGARET M. MANIFOLD, widow of sd.JOHN,showing that he died at his residence 25 Sept.1878; intestate;no children. She (MARGARET) is the sole distributee. JOHN,decd., was a partner with the late N.B.JOHNSON. Their affairs were very complicated and intertwined. She feels unable to cope with the hardware store, sawmill, cotton plantation, etc., and requests that S.W.FERGUSON be appointed Adm.in her place,and that her husband's estate be joined with that of N.B. JOHNSON,decd.,as JOHNSON's widow so desires.//ELIZABETH J.JOHNSON, widow of N.B.JOHNSON,makes the same request,stating that she has 4 children-"M.W.JOHNSON an adult child by a former wife",and 3 minor children of her's and N.B.'s. At one time J.Y.JOHNSON,brother of N.B. was the Adm.of his estate,but J.Y. has since moved from this state. ELIZABETH asks S.W. FERGUSON to Adm.both estates.// Included in Pkt. is a note stating that a WILL of JOHN MANIFOLD's had been found,but there is no copy in this Pkt.,nor recorded in WILL Bk."1".(See next pkt.)

PKT.#553 B:EST.JOHN MANIFOLD,decd.-S.W.FERGUSON,Adm.
WILL of JOHN MANIFOLD: written 24 Sept.1878 in which he states that "1/2 of N.B.JOHNSON & CO. belongs to me,other 1/2 to N.B.JOHNSON's heirs. My 1/2 to go to my wife MAGGIE." MAGGIE to be Exect. Wit:S.ARCHER, JOS. S.WILDER.(NOTE: Buried in "Old Greenville Cem."-*Margaret Manifold-1838/1898:John Manifold-1830/1878:Sarah Manifold-1799/1875*

PKT.#554:EST.JOHN H.SANDERS,DECD.-MARY SANDERS,ADM.
(Inside this Pkt.the number of this Est.is #559) Petition for L.\Adm.filed by MARY SANDERS, 6 Dec.1878, stating that she is the widow of JOHN H. SANDERS,who decd.1 Oct.1878,living at the time of his death in Wash.Co., Ms.leaving small personal property-$400.//Adm.dismissed Oct.1880.

PKT.#554 1/2:EST.A.B.TRIGG,decd.-SUSAN P.TRIGG,Exectx.,
who petitions 3 July 1879 for L.\Adm., for her late husband's est. She stated that ABRAM BIRD TRIGG decd.22 Sept.1878,leaving a WILL,which she now presents for Probate. No estate, just a few "desperate debts".// W.R. TRIGG,bro.of sd.decd., was a witness to WILL when it was written in 1872; **WILL OF ABRAM BIRD TRIGG-** written 3 Aug.1872-leaves 2/3rd of Estate to SUSAN P.TRIGG, 1/3rd to "my child MARY TRIGG." Wife,SUSAN,to be Exect. Wit:S.ARCHER, S.D.FINLAY, W.R.TRIGG.(**Note:** Listed on the Confederate Monument,"Old Greenville Cemetery" *A.B.TRIGG-VIRGINIAN*

WASH.CO.,MS.PKT.GLEANINGS
PROBATE COURT 1871-1884

PKT.#555:EST.SIMON FLIESHER,decd-NATHAN GOLDSTEIN,Adm.
who filed Petition for L.\Adm.,2 Dec.1878,showing SIMON decd.--day of --1878,at his residence in Greenville;no widow;2 minor children;no property except a horse and dray worth @$100. He owned an endowment with BENIE BRITTRS(?) LODGE to be paid over to the Orphan Asylum where the 2 children will be sent. Petitioner is nearest relative to minors.// VOUCHER for travel expenses for "custodian" and orphans to Asylum-$32.50(Asylum and children unnamed.)Adm.\Bd.$200.

PKT.#556:EST.MARSHALL BURDETT,decd.-R.BURDETT,Adm.
Filed 2 Dec.1878,Petition for L.\Adm.by RICHARD BURDETT,showing that MARSHALL decd.1 Nov.1878 at his residence in Wash.Co.,Ms.;intestate, owning a small personal estate-stock,farm implements,etc.; your petitioner is brother and next of kin.//Adm.\Bd.$2000,with JOHN M.LEE,W.E.HUNT as sureties.//INV.& APPRAISAL 8 Jan..1879.

PKT.#557:EST.JULIUS ROCHLITZ,decd.-JOHN HANWAY,Exect.
Petition by heirs of "our father "JULIUS THEODOER ROCHLITZA(also spelled RACHLITZ,ROCHLITZ) who decd. in Greenville,Ms.in America, giving their Power of Atty.and authority to the Imperial German consul,MR.GERLICH,at St.Louis,Mo.,asking him to acknowledge the LAST WILL and Testament,and to collect from the Estate of sd.decd. MR.GERLICH may transfer this P\A to a substitute. (As best deciphered)Ogbin near Litton,Bautzen and Berlin-10 Mar.1879 and signed by: ELEANOR AUGUSTA ANNA ULBRICH, nee RACHLITZ and her husband FREDERICK WILHELM ULBRICH,a trader of Ogben; ROBERT ADOLPH THEODORE RECHLITZ;CARL THEODORE MARC RACHLITZ.//In Royal Court,Litton-11 Mar.1879,witnesses prove signatures of above heirs// Attached: United St.Consulate at Manneheim:"I,EDWARD M.SMITH,CONSUL OF U.S.A.at Manneheim,Germany,attest to authenticiy of signatures.// ATTACHED: St Louis,Mo. RUDOLPH SCHULENBURG attests to the true translation of above documents from those written in German,to English,before Vice-Consul WM.KROOP of U.S.A.-Dresden,Germany.//Attached:are German documents-apparently the original ones named above.//Pkt contains a copy of WILL OF JULIUS ROCHLITZ ,of Wash.Co.,Ms. written 6 Sept.1878. He appoints JAMES CONNELL,JOHN HANWAY as exects.and instructs them to sell his estate and "for the proceeds to go to my children":ANNIE ROCHLITZ, ROBERT ROCHLITZ, MAX ROCHLITZ-to share and share alike. Wit:HERRMANN SOMMERS,F.C.BOHNERT.//Petition for L.\Adm.by JOHN HANWAY,11 Nov.1878, shows that JULIUS ROCHLITZ decd. 8 Sept.1878,leaving a WILL. He was a fisherman by trade and carried on his business in co-partnership with

WASH.CO.,MS.PKT.GLEANINGS
PROBATE COURT 1871-1884

PKT.#557;ROCHLITZ,cont.
F.DUCHMON,now the surviving partner. Sd.decd.owned no real estate,but did own 1/2 interest in fishing boat,tackle,etc. + 1/2 interest in 2 U.S. Bonds + 1/2 interest in $1600 in currency-All of which is worth @$800,to be divided between 3 children,now residing in Germany. The co-executor has decd.(JAMES CONNELL),leaving JOHN HANWAY as sole exect.//Oct.1882: Discharge of HANWAY as Adm. Heirs split $104.(Lawyers and court fees got the rest of it.)

PKT.#560:EST.D.E.BROOKS,et ux-SAML.B.LAWSON,Adm.
LAWSON filed a petition on 9 Dec.1878 to consolidate the Adm.of the 2 estates of D.E.BROOKS and FANNIE C.BROOKS,decd. Petitioner (LAWSON)is the brother of the late FANNIE C., who decd.in Greenville, 4 Sept.1878; intestate;small personal est.;that during her lifetime FANNIE was the wife of DAVID EMERSON BROOKS,who decd.intestate(Sept.2,1878);without children,dying 3 days prior to the death of sd.wife;small estate. LAWSON requests to be Adm.of both ests. (Note: both victims of Yellow Fever)

PKT.#562:EST.KAROLINE HABICHT,Dec.-JOHN HABICHT,Adm. who petitions for L.\Adm.,showing that KAROLINE was his wife who decd.16 Sept.1878;intestate;no children or descendants of any;your petitioner is the sole heir to small Ins. Policy by the German Life Association of N.Y.

PKT.562 1/2:MARY SHANNAHAN and FANNY E.SHANNAHAN,minors -T.M.SHANNAHAN,Grdn. who petitions for Grdnp.,showing that MRS.ANN SHANNAHAN decd.5 Sept.1878. She was the widow of DAN SHANNAHAN, decd.;leaving as survivors 2 minor children,named above. MARY is 11, FANNY ELLA @9. They are the neices of your petitioner (T.M.). MRS. ANN SHANNAHAN left a Lot of land in greenville,on which was a dwelling house inhrited from her husband,Dan.:T.M. states that since the death of DAN,he has occupied sd.house,keeping the widow and children with him. He would further show that one of the children will now be sent to the Catholic Orphan Asylum He has talked with Rev.F.C.BOMART and other friends and feels that $20 per month is fair rent for the house - sd.sum going to the children.//THOS.W.WARREN,Clerk,said he felt $25 was the correct amount for rent. Filed 10 Dec.1878.

PKT.#563:EST.MARTHA G.POWELL,minor-THOS.W.POWELL,Grdn.
who petitions for L.\Grdnp.11 Dec.1878,showing that the late B.FRANK JAMES,resident of Wash.Co.,decd.7 Oct.1878, leaving surviving as his sole

WASH.CO.,MS.PKT.GLEANINGS
PROBATE COURT 1871-1884

PKT.#563:cont.
heir,MARTHA G.POWELL,his 1/2 sister,a minor of tender yrs. Your petitioner (THOS.W.)is the Uncle and next of kin in this state. He has had complete control of sd.minor for last 12 yrs., maintaining and supporting her entirely during the entire time.She requests that he be appointed her Grdn. THOS.W.POWELL has also executed Bond as Adm.of Est.of B. FRANK JAMES, decd. Minor to get income of @$750 per yr.//Annual a/c shows that E.F. EUBANK rents 'Oak Grove Plt.' and 'Opossum Ridge Plt.' @$3.50 per ac. - 250 ac.//29 Oct.1880-MARTHA G.POWELL has married J.C.HAMNER.

PKT.#565:LYMAN STOVALL,decd.-J.E.NEGUS,Adm.
who petitions for L.\Adm. showing that STOVALL decd.5 Sept.1878, leaving money and personal property @$250;a WILL in which he left everything to one HATTIE TRAMMILL and her father,who has since decd. NEGUS is her Grdn. by her request. STOVALL decd.leaving no heirs at law or relations known to petitioner. Filed 3 Jan.1879//WILL OF LYMAN STOVALL is annexed. He left everything to HARRIET TRAMMILL,except his tools and gun,which he left to her father JEFF TRAMMILL. Wit:by Rev.T.PAGE,Pastor of Methodist Church, and THEO.HABICHT.No dates.//2 July 1879:Witnesses give proof of sd. WILL, and GEORGE BILLINGSLEY attests to accuracy of signature on WILL.//GRDN,.\BD.-$203.//Estate closed 12 Oct.1892.(See next Pkt.)

PKT.#566:EST.HARRIET TRAMMELL,minor-JAMES E.NEGUS,JR.GRDN.
2 Jan.1879,NEGUS files petition for L.\Grdnp.for HARRIETT E.TRAMMELL, minor over 14, resident of Wash.co.,Ms.,who chooses NEGUS as her Grdn. She is an orphan with no blood relations living.

PKT.#569:EST.ALICE CHIASA,Ward,minor-S.O.SHOREY,Grdn.
Petition for L.\Grdnp.filed 6 Jan.1879,by S.O.SHOREY who states that he is the step-father of ALICE CHIESA, minor under 10,whose mother decd.of yellow fever in Greenville (Ms.),whose father has long since been decd. SHOREY claims that the minor's mother asked him to take care of her child while on her death bed. She has no estate.//6 Jan.1879 - Grdnp.\Bd.to SHOREY -$100//Mar.Term 1879:Petition for L.\Grdnp.by JOHN CHURCH,who states that he is 1/2 brother of the minor ALICE CHIASA,who is 8 yrs.old. and that ALICE hardly knows SHOREY. CHURCH declares that he and his wife have no children of their own and would welcome ALICE to their comfortable home. He further states that SHOREY is (now) a single man, absent from home and county for long periods of time,and the child is left with a dau.of SHOREY's who has a weak and wandering mind and is often cruel to

WASH.CO.,MS.PKT.GLEANINGS
PROBATE COURT 1871-1884

PKT.#569:CHIASA,cont.
ALICE. She won't let ALICE see her relatives. CHURCH asks that the Grdnp. allowed SHOREY be revoked and given to him.//Apr.1879: DEPOSITION by JAMES MURRAY in case JOHN CHURCH,et ux vs C.O.SHOREN, in which MURRAY gives an unfavorable, graphic picture of Mr.SHOREY's moral character.//16 May 1879:DEPOSITION by J.A.NEWMAN,SAM T.WILLIFORD,LOUIS SCHLESINGER swearing to good character of JOHN CHURCH.//24 May 1879:DEPOSITION: by MRS.W.B.WHEATLY and MRS.CHARLES WHITE who state that ALICE has not a place to sleep nor is she strong enough to last at the SHOREY's. They declare that JOHN CHURCH can afford to take care of her.//29 May 1879: Petition for Grdnp.of ALICE by JOHN CHURCH,next of kin,attested to by NELLIE PENNY and FANNY PUTNAM CHURCH,wife of JOHN CHURCH,who swear they know O.M.SHOREY personally and know that his financial means are the most pecunius kind. ALICE is young,JOHN CHURCH is a married man,has a comfortable house in Greenville,is next blood kin,willing and able to care for sd.minor. They go on to say that SHOREY,who claims possession of sd. minor child by reason of having married her mother a few months prior to her death,had practically abondoned sd. mother and child up to a short time before her demise of Yellow Fever. That the child had no bed,slept on the floor. Petition signed by MRS.CHURCH,nee FANNIE PUTNAM CHURCH, E.A. PUTNAM,BETTIE ----(Note:the signatures do not match the names at top of this document.)//31 May 1879: GRDNP.\BD. states that ALICE CHIASA is minor heir of LAURA L.SHOREY,nee CHIASA. Bd.for $250.//31 May 1879: Court Order granting Grdnp.to JOHN CHURCH.

PKT.#570:EST.N.J.NELSON,decd-MARY NELSON,Adm. who petitions for L.\Adm.8 Feb.1879,stating that she is the widow of NEWMAN J.NELSON,who decd.18 Sept.1878;intestate;at his residence in Wash.Co.;no personal estate except that exempt for widow's part,except for a claim against JOHN HANWAY for $300 judgement in a case before the Supreme Court of Ms.// 13 Dec.1879 an allowance of $900 to widow since she has a grandchild of NEWMAN J.'s living with her,whom she treats as though she were her own child.

PKT.#572:EST.LELIA PERKINS,minor-D.A.LOVE,Grdn. who filed Petition for Grdnp.10 Mar.1879,stating that LELIA is a resident of Wash.co.,a minor under 14, no father or mother living. Minor has no property in Ms.,but owns some in Iowa and Tenn.Petitioner is husband of the aunt of LELIA// 10 Mar.1879: Grdnp.\Bd.for $1000 shows that LELIA is the minor heir of

WASH.CO.,MS.PKT.GLEANINGS
PROBATE COURT 1871-1884

PKT.#572;PERKINS,cont.
DANIEL P. and CAROLINE PERKINS,both decd.// On 7 Feb.1881,D.A.LOVE states that LELIA is one of 2 children of CAROLINE HEDGES, who decd.in Memphis,Tn.;leaving a WILL,which was probated in Bolivar Co.,Ms.;leaving every thing to sd.LELIA PERKINS and ---- HEDGES. About $20,600 was attached by creditors in Shelby Co.,Tn. LOVE has learned the expectancy of sd.Ward is more than anticipated, and asks that the Grdn.\Bd.be raised. Claims against the estate are still in litagation.

PKT.#573:EST.J.S.TATLEY,decd-C.S.JOBES,Adm. ,a citizen of Attala Co.,Ms.who states that TATLEY,of wash.co.,Ms.decd.10 Mar.1879,intestate; leaving a small estate-1 mule + 1 outfit for levee work,wheel barrows, shovels,ect.which are now in Issaquena Co.,Ms.where TATLEY was working on a levee contract at the time of his death. JOBES claims that the Miss. Levee Commission owes TATLEY $1500. TATLEY had a contract along with THOS.SWEENEY and GEORGE B.LEWIS to construct the Duval Levee in Issa.Co. JOBES is a friend and creditor of sd.decd.//Adm.\Bd.$2500 with surety by JOHN P.FINLAY,I.ISENBERG.//Attached is a petition by JOHN TATLY, brother of the decd.,who states that J.S.decd.leaving surviving him,his father JOHN TATLEY, JOHN TATLEY,JR.-your petitioner, LAMBERT TATLY, and ELLEN TATLEY. Only JOHN,JR.resides in Ms.and asks that C.S.JOBE act as Adm. All filed 17 Mar.1879.

PKT.#574:EST.C.R.BASS,Decd.-E.MONASH,Exect.
Pkt.contains 'Original WILL',filed 19 Mar.1879,Wash.Co. Will Bk."1",p.411 (Abst.Vol.II this series.)Written in pencil on small lined paper.//Petition for L\Adm.by MONASH states that BASS left a large and valuable estate, and work on the plantation must proceed. He needs a court order to carry on the business.// 22 MAR.1879: Petition for probate by Exect.H.J.JOHNSON shows that BASS decd.13 Mar.1879, leaving a WILL, a large estate, 'Riverside Plt.'+ property in Texas,and in Tenn.//22 Mar.1880: Petition by Exect. for release from Adm., stating they had complied with all terms of WILL when to their astonishment the decd.'s Mother filed a claim for $10,160. Then a former brother-in-law of sd.decd. probated a claim against the sd.estate for $18,000 in Circuit Court of Wash. Co.,Ms. and the latter had brought suit against the executors for the sd.sum. The executors could wind up the affairs of BASS's estate, except for these ridiculous charges, and they refuse to function further under these conditions,as the time they have taken away from their own affairs has been considerable. E.MONASH wishes to go to Europe,and JOHNSON has enough to do to attend to(cont.)

WASH.CO.,MS.PKT.GLEANINGS
PROBATE COURT 1871-1884

PKT.#574:BASS,cont: his own affairs. If not released they demand that "Riverside Plt."be turned over to them to work,until all debts are paid. (Note: very incredulous,outraged Petition) //29 Apr.1880: Petition for L.\Adm.by EUGENIA P.BERTINATTI,who states that the Exect.have been discharged and as mother of the decd.,C.R.BASS,she wishes L.\Adm.//Granted Final a/c shows that the bodies of C.R.BASS and his father have been removed to Georgetown,D.C.,Feb.1880, as set up in WILL of C.R.BASS.(Note: Named in WILL OF C.R.BASS: Mother-EUGENIA P.BERTINATTI;sisters ELLA ANN INCHISA and EUGENIA BASS,both decd.and some of their BATE kinfolk.)

LOOSE PAPER :
Found in Pkt.#574: Dated 21 Mar.1879.A small document states that BEN T.WORTHINGTON is the natural Grdn.of ELLEY WORTHINGTON.

PKT.#575:EST.A.J.H.CROW,decd.-MARY JAMES,Adm. who petitions for L.\Adm.25 Apr.1879 (with MARY J.BAKER scratched through, and MARY JAMES written above it.) MARY JAMES,a resident of Wash.co. was a sister to A.J.H.CROW,decd., a citizen of Wash.Co.,who died in Natchez 11 Feb.1879; leaving a small estate, worth @$1200. She's the only surviving heir.// Adm.\Bd.$1200 with H.L.BAKER, F.I.CRAIG as sureties. Oct.1879

PKT.#576:EST.DANIEL E.YOUNG,decd.-MATTIE A.J.YOUNG,Adm.
who petitions for L.\Adm.26 Apr.1879,stating that her brother DANIEL E.,a citizen of Wash.Co., decd. in Greenville Sept.1879, leaving a small estate. She is the only heir//Bond $100.

PKT.#577:EST.MARY GRIFFIN,et al,minors-JOHN GRIFFIN,Grdn.
Petition of MARY GRIFFIN, LAURA GRIFFIN, HELLEN GRIFFIN, DONALD C.GRIFFIN, G.G.GRIFFIN shows that JOHN K.LANE,late of Jeff.Co.,Ky. decd. there Dec.1877;intestate;owning an Insurance Policy of $3000 for the benefit of one SARAH GRIFFIN and her 8 children-FRANK, JOHN, WILLIAM, MARY, LAURA, HELLEN, DONALD C., G.G. Your petitioners are heirs-at-law of JOHN K.LANE,decd. MARY, LAURA, HELLEN are under 21 and over 14, and choose their father JOHN GRIFFIN as their Grdn. Donald C. and G.G. are under 14.//Grdn.\Bd.$3000 with JAMES RUCKS,ALEX YERGER,JOHN H.BOWEN, WM.GRIFFIN as sureties. 5 Apr.1879

PKT.#578:EST.MARGARET WILLIAMS,decd.-R.W.THOMAS,M.D.Adm.
DR.THOMAS filed Petition for L.\Adm.25 May 1879,stating that has been a practicing physcian in Greenville,Ms.for more than 5 yrs.and was acting in

WASH.CO.,MS.PKT.GLEANINGS
PROBATE COURT 1871-1884

PKT.#578:WILLIAMS,cont.
that capacity at the time of the Yellow Fever Epidemic in 1878. He was attending MARGARET WILLIAMS,who decd.17 Sept.1878,intestate possessed of a Lot and tenement in Greenville on West side of Mulberry St.,+ personal property-furniture,etc. Her entire estate is not worth more that $150. His bill was for $100 for medical services during her last illness.12 Sept.-Sept.17,1878.

PKT.#579:EST.HENRIETTA LEE,alias ROGERS,decd.-R.W.THOMAS, M.D.,Adm. Dr.THOMAS states that HENRIETTA LEE owed him $100 for medical services during her last illness-from Sept.8 to Sept.15,1878. In May Term 1879,a petition by Dr.THOMAS states that HENRIETTA decd.15 Sept.1878,intestate;owning a house and Lot in Greenville on Mulberry St. No kin has applied for L.\Adm.//Bond $100//July 1879, DR.THOMAS files a complaint against DOC ANDERSON and his wife who have kept him out of possession of the house and Lot of HENRIETTA LEE,alias ROGERS. He also files a similiar complaint that FANNY WASHINGTON won't let him have the house and Lot of MARGARET WILLIAMS,decd.

PKT.#579 1/2:EST.LOU PERRY,ELIZA HOUSTON,ANN HOUSTON, minors-CAROLINE COLLIER,Grdn.
Petition for L.\Grdnp.by NAT PENNER, shows that JONAS HOUSTON and his wife BENTON HOUSTON,decd.in Greenville,Ms. Sept.1878 of Yellow Fever, leaving the following children: LOU PERRY age 7; ELIZA HOUSTON-4; ANNA HOUSTON-3, all 3 the children of sd. BENTON HOUSTON. Your petitioner is brother to sd. BENTON, decd. and nearest of kin. He can support and maintain sd.children. Filed 30 June 1879.//1 July 1879: Petition by CAROLINE JOHNSON, who shows that JONAS HOUSTON and his wife BEATON HOUSTON, decd.Sept.1878 of Yellow Fever, leaving 3 children-LOU PEERY age 7;ELIZA HOUSTON-4;ANNA HOUSTON-3,all 3 the issue of sd. BEATON,decd. Petitioner states that she has the care and support of sd.minors,is blood kin. Signed CAROLINE JOHNSON marked out and COLLIER written in.//14 July 1879:Petition of PENNER dismissed and CAROLINE appointed Grdn.with Bond $100.PAUL WOODRUFF,HAM GREEN,LEM COLLIER -husband to CAROLINE, signing as sureties.

PKT.#580:EST.MIKE DUFFY,decd.-PAT DUFFY,Adm. who files Petition for L.\Adm.in Oct.1879,showing that MIKE,who was his brother, decd. Oct. 1878; intestate; estate valued at $1500; no wife or children.

WASH.CO.,MS.PKT.GLEANINGS
PROBATE COURT 1874-1881

PKT.#581:EST.TIM O'CONNOR,decd.-JOHANNA KINSELLA,Adm.
Petition for L.\Adm.Filed 11 Oct.1879, by JOHANNA O'CONNOR, widow of TIMOTHY O'CONNER,late of Wash.Co.,Ms., who shows that TIMOTHY decd.22 Jan.1877, intestate; leaving surviving him 3 children, the offspring of marriage with your petitioner(JOHANNA). ARTHUR-age 6;KENNEDY-4; NORA-3 the only heirs. TIM owned a home on L.13 & 14, Block 13 of Original Town of Greenville,on Mulberry St., and a saddle shop,which has been sold.//Dec.1879:$1000 set aside for the widow and children's support.// Adm.\Bd.$100 with JOHN KINSELLA signing as surety.// Next document dated 1887 - JOHANNA O'CONNOR, now KINSELLA, states that she hasn't reported an annual a/c, because the O'CONNOR estate is depleted.// CITATION published Nov.1889, in which NORA and ARTHUR are named,but not KENNEDY. {NOTE; 'OLD GREENVILLE CEM.' by Payne": *Johanna Kinsella (WIFE OF John K.)1854-1907// Arthur O'Connor 1873-1911// Nora O'Connor Healion 1872-1966; Joseph E.Healion 1871-1939 }*

PKT.#582:EST.SALINA MORRIS,decd.-B.HASBURG,Adm. filed L.\Adm. Feb.1879,showing that SALINA decd.7 Oct.1878,intestate;leaving an Estate worth @$1500 + an Insurance Policy on the life of DAVE MORRIS, decd., father of sd.SALINA. B.HASBURG is next of kin to SALINA. {Note: Both DAVE MORRIS and his infant dau.SALINA,and MRS.B.HASBURG died in Yellow Fever Epidemic, Fall of 1878.}

PKT.#583:EST.STEWART WHITE,decd.+Grdnp.of GEORGE WHITE-MRS.CAROLINE WHITE petitions for L.\Adm.and L.\Grdnp., stating she is the widow of STEWART WHITE, decd. of Wash.Co., who died 29 Sept.1879, intestate;leaving 1 child-the offspring of marriage with your petitioner, GEORGE WHITE who is 9 yrs.old. The Estate consists entirely of an interest in real estate of MRS.G.A.TAYLOR for $150, and an interest in a Quit Claim Deed from GEORGE LANFORD. There is nothing to Adm., but creditors are prosecuting suits in Court and she must defend. Filed 31 Oct.1879

PKT.#586:EST.J.BOWMAN STIRLING,Testator-PENELOPE J.STERLING, Adm. who files for L.\Grdnp.on 11 Dec.1879,showing that J.BOWMAN STERLING decd. leaving 3 children-JAMES STEWART STIRLING, MARY C. STIRLING, JACOB BOWMAN STIRLING ,minors. Their father died intestate* leaving a small estate worth @$1500 for each child and PENELOPE is applying as mother and natural Grdn. Also for L.\Adm.//Adm.\Bd.$2000.
*{Note:WILL OF J.B.STERLING filed Wash.Co.,Ms.WILL Bk."1",p.414,and abst.in Vol.II of this series. In addition to those named above,he named his

WASH.CO.,MS.PKT.GLEANINGS
PROBATE COURT 1874-1881

PKT.#586:STERLING,cont.
sister-in-law MARY McCAUSLAND,1st wife of "my brother WM.H.STERLING".
The surname is spelled interchangeably STIRLING AND STERLING.)

PKT.#587:(CHANCERY COURT)THOMAS J.B.TURNER vs SAM BROWN, et al. Suit covers time period of 7 yrs. Original Bill missing.:8 Feb.1869, SAM BROWN and partner J.L.ROYSDAN bought some land in Wash.Co.,Ms. They were at that time living in Rutherford Co.,Tn. The sd. suit seems to be built on the premise that SAM and his partner were to continue a schedule of payments for sd.land when SAM claimed that the land had been misrepresented". Land in question-SW1/4,Sec.17,T18N,R7W: W1/2 SE1/4,Sec.20, T15N,R7W : E1/2 of Sec.19,and part of W1/2 of 19. ROYSAN sold out to a Firm known as JORDAN MILLER & CO. A member of that firm,J.L.CARNEY, was the son-in-law of one THOS.J.B.TURNER,who put the sd.land up for sale. Later VIRGINIA MILLER states that S.H.MILLER, one of the partners in JORDAN MILLER & CO.,has decd. and he will be represented in sd.suit by S.H. SPARKS,Exect. All parties lived at this time in Murfreesboro,Tn. BROWN contends that the amount of cleared land was exaggerated and the timber actually was on someone else's land.// In Aug.1874, the MILLER HEIRS are listed as VIRGINIA P.MILLER,WIDOW; CARRIE MILLER; ELECTRA MILLER; S.H. MILLER,(Jr.)minor heirs of S.H.MILLER,decd.all non-residents of Ms.// Sept. 1874: ANSWER of J.L.CARNEY,age 37,now living in Florida,an Agent of THOS. J.B. TURNER, objects to SAM BROWN's cry of misrepresentation. Signed in Duvall Co.,Fla.//ANSWER of JOHN JORDAN and JESSE SPARKS, as Exect.of last WILL and Testatmen of S.H.MILLER,decd.,filed Davidson Co.,Tn.1874 : JOHN W.JORDAN age 43, Nashville,Tn.; in the hotel business; lived in Murfreesboro,Tn.in 1869,70;owned 1/6th of the land in question. He avows that CARNEY did declare 200 ac.had been cleared. JORDAN has declared bankruptcy.//Pkt. includes descriptions of visits to the plantation in question, where they were shown the land. [Note: Depositions seem to indicate the place had been cleared, but neglected and allowed to grow back up.]//Court decreed that SAM BROWN couldn't have been as gullible as he pretended,and must pay the payments due or lose his equity.//The land was sold at the Sheriff's Sale and bought by WM.A.RANSOM for $370 (1000 ac.).

PKT.#588:EST.WADE HAMPTON,JR.Testator-S.W.FERGUSON,Adm.
whose Petition shows that WADE,JR. decd.late of Wash.Co.by his WILL made S.W.FERGUSON the Exect.of his Estate. He left 3 horses and some household furnishings,not more than would be exempt to his widow, in Wash.Co.,Ms. Also property in Issa.Co.,Ms.-13 head mules and horses in poor condition,

WASH.CO.,MS.PKT.GLEANINGS
PROBATE COURT 1874-1881

PKT.#588;HAMPTON,cont.
1 wagon much used, a portion of a cotton crop not yet shipped. S.W.seeks Adm. and asks that the APPRAISAL be conducted by W.G.TUTT,J.E.HAUFF, E.J. BRYAN, C.WORTHINGTON, V.F.ERWIN.//Copy of **WILL OF WADE HAMPTON, JR.** (Recorded WILL Bk."1",p.415,Abst.Vol.II,this series.) Written at 'Wildwood Plt.'the habitation of sd.testator for 10 days prior to his death on 22 Dec.1879.//VOUCHERS: To Dr.W.G.ALLEN for visiting BOB WATSON on 'Wildwood'-2 Oct.1879-obstetrics for WATSON's dau.: Paid KATE P.HAMPTON, widow,$5512. She also got the mules,furniture,etc.: Received by WADE HAMPTON,$1960 from Estate of WADE,JR.,1879, from Crop proceeds at 'Wildwood' and ' Richland Plts'.:WADE.JR. to STEPHEN STEWART Jan.3,1880 on 'Wildwood' and 'Walnut Ridge Plts.':To W.H.GILMORE; To J.A.NEWMAN for metal casket-$140-Billed 31 Dec.1879: To W.G.TUTT.//S.W.FERGUSON attests to waiver of Adm.rights by Widow KATE HAMPTON and C.F.HAMPTON,6 Jan.1880.// <u>Steamers</u> used by MAJ.WADE HAMPTON,JR. billed to Duncansby (Ms.) **Memphis & St.Louis Pkt.Co.**- 1879: **Silverthorn** -Dec.1879: **Josephine Shingler** which brought a cask of china to MRS.HAMPTON Dec.1879; **J.M.White** : **Joe Kinney** of Kansas City Pkt.Co.// Plantation records give the names of the following employees:PLENTY CLEMENS,RAMEL LEWIS,WM.FOSTER;TONEY ERWIN;WM.GREEN;CHARLES JONES;ISAIAH WATSON; BOB WATSON;ISREAL GREEN;JOE STANLEY;JONATHON ROBINSON;CAESAR SPENCER;STEPHEN GREEN;PRINCE MACK; WILSON ---; ABRAHAM LADSEN; SWARTZ BELL;SHED MILLER for running engine at 'Richland'; Wm.Goodwin,an old servant.

<u>**PKT.#589:W.G.TUTT,decd.-J.E.HAUFF,Exec.**</u>   No Bond. L.\Adm.granted 20 Feb.1880,showing that TUTT decd.leaving a WILL and filed it for probation. WILL Bk."1"p.423. 1 Old buggy and the salary he made for managing estate for WADE HAMPTON,decd. Filed 31 Jan.1880//Proof of Will// VOUCHER: J.A.NEWMAN, funeral expenses-casket,etc.$135.

<u>**PKT.#592:EST.THOMAS G.PERRY,.et al,minors-ALBERT WHITEWAY, Grdn.:**</u> 16 Apr.1883:Dominion of Canada,Ontario,Wentworth Co.,Hamilton: Consulate of U.S.A.,FRANK LELAND,Consul,certifies that the signatures of MARY SPENCE and THOS.B.SPENCE are true signatures.//MARY SPENCE and her husband THOS.B.SPENCE, ANSWER to Petition for Grdn.by WHITEWAY for the children of THOMAS PERRY,decd.,and for the sale of the property of JAMES PERRY,decd. MARY was a sister of JAMES PERRY,decd. and joint heir, and entitled to share equally with the children of THOMAS PERRY.//

WASH.CO.,MS.PKT.GLEANINGS
PROBATE COURT 1874-1881

PKT.#592:PERRY,cont.
26 Apr.1883: Court Order to ALBERT WHITEWAY,Grdn.,to pay attorney fees to C.W.CLARKE,Solicitor, for filing Petition and papers.(Not in this pkt.) States on cover of this document-Filed 20 Feb.1880//23 July 1883: Report of Grdnp.-VOUCHERS; Bill paid to FRANK G.PERRY, Wetherbee's of Greenville for work done on house. Attached is a report by WHITEWAY, Grdn.of F.G. PERRY,THOS.H.PERRY, SIDNEY L.PERRY, CATHERINE (called CARRIE) PERRY. He states he was appointed JULY 1880, and has rented out property, paid taxes, paid support for minors. FRANK G.PERRY became of age on 22 Feb. 1882 and has assisted in supporting the children.//Bill for $456 repairs on house; sale of personal estate of JAMES PERRY,decd.,$246; sale of real estate $204. Grdn.WHITEWAY states he did not keep vouchers on his Wards as they have lived in his family and were clothed and educated at his expense.//Apr.1887, Court allows expenditure on real estate to support minors.//31 Oct.1888. Regarding the Grdnp.of SIDNEY L.and CARRIE PERRY, minors, THOMAS H.PERRY,brother of sd.minors, has no objection to settlement proposed in Petition of Guardianship of sd. minors for authority to compromise with claim against them by ELLEN WHITEWAY.//30 Apr.1889: Commissioners review condition of property of the minors,and allow money to move a house-the residence of ALBERT WHITEWAY FAMILY and PERRY minors from the (Ms.) River's edge and repairing same. They also approved moving another small house.//Final report of ALBERT WHITEWAY, Grdn.7 Nov.1888,shows that in the Spring of 1885,the 2 minors,SIDNEY L. and CATHERINE PERRY,with their 2 brothers FRANK.G. and THOMAS H.PERRY, and their sister ELLEN WHITEWAY owned 3 dwelling houses and a house used as a shop,located in Town of Greenville,all situated on the Bank of Ms.River. The encroachment of the River made FRANK.G. remove all 3 houses at his own expense. The largest he placed on L.2,Block 17,3rd addition,the other 2 on L.1,2, Main & Theobald..lots belonging to FRANK G. Report further says that FRANK G. decd.29 Apr.1888,Testate,leaving everything he owned to his sister,ELLEN WHITEWAY,with the stipulation that the amount owed by the minor brother and sister to ELLEN "would be compromised." ELLEN (PERRY) is now the wife of ALBERT WHITEWAY. (NOTE:' Old Greenville Cem."by Payne: *F.G.Perry 1861-1888//Sidney L.Perry 1872-1927// Annie Ede Perry 1884-1952//Whiteway Children-n\m//Mrs.T.- Perry d.1938\9//Carrie Perry Aiken (wife of W.B.Aiken) 1870-1905//William Bryant Aiken 1861-1938*)

PKT.#593: Est.HEARD,Comegys,minors-Grdn.
Petition for L.\Grdnp. filed 20 Jan.1880 by COLUMBUS HEARD, a citizen of

WASH.CO.,MS.PKT.GLEANINGS
PROBATE COURT 1874-1881

PKT.#593;HEARD,cont.
Wash.Co.,Ms.who states that on 5 Jan.1880,NATHAN A.HEARD of Wash.Co. decd.;intestate;leaving 2 minor children-CHARLES A.HEARD,AND NATHAN A. HEARD, and a grandson JOHN P.COMEGYS. They are entitled to a payment of a Life Insurance Policy. Petitioner (COLUMBUS)is the brother of NATHAN A. and CHARLES A. HEARD and Uncle to JOHN P.COMEGYS. Signed by J.C.HEARD// Grdn.\Bd.$3000.**(Note:** "Old G'ville Cem."by Payne: *Jennie Schall Heard d. 1913//Joseph Columbus Heard d.1918//Chas.A.Heard 1862-1898* }

PKT.#595:EST.ELLA INCISA DE CAMERANNA,decd.-WILL recorded Wash.Co.,Ms.Will Bk."1"p.412-(Abst.Vol.II this series) She names her husband ALBERTA INCISA DE CAMERANNA to get land given her by R.C.BRINKLEY; Mother EUGENIA BERTINATTI;Brother C.R.BASS; Gr.mother ANN F.BATE// Authenticity of WILL proven in Gallatin,Tn.28 Jan.1880//Petition of husband to have sd.WILL probated (in Ms.)24 Mar.1880,stating that ELLA decd. May 1871 in Tn.,leaving a WILL probated in Tn. He asks that the same be probated in Wash.Co.,Ms. She owed nothing and is owed nothing.//Granted.

PKT.#596:EST.JAMES B.SILLERS,minor-MRS.ANNA E.SHUTE,Grdn.
Grdn.\Bd.$100 with J.O.SHUTE,and Wm.SILLERS as sureties.//Petition for L.\Grdn.Filed 7 May 1880 by ANNA SHUTE,who is the mother of JAMES B. SILLERS,minor age 10,the son of your petitioner and her 1st husband JAMES SILLERS,who decd. 9 yrs.ago. Sd.minor is to inherit from his grandfather, WM.SILLERS,an undivided 1/4th interest in a tract of land in Claib.Co.,Ms. known as 'Evergreen Place',containing in all 582 ac.in Sec.12,T12,R2E. The land is to be divided,with the boundary embracing a dwelling house. The minor,JAMES B.,lives with his Mother in Wash.Co.,Ms.// Pkt.contains a Conveyance by HENRY T.ELLITE to CAROLINE SILLERS,by DEED 14 Jan.1868- (Recorded Bk."NN"p.450 Claib.Co.,Ms.) CAROLINE was the grandmother of sd. minor, JAMES B.SILLERS. She decd.intestate,leaving as survivors 3 children one of whom was JAMES SILLERS,who had died before his Mother,and who was the father of sd.minor,James B. Also surviving CAROLINE was her husband,WM.SILLERS,who is still living and has a life tenancy in 'Evergreen'. ANNA E.SHUTE states she is in dire need, having a number of children by her 2nd marriage, and she is reduced to running a boarding house. The other children of CAROLINE and WM.SILLERS gave their interest to their father so JAMES B.is the only one with any interest left. ANNA seeks sale of the property. She also states that the nearest relatives (living in this state) of sd.minor,JAMES B.SILLERS,are his grandfather WM.SILLERS, and his maternal grandmother NANCY BARROWS. Filed 7 May 1880// (Cont.)

WASH.CO.,MS.PKT.GLEANINGS
PROBATE COURT 1871-1884

PKT.#596:SILLERS,cont.
14 June 1880:Grdn.\Bd.$500 with ANNA SHUTE as principal and her husband JAMES D.SHUTE and WM.SILLERS as sureties. WM.SILLERS recommends that they sell the undivided 1/4th interest in 'Evergreen Place'//12 July 1880: Order to send CITATIONS to CALHOUN HAILE-uncle of JAMES B.,minor;ANNA (NANCY)BARROWS both of Bolivar Co.,Ms.and to WM.SILLERS-Claib.Co.Ms.// Wm. SILLERS has moved from Ms.,but CALHOUN HAILE,uncle,and JAMES D. SHUTE, step-father of sd. minor,think it wise to sell.//Land put up for sale (1/4th undivided portion)and WM.SILLERS bought it for $100.//13 Apr.1882 WM. SILLERS petitions Court to be released from Grdn.\Bd., stating that ANNA E. has moved to Ark.and taken JAS.B.,minor,with her.(Note: ANN (NANCY)FLY lOOR marr.WM.HAILE 1827 in Woodville,Ms.and they had 3 ch.- CALHOUN,JOHN JOOR,EMILY HAILE who marr. Dr.BEDON. NANCY(lOOR) HAILE marr. 2nd BENNET H. BARROW(his 2nd) and they had 2 girls-ANN E. who marr.1st JAS.SILLERS, 2nd to JAS.SHUTE; and MARTHA ALENA. From "Old G'ville Cem."BY Payne:*Nancy loor Barrow 1811-1888 & Capt.Calhoun Haile 1828-1893*)

PKT.#597"EST.HENRY JOHNSON BLACKBURN,et al minors-MRS.A.B. CARSON,Grdn. who filed L.\Grdnp.18 May 1880,stating that she is MARY BELLE CARSON,her husband is ANDREW B.CARSON. She is the mother of the following children: HENRY JOHNSON BLACKBURN,20 yrs.old; E.JULIA BLACK- BURN,18; LOU.E.BLACKBURN,16; PRUE H.BLACKBURN,12. Their father, the late GEORGE T.BLACKBURN is decd. and all minors live with their mother and step-father. Sd.minors are due to inherit from their AUNT E.F.BLACK- BURN $1500 or $1600. The Aunt's WILL has been probated in Ky.and they need a Grdn.,to collect their share.//Grdn.\Bd.$2000 with SAM WORTH- INGTON as surety.(Note:" Old G'ville Cem."by Payne: *Henry Johnson Blackburn 1859-1927*)

PKT.#598:EST.JOHN ORVILLE and MARY LEON RIVES, minor heirs-at- law of ANNIE M.RIVES,decd. Petition for L.\Grdnp.by NATHAN GOLDSTEIN, 3 June 1880,who states that NANNIE M.RIVES decd.17 Apr.1880 in Wash. Co.,Ms.;leaving surviving her husband JAMES W.RIVES and 2 minor children JOHN O.age 4 and MARY L.age 2; a Life Insurance Policy worth $3000. Their father declines to qualify as Adm.and asked GOLDSTEIN to accept.//May Term 1881:BENJ.F.MOORE,Talif.Co.,Ga.applies for L.\Grdnp. for the 2 minors who are now living in Ga.-Bd.$10,000//GOLDSTEIN's Grdnp.is terminated Apr.1882 as minors are non-residents of Ms.//VOUCHER;To Mrs.LEONORA L. GOLUCKE of Crawfordsville,Ga.-$144 per yr.for board of sd.minors.

WASH.CO.,MS.PKT.GLEANINGS
PROBATE COURT 1871-1884

PKT.#599:EST.JOHANN GETTFRIED SIENPPENDOEFER,decd-Adm.by JENNIE D.SIENPPENDOEFER ,who filed for L.\Adm 6 July 1880,stating that she is the widow of the decd.,and the mother of his only child - an infant. JOHANN decd.Wash.Co.,Ms.,26 Sept.1878 of Yellow Fever.They lived in Greenville, but the decd. had $100 in Ga.

PKT.#600:EST.M.MORRIS,decd.-SAM HARRIS,Adm. who petitions for L.\Adm.9 July 1880,stating that MORRIS decd.8 July 1880. Attached,if the Court will accept same,is the NONCUPATIVE WILL of sd.MORRIS,decd.,by birth a foreigner,but who lived in Wash.Co.,Ms. No relatives in this state,a merchant with stock worth @$2000. DR.JAMES M.SMITH attests to WILL of M.MORRIS-"Iwill leave my property to HARRIS and to MARK (ROSENBURG)-handyman,that they will do what is right by my family and the nearest Jewish Institute," Dr.SMITH said he could get no more information from him.//9 July 1880:Proof of heirship by ISADORE BROH,brother of M.MORRIS, alias MORITZ BROH,who decd.June 1880. ISADORE states that MORITZ was never married;their father was GABRIEL HIRSCH BROH and their mother was CECELIA BROH nee LE VITSKI. The father-GABRIEL decd 20 yrs.ago at Lekno in Prussia;the mother decd.8 July 1878 in Chicago,Ill. Both decd. before MORRIS,alias MORITZ,leaving 7 children,6 of whom are still living:
   FRANCES BROH,age 37, marr. to JULIUS STEIN living Boston,Mass.
   PAULINA-34-wife of GUSTAV WOLF, living in Houston,Tx.
   YETTA-33- marr.JULIUS ROTHSCHILD, living Boston
   JULIA-30-marr.JACOB MORRIS, living Chicago
   SARAH-35- marr.---HERTER, lives Berlin,Prussia
   ISADORE-26-living in Chicago with his sister JULIA
   RACHEL who decd.@40 yrs.ago at Lekno,Prussia at age 18,never marr.
Filed 6 Sept.1882//Heirs divide $294,Oct.1883.

PKT.#601:EST.J.BOWMAN STIRLING,decd.-PENELOPE J.STIRLING, Adm. with WILL annexed.(See Pkt.#586)(Pkt.badly rotted) Petition for L.\Exect.by widow PENELOPE,filed 19 July 1880, who states that her late husband,J.BOWMAN STERLING decd.2 Dec.1879,a resident of Wash.Co.,Ms. He had written the WILL himself and it was found and duly filed with the Court Clerk 16 Dec.1879.//In Apr.1881: J.A.V.FELTUS sought to be released from Exect.Bond,"feels danger by reason of said surety". Bond was for $1000,and co-signed with HENRY SCOTT.//Petition by PENELOPE for closing Estate and dismissal from Exectx.-14 Apr.1885, naming heirs JULIA ANNA STERLING, LOUISA BUTLER LUTHICOM (sp.?), MARY CORNELIA THOMPSON - their residence and P.O.Box is Helena,Ark.and J.BOWMAN STERLING(JR.) a

WASH.CO.,MS.PKT.GLEANINGS
PROBATE COURT 1871-1884

Pkt.#601:STIRLING,cont.
resident of Ms.// Exceptions filed by JULIA ANNA STERLING and MARY CORNELIA THOMPSON.//VOUCHERS and other papers are falling apart.

PKT.#602:EST.WILLIAM GREEN,decd.-PETER GREEN,Adm. who files Petition for L.\Adm.,stating that his father,WM.GREEN of Wash.Co.,decd.7 Aug.1880,leaving surviving him JOHN GREEN,JOSEPH GREEN,LORENZO GREEN and your petitioner (PETER), all over 21 and ELLEN GREEN his wife "who is not the mother of these children." Left a WILL (Recorded WBk."1"p.423, Abst.Vol.II this series.no additional infor.) and small estate.

PKT.#604:EST.REUBEN SMITH,decd.-LOMAX ANDERSON,Adm. who petitions for L.\Adm.showing that REUBEN decd.28 Oct.1880;intestate;no relation capable of adm.estate. He owned some personal property on 'Magenta Plt.'//Adm.\Bd.-$100.

PKT.#606:EST.A.C.WEST,decd.-WINSTON E.WEST,Adm. who petitions for L.\Adm.stating that A.C.decd.10 Nov.1880,intestate;a resident of Wash. Co.;no wife or children. Your petitioner (Winston) is his brother. Filed 2 Dec.1880.//Adm.\Bd.signed by JENNIE D.WEST, D.HARRINGTON-$1000.

PKT.#608:EST.FANNIE E.BURDETTE,et al,minors-RICHARD BURDETT Grdn. who petitions for L.\Grdnp.showing that his 4 Wards-FANNIE E.;EMMA H.;WILLIE M.;NANNIE L.BURDETTE own an interest in a tract of land on Deer Creek in Wash.Co.,Ms.with MARY LILES holding the other interest. Filed 7 Mar.1881//[Note: Pkt.falling apart,difficult to read.] Apr.1881:Petition by RICHARD BURDETTE,Grdn.of the above named minors-FANNIE,EMMA, WILLIE, NANNIE who are his own children, all under 14, and he is seeking settlement between his children and his mother-their grandmother-MRS.MARY LILES (Sp.Lyles,Lisles,Liles)in a dispute over some land that RICHARD had bought, putting it in the name of his mother during her lifetime,and then to have it revert to his children,all undivided interest. Land description:Sec.2, T17N, R7W @118 ac.along Deer Creek known as 'The Gaddis Place". His mother has since sold her life interest in said place to a manager,who deprives Petitioner (RICHARD) of any control. His mother is only 64 yrs.old and in good health,liable to live a long time,and RICHARD thinks it would be in the best interest of his children to sell their interest in the land,and invest the money in land close to his residence which he can control. RICHARD further states that the minor's next of kin in Wash.Co. is their mother and his wife-MINERVA BURDETT, and J.COLUMBUS HEARD,the (cont.)

WASH.CO.,MS.PKT.GLEANINGS
PROBATE COURT 1871-1884

PKT.#608:BURDETT,cont.
children's uncle.//Summoned to appear in Court were MINERVA BURDETT, MARY LILE,J.C.HEARD-Mother,Gr.mother,Uncle of sd.minors. Petition to sell granted.//Sold to JOHN W.HAMER for $500.

PKT.#609:EST.ARTHUR,KENNEDY,NORA O'CONNOR,minors- Petition for L.\Grdnp.filed 4 Apr.1881,by JOANNA O'CONNOR,shows that she is the widow of TIMOTHY O'CONNOR,late of Wash.Co.,who decd.22 Jan.1877,leaving children ARTHUR,now 8;KENNEDY 6;NORA 5. They own a dwelling house in Greenville worth $2000.//ANSWER of ALEX ANDERSON and ELLA ANDERSON, his wife and nearest relatives of sd.minors.// By 1885 JOHANNA O'CONNOR is JOHANNA KINSELLA. JOHN KINSELLA bought the house.//DEED of Conveyance to HENRY A.O'CONNOR, HONORA O'CONNOR, 25 Jan.1887 from JOHN KINSELLA.(No mention of KENNEDY)

PKT.#610:WILL OF JANE E.COURTNEY,decd. Filed Oct.22,1880 and recorded Will Bk."1".p.424,425(Abst.Vol.II this series.) Written 7 July 1877 names nephew W.L.GAY, sister CAROLINE A.GAY and THOS.KELLY//Petition for L.\Adm.by W.L.GAY who said that JANE decd.--day of --18--,leaving a Will witnessed by W.A.HAYCRAFT who decd.5 Sept,1878,and MAMIE BOWEN, MARY H.YERGER. W.L.seeks probation of WILL.//

PKT.#612:EST.EMMA G.JENKINS vs H.P.LEE,Grdn.(Chancery Court)
(1/2 of these documents have disintegrated) Pkt.contains an envelope marked "Court of Probate,Charleston Co.,S.C." Copy of these Grdnp.Letters of JENKINS minors Filed 14 Oct.1881 in Wash.Co.,Ms.//JENKINS minors EMMA G. age 15;CAROLINE L. 13;ESTELLA G.11;JAMES G. 7;MARY G.-Minor children of PAUL G.JENKINS who applies for Grdnp.of his children 21 May 1881-granted in S.C.//CITATION; issued Wash.Co.,Ms. to JOHN A.SCOTT, SARAH E.LEE, FANNIE E.SCOTT to appear and state if they object to sale of land of sd.minors. H.P.LEE is their Grdn.in Wash.Co.,Ms.// 20 Apr.1881:WM. G.YERGER states he is familiar with the land as set out in the estate of JOHN A.SCOTT,decd.to the heirs of JAMES GUIGNARD,decd. This land was a part of 'Scotland Plt.'//Petition of Grdnp.by LEE impossible to read//Aug. 1881:Grdn\Bd.by REV.PAUL G.JENKINS $1000 for Estate of EMMA GUIGNARD JENKINS,CAROLINE LaROCHE JENKINS,ESTELLA McNISH JENKINS, JAMES GUIGNARD JENKINS, MARY GAMBUELL JENKINS shows that the total value of sd.tract of land is worth $4000,but $1000 represents their share. Petitioner further shows that the minors are the heirs of Mrs.SUE JENKINS, decd. and that they reside in S.C. They received $942 for sale of land.

WASH.CO.,MS.PKT.GLEANINGS
PROBATE COURT 1871-1884

PKT.#613:EST.PETER DeSOUTER,decd.-ALBERT VORMUS,Adm.
(Name also sp.DeSOTO, DESOUTES) VORMUS petitions for L.\Adm.29 Apr. 1881,stating that PETER decd.intestate;leaving a small estate-some land in Greenville, but his debts are 6 times his assets. VORMUS says he is a countryman and friend of the family before coming here.//Adm.\Bd.$100 co-signed by SOL BRILL and LOUIS VORMUS as surety.//Notification of heirs names :brother JOHN DeSOUTER, Belguim; a brother living in Washington City,Dist.C.;a sister ----;2 children of a brother who live in Belguim. VORMUS says the house is now in possession of JOHN DeSOUTER. Filed 27 Oct.1881// Estate declared insolvent.

PKT.#614:EST.VICTOR M.FLOURNOY: CHARLES E.BLACK,New Orleans,La. attests to WILL of FLOURNOY,decd.,stating that sd.WILL has been probated in Fayette Co.,Ky and orders it to be probated in Wash.Co.,Ms. 6 June 1881// Only this one document-no cover.

PKT.#617:EST.PAT WALSH,decd.-H.M.SNOWBERGER,Adm. who petitions for L.\Adm.,4 July 1881,showing that WALSH decd.June 1881 a resident of Wash.Co.,Ms.;intestate;small property. Your petitioner (SNOWBERGER) is the Undertaker who buried WALSH at his own expense, saying he was a railroad worker with no funds,or relatives.//Adm.\Bd.$100.

PKT.#618:EST.ROSALIE BAER,decd.-BERNARD BAER,Adm.
3 Aug.1881:JACOB ALEXANDER submits Noncupative WILL of Rosalie Baer. She left the house and furnishings to husband BERNARD BAER,and everything else to go to the Jewish Widows and Orphans Home in New Orleans. BERNARD contests the WILL.//BERNARD BAER petitions for L.\Adm. 4 Aug.1881 saying that ROSALIE,his late wife,decd.intestate;leaving a small estate, and he is the sole heir.// 9 Aug.1881: J.ALEXANDER filed a petition for L.\Adm.for estate of ROSALIE BAER, who decd.28 July 1881 at her home in Wash.Co.,Ms.making a Noncupative (verbal)WILL appointing your petitioner (ALEXANDER) as Exect.with witnesses THEODORE POHL,W.R.TRIGG,JULIA LEVY,B.BAER,and your petitioner. ALEXANDER states that he expected B.BAER to contest WILL.//Adm.\Bd.$300.//In her WILL ROSALIE asked that ALEXANDER put tombstones on graves of her 1st husband and "my dau.and my grave". After this is done,everything else to the Jewish Home. B.Baer has "this place" and nodding at ALEXANDER and POHL she said,"They have always done right by me and I trust them to do my will."// B.BAER's Adm.is revoked and ALEXANDER is appointed Adm. 7 Sept.1881.//Agreement between BAER and ALEXANDER shows that Baer must erect tombstones to

WASH.CO.,MS.PKT.GLEANINGS
PROBATE COURT 1871-1884

PKT.#618:BAER,cont. ISAAC KINTZLER,decd.-1st husband of ROSALIE BAER,and her child AMELIA, paying at least $100. If he doesn't comply by a reasonable time,ALEXANDER can do so and send the bill to Baer.

PKT.#619:EST.CLARENCE JOYES,decd.-JENNIE A.JOYES,Exectx.
JENNIE files Petition for L.\Adm. and Probate of Will on 6 Sept.1881, showing that her late husband decd. 27 Aug.1881,at his residence in Wash. Co.,leaving a WILL,and a small estate. (Will recorded WBk."1"p.426-left everything to widow JENNIE) Will written 13 Aug.1881.

PKT.#620:EST.SAML.J.ABELL,decd.-MRS NANNETTE SWITZER,Adm.
who files Petition for L.\Adm,stating that she is the mother of Saml.Abel, who decd.intestate on 21 Apr.1880 at her residence which was his home. He was unmarried;his heirs at law are WILLIAM ABELL,NANNETTEJAMES nee ABELL;FANNY POWELL nee ABELL;MRS.MOLLIE WELLS nee ABELL;brother and sisters of the decd. SAML.left 2 horses and a Life Insurance Policy for $1000.//Adm.\Bd.$1000 with THOS.W.POWELL,BENJAMIN JAMES as sureties. Filed 23 June 1881(Note: NANNETTE JAMES marr.1st ,1850,JAMES ABELL and they had the following ch:Nannette,Mary E.,Jas.Wm.,Frances, Samuel, Susan, Edgar. NANNETTE (JAMES)ABELL marr. 2nd 1866 JOHN T.SWITZER and they had Minnie. See "Keystone Cemetery Records" this vol.)

PKT.#621:EST.S.T.STANDARD,decd-B.STERN,Adm. who petitions for L.\Adm. showing that S.T. decd.10 Oct.1878,leaving a small estate-$300, but owes $500. The widow of sd.decd.has removed his personal property from this county. No one has appeared for L.\Adm. 4 Oct.1881//Bd.$500

PKT.#622:WM.M.WALLACE,decd.-GEORGE G.JOHNSON,Adm.
Petition for L.\Adm.by KATE BURNES,who shows that WM.M.WALLACE decd. 22 Dec.1881 at his residence in Wash.Co.Ms.;intestate. She was his neice, and next of kin in this county,with no other kin in this state. Wm.never married;but had 2 brothers-1 of whom was KATE's father who decd.7 yrs.ago. The other brother is PATRICK WALLACE who is still living so far as KATE knows-in Canada,she thinks. KATE has a sister and a brother-MARIAN WALLACE wo intermarried with one QUIGLEY and they are living in St.Louis;and PATRICK WALLACE of Colo. KATE and her husband JAMES BURNES are new here,they cannot make up the bond-but Wm.M.'s property is in the hands of strangers, and it need attention. She said she was denied the right to see her uncle when he was dying. She thinks that GEO.G. JOHNSON is a worthwhile person in this area,a planter,and requests that he be

WASH.CO.,MS.PKT.GLEANINGS
PROBATE COURT 1871-1884

PKT.#622:WALLACE,cont.
appointed Adm.// Petition of distributees names : PATRICK J.WALLACE,bro of WM.M.WALLACE,decd.;MARY A.QUIGLEY,PATRICK WALLACE,KITTY BURNES as heirs of decd. bro.JOHN P.WALLACE.// Many VOUCHERS.

PKT.#623:EST.A.A.WIRTH,decd.-I.ISENBERG,Adm. who petitions for L.\Adm. showing that WIRTH decd.30 Mar.1882,intestate; leaving small estate;was living at Arcola,Ms.;no kin in this State. Filed 1 Apr.1882//

PKT.#624:EST PATRICK DUNN,decd.-FANNY DUNN,Exectx: who petitions for L.\Adm.showing that PATRICK decd.Feb.1882 at his residence in Greenville,leaving a widow and 2 children-WILLIE THOMAS and FANNIE LEE DUNN.Small amt. of household furniture +small tract of land in Claib.Co.,Ms ["Old G'ville Cem..*P.Dunn 1837-1882/Mary Frances Ryan Dunn (w.of P.Dunn) 1854-1904/ Wm.Thos.Dunn 1874-1908*]

PKT. #625:EST.D.DICKINSON BELL,decd.- Petition for L.\Grdnp.Filed 13 Apr.1882 by D.C.MONTGOMERY of Wash.Co.,Ms.showing that CAROLINE D.BELL is a minor under 21,and has been in his custody for last 10-12 yrs. She is the neice of his wife, lately decd. CAROLINE has a brother, JAMES BELL, living in Vicksburg and a sister MRS.FRANCES DENNETT who is also living with the MONTGOMERY family. CAROLINE has an interest in an estate in Bolivar Co., Ms., and MONTGOMERY has received correspondence from an attorney in Mansfield,Desota Parish,La.,who writes that there is a small real estate-160 ac.,which was entered by the BELL children's grandfather. CAROLINE, JAMES, FRANCES are the only surviving heirs of the late DAVID DICKINSON BELL who was the only son of JAMES BELL,decd.who resided in Tn. CAROLINE needs a Grdn.to recover the land.// Adm.\Bd.$100 with W.E. MONTGOMERY as surety. Filed 13 Apr.1882.(Note:From "The Montgomery Papers": Dr.Daniel Cameron Montgomery's 1st wife was FANNY SEMMES HARRIS,who was the aunt of the Bell children. He marr.2nd MARY NELSON (FINLAY)SIMS,widow,and they had 1 son,D.C.,Jr.)(NOTE: Buried "Old G'ville Cem."*Frances Semmes Harris Montgomery 1845-1881*]

PKT.#626:EST.JAMES C.MOORE,decd.-JOHN M.McCUTCHEON,Adm.
Petition for L.\Adm.by JOHN H.MOORE, stating that JAMES C.MOORE decd.6 Oct.1881,leaving as heirs JOHN H.MOORE,EMILY BABB,MARY V.MOORE. None wants to Adm.the estate of their brother,the sd.decd. Filed 15 Apr.1882. JAMES owned an undevolped 1/2 interest in land in Wash.Co. located in Sec.10,T19N,R6W.The named heirs requested that McCUTCHEON be appoint.

WASH.CO.,MS.PKT.GLEANINGS
PROBATE COURT 1871-1884

PKT.#626:MOORE,cont.
Adm.-signed JOHN H.MOORE,M.F.MOORE,L.H.BABB,E.M.BABB.(Note:"Old G'ville Cem." by Payne: *John H.Moore 1849-1903/ Eliza B.Moore 1853-1932/James C.Moore 1858-1881/Annie Moore 1881-1961 Charles A.Moore 1876-1917*)

PKT.#627:WILL OF E.D.WYATT formerly of Sommerville,Tn. but now of Greenville,Ms.-Written 10 Nov.1876-Filed 15 Apr.1882 gives all of her Estate to BELLE B.GREEN of G'ville. Wit:by C.M.McGARTH,CHAS.W.CLARKE, W.M.GREEN,Jr.// Attached is a petition by BELLE B(ott).GREEN saying that ELIZABETH D.WYATT decd.1881,owing no debts,no property in Ms.,but left some real estate in Tenn. (Not recorded in Will Bk."1")

PKT.#628:EST.JOHN SMITH,minor-HARRY SCOTT,Grdn.
Petition for L.\Grdnp.filed 28 Apr.1882 by DEBEY SMITH,the grandmother and next of kin living of sd.minor JOHN SMITH,the son of her dau.AMANDA HILL. DEBEY asked that he be bound to HARRY SCOTT so that he may be educated and cared for. (Note: There are no indenture papers in file)

PKT.#629:MRS.ANN WORTHINGTON,Test.-THOMAS WORTHINGTON, Adm.: Pkt.contains WILL of ANN WORTHINGTON,recorded WBk."1"p.427// Petition to probate sd.WILL filed by THOMAS WORTHINGTON stating the decd.was his mother,who died 19 Mar.1882 at her residence in Wash.co.,Ms. Filed 25 Apr.1882.//Petition for L.\Adm.by THOS.who states that she left 4(other ?) children,and that he is one of them.//Power of Atty.-June 5, 1882,by BEN T.WORTHINGTON,JAMES ANN PEAK,MRS.TENIE W.VALLIANT, ISAAC M.WORTHINGTON to THOMAS WORTHINGTON- joint heirs of MRS.ANN WORTHINGTON. Signed over to THOS.(WILL abst.Vol.II,this series.)

PKT.#630:EST.THOMAS W.POWELL,decd.-FANNIE A.POWELL,Adm.
who files Petition for L.\Adm.1 Jan.1882,stating she is the widow and sole heir of THOS.W.who decd.1882,leaving no children,no other heirs. Est.worth $3000.//Adm.\Bd.$4000 with NANNETTE SWITZER,H.J.BAKER,F.J.CRAIG-sur.

PKT.#631:WILL of EMORY CLAPP Recorded WBK."1",p.421,422-Abst. Vol. II,this series. Official document from Parish of Orleans,La. shows next 8 pages of printed matter contains true and correct copy of WILL and atta-ched testimony concerning WILLS of EMORY CLAPP,decd.// Petition of PAM-ELA STARR CLAPP,widow of EMORY CLAPP,decd.,states that he decd. in N.O. several yrs.ago,leaving 2 WILLS-1 dated 18 Oct.1871,another dated 3 May

WASH.CO.,MS.PKT.GLEANINGS
PROBATE COURT 1871-1884

PKT.*631:CLAPP,cont.
1880,with a codicil dated 13 July 1880. WILL to be recorded in Wash.Co., Ms.,where he owned property.//Named in (1st) WILL is wife PAMELA STARR CLAPP;mother MRS.PHINEAS CLAPP ALLEN;1/2 bro.JOHN FORSYTH ALLEN; namesakes EMORY STARR FRY and EMORY BROWN THOMPSON; 2 adopted daus. -LILY CLAPP and SALLIE CLAPP.//2nd WILL names the same as above,but adds the name of grandson EMORY CLAPP DAY,son of SALLIE CLAPP DAY.// Codicil adds the name - JOHN T.ALLEN.

PKT.*632:EST.WM.A.CLEATON,decd.-A RENNATH CLEATON,Admx.of Cletonia,Ms.(her name spelled ASENATH on inside of Pkt.)ASENATH files Petition for L.\Adm.as widow of Wm.A.CLEATON who decd.25 July 1882; intestate;leaving a large real estate & personal estate on Deer Creek. Real Est.worth $15000;Pers.-$1800. Also leaving a liability and mortgage of $3000. Heirs listed as your petitioner (ASENATH), CHARLES age 22; EDWARD 21; JOSEPH 18; AMANDA 15; MARY 11 all of whom live at late residence in sd.county (Wash.) Filed 6 Aug.1882.//Adm.\Bd.by JEFF F.TILLMAN (who asked to be released from same in Dec.1882) and W.E.SATTERFIELD - $2000.// Final a/c filed Mar.1883//Feb.1884: Summons to CHARLES CLEATON,EDWARD CLEATON,JOSEPH CLEATON, and DAVID FRILEY,who is Grdn.of minor heirs of CLEATON ESTATE + ANDREW *CLEATON and MARY CLEATON...to show cause why the Est.should not be closed.*(Name written AMANDA in petition for L.\Adm.,ANDREW in summons.)(Note: Cletonia was a stop on Deer Creek just below and east of Hollandale.)

PKT.*633:EST.LeROY PERCY,decd.(WBk."1"p.428,Abst.in Vol.II,this series.) Petition of W.A.PERCY shows that LEROY PERCY decd.27 June 1882; they were brothers;and W.A.presents the WILL for Probate.All of the decd.'s property was in Wash.Co.,Ms.,which he left to W.A.,leaving no debts. Filed 7 Aug.1882.//Interrogation of wit. to WILL-JOHN P.FINLAY, C.McGRATH, WM.G.YERGER. 27 June 1882,all living G'ville. McGrath stated that he was 45,and that Mr.PERCY was about 58 yrs.old when the WILL was written in 1873: WM.G.YERGER gave his age as 42,and JOHN P.FINLAY as 33.//(NOTE: "Old G'ville Cem.Rec."-Payne: *Caldwell McGrath 1837-1886/ John P.Finlay 1848-1913/ Leroy Pope Percy 1825-1882/ William Alexander Percy 1834-1888/ Wm.Gwin Yerger 1840-1899/*)

PKT.* 635:EST.LULA WITKOWSKI,et al,minors-FLORA WITKOWSKI, Grdn. who filed petition for L.\Grdnp.,21 Nov.1882,showing that her late husband GUSTAVE WITKOWSKI decd intestate,leaving 3 children,the fruit

WASH.CO.,MS.PKT.GLEANINGS
PROBATE COURT 1871-1884

PKT.#635:WITKOWSKI,cont.
of their marriage-LULA,CLARENCE,SADIE,minors under 14;leaving an Insurance Policy worth $3000 with Knights of Pythias. FLORA seeks Grdnp.of her children.//Grdn.\Bd.$2500 with MORRIS WEISS,NATHAN GOLDSTEIN as sureties.//Final a/c 18 Mar.1901, shows that their surname has been changed by the courts from WITKOWSKI to WITT, as well as that of their mother and Guardian, signed CLARENCE WITT,SADIE WITT,FLORA*WITT PHILLIPS nee WITT- each over 21. Document also states that MORRIS WEISS has decd.,leaving all his property to his widow HANNAH WEISS,who has also since decd.-leaving as her only heirs your petitioner (FLORA WITT) EMMELINE GOLDSTEIN, MALINDA HIRSCH, JAKE and L.D.WEISS.
*(In signature she signs LULA WITT PHILLIPS)

PKT.#636:EST.McKINNYE L.COOK,decd.-DAVID FRILEY,Adm. who files for L.\Adm.on 3 Nov.1882,showing that COOK decd.9 Sept.1882 at residence of J.T.ATTERBERRY;intestate;leaving a personal property of $700. FRILEY is a creditor,no heirs listed//ADM.\BD.$100 with JOHN T.ATTERBERRY, ISADORE KERSTEIN as sureties.

PKT.#637:EST.J.L.HAMER,decd.-LEOPOLD GLDSMITH,Adm.
(Name also sp.HAMMERS) LEOPOLD files Petition for L.\Adm.19 Dec.1882 with SOL GOLDSMITH of firm of GOLDSMITH BROS. and THEO POHL, E.G. MARSHALL,showing that HAMMER decd.2 Dec.1882,leaving a personal estate of $1500;intestate;they are creditors and seek temporary Adm.//Adm.\Bd. set at $3000// LEOPOLD resigns as Adm.stating that J.A. OVERBY had applied for L.\Adm.(See next Pkt.)

PKT.#638:EST.J.L.HAMMERSdecd.-J.A.OVERBY,Adm. who files for L.\A. who shows that HAMMERS decd.19 Nov.1882;intestate;personal property of general merchandise + store fixtures in town of Cletonia, near Overby Station in Wash.Co. Petitioner is creditor as Hammers owes him $1530. Next of kin is AARON HAMMERS of Hinds Co.,Ms.;ELIZABETH ,ANNA,LOULA E. & WILLLIE HAMMERS of Wash.Co. Sworn to 1 Dec.1882;Filed 4 Jan.1883.// Overby Station-3 Jan.1883: Personal letter to C.M.JOHNSON,Clerk of Chan. Court of Wash.Co.,written by T.R.HAMMERS who states that his son decd. intestate Nov.1882,unmarried,no relatives of age who wants to Adm.estate and requests that OVERBY be appointed Adm.//Apr.21,1884: Annual a/c shows the store has burned,but OVERBY collected $601 in Insurance.

PKT.#639:EST.JANE C.NIXON,decd.: W.H.HICKSON of Sharkey Co.,Ms.files

WASH.CO.,MS.PKT.GLEANINGS
PROBATE COURT 1871-1884

PKT.#639:NIXON,cont.
Petition for L.Adm.for Estate of JANE C. of Wash.Co. who decd.4 Sept.1882, in Wash.Co.;intestate;personal property worth $175.Petitioner is creditor. Filed 31 Oct.1882//The Commissioner to appraise sd.property states that JOHN NIXON,the son of the decd.JANE C.NIXON, refused to show the property and is in possession of 2 mules,3 cows & calf,a feather bed,1 wagon.

PKT.#640"EST.ALEX.G.FRASER,decd.-W.A.POLLOCK,Adm. with Bond @$6000,with CHARLES H.GANITH as surety.//Petition by GEORGE G.FRASER, of Fall River,Mass.; DAVID R.FRASER of Santa Rosa,Calif.; CATHARINE S. FRASER of R.I.; JANE F.HOLT of R.I.; ELLEN C.EASTERBROOKS of Newport, R.I.; MARGARET A.STONE of Binghampton,N.Y.; ABBE JANE ROUNSVILLE of Fall River,Mass.; SARAH L.FRASER of Fall River,Mass.; GEORGE ROBERT FRASER of Ripon,Wis.;JANE FRASER of Ripon,Wis. Petition shows that ALEXANDER G.FRASER decd.15 Oct.1882 in Hot Springs,Ark.,intestate,leaving no debts except for medical bills and a hotel bill at Hot Springs covering the time of his last illness, + funeral expenses-leaving @$5775 by a note of JOHN COMPTON's and A.B.FINLAY & CO. of Wash.Co.,Ms. Each of his relatives are in a distant state. They (named above) request that W.A.POLLOCK be granted L.\Adm..//In signatures for the Petition above-JANE BESSETT signs as Grdn.for GEORGE Y.and JANIE C.FRASER. Others signing-MARG.A.STONE; ELLEN C.EASTERBROOKS; CATHARINE S.FRASER; JANE F.HOLT; ANN FRASER (not mentioned above);GEORGE G.FRASER; ABBE JANE ROUNSVILLE; SARAH L. FRASER; DAVID R.FRASER-dated 6 Dec.1882//Feb.7,1888:CITATION notice to all the ones named in original Petition,one exception-SARAH L.FRASER is now SARAH.L. DAVIS//Amount paid each named heir on 8 Oct.1887:
   GEO.Y.;MARG.A.;ELLEN;CATHARINE;JANE F.;DAVID R.and GRDN.JANE BASSETT received $283.52 each.
   ABBE JANE and SARAH L.DAVIS rec.$146.76 each.
Annual a/c stated that 3/4th of sd.estate had already been divided in April with a whole share worth $591.25.

PKT.#641:EST.P.M.BRITT,decd.-MAGGIE BRITT,Adm. who petitions for L.\Adm.showing that her husband,P.M.,decd.4 Jan.1882,with her as his sole heir;no children;leaving a small estate. Filed 23 Jan.1883.

PKT.#643:EST.WM.A.CLEATON,decd.-DAVID FRILEY,Adm. who filed a Petition for L.\Adm.2 Feb.1883 (See Pkt.#632) showing WM.A.CLEATON decd.25 July 1882;intestate;leaving a large estate-between $10,000-$15,000 + personal estate;leaving as heirs, a widow-ASENATH; and 5 ch.

WASH.CO.,MS.PKT.GLEANINGS
PROBATE COURT 1871-1884

PKT.#643:CLEATON,cont.
CHARLES age 22;EDWARD 21;JOSEPH 18;AMANDA 15;MARY 11 all living a the residence of the decd. FRILEY further shows that MRS.ASENATH CLEATON, the widow,was appointed Adm.in Aug.1882 with J.F.TILLMAN and W.E. SATTTERFIELD as her sureties,but in Nov.1882,TILLMAN wanted out of the Bond,and as ASENATH couldn't raise the Bond money,the estate had no Adm. All parties consent to FRILEY's appointment.//In March 1883,FRILEY asks permission to rent out the plantation.// Pkt.contains another petition by FRILEY,seeking to become the Grdn.of MARY,minor,who is under 14-Filed Apr.1883 and JOSEPH,AMANDA,both over 14,ask FRILEY to be their Grdn.//

PKT.#644:EST.NELLIE THOMAS,alias NELLIE KANATZER,decd.
(WBk."1",p.428,Abst.Vol.II,this series) In her WILL,written 16 Apr.1877 NELLIE asked H.F. KRIGER to be the grdn.to her minor children and also to be Exect.of her Est. The Petition for proof of sd. WILL,shows that NELLIE decd. 1 Feb.1883 in Wash.Co.;leaving a WILL. She had first been married to JOHN KANATZER, who died, then to MR.THOMAS from whom she separated, and after that, kept the name of her former husband. KRIGER accepts the Grdnp. of all children except WARREN DAVIS. Minors named are: CORA KANATZER, JOSEPH KANATZER, ADA KANATZER, EVA KANATZER, AMELIA KANATZER. Pkt.contains a copy of the WILL,Codicil,Proof of Validity of WILL. The Codicil states that since she made her WILL,she had come into some property,a part of 'Wildwood Plt.'conveyed to her by REBECCA YERGER, and she (NELLIE) gave this property to her son WARREN DAVIS. She desires to take this gift back,and in place of it,give WARREN DAVIS $1500 cash...Signed NELLIE KANATZER.//DEPOSITION by W.YERGER,who acknowledged that Nellie signed the codicil,and stating that she was about 40 yrs.old at the time of her death in1883.//DEPOSITIONS by H.W.CONNERS, R.S.TOOMBS, W.A. EVERMAN, W.G.YERGER.//In documents giving the minors an allowance, all children are named but WARREN.//14 Oct.1885:CITATION to CORA,LACEY,AMELIA ADA,EVA,JOSEPH KANATZER and WARREN DAVIS to be served in Wash. Co.// CORA,JOSEPH and WARREN were so served,but the others "were not found in this county";later found and served in Adams Co.,Ms.//Final a/c-each interest was 1/6th portions,with each receiving $202.98.(See next Pkt.)

PKT.#645A_B:CORA KANATZER,et al,minors-C.M.JOHNSON,Grdn.
Facts picked from VOUCHERS:1883-4,MRS.H.E.MOORE boarded CORA for the yr.//In Pet.for L.\Grdn. KRIGER states that all the children were NELLIE's by a 1st and 2nd marriage. They all lived with the KRIGERS in Feb.,Mar. 1883, except WARREN DAVIS, and that JOSEPH stayed on until 1884.//

WASH.CO.,MS.PKT.GLEANINGS
PROBATE COURT 1871-1884

PKT.#645A-B:KANATZER,cont.
VOUCHER:signed by MRS.JOHN FLEMING of the Protestant Orphan Asylum in Natchez-Dec.1883-acknowledging the receipt of $50 for board of the KANATZER children of Greenville.// Tax Receipts for Est.JOHN KANATZER for 168 ac.valued at $1486,located in Sec.30,31, 35; T18N; R8W Wash.Co.// Acknowledgement from Orphans Home in Natchez for ADA, EVA (ENA?), AMELIA-Nov.1886,also for 1889.//VOUCHER; for child's carriage charged to MRS.CORA LACEY on 10 June 1886//AMELIA was a student at Blue Mountain College,Ms.1889,90,91 and living with CORA// Final a/c for CORA LACEY 24 Oct.1887 (**Note**:Wife of ROBT.H.LACEY) //In 1890-91,EVA attends Blue Mt.College.//ADA HENDEL nee KANATZER comes of age 24 Mar. 1891-she signs as MRS.M.B. HENDEL//In 1889, EVA requested that C.M. JOHNSON be appointed her Grdn. as KRIGER is about to be released as such. Request sent from Tippah Co.,Blue Mt., Ms.//Mar.1891-C.M. JOHNSON states that WARREN DAVIS has instigated a suit vs KRIGER and the minors,and JOHNSON had to hire a lawyer,who was paid out of the estate. Case went to the Supreme Court of Ms. Minors named in sd.suit were EVA,AMELIA,JOSEPH and ADA HENDEL nee KANATZER //1892, JOSEPH has nearly reached his majority// CITATION:sent to Texas to EVA HERRON and her husband R.L. HERRON to appear 7 Oct.1895 for final a/c by JOHNSON.//(**Note**:"Old G'ville Cem." by Payne:*John Kanatzer 1838-1876/Nellie Kanatzer 1845-1883/ Cora (Kanatzer)Lacey 1868-1895/ Mary Lacey b.Queentown,Ire. 1832-d.1886*)

PKT.#646:EST.KITTIE ELKAS,decd.-LOUIS ELKAS,Adm. who petitions for L.\Adm.,saying that his wife,KITTIE ELKAS decd. at Leota,Ms.17 Dec. 1882,intestate; also leaving their 2 children-ISAAC and CARL ELKAS; no debts;but she had a certified check on 4th National Bank of St.Louis for $2000.Filed 15 Feb.1883.

PKT.#650:EST.SAMUEL WESTBROOK,minor-MATILDA WESTBROOK, Grdn. (See Pkt.#541A-B) MATILDA petitions for L.\Grdnp. on 5 Mar.1883, stating that she is a resident of Wash.Co.,Ms.and that SAML.WESTBROOK is her son and a minor under 14. Saml.has several hundred dollars in the hands of CHARLES T.WORTHINGTON which came to sd.minor under the Last Will and Testatment of his grandfather,J.WESTBROOK. C.T.WORTHINGTON has asked to turn the money over to someone with authority,and she seeks Grdnp.//Grdn.\Bd.$1000 with THOS.REDD,S.R.McDOWELL as surety. 23 Feb. 1883//Court orders WORTHINGTON to turn the money over to MATILDA.

WASH.CO.,MS.PKT.GLEANINGS
PROBATE COURT 1871-1884

PKT.#653:EST.J.A.TILLMAN,decd-ANNIE B.TILLMAN,Exec. with Bond $2000 and J.F.TILLMAN,DAVID FRILEY as sureties.(WILL in WBk."1" p.432, Abst.in Vol.II this series)//May 1883,ANNIE B. TILLMAN petitions for Probate of the WILL of her brother, J.A.TILLMAN,who decd.at his residence in Wash.Co. on 22 Mar.1883,naming J.F.TILLMAN as co-exectr. J.F. declines to qualify. WILL written 20 Mar.1883 on Deer Creek, J.A.TILLMAN leaves the land he and his brother J.F. had bought from the WEST estate,to his sister, ANNIE B.TILLMAN+ more purchased recently from JUDGE H.W.FOOTE. Wit:by S.H.WOOD,J.R.JOHNSON,WM.WOOD,AUGUSTUS CHEW and recorded May 1883. (Note: Judge HEZEKIAH WILLIAM FOOTE and his 3rd wife SYBELIA MESSINGER lived in Macon,Ms. They owned property below Hollandale)

PKT.#654:EST.REBECCA R.SATTERFIELD,decd.-EMMA K.SATTERFIELD,ADM. who Petitions for L.\Adm.June 1883,stating that REBECCA R. was the first wife of W.E.SATTERFIELD. She decd.at her residence in Wash. Co.,Ms.@1875;and her husband,W.E.,was appointed Adm.of her Est., which consisted of 1/3rd interest in an Insur Policy for $1666. Your Petitioner (EMMA K.),the 2nd wife of W.E.SATTERFIELD, further states that W.E. decd.7 Feb.1883,testate, appointing his widow,EMMA K.,as his exectx. W.E. left 2 minor children by his first wife and EMMA K. is their Grdn.,who is now seeking to be appointed the Adm.of REBECCA R.'s estate in order to collect their share of the Insurance Policy. (NOTE: Named in the WILL of W.E.SATTERFIELD were the children MILLING MARION,VINES JOHN,EMMA YEISER. Believe EMMA YEISER to have been W.E.and EMMA K.'s child)(See Pkt.#512)

PKT.#655:EST.IDA LOUISE WHITE,minor-CHARLES S.WHITE,Grdn. who petitions for L.\Grdnp.stating that some years back he had intermarried with AMANDA B.GRAY,who has since decd.in Wash.Co. They had 1 child,IDA LOUISE WHITE,minor,1 1/2 yrs. She is due an inheritance from her decd.mother's relatives in N.Y.-about $175 + an interest in some real estaste in Greenville,Ms.@$150. Filed 30 June 1883.

PKT.#656:EST.ELLEN H.GREY,ANNIE E.GREY,minors: 2 July 1883: Petition of ELLEN H. and ANNIE E.GRAY,minor heirs of LOUISE GRAY,decd.asks that their Grdn. papers be awarded to their father J.P.GRAY,they are over 14.They are intitiled to an interest from their grandfather-M.B.HOYT-$175, resulting from the sale of property in Lewis Co.,N.Y.//Grdnp\ Bond for $500 with ALICE GRAY,JOHN P.FINLAY as sureties.(Note: Correct sp.isGRAY.)
("OLD G'ville Cem.": Payne: *Louise Gray (w.of J.P.Gray)1837-1881/ Lawrence T.Wade 1864-1924/ Lillian Gray Wade 1864-1938*)

WASH.CO.,MS.PKT.GLEANINGS
PROBATE COURT 1871-1884

PKT.#657:EST.PEGGY GREEN,decd.-HARRIET SINGLETON,Adm. who files Petition for L.\Adm.stating that PEGGY decd.Nov.1882; intestate;in Greenville at her residence; leaving 1 child-VENUS STEWART,who is over 21; a small estate-a house and Lot on Mulberry St.in G'ville. HARRIET claims that PEGGY owes the SINGLETON's money for caring for her in her last illness. Filed 9 June 1883.//Sept.1883-SINGLETON's seek sale of HARRIET's property.//Fee Bill from Chancery Court for case #809 & #932 -HARRIET SINGLETON,JULY SINGLETON// SUMMONS to VENUS STEWART Sept.1883//ANSWER of VENUS(badly torn) denies that PEGGY owed so much to the SINGLETONS//Property sold to E.H.THOMAS in 1884 for $107.

PKT.#658:EST.JOHN WILSON,decd.-S.W.FERGUSON,Grdn. Petition,30 Oct.1886 by SARAH WILSON,who states that JOHN decd.Aug.1883,leaving surviving, his widow (SARAH), who is the mother of 2 children: AMELIA WILSON and EUGENE WILSON,-at least "it was supposed that he left one son,EUGENE". JOHN decd.testate,with S.W.FERGUSON as Grdn.to the 2 children,with instructions to FERGUSON to collect rents, etc.until EUGENE returns-they don't know where he is. Since the Will was written,(19 Jan. 1883) AMELIA has decd.in Washington City (D.C.). EUGENE left home without consent of either parent,and SARAH had heard a rumor that he had died in St.Louis,no other word,and believes him dead. She claims rent money from her husband's estate as only surviving heir.//Pkt.contains copy of WILL OF JOHN WILSON (WILL recorded in WBk."1"p.434,Abst.Vol.II, this series.). In WILL, the daughter's name is <u>ADELIA</u>.//S.W.FERGUSON confirms SARAH's story and asks permission to turn everything over to the widow-SARAH- and to be discharged.Filed Oct.1888. Next Pkt.#659:**ADELIA and EUGENE WILSON,minors,** reviews the same set of facts.,no additional information.

PKT.#661:EST.BERTHA HIRSCH,et al,minor-HENRIETTA HIRSCH, Grdn.:Inside of Pkt.,name is spelled <u>HANNAH</u> Hirsch, who files Petition for L.\Grdnp.,showing JACOB HIRSCH decd.28 Mar.1883,leaving his widow-your petitioner-and children BERTHA over 14;ROSA,HARRY (also spelled HENRY); JULIA;LEOPOLD;SAIDA all under 14. HANNAH seeks Grdnp.//Grdn.\Bd.$3000 with THEO POHL,D.LEMLE as sureties.

PKT.#662:EST.FANNIE A.LISBONY,decd.-W.E.HUNT,Sheriff,Adm.
No one qualified for Adm.,so the Court appointed HUNT.Filed 1 Oct.1883// SUMMONS to ARTHUR M.LISBONY,minor and R.S.GOLDEN,Grdn.of ARTHUR,to show cause why the final a/c cannot be allowed.-Aug.1890//Petition by W.A.LISBONY on behalf of himself and son ARTHUR M.LISBONY,only heirs at

WASH.CO.,MS.PKT.GLEANINGS
PROBATE COURT 1871-1884

PKT.#662:LISBONY,cont.
law of MRS.LISBONY,decd. W.A.seeks 1/2 of $106.//He received 1/2 and ARTHUR's Grdn.,MR.GOLDEN,received the other 1/2-10 Oct.1890.

PKT.#666:EST.RACHEL LANE,decd.-G.H.LAMB,Adm. : Petition for L.\Adm.,Filed 3 Dec.1883, by W.F.RANDOLPH,creditor,who states that RACHEL decd.intestate,and asks that the court appoint I.H.LAMB as Adm. LAMB is an Agent of RANDOLPH's,and living on the property in question.// Inventory made on 'Woodstock Plt.'by W.G.CARTER,PETER MOORE,THORNTON KEEN,PAT DONLEY,W.B.RAGAN//Adm.\Bd.$500//Sale of property ordered by Court//VOUCHER filed by ISABELLA JOHNSON,23 Apr.1884 for a/c-1 pair child's shoes,1 boy's hat and coat//SUMMONS to POLLY JANE BILLUPS on MARSH BURDETTE's place,and KING BANKS at Storm's Landing,%J.S.RICH- ARDSON; and ISABELLA JOHNSON.//No heirs listed.

PKT.#667:MARY W.RIVES,decd.-G.M.WADDELL,Adm. Petition rel- inquishing L.\Adm.,by MARTHA A.MURF (She signs MATTIE) who shows that MARY W.RIVES decd.9 Oct.1883 in Wash.Co.,Ms.;testate;A.M.WADELL was appointed Exect.in sd.WILL, but MATTIE MURF is next of kin and declines to qualify as Adm.but she does seek probate of sd.WILL.//WILL and PETITION for Probate of same,presented to Court. Exect.DR.WADELL testifies//WILL of MARY W.RIVES left 2/3rd of her property to dau.MRS.M.A.MURFF and her children;and 1/3rd to JOHN ORVILLE RIVES and MARY LEONE RIVES,who are the children of "my dau.ANNIE M.RIVES,decd."//(WILL WBk."1"p.447,Abst. Vol. II this series.)//Adm.\Bd.with JOHN S.JOOR and GEORGE C.WADILL as sureties-$2500//Fat Pkt.-full of VOUCHERS// 3 Sept. 1885,J.O.RIVES and MARY L.RIVES, heirs of MRS.MARY W.RIVES are non residents of this state and living in Ga.,and have no Grdn.in Ms. Signed A.M. WADDILL//Oct.1885: SUMMONS to MRS.M.A.MURFF in Alcorn Co.,Ms.//Apr. 1886: SUMMONS to MRS. M.A.MURFF at Winona.Ms.,Montgomery Co.//SUMMONS to JOHN ORVILLE RIVES and MARY LEONE RIVES,Tal.Co.,Ga.delivered 1 Oct.1885. JAMES W.RIVES states that the children are his and ANNIE's,now decd.

PKT.#668:EST BERTHA HIRSCH,etal,minors-HENRIETTA HIRSCH, Grdn. who files Petition for L.\Grdn.,7 Jan.1884,stating that she is the widow of JACOB HIRSCH,decd.and their children are BERTHA17,ROSA 13, HARRY 12, JULIA 8, LEOPOLD 6, SAIDA 1. The sd.minors have a possible inheritance in Province of Alsace,now in litagation-@$100// Oct.1887, HENRIETTA seeks discharge from Grdnp.\Bd.,saying no money was coll- ected, and further shows that BERTHA DREYFUS nee HIRSCH is of full age, and answers of other minors allow discharge//Granted.

DEATH NOTICES FROM THE GREENVILLE TIMES

The following section of MARRIAGE and DEATH notices was taken from 'THE STOCKWELL PAPERS', a collection transcribed from newspapers, some no longer extant, and made available by Ms. EUNICE STOCKWELL during the 1930's. Copies are in the Greenville, Ms. Library, and the State Archives, Jackson, Ms.

1890

Jan.4: ROLLINS, MR. WILLIAM R., a resident of G'ville for the past ten yrs. *[b.1844-d.1890]*

Jan.5: SCHLESINGER, ABRAHAM, of meningitis, aged 6 yrs. The decd. was the infant son of MR. and Mrs. L. Schlesinger.

Jan.10: DUNN, ORVILLE BLANTON, of pneumonia, at the residence of his brother, Dr. S.R. Dunn.

Jan.24: GERALD, MRS. LULA, of pneumonia, at the residence of Mrs. John Black.

Feb.18: WRIGHT, CALDWELL, infant son of Mr. and Mrs. Price Wright. [G'ville Cem.-n/d]

Feb.18: COX, MALCOLM, aged 15, at the residence of relatives in Arkansas. The decd. was the only child of Mr. Jack Cox and the nephew of Mrs. Kate Kretschmar.

Feb.23: PAXTON, MRS. MARY N., wife of A.G. Paxton, in Indianola, Sunflower Co. The decd. was a daughter of Mr. Hal T. Noland, of this county and was born in 1862. (Buried in Warren Co., Ms.)

Feb.28: WORTHINGTON, WILLIAM, in Enterprise, Miss. in the 58th yr. of his life. Mr. Worthington was born in Ky. in 1832, but spent his youth and early manhood in this county, which was his home for the greater part of his life. He was a brother of Messrs. Ben T. and Thomas Worthington of this county, Judge Isaac Worthington and Mrs. J. Peak, of Chicot County, Ark. and Mrs. L.B. Valliant of St. Louis.

April 6: MONTGOMERY, MRS. J.M. at the residence of Dr. D.C. Montgomery. The decd. was the wife of Mr. J.M. MONTGOMERY.*[CARRIE MOSBY 1859-1890 wife of J.M. Montgomery, and the dau. of C.S. and E.G. MOSBY]*

May 10: TOY, MR. I.N., at his home in Greenville. *[1831-1890]*

May 28: BLOCKETT, MRS. BETTIE ERWIN, at her home in Atlanta, Ga. Mrs. Blockett was a great-granddaughter of Henry Clay, and a neice of Messrs. Johnson and J.W. Erwin of this county. As Miss Bettie Erwin, she lived in Washington Co. ten or fifteen yrs. ago, a beautiful and greatly admired member of its young society.

June 2: CAPERTON, J.C., at his plantation near Carolina Landing.

June 6: RUCKS, MRS. S.B., aged 54 yrs. Her husband was the late Judge James T. Rucks, who died at Friars Point, in 1878. [SALLIE B. RUCKS 1835-1890]*

Sept.25: PURCELL, SAMUEL H., at Alton Park, Va., aged three yrs. The decd.

*From: "OLD" GREENVILLE CEMETERY by Payne

DEATH NOTICES FROM THE GREENVILLE TIMES

1890

was the son of Mr.and Mrs.Samuel H.Purcell.
Oct.5: SULKE,MR.BERNARD,at his residence in G'ville.
Oct.26: UHL,CLARA P.,"In the communion of the Catholic Church,in the confidence of a certain faith."
Oct.15: URQUHART,JOHN A.MILLER,suddenly in Kansas City,son of Mrs.E.C. Urquhart,of this county,aged 22. *[1868-1890]*

1891

Jan.25: HARTMAN,MRS.BELLA L.,wife of Lee Hartman and sister of E.G. Marshall, at her residence in G'ville.
Feb.5: GRAVITT,MRS.W.H., aged 44 yrs., died at Baird, survived by husband and children.
Feb.9: BIDDLE,MRS.FRANCIS A.,nee Clark,aged 67 yrs. Mrs. Biddle was the mother of Mrs.S.B.Lawson,of Leota. She was the daughter of D.W. and Anne Clark of Jefferson Co.,Ky.
Feb.15: SKINNER,MRS. CAROLINA M., beloved wife of N.C.SKINNER,M.D., in the 65th yr.of her age. *[1828-1891]*
April 2: O'HEA,MAJOR RICHARD A.: On Saturday last, Major R.A.O'Hea peacefully laid down the burdens of life. He was at Longwood, in the southern part of the county...Major O'Hea was a native of the Emerald Isle...and was about 73 yrs.of age and unmarried.
April 25: GREENWALD,JAKE, a former citizen of G'ville, in Memphis at the Peabody Hotel.
May 15: SCHLESINGER,MR.ISAAC, of the law firm of Nelson and Schlesinger. The decd. was buried in his old home, Woodville,Ms.
May 21: SCHLESINGER, IKE, survived by wife and two children.
May 22: SCURLOCK,MR.W.T., aged 66 yrs.; at his residence in G'ville. The decd.was born in Sumner Co.,Tenn.and lived in G'ville for the past 7 yrs.
June 17: SWAIN,S.R.   *[Samuel R.Swain 1838-1891]*
July 7: LENGSFIELD,MRS.ELIZABETH, at her residence in G'ville.
   [Elizabeth Hackett Jackson Lengsfield 1818-1891]
July 7: ANDERSON,CECILE, little dau. of Mr.and Mrs. A.Anderson.
July 9: McLEMORE,THOMAS, 4 yr.old twin son of Mrs.T.N.McLemore.
Aug.27: BUTTS,W.R.
Sept.10: GRIFFIN,J.D.,aged 72 yrs.,survived by a son,J.E.Griffin.
Oct.24: WEEMS,MRS. MARY B., of Arcola, a native of Georgia. She was married in 1869 and has since lived in Wash.Co. She is survivied by her husband "Squire" Weems and her daughters Bessie & Julia.
Oct.30: HEBRON,NETTIE P.
Nov.31: GREEN,W.H.
Dec.4: SMITH,MRS.SALLIE, w.of L.Pink Smith,editor of the G'ville Democrat

*From: "OLD"GREENVILLE CEMETERY by Payne

DEATH NOTICES FROM THE GREENVILLE TIMES

1891
Dec.10: YERGER,JAMES R., died in Jackson (Ms.)

1892
Jan.8: SHAW,MRS.CHARLES,dau.of Mrs.Lyman G:Aldrich of Natchez.
Jan.8: WADE,GEORGE, in Bolivar Co.,son-in-law of Dr.C.M.Curell.
Feb.5: DUNN,EDNA BURKE,five yr.old dau.of John N.and Mrs.Mary Dee Dunn. *[1887-1892]*
Feb.18: GOODMAN,JONAS
April 2: MURPHY,J.W.,aged 50 yrs.pioneer of G'ville,survived by 5 children.
April 2: FLOURNOY,MRS.E.J., aged 70 yrs., mother of Mrs. W.W.Worthington and Mrs.A.F.Wickliffe.
April 2: FISHER,JOHN W.
April 3: GRIFFIN,JOHN DRYDEN, 8 yr.old son of Mr.and Mrs.John L.Griffin.
May 7: GRAINGER,MRS.NELLIE CORRIGAN, wife of Dr.R.A.Grainger. For 11 yrs.a devoted companion to Mrs. H.B.Theobald.
Sept.17: LOVE,JOSEPH T.,aged 62 yrs.
Oct.15: YERGER,MRS. MAY H. *[Mary H.Yerger 1817-1892]*
Dec.8: STIRLING,MRS.SARAH HANNAH,on the plantation (Berkley) where she was born,April 15,1836. The dau.of the late John A.Miller. [1835-1892]*

1893
Mar.12: ISENBERG,ABE,aged 18 yrs.,in Cincinnatti,of Typhoid fever.
May 3: PHILLIPS,JENNIE,dau.of Mr.and Mrs.S.F.Phillips,near Arcola.
May 31: DAVIS,ELIZA COCKS,wife of T.F.Davis of Rosedale.
July 29: DABNEY,MRS.LOLA BLANTON,eldest dau.of Dr.and Mrs.O.M.Blanton and grand-daughter of the late Mrs.H.B.Theobald. *[Lola Angeligne Blanton Dabney 1854-1893]*
July 30: YERGER,JAMES ALLEN, 2nd son of Capt.and Mrs.W.G.Yerger. *[1872-1893]*
Aug.7: PETTIT,JOHN A., son of Dr.A.and Czarina F.Pettit, at Avon.
Sept.28: BUCHANAN,LULA LEE, dau.of Mr.and Mrs.W.H.Buchanan,aged 17 yrs.
DEC.3: ALLEN,MRS.SARAH B., at the home of her brother,Mr.John V.Bell.
Dec.6: WILLIAMS,MRS.C.M., a citizen of G'ville for many yrs.
Dec.27: DUFFY,PATRICK, sexton of the G'ville Cemetery.

1894
Jan.24: BARTLETT,LUDIE,wife of Capt.Henry J.Johnson,of Aldomar,Wash. Co., Ms. Born in Covington,Ky., Jan.1,1845. Survived by husband and 4 children, Misses Anne T.and Narcisse Johnson, and Messrs. Charles and Edward B. Johnson, and a step-daughter, Mrs.Peyton Kincead of Ky., and step-sons, Wm. Henry, George G., C.M. and R.A.Johnson. *[1847-1894]*
Feb.13: PERCY,MRS.FANNIE WILLIAMS,aged 71,at her home in G'ville. The decd.was a native of Knoxville,Tenn.,a dau.of Judge Thomas L.Williams,

*From: "OLD"GREENVILLE CEMETERY by Payne

DEATH NOTICES FROM THE GREENVILLE TIMES

1894

prominent jurist of that state. She was the wife of Dr.J.Walker Percy,an elder brother of the late Col.W.A.Percy, who died at their home on Deer Creek in 1888. For the past 20 yrs.Mrs. Percy has lived with her son-in-law, Capt.J.S.McNeily,of G'ville. *[1825-1894]*

Feb.22: NELSON,MR.N.T., one of the oldest and best citizens of G'ville. He was a Mason. *[1835-1894]*

Feb.23: NEILSON,COL.CHARLES P.,aged 59 yrs. Col.Neilson came to G'ville in 1889 from Woodville,Miss. He served with distinction and honor throughout the war with the rank of Colonel in the Confederate Army. He leaves a widow and 3 daughters,Mrs.N.C.Skinner,Miss Neilson, and little dau.Nannie.

Feb.25: OURSLER,MRS.MARY E.,aged 63, a member of the Methodist Church.

Feb.27: SHANAHAN,MR.TIMOTHY M.aged about 80. He was born in Ireland and was one of the earliest settlers in G'ville, building one of the first houses in the city in 1865.

Feb.28: GILDART,ROBERT EDWARD, little son of Capt.and Mrs.W.K.Gildart, from membranous croup.

Mar.9: DAVIS,MARY DAVIS,infant daughter of William and Sallie Davis,aged 2 yrs.,11 mos.,26 days.

April 12: JONES,EMMA, a few days ago in Crystal Springs.

May 4: IREYS,BETTIE TAYLOR,aged 44,wife of Henry T.Ireys.[1849-1894]*

May 4: SPIERS,R.H.,aged about 35.He was prominent in the Methodist Church and was a prosperous merchant. He came to Greenville from Virginia... was married a few yrs.since to Miss Kate Shelby.*[R.H.SPI ARS 1860-1894]*

June 1: JOHNSON,WILLIE HUNT,youngest daughter of Mr.and Mrs.C.M.Johnson, nearly 2 yrs.old. *[1892-1894]*

June 24: MILAM,B.L.,in Leland,a member of the Stoneville Jackson Lodge, and a well known figure in G'ville and Leland. For some yrs.past he was engaged in railroad work.

June 24: GIDDEN, baby daughter of S.W.Gidden.

Aug.25: McGRATH,MRS.ALICE E.,aged about 55, at the home of her dau., Mrs. Magruder. She was a native of Washington County, being the dau.of Mr.John Penrice,one of its earliest settlers. She was married to Caldwell McGrath of Ky. *[1839-1894]*

Sept.15: STERN,MRS.FANNIE,aged 55 yrs.,wife of Mr.B.Stern.

Oct.7: SMYTHE,MRS.M.S.,at the home of her son Dr.J.D.Smythe. The remains were interred at the former home in Carthage,Miss.,where the greater part of her life was spent.

Nov.21: CARSON,ANDREW B. at his home in G'ville. Born in Washington County 60 yrs.ago. Served as Sheriff of the county during the troubled period succeeding the war. *[d.1894]*

*From: "OLD"GREENVILLE CEMETERY by Payne

DEATH NOTICES FROM THE GREENVILLE TIMES

1894
Dec.15: LEMLER,NORVELL, the youngest son of Mr.and Mrs.Max Lemler.

1895
Jan.25: WALSH,MRS.CARRIE A.,wife of Mr.M.E.Walsh,at her home in G'ville.

Feb.8: HOLMES,MRS.EMMA,at Arcola. Mrs. Holmes, nee Parnell, was born in Dallas County,Ala., in 1832 and married Mr.Holmes in 1855.

Feb.18: WASSON,MR.D.C., able lawyer and splendid citizen. Mr.Wasson came to G'ville 6 yrs.ago from the eastern part of the state,where he was reared. He succeeded here as a lawyer, and before ill health forced him from his office enjoyed a lucrative practice.

April 20: ENOS,MR.EDWARD, at the home of his dau.,Mrs.S.J.French. Mr.Enos was one of the first settlers of the present town of G'ville,coming here in 1866,first to manage the plantation of Mr.Roach and afterward engaging in the hotel and merchandising business.

May 4: ISENBERG,MISS MATTIE, young daughter of Mr.and Mrs.I.Isenberg.

June 27: ROSE,MR.E., well known citizen of Leland.

June 27: TURNER,DR.E.R., also a well known citizen of Leland.

June 29: AXMAN,CHARLES,aged about 65 yrs. *[d.1895]*

July 30: LEMLE,MR.D.,at his home in G'ville,aged about 70 yrs.

Sept.7: TAYLOR,MRS.SUSAN P.,aged 81 yrs. She was one of the oldest inhabitants of the county and was a sister of Miss Paulina Mosby,and the mother of Mrs.P.McCutcheon and the late Mrs.Henry T.Ireys.[1815-1895]*

Sept.7: HUGHES,MISS SALLIE,at the home of Maj. James A.Deaton, in G'ville.

Sept.10: DARLING,DR.JOSEPH,in G'ville at the home of his sister,Miss Darling.

Sept.10: LACEY,MRS.ROBERT H.,at her home in G'ville; Mrs. Lacey was the eldest dau.of Mr.and Mrs.John Kanatzer of this county. *[1868-1895]*

Sept.12: McCLAIN,MRS.WALTER

Sept.14: WEST,WINSTON E.,aged 50 yrs.,at his home in Hollandale.(Ms.)

Sept.24: CASEY,CHARLES G.,aged 34 yrs.,at his home near Hollandale.

Oct.2: PERRIN,MR.SAM W.,a resident of G'ville for twenty yrs. He came to this county from Painville,Va. *[1847-1895]*

Oct.6: O'BANNON,MARY,aged 9 yrs. The decd.was the youngest dau.of Mr.& Mrs.D.B.O'Bannon. *[1886-1895]*

Oct.15: BEDON,MISS WILLIE,at the home of her sister,Mrs.J.M.Lawrence,aged 17. Miss Bedon was the youngest dau.of the late Dr.and Mrs. Bedon of this county,a neice of the late Capt.Calhoun Haile,and Mrs.Harry Smith of G'ville

Oct.16: BRANTON,ROBERT,twin son of Mr.& Mrs.J.E.Branton,at Burdette,this county,aged 4 mos. *[Robert Pollard Branton aged 4 mos.-1895]*

Nov.1: CARSON,MRS.E.J.,aged 95 yrs.,at the residence of Mrs.M.B.Carson on Washington Ave.,G'ville. *[Elizabeth J.Carson d.1895]*

*From: "OLD"GREENVILLE CEMETERY by Payne

DEATH NOTICES FROM THE GREENVILLE TIMES

1895

Dec.5: KNOX,MISS MATTIE, aged 43, at her home in the south end of this county. Miss Knox was a lifelong resident of Washington County and her ancestors,the prominent and distinguished Knox and Shelby families, were among the original land grantees of the Delta.

Dec.21: QUINN,MRS. aged about 96 yrs., the mother of City Marshall William Quinn.

1896

Jan.27: GOLDSMITH,HAZEL FLORENCE,aged 6 yrs.,dau.of Mr.& Mrs.S.Goldsmith

Jan.27: FRANKEL,RUBY,aged 5,dau.of Mr.&Mrs.Frankel of Leota.

April 13: POHL,MR.THEODORE, at the age of 62. For many yrs.the decd.acted as secretary of the County Democratic Executive Committee. He also held a responsible position in the G'ville Building Association. He was a native of Alsace, and had been in G'ville for more than 20 yrs.

April 30: GORMAN,ADDIE LUELLA, little dau.of Mr.and Mrs.J.H.Gorman.

May 3: ROSELLA,JAMES CARROLL,son of James and Mollie Rosella,age 3 yrs.

May 5: CLAY,JR.MR.GREEN, in San Antonio,Texas. The death of Mr.Clay is rendered doubly melancholy by the fact that he was married only a few months ago to Miss Louise Campbell.

July 15: COWAN,MR.J.C., of typhoid fever.

July 28: YOUNG,MRS.MARY, at the home of her father, Mr.Killian of Mayersville,(Ms) wife of Dr.J.L.Young, of this city. The decd.was buried at the old graveyard at the foot of Lake Washington. (Greenfield)

Aug.4: STARLING,MRS.MARIA HENSLEY, at the home of her sons, Major William Starling and Mr.Lyne Starling.

Aug.14: KENNEDY,MRS.MAGGIE,in Chicago,Illinois,widow of Edward Kennedy and dau.of Mr.F.Biggins*[Maggie Kennedy b.9 Aug.1858-d.13 Aug.1896 /Edward Kennedy b.at Castlecomer Co.,Kilkenny,Ire. 1844-d.26 Oct.1893/ Francis Biggens b.12 Nov.1816-d.4 Oct.1896/ Jane Biggens(w.of Francis Biggens) d.13 Nov.1885-age 55 yrs.]*

Sept.12:BARNES,MRS.HARRY M. at her home in Winterville, aged 48. Mrs. Barnes was a native of Hartford,Connecticut, but for many yrs.past has been a resident of this county.   *[d.1896]*

Sept.20: PERRY,MR.OLIVER HAZARD, at the home of his father, near Nicholasville,Ky. Mr.Perry was a native of Ky.and a direct descendant of Commodore Perry, the hero of Lake Erie.

Dec.12: HOOD,MRS.MARY SHIELDS,wife of Mr.Thomas H.Hood,at the home of her mother. *[1872-1896]*

Dec.16: BOWEN, ALLEN,little 6 yr.old dau.of Mr.and Mrs.John H.Bowen.
  [Allen Campbell Bowen 1889-1896]

*From: "OLD"GREENVILLE CEMETERY" by Payne

DEATH NOTICES FROM THE GREENVILLE TIMES

1896

Dec.24: NELSON,MRS.MARY, aged about 75 yrs. In the death of Mrs. Nelson, G'ville loses one more of its old and honored residents-one of those few ... who were distinguished members of the old-time social regime of the county before the war. Mrs. Nelson and her husband,the late Judge Newman J.Nelson, who decd.from yellow fever in 1878, came to G'ville from the county early in the 70's. *[Mary Ward Nelson 1826-1896]*

Dec.28: BAGLEY,Dr.W.M., of pneumonia. The decd.came here from Missouri and married Mrs. Jennie Harvey Joyce,a sister of Mr.W.R.Harvey.

Dec.20: TUPPER,MRS.FRED, of Benoit(Ms.) Mrs.Tupper was well-known in G'ville and a life-long resident of Bolivar County, where she has many relatives.

1897

Jan.12: SHELBY,MRS.ELIZABETH, aged 63. The decd.'s maiden name was Elizabeth Cornelius. She was from Huntsville,Ala. At 17 she married Jefferson Wilkerson and moved to her home 46 yrs.ago. Mr.Wilkerson died in 1866 and in 1870 Mrs.Wilkerson was married to O.L.Shelby.

Feb.11: LEYSER,DR.D.S., at Memphis. The decd. was a resident of G'ville.

Feb.11: LILE,MRS.MARY, in Washington,D.C., at the home of her sister. The decd. was formerly of Washington County,Miss. She was an aunt of Messrs.Richard and Marshall Burdette, and a great-aunt of Mrs.J.B.Hebron. (Note:Error- Mary Lile was the _Mother_ of Richard and Marshall Burdette. See Probate Pkt.#608,this Vol.)

Feb.12: HOLMES,HINDS JR., only son of Mr.& Mrs.Hinds Holmes, aged 19.
 [1877-1897]

Feb.12: GUGGENHEIM,M.S., at his home in G'ville, aged about 45.

Feb.16: WORTHINGTON,MR.W.MASON, at his home in G'ville. Mr.Worthington's family in ante-bellum times was one of the wealthiest and most influential in the Delta. At his father's death he inherited the magnificent "Wayside" plantation,together with the other estates in the county. He founded the Bank of Greenville and was its president until he resigned to look after his plantations, being succeeded by Mr.W.A.Pollock. Becoming heavily involved at the time when a succession of disadvantageous yrs. brought failure to so many planters, he made over all of his entire property to his creditors and went to Texas to begin the world anew, but returned a few yrs.ago to G'ville, where he remained until his death. He married Miss Stone,of Ky.,who survives him with a family of 4 daughters and 1 son.
 [1835-1897]

Feb.23: HANWAY,MR.JOHN, aged about 70,at his home in this city. Mr.Hanway was born at Lara,near Maynooth,Ireland,and came to America in his youth.
 [1815-1897]

---

*From: "OLD"GREENVILLE CEMETERY" by Payne

DEATH NOTICES FROM THE GREENVILLE TIMES

1897

Mar.1: FORTNER,MR.SED. On this date a party of Italians went into Lake's Hardware store to buy a pistol. Mr.Fortner waited on them, and, after selecting two pistols, one of the Italians, Marcus Bartino, pulled an old pistol out of his pocket. He was examining it and comparing it with the new ones when it went off and Mr.Fortner was shot through the heart. The terrible affair was plainly an accident and the Italian was crazed with grief at what he had done. Mr.Fortner was not well-known in G'ville, having only lived here a short time. He was a brother of Douglas Fortner of Winterville and leaves a mother and father at Terry, Mississippi.

Mar.13: STRAUSS,MR.GERSON,aged 78 yrs. He was the father of Mrs.Lee Hexter of G'ville,and has made his home with his daughter for some yrs.

Mar.28: WRIGHT,MR.J.PRICE, at the home of Mr.& Mrs.J.C.Greenley, a victim of consumption.

April 27:McDONALD,MRS.LULA PENNY,at her home in Greenwood,Miss.
   [1871-1897]

April 22:CARR,DONALD,son of John and Sarah L.Griffin,in G'ville.
 *[Donald Carr Griffin 1866-1897/ John Lane Griffin 1854-1895
   Sarah Lane Griffin 1829-1900/John Griffin 1826-1903]*

May 24: GEORGE,MR.SAM B., at his home in G'ville.

May 30: HARRIS,MR.SAM, at his home in Avon,aged 55.

June 9: YERGER,MRS.SALLIE M.,wife of Mr.Hal Yerger,a brother of the Hon. W.G.Yerger, of G'ville. She leaves a family of 3 sons and 1 daughter,and one brother and sister,Mr.Harvey Miller and Mrs.Shortridge of New Orleans.

June 9: JAMES,Mr.Ed.C.,at his home near Lake Washington.

June19: BODDIE,MAMIE SHIELDS,infant dau.of Mr.& Mrs.Van B.Boddie.*

June19: ABLE,WILL, shot in a gun duel at Avon. [age 40]

June19: JAMES,PAUL,shot in a gun duel at Avon. [age 25]

(Note: Paul James was the son of Mr.Ed.C.James,and a cousin of Will Able. Will and Paul killed each other in a shoot-out.)

June 24: WILCZINSKI,MR.JOSEPH,at his home in G'ville.

July 11: WATERS,MRS.N.C.,w. of Mr.H.Waters,aged 61,at her home in G'ville.

July 26: MONTGOMERY,MR.F.P.,at the residence of Mrs.E.R.Wortham in G'ville, at the age of 80. Mr.Montgomery had spent most of his life in California, coming to G'ville about 3 yrs.ago,making his home with his neice,Mrs. Wortham. He was a member of the Montgomery family so numerous in G'ville and the county,and so closely identified with society and public life for generations past. *[1818-1897]*

July 29: GRAVITT,MR.W.H.,at the home of his son-in-law,Mr.W.H.Neal,in G'ville. *[Listed on Confederate Monument as a Kentuckian]*

Aug.2: ISENBERG,MR.ISAAC,in Philadelphia.He was one of the old citizens of

*From: "OLD"GREENVILLE CEMETERY" by Payne

DEATH NOTICES FROM THE GREENVILLE TIMES

1897

G'ville...has been closely identified with its public life for the past 25 yrs.
Aug.10: HARBISON,GEORGE LYNN,infant son of Mr.&Mrs.Joseph Harbison.
 [1895-1897]
Sept.21: DARET,ADRIEN,aged about 60. He was a Confederate veteran with a record of brave service. *[A.DAR RETI - listed on Confederate Monument as a Frenchman]*
Oct.7: JOHNSON,DR.McWILLIE, at his home in Leota,of typho-malarial fever. Dr.Johnson was the son of Dr.& Mrs.R.B.Johnson,of Kirkwood,Miss. He married Miss Kate Stinson,daughter of Mr.W.B.Stinson,of Canton,Miss.
Oct.12: McNAMARA,MR.JOHN, after a long illness.
Oct.13: SOMMER,MR.HERMAN,SR.,
Oct.15: WYCHE,MRS.JULIA D., an old and honored citizen of G'ville.
Oct.26: NURSE,MR.SAMUEL. *[1843-1897]*
Oct.31: BARRINGTON,MR.E.H., was caught between the Goyer platform and a moving train,sustaning injuries which resulted in his death.
Nov.13: WAGAMON,MRS.LOUISA, at the residence of Mr.W.Schilling. The decd.was the mother of Mrs.Schilling. *[Louise Wageman 1826-1897]*

1898

Jan.25: LEE,JOANNA,6 yr.old dau.of Mr.& Mrs.John M.Lee,at the home of her grandmother,Mrs.J.P.Harshe. *[1891-1898]*
Mar.3: RICE,MR.D.McKAY, a prominent young man of Memphis,at the King's Daughter's Home.
Mar.11: O'BANNON,JUDGE D.B.,at his home in G'ville,after a severe illness of short duration. For more that 30 yrs.Judge O'Bannon has been a well-known figure in the public life of Washington Co.,having come to this state from Virginia,the state of his birth,when a young man. *[Dagobert B.O'Bannon 1822-1898/Mary P.,wife of D.B.O'Bannon 1851-1886]*
Mar.15: WILZIN,MR.NATHAN
Mar.17: HEARD,C.A.,shot and killed at Leland. *[1862-1898]*
Mar.19: MONTGOMERY,DR.C., of pneumonia,after a short illness. Dr.Montgomery was the oldest practicing physcian in G'ville and a man universally loved and honored,not only for his professional attainments, but for the exalted character of his public and private life. A large circle of relatives and friends mourn his loss,including his brothers, Capt.J.M. Montgomery, Maj.Eugene Montgomery, his wife and sons, his neices and step-sons, to whom he always stood in the relation of a tender father,and the families of Montgomery, Finlay, Archer, and others, including a great number of the best citizens of the county.
April 17:HARSHE,MRS.JOANNA P., at her home in Belle Air. She had been a resident of G'ville for about 20 yrs.and was greatly honored and loved by

*From: "OLD"GREENVILLE CEMETERY" by Payne

DEATH NOTICES FROM THE GREENVILLE TIMES

1898

all who knew her. She leaves a daughter,Mrs.John Lee,and 2 sons,Messrs. M. Neil Harshe and Robert Barnette Harshe,and a grandson,Mr.Heddens Montgomery. *[1832-1898]*

April 21: LEWIS,Rev.Dr.J.M.,after a short illness,of pneumonia,aged 69 yrs. Dr.Lewis came to G'ville about 10 yrs.ago and was for several yrs.pastor of the Baptist Church of this place ... He served with gallantry through the war between the states, being at the time of his death a member of the G'ville Camp of Confederate Veterans. He leaves a devoted wife, 2 daus. Miss Effie Lewis,of G'ville and Mrs.Houston Woods of Ky.,and a son, Mr. Vivian Lewis of Chicago.

April 20:HEAD,MR.DAN,after a long illness,aged 38. *[1860-1898]*

May 13: RANSON,RICHARD POLIS,infant son of Mr.&Mrs.Ransom,aged 3 mos.*

June 17: GOLDSMITH,MR.SOL

June 9: HUNT,PRUE,aged 16 yrs.,9 mos.,daughter of William E.and Maria C.Hunt. *[Prudence B. Hunt 1881-1898]*

July 14: RYAN,JIMMIE,little son of Mr.& Mrs.Jim Ryan. *[1891-1898]*

Dec.12: DEATON,MAJOR JAMES A., at his home in G'ville. *[James Alexander Deaton 1840-1898]*

Dec.22: MANIFOLD,MRS.MARGARET, at her home in G'ville. She was one of the oldest residents of G'ville,having lived here continually for about 30 yrs.

[1838-1898]

Dec.?: LANGER,MR.A.B.,in G'ville during the last of December.

1899

Jan.9: YERGER,JACOB SHALL,after a long illness. He was the eldest son of the late Hal Yerger and grandson of J.Shall Yerger,who in his lifetime was one of the most eminent jurist and public men of Miss. The decd. was also a nephew of the Hon.William G.Yerger of G'ville.

Feb.14: SKINNER,DR.N.C.,aged about 75,at his home in G'ville. Dr.Skinner was one of the oldest settlers of the Delta,having come to this country from North Carolina when a young man. *[1826-1899]*

Mar.1: HANWAY,Tim,aged 12,youngest son of Mrs.John Hanway. *[Timmie B.Hanway 1887-1899 son of J.V. and A.Hanway]*

Mar.2: HOLLAND,MR.GOERGE, after a brief illness. *[1857-1899]*

Mar.2:PETTIT,MR.J.J.,one of the prominent citizens of the county.

Mar.8: WEST,MARY DULANEY, at Memphis,Tenn., daughter of the late Dr. Dulaney of Jackson,Miss.and beloved wife of Charles H.West,Chief Engineer of the Levee Board.

Mar.22: NASON,MYRTLE, 6 yr.old dau.of Mr.& Mrs.J.R.Nason.

Mar.22: GILLESPIE,MRS.A.A.,run over and killed instantly by train entering

*From: "OLD"GREENVILLE CEMETERY" by Payne

DEATH NOTICES FROM THE GREENVILLE TIMES

station at Estill, Miss.

1899

April 8: BELL, ALICE FISHER, dau.of Mr.& Mrs.J.W.Bell.
April 21: YAGER, LULA, dau.of the late Mrs.Mary Yager, at Ocala, Florida.
[Luella M.Yager 1877-1899]
May 31: ROSENSTOCK, MRS.MORRIS, of Avon. Mrs.Rosenstock was a dau.of Dr.Peters, one of the old southern gentlemen of the Delta, and in her youthful days as Miss Minnie Peters was a great favorite in Delta society.
June 15: RANSON, MR.ROBB L., shot and killed himself in the office of the Delta Grocery Company.
June 28: BRAWNER, CAPT.L.T., at the G'ville Inn.
June 30: DARLING, MRS.ELIZABETH, aged 73. She leaves a dau., Miss Ella Darling, who has the sympathy of many friends in her bereavement.
July 2: THOMPSON, MR.JOHN B., at Senatobia, Miss., Mayor of Leland and one of the leading young business men of Washington County.
Aug.16: BYRAN, MR.J.HARRY, civil engineer...at the Leota House.
Sept.5: SESSIONS, MR.HORACE W., real estate dealer, in Birmingham, Ala.
Sept.7: McGEE, MRS.B.O., wife of Mr.B.O.McGee of Leland, Miss.
Sept.6: FOSS, MRS.E.T., at the home of her son.
Sept.10: MONTGOMERY, MR.W.P., son of Mr.& Mrs.W.E.Montgomery, in Natchez.
Oct.14: BILLINGSLEY, MR.GEORGE E., formerly a citizen of G'ville, where he acted as manager of the G'ville Oil Works, and who left here in 1890 or 91 for the west, died at his home in Guthrie, Okla.
Oct. 2: YERGER, CAPT.W.G., a prominent lawyer of Washington County and of the State, a brave and manly soldier and officer in the Confederate Army.
[William Gwin Yerger 1840-1899]
Nov.15: KENNEDY, JOHN J., at his home.
Nov.10: TAYLOR, MR.HINTON, at Percy Station, aged 61. Mr.Taylor was a Confederate veteran, a member of Co.A, First Miss.Artillery.

1900

Jan.4: PIERCE, FRANK, little son of Mrs.Annie Pierce and grandson of Mrs.B.F.Gray. *[Frank M.N.Pierce 1893-1900]*
Feb.26: STANTON, MRS.FANNIE.
Mar.23: BARNES, ESTELLE, eldest dau.of Mr.& Mrs.J.F.Barnes, at the home of her cousin, Mrs.Rebecca Williams, Jackson, Miss.
Mar.24: JOHNSON, MR.EDWARD B. *[1872-1899]*
Mar.26: WINTER, WILLIAM S., at the King's Daughter's Hospital of this city.*
May 27: BAREFIELD, SAM, near Hollandale. Mr.Barefield came from South Carolina and settled in Warren Co.in 1823, but for the past 35 yrs.he has been a citizen of Deer Creek in Washington County.
Oct.1: ARCHER, DR.FINLAY, at the home of his parents; age 21 yrs..

*From: "OLD"GREENVILLE CEMETERY" by Payne

DEATH NOTICES FROM THE GREENVILLE TIMES

1900

Oct.28: MUSGROVE,CARRIE YERGER,dau.of Mayor and Mrs.Wm.Yerger. *[1868-1900]*

Dec.?: STARLING,MAJOR WILLIAM, formerly president of Levee Board. *[1839-1900]*

Dec.30: ROBB,MRS.ANNA L.,aged 85, a resident of Wash. County from 1864 until 1890. Mrs.Robb spent the last few yrs.of her life in Nashville,Tenn.

1901

Jan.13: WEISS,MRS.HANNAH, at the age of 70.

Feb.2: ROSENFIELD,MR.SIMON, long a resident of G'ville.

Mar.13: McKIE,MINNIE, little dau.of Capt.and Mrs.McKie.

April 1: McDOWELL,S.R.,aged 60. Mr.McDowell was a brave soldier in the Confederate Army, a true friend and a splendid citizen.

April 10: ANDERSON,CAPT.FRANK. He was a citizen of Vicksburg (Ms.)when the war broke out and enlisted in Capt.L.C.Moore's Company of Volunteers and was transferred to another company in the 48th Mississippi Regiment and became a sargeant. He was a gallant soldier,and it was such men as he that made General Lee's army invincible. *[Frank Woodson Anderson 1845-1901]*

April 26: DAWSON,MRS.L.A.,one of the oldest citizens of G'ville, at the home of her daughter Mrs. Lowenburg.

May 15: COPPEE,H.L.ST., prominent engineer in the Government River Service,an honored citizen,member of the Board of Trustees of the city's public schools,and a polished gentleman and a Christian.

June 1: ROMANSKY,SOLOMAN,aged about 60, at Mineral Wells,Texas. For the past 15 yrs.an honored merchant of G'ville.

June 6: LYON,CAPT.G.W.,aged 77,one of the oldest river men on the "Father of Waters",at his home here.

June 12: TILFORD,MISS GRACIA, aged 16, only child of Robert and Claudia Walton Tilford, and granddaughter of Mrs. Gracia Walton, at Asheville, North Carolina. *[1884-1901]*

June ?: JACKSON,JOHN C., at St.Charles.La.,oldest son of Mr. & Mrs.N.T. Jackson,formerly of G'ville,now of Edwards,Miss. *[John Cunyus Jackson 1866-1901]*

June 14: VORMUS,ALBERT, after a short illness.

July 3: ESKRIDGE,ELEANOR VALLIANT, aged 17 months, at Castillian Springs,Miss. *[1900-1901]*

July ?: CARTER,ROBERT HILL, aged 60,resident of the Delta and of Carter's Point for half a century,at Woodstock Plantation. *[1834-1901]*

July 18: CHAPELL,HENRY J.,formerly of Vicksburg, son of the late Carter Chapell who for many yrs.was Clerk of the Vicksburg Court.

*FROM: "OLD"GREENVILLE CEMETERY by Payne

DEATH NOTICES FROM THE GREENVILLE TIMES

1901

July 18: JOHNSON,MRS.ALICE HUNT,widow of the late Claude M.Johnson and a sister of Capt.Hunt and D.F.Hunt. *[1858-1901]*

July 25: PERCY,MRS.WILLIAM A., in a sanitarium in Kenosha,Wisconsin, where she had been for several weeks.

Sept.11: ROSENBURG,M., planter and merchant of Avon, at King's Daughter's Hospital in G'ville.

1902

Feb.3: LEE,CLARENCE PERCY, at Pueblo,Colorado; youngest son of Maj.& Mrs.William Henry Lee,now decd.,a native of G'ville where he spent his youth. Survived by John M.Lee and Harry Percy Lee, brothers, and 2 sisters, Mrs.S.W.Ferguson and Mrs.Archer Harmon.

Feb.20: BENOIT,MRS.A.W., in Memphis,a native of Washington County and a dau.of William C.Blanton. *[Ida Blanton Benoit 1859-1902]*

April 11: HAMPTON,GENERAL WADE, officer in the Confederate Army and a leader in southern politics. He was well known in the Delta where he owned extensive properties and where he spent much of his time between the yrs.1866-1885.

May 8: FORTNER,MRS.JOSIE HUESTON, at the home of her parents, Capt.& Mrs.Hueston at Avon.

May 7: YAGER,GEORGE A.,aged 24 yrs.,a native of G'ville.

May 7: WORTHINGTON,ED.T.,at his home Wayside,Miss.,aged 60 yrs. A lifelong resident of Wash.Co.,he served as a Confederate soldier during the war

May 13: SOMMER,HERMAN B., resident of G'ville,at Hot Springs,Ark.
  [1861-1902]

MAY 14: JOHNSON,GEORGE G.,prominent merchant and planter.Born at his father's home on Lake Washington,he spent his life in this section.
  [1854-1902]

June 12: WILLIAMS,DAN of Washington County,at Mississippi City.

June 12: ECKSTONE,LOUIS,aged 85,for 30 yrs.a resident of G'ville.

July 16: McLEAN,DAN,little son of Mr.& Mrs.Dan McLean.*[1900-1902]*

July 30: IKERD,WILLIE,infant son of Mr.& Mrs.Lee Ikerd.

July 31: BAKER,EDGAR WOOD,resident of G'ville.

July 31: COHN,D.,in G'ville where he had come recently to make his home.

Aug.27: BRYAN,MRS.,wife of E.J.Bryan and mother of Mrs.N.T.Winter,and the Misses Maude and Daisy Jo Bryan.*[Josephine Owen Bryan 1847-1902]*

Sept. 7: LORD,STACEY, a fine type of citizen and resident of G'ville for several yrs.

Sept.9: CHIPMAN,ALMA, daughter of Mr.& Mrs.T.J.Chipman.

Oct.24: REBUHN,MRS.HENRIETTA, an aged lady, mother of Mrs.Charles Roy.
  [1834-1902]

*FROM: "OLD"GREENVILLE CEMETERY by Payne

DEATH NOTICES FROM THE GREENVILLE TIMES

1902

Oct.27: HIGGINS,MRS.S.E., in Memphis,formerly a resident of G'ville.
Nov.5: SUTTON,BEN H., a Confederate Veteran and long a resident of G'ville.
Nov. ?:KAPLAN,ADOLPH,5 yr.old son of Mr.& Mrs.D.Kaplan of Hollandale.
Dec.27:GREEN,J.R., a resident of G'ville . *[1868-1902]*

1903

Jan.9: BROWN,MRS.MATTIE McKIE,wife of Dr.James Spencer Brown in San Antonio,Texas.
Jan.21:SCHWARTZ,MRS.BERTHA,wife of Simon Schwartz.
Mar.12: NEGUS,MAJOR JAMES ENGLE,b.in Mound Brook,N.J.,1842; came to G'ville about 1870. At the time of death was President of the 1st Nat.Bank.
Mar.19:LEE,MRS.ANNIE HARSHE, wife of John M.Lee. *[1864-1903]*
April 7: SHAW,TRUMAN B., aged 71 yrs.,one of G'ville's oldest citizens,at Indian Head,Maryland.
April 16: LOVE,D.A.,at Biloxi,a citizen of Wash.Co.since 1859. Served 4 yrs.in Confederate Army-Co.D.28th Miss.Cavalry.
April 19: BOURGES,MRS. CAMILLE GENERELLEY, wife of Capt.Ernest Bourges. Survived by her husband and 4 daughters, Mrs.LeRoy Percy, Mrs. George Pearce, Mrs.Edward Mount, and Mrs.Lelia Jackson. *[1841-1903]*
July 9: DUDLEY,MRS. LOU JOHNSON, in her home in New York.
Sept.24: ROUSSEAU,ALMA BELLE.
Oct.1: GRIFFIN,JUDGE JOHN L.,aged 77 yrs.;one of Wash.Co.'s oldest and most beloved citizens-honored for his learning,his brilliant mind and the integrity of his character. *[1826-1903]*
Oct.4:SKINNER,MRS.SALLIE, at the home of her daughter in Vicksburg.
Oct.8: HALLETT,CAPT.GEORGE H., a Confederate soldier,public spirited citz.
Oct.21: LOVE,W.D., at his home in Arcola.
Nov.14: JETER,MRS. LOUISE,wife of Thomas Jeter.
Nov.14:VINCENT,MARY JEANETTE,little dau.og Mr.& Mrs.H.G.Vincent.
 [1899-1903]

1904

Feb.3: KIRBY,MRS.SALLIE, at the resident of her dau. Mrs.Harry Ferguson where she was making her home.
Feb.4: BUCKNER,MRS.LOUISE, at the home of her dau.,Mrs.J.H.Robb,where she was making her home.
Mar.1: BARNES,H.M., a resident of Wash.Co.for 37 yrs.
April 2: WINTER,CAPT.C.A., a well known citizen.
April 10: SMITH,ALBERT, son of Mrs. Anna Smith
May 21: DRUMMOND,W.H.,at St. Luke's Hospital in Memphis.*[1836-1904]*
June 6: BORUM,EDITH KILBEY, dau.of Rev.& Mrs.W.A.Borum.*[1898-1904]*
July 2: STORM,EDWARD, aged 64, at his home in Benoit...

*FROM: "OLD"GREENVILLE CEMETERY by Payne

DEATH NOTICES FROM THE GREENVILLE TIMES

1904

July 9: HAWKINS,UNCLE HEZEKIAH, ex-slave,at the home of Mrs.Jos.Hirsch.
Aug.7: DUNN,MRS.MARY FRANCES, eldest dau.of Mr.& Mrs.Thomas Ryan of Port Gibson. *[1854-1904]*
Aug.9:WARFIELD,THOMAS B.,for many yrs.a resident of Wash.Co.
Sept.18: HUNT,VIRGINIA,eldest dau.of Capt. & Mrs.W.E.Hunt.*[1870-1904]
Oct.8: TRIGG,JUDGE WYNDHAM R., for many yrs.a prominent citizen of G'ville. *[1834-1904]*
Nov.4: BATES,MRS.A.C. at the home of Mrs. J.A.Dugger.
Dec.8: STARLING,MARY CABLE, dau.of Mr.& Mrs.Charles Starling,fatally burned when a lamp exploded in her home. *[1887-1904]*
Dec.25:IREYS,CAPT.HENRY T.,JR., for many yrs. a resident of G'ville,in the home of his wife's parents,near Frankfort,Ky.

1905

Jan.27:EVERMAN,MEREDITH D., only son of Mr.& Mrs.W.A.Everman. *[Meredith David Everman 1875-1905]*
Feb.18:PETERS,MRS.HALLIE HOOE, aged 69,widow of Dr.Matthew Peters, at home of her granddaughter, Mrs. Brooks in Leland. Mrs.Peters was one of Wash.Co.'s oldest citizens having lived before the War on her husband's plantation near Egg's Point. After her husband's death she resided with her dau.,Mrs.J.J.Pettit at Avon.
Mar.2: HALL,MRS.JAMES, long a resident of Wash.Co.,having lived many yrs.at Leota,later a resident of G'ville; at home of her dau. Mrs.L.C.Goode. *[Sarah O'Bannon 18_2-1905, (widow of Leonard Haire and of James P.Hall).]*
April 10: ALVERSON,WILLIAM M.,killed by a stroke of lightning during a terrible rain and thunder storm at Ditchley.
April 26:WARD,JOHN W. at his home in G'ville. In 1868 he founded the Greenville Times which after a few yrs. he sold to Capt.J.S.McNeily. He was a veteran of the Mexican War and served with the Confederate troops during the Civil War. *[1824-1905]*
May 11: TILFORD,ROBERT W., a native of Frankfort,Ky.for many yrs., a prominent figure in the social and public life of G'ville,having been Mayor and Councilman. *[d.1905]
May 18: McRAE,ROBERT STEWART, aged about 57; a native of Louisiana.
June 19:ARMSTRONG,MRS.JULIA,wife of Hugh Armstrong.
July 6: CAMPBELL,W.R., a native of Wash.Co.,son of W.R.Campbell,Sr.,an early settler. W.R.Campbell,Jr.was a member of Co.D.8th Mississippi Regiment,Wash.Co.Cavalry C.S.A.
July 14: JOHNSON,R.A., son of Henry J. and brother of Claude M., George G.Johnson and Mrs.E.H.Taylor.

*FROM: "OLD"GREENVILLE CEMETERY by Payne

DEATH NOTICES FROM THE GREENVILLE TIMES

1905

Aug.6: AIKEN,MRS.CARRIE PERRY, wife of W.B.Aiken. *[1870-1905]*
Aug.6: CROSBY,MRS.JULIA BUCHANAN, aged 69 at home of her son, Henry T.Crosby. *[1841-1905]*
Aug.7: JOHL,MRS.FANNIE, aged 73 yrs.
Aug.8: WALDAUER,EDITH MAY, little dau.of Louis and Lillie Johl Waldauer.
Aug.10:GRADY,E.D.,died in Colorado. Supt.of Wash.Co.schools formerly teacher in High School.
Sept.7: REBUHN,HENRY,at home of his dau.Mrs.Charles Roy. *[1824-1905]*
Oct.27: DUKE,MAMIE, wife of J.W.Duke at home of Mr.& Mrs.A.R.L.Duke.

1906

Jan.20:BRANDON,GERALD PHILLIPS *[1869-1906]*
Jan.20:MOYSE, LEON, survived by several sons and 2 daus.

MARRIAGE NOTICES FROM THE GREENVILLE TIMES

1890

Jan.5:WULF-BEST: Mr.Henry F.Wulf and Miss Willie F.Best, in G'ville, by Rev.G.T.Storey.
Jan.13:LEONARD-BROWNELL: Mr.J.J.Leonard of Memphis, and Miss F.E.Brownell of this city, at the Catholic Church,by Rev.Father Korstenbrock.
Jan.15:BAIRD-MONTGOMERY: Hon.T.R.Baird and Miss Annie Louise Montgomery, at Indianola,Miss., by Rev.Stevenson Archer.
Jan.21:RODWELL-LONG: Mr.William E.Rodwell and Miss Fannie Long of Yazoo City,at Yazoo City.(Ms.)
Jan.22: WINZBURG-LABENBURG: Mr.Seymour Winzburg and Miss Nettie Labenburg, at the residence of the bride's mother in Port Gibson,Miss.,by Rev.Dr.Samfield.
Jan.29: RYAN-SHANNAHAN: MR.J.J.Ryan and Miss Frances Shannahan, at the Catholic Church by Rev.P.J.Korstenbrock.
Feb.3: LAWRENCE-BEDON: Mr.James M.Lawrence and Miss Leonella Bedon,at the residence of the bride's sister,Mrs.G.B.Lancaster,by the Rev.S. Archer.
April 6: HARDY-CLOCK: Mr.Ed.B.Hardy and Miss Fannie S.Clock,at the residence of the bride's parents,by Mayor J.H.Wynn.
April 16: CRAIG-BIVINS: Mr.M.W.Craig and Miss Louise Bivins,by Rev.Dobson.
May 17: MR.&MRS.JOHN A.METCALFE reached G'ville by steamer from Vicksburg and then proceeded by skiff to Brighton Plantation where they will be at home to their friends.
May 28:BATES-DOYLE: Mr.Tunis L.Bates and Miss Madge Y.Doyle
Sept.16:SEARLES-MOUNT:Mr.T.M.Searles,of V'burg and Miss Annie E.Mount of G'ville. The bride is dau.of Mr.Thos.Mount,cashier of 1st Nat.Bank of G'ville.

*FROM: "OLD"GREENVILLE CEMETERY by Payne

MARRIAGE NOTICES FROM THE GREENVILLE TIMES

1890

Oct.15: ROY-REBHUHN: Mr.Charles Roy and Miss Lillie Rebhuhn at the residence of the bride's father, by the Rev.Stevenson Archer.
Oct.21: GRIFFIN-URQUHART: Mr.William Griffin and Miss Corinne Urquhart
Nov.12:SYKES-WILLIAMS: Mr.I.H.Sykes of Columbus,Miss.and Miss Lida Williams of this city,Rev.Granville Storey officiating.
Nov.12: AMERINE-NEELY: Capt.M.H.Amerine, of Montgomery,Ala.and Miss Effie Neely of this city,at the Poplar St.Baptist Church,by Dr.Strictland.
Nov.27:SPIERS-SHELBY, Mr.R.H.Spiers and Miss Katie Shelby,at the Methodist Ch.,by Rev.R.M.Standifer.
Dec.10:METCALFE-RICHARDSON: Mr.Frederick Metcalfe and Miss Emma Richardson,in Monroe,La.
Dec.23:HARDY-DAVIS: Dr.James W.Hardy and Miss Cora Davis,at Winterville.
Dec.25:COOVERT-SINON: Mr.John C.Coovert of this city and Miss Florence C.Sinon of Bristol,Tenn.at the home of Mr.& Mrs.W.S.Clack.

1891

Jan.20:HINDS-ALEXANDER: Mr.S.A.Hinds and Miss Mattie Alexander of Rosedale,Ms.both formerly of this city.
Feb.12:COHEN-FLETCHER:Amelia Fletcher of G'ville to Dave Cohen of Aspen,Colo.,at Temple of the Hebrew Union by Rabbi J.Bogen.
May 10: CANADA-SHORES: by Mr.Thomas J.Canada and Miss Ida Shores,
May —:BRAZELTON-THOMPSON:Mr.A.J.Brazelton and Miss Mary C.Thompson, at the residence of Mr.George Griffin, LaGrange,La.
July 30: MILAM-STOVALL: Addie Stovall,dau.of Dr.Stovall,to Capt.B.L.Milam.
Sept.3: KANATAZER-JETER:Ella Jeter to Joe Kanatzer.
Sept.24:HARBISON-SUTTON: Sarah C.Sutton to J.B.HARBISON
Nov.28:WEBB-WORTHINGTON: Carrie,2nd dau.of Geo. Worthington,to J.G.Webb.
Dec.17:PEARSON-WORTHINGTON: Francis Mona,dau.of Geo.P.Worthington to John Reed Pearson,of Jacksonville,Florida.

1892

Feb.27: HEXTER-MOYSE: Belle Hester to Alphonse Moyse,at the Synogogue.
Aug.6: GIDEN-CORDON: Eugenia K.Gordon to Mr.Wm.B.Gidden, at Port Gibson.

1893

Mar.19:DAVIS-DAVIS: Miss Lula Davis to James L.Davis in Winterville.
June 6: BENJAMIN-GOLDSMITH: Miss Rachel Goldsmith to Emanuel V. Benjamin of Cincinnatti,Ohio.
June 10: TILLOTSON-OURSLER:Miss Belle Oursler to W.W.Tillotson.
June 14: BULL-ARCHER: Alice,dau.of Rev.& Mrs.S.Archer to Samuel B.Bull,Jr.
July 6:HEBRON-DEAN, at Senatobia,Miss; Miss Lula Dean to John L.Hebron,Jr.
Oct.30:BLACKBURN-SCOTT:Dr.E.C.Blackburn and Miss Willie Scott,at the home of the bride's mother,near Wayside,Miss.

MARRIAGE NOTICES FROM THE GREENVILLE TIMES

1893

Dec.19:MILLER-VALLIANT: Mr.Harvey Miller and Miss Mary Valliant.
Dec.19: HEBB-STERLING: Mr.Hebb of Baltimore,and Miss Mary Sterling,of Lake Washington.

1894

Jan.3:WEISS-HIRSCH:MR.M.Weiss and Miss Julia Hirsch,at the Synagogue.
Jan.3:TAYLOR-JOHNSON,Mr.Edmond Taylor and Miss Bessie Johnson,at the residence of the bride's father,Dr.W.C.Johnson,Springdale,Tenn.
Jan.9:JORDAN-SMITH:Mr.C.E.Jordan and Miss Mary E.Smith,at the residence of the bride's father on Walnut St.,by Rev.T.Y.Ramsey.
Jan.15:HILZIM-LAMB: Mr.Percy T.Hilzim and Miss Georgia Lamb, at the residence of the bride's father,Mr. George Lamb,by Rev.Dr.Lewis,uncle of the groom. The honored Grandfather of the bride, Ex-Governor Robert Lowry gave the bride away.
Jan.16:BRANTON-BARRY:Mr.Peter R.Branton and Miss Ada Q.Barry of Water Valley,at the residence of Mr.John Branton on Deer Creek,by Rev.S.Archer.
Jan.24:MILLER-MORSON:Mr.Sidney S.Miller and Miss Katie B.Morson, at the residence of the bride's father on Sunflower River,Rev.S.Archer officiating.
Feb.2:KENNEDY-RYAN: Mr.John J.Kennedy and Miss Alice Ryan,at St.Peters Church in New Orleans.
Feb.6:MUSGROVE-YERGER:Mr.Edgar Musgrove of New Orleans,and Miss Carrie Yerger of G'ville,at the home of the bride's parents,by Father Korstenbrock.
April 1:JOHNSON-STONE: Mr.Ben Johnson and Miss Alice Stone, at St.James Episcopal Church by Dr.William Cross. Mr Johnson is a graduate of West Point and is now Cotton Tax Collector for the Miss.Levee Board.
April 19: CALHOON-INGRAM: Mr.Albert B.Calhoon and Miss Eva K.Ingram, at the residence of J.H.Leavenworth,by Rev.S.Archer.
April 30:McCOY-ARCHER:Mr.Will McCoy and Miss Annie Mary Archer,at the residence of the bride's father,Rev.Stevenson Archer,who officiated.
May 17: WOOD-LEWIS:Mr.Houston Davis Wood,of Franklin Co.,Ky.,and Miss Eugenia Richmond Lewis,at the residence of Dr.James M.Lewis,father of the bride,who officiated.
July 5:HENSON-STUART:Mr.A.G.Henson and Miss Willia Stuart,at Arcola.
Sept.11:SAWYER-LOWERY:MR. Ed G.Sawyer,Chief Electrician in the G'ville Electric Light works, and Miss Mattie V.Lowery, at St.James Episcopal Ch.
Oct.10: MYERS-JETER:Mr.Will Myers and Miss Dora Jeter,at the residence of the bride's brother,Mr.Thomas Jeter,by Rev.Ramsey.
Oct.14:ROBINSON-SELLARS:Mr.H.B.Robinson,of G'ville,and Miss Lela Sellars,of near Hazelhurst,Copiah Co.,Miss.,at the home of the bride's parents,Rev.B.W.Lewis officiating.

MARRIAGE NOTICES FROM THE GREENVILLE TIMES

1894

Oct.17:ROTCHILD-GENSBERGER:Mr.Louis Rotchild,of Gunnison,and Miss Helen Gensberger,at the Temple,by Rabbi Bogen.

Nov.28:JONES-BELL:Mr.J.Rabun Jones and Miss Alice Bell,at the Presbyterian Church, by Rev.S.G.Miller.

Dec.-:SHIPMAN-SHELTON:Mr.W.W.Shipman,of West Point,Miss.and Miss Amela Shelton,of G'ville.

Dec.12:MONTGOMERY-STANTON:Mr.Heddens Montgomery and Miss Annie Stanton,of Natchez,at Natchez,Miss.

1895

Mar.1:BODDIE-SHIELDS:MR.Van Buren Boddie and Miss Fay Shields,in St.James Church,Rev.George Neide,of Greenwood,Miss.officiating.

Mar.14: GILLILAND-SMYTHE: Mr.E.C.Gilliland of Memphis and Miss Jennie Smythe,by Rev.S.G.Miller.

June 8: SMITHDEAL-SMITH: Mr.George H.Smithdeal of Salisbury,N.C.,and Miss Nannie B.Smith of G'ville.

Sept.18: SENN-WETHERBEE:Ensign Thomas J.Senn of the U.S.Navy and Miss Percie Wetherbee, at the Baptist Church,Rev.M.E.Broadus officiating.

Oct.2: RIGGS-TRIGG:Mr.Frank Riggs &Miss Ellen Trigg,by Rev.R.M.Standifer.

Oct.10:JONES-BEARDSLEE: Mr.H.P.Jones of Memphis,and Miss Meta Beardslee of Swain,by Rev.D.J.M.Lewis.

Oct.-:DAMSON-SOMMER: Mr.Thomas Damson and Miss Maggie Sommer at the home of the bride's father,Rev.Father P.J.Korstenbrock officiating.

Dec.18: CLAY-CAMPBELL:Mr.Green Clay and Miss Louise Campbell at the home of the bride's mother.

1896

Jan.8: METCALFE-JEFFREYS: Mr.Harley Metcalfe and Miss Sallie Jeffreys, at St.James Church, by Rev.Quincy Ewing.

Jan.16:LAWLOR-OURSLER:Mr.James L.Lawlor and Miss Ludie Oursler,at the home of Mr.& Mrs.Tillotson,by Rev.T.Y.Ramsey.

Jan.29: JACOBS-GENSBURGER:Mr.Sam Jacobs and Miss Sara Gensburger at the Temple,by Dr.Bogen.

Feb.12:ROBINSON-DUNN:Mr.Harry C.Robinson and Miss Marian Dunn at the home of the bride's parents,by Father Korstenbrock.

May -:THOMAS-WAITE:Mr.Lloyd Thomas of G'ville,Miss Kate Waite,daughter of Mr.James Waite of this city.

May 15:RATLIFF-MATTHEWS:Mr.R.L.Ratliff of New Orleans and Mrs.R.C. Matthews,of G'ville,at the home of Mrs.D.C.Wasson,by Rev.Q.Ewing.

May 25:STONE-IREYS:Mr.Alfred Holt Stone and Miss Mary Bailey Ireys,both of G'ville, at the First Presbyterian Church,by Rev.S.Archer.

Aug.5:ISENBERG-BLOOMENSTEIL: Mr.Will Isenberg and Miss Blanche

MARRIAGE NOTICES FROM THE GREENVILLE TIMES

1896

Bloomensteil,of Port Gibson,Miss.
Sept. -: IREYS-HOGE:Mr.Henry T.Ireys and Miss Evelyn Hoge, at Ingleside,the country home of the bride's parents,Col.& Mrs.Charles E.Hoge.
Oct.28: SEEGER-FREDRICHSEN:Mr.Julius Seeger and Miss Marie Fredrichsen, at the home of the bride's parents on Broadway,by Rev.Q.Ewing.
Nov.4: KLINGMAN-BELL:Mr.E.E.Klingman and Miss Sarah Bell, at the Presbyterian Church,Dr.J.W.Primrose officiating.
Nov.11: MANN-MEYERS: Mr.Albert W.Mann and Miss Lily Meyers,at the home of the bride's mother, by Dr.J.W.Lewis.
Nov.18: HALLETT-NICHOLS: Mr.Harry Hallett and Mrs.S.A.Nichols, at Meridian,Miss. Mr.Hallett is the son of Mr.George Hallett of G'ville.
Dec.15: WOOD-JOHNSON:Mr.Emile P.Wood and Miss Lizzie Johnson,at the home of the bride,by Rev.Ewing.
Dec.29: PHILLIP-WITT:Mr.Julius Phillip of San Francisco, and Miss Lulu Witt.

1897

Jan.20: TURNER-GORDON: Mr.V.H.Turner and Miss Sarah S.Gordon,at the residence of Mr.W.B.Gidden,near Hampton,by Rev.S.Archer.
Feb.24: PEPPERMAN-ORGLER:Mr.Marx Pepperman and Miss Dora Orgler at the Temple by Dr.Bogen.
April 27,1896: REED-MEGGET:Mr.Whitmil H.Reed and Miss Bessie Megget,at St.James Episcopal Church, by Rev.Ewing.(This Notice was placed in this sequence, possibly the date 1896 is an error,and should read 1897)
May 18: WATERS-WILLIAMS: Mr.John H.Waters and Miss Cora Williams,both of G'ville,at the Baptist parsonage,by Rev.Mr.Barr.
June 9: KIRKLAND-GREGO:Mr.G.H.Kirkland and Miss Camille Grego,at Leland.
June 15: SHANDANNAIS-MYERS:Mr.Oliver Shandannais and Miss Malinda Myers,at the residence of Mrs.Charles Rogers,by Rev.W.M.Burr.
June 17: RUSSELL-McKINNEY: Mr.DeVrance Russell,of Hollandale and Miss Madie McKinney of Arcola,at the Arcola Parsonage by Rev.Mims.
July 26: SMITH-BERRY:Mr.Greenway Smith and Miss Claudia Berry,at the home of the bride's parents in Waco,Texas.
Dec.28: GOLDMAN-SCOTT:Mr.Bernard B.Goldman and Miss Hennye Scott.

1898

Jan.19: REUTER-HALLET:Mr.Max Reuter and Miss Laura Hallet,at St.Josephs Catholic Church,by Rev.P.J.Korstenbrock.
Jan.27: HARRISON-PRIMROSE:Mr.Sidney W.Harrison and Miss Sarah Primrose
Jan. -: LOYD-SKINNER: Mr.F.A.Loyd and Miss Carrie Skinner,dau.of a prominent G'ville attorney.
Mar.17: TODD-CARLETON: Mr.Miller Todd,employed by the Government and stationed on the Government Fleet,and Miss Sue Carleton of Chicot Co.,Ark.

MARRIAGE NOTICES FROM THE GREENVILLE TIMES

1898

Mar.24:CORNISH-WYCHE: Mr.Jeff Cornish and Miss Devereux Wyche, at the home of the bride's brother and sister, by Dr.J.E.Thomas of the Meth.Ch.
April -:RICE-LAWSON:Mr.S.A. Rice of Hillsboro,Texas and Miss Florence A.Lawson, at the residence of the bride's father and mother in Leota.
April 14: McCUTCHEN-HARBISON:Mr.S.Proctor McCutchen and Miss Georgia Lee Harbison at the Presby.Ch.,by Rev.J.W.Primrose.
April 20:SMITH-DUDLEY:Mr.L.Pink Smith &Miss Anna Dudley of Gonzales,Tex.
May 29:FASS-BERGMAN:Mr.Nathan Fass &Miss Lillian Bergman at theTemple.
June _ :LESSER-FLETCHER:Mr.Julius Lesser and Miss Sara Fletcher,-Temple.
Oct.12:BORODOFSKY-GENSBERGER :Mr.J.S.Borodofsky of Arcola and Miss Flora Gensberger of G'ville at the Temple by Dr.Joseph Bogen.
Nov.23:DETERLY-MANN: Mr.M.S.Deterly and Miss Carrie Mann,at the home of the bride's parents.
Nov.23:ZADEK-WOOLF:Mr.I.Zadek of New Orleans and Miss Katie Woolf.

1899

Jan.19:WASSON-OLIVER:Mr.Ben F.Wasson and Miss Rebekah Oliver at the home of the bride in Woodbury,Tenn.
Jan.24:NEWMAN-WOOLF:Mr.Adolp Newman and Miss Bella Woolf of St.Louis.
Jan.-:CHILDRESS-ADAMS:Mr.C.S.Childress and Miss Julia Adams, at the Presbyterian Church by Rev.S.Archer.
Feb.2:HARRIS-CADENHEAD:Mr.C.E.Harris and Miss Maggie Cadenhead,at the residence of Mrs.W.H.Cadenhead,by Rev.Wm.Burr.
Feb.6:SOMMER-RHOMER: Mr.Ludwig Philip Sommer and Miss Agnes Rhomer.
Feb.8:McCLAIN-VAUGHT,Mr.Daniel L.McClain and Miss Mary Belle Vaught, at the residence of Mrs.Mary P.Vaught,by Rev.Korstenbrock.
Feb.14:KEENAN-HALL:Mr.Edward Keenan,Jr.of New Orleans and Miss Fannie Hall, at Leota House,by Rev.Archer.
Mar.9:WILKINSON-KIMBALL: Mr.Charles L.Wilkinson of Huntington,Miss.and Miss Alberta Kimball of Ark.,at the Hotel Newman.
April 4:ESKRIGGE-VALLIANT,Mr.Herbert Eskrigge and Miss Louise Valliant, at St.James Episcopal Church.
June 8:GILLESPIE-VAUGHN: MR.Charles G.Gillespie and Miss Edith Vaughn at the St.James Episcopal Ch.by Dr.Q.Ewing.
June 8: MONTGOMERY-ROBERTSON: Dr.S.A.Montgomery of Baird-Smith Company and Miss Pattie Robertson of Forest,Miss.
June 14:GARY-CROWELL:Mr.Albert Gary and Miss Lily Crowell- Baptist Ch.
Aug.16:RICHARDSON-JACKSON: Mr.Cabell Breckenridge Richardson,Jr. and Miss Josie Dele Jackson at the Methodist Church.
Oct.17:HARBISON-GEORGE: Mr.R.Taylor Harbison,Jr. and Miss Susie George.
Oct.11: BARRETT-MERRILL: Mr.Lucien Barrett and Miss Emma Merrill.

WASHINGTON CO.,MISS.
WILL BOOK "2"

P.1:**WILL OF C.P.NEILSON** ,decd.(Charles Purvis Neilson) of Greenville- "sound of mind but bad physical health". Denies ownership of "The Neilson Building",stating that the land on which the building sits, was bought "by my wife with her own money...the building was erected under contract made with her and the payments arranged by her alone...my only means of support for me and my family for last 3 yrs." Will names Wife:NANNIE SIMS NEILSON,exectx. WILL written 13 Mar.1894-Filed 19 Apr.1894. Witnessed by J.S.WALKER,G.R.DELAUREAL,M.D.LANDAU. The county clerk is C.M.JOHNSON,with J.A.SHALL,Dep.Clk.[**Note**: C.P.NEILSON was a confederate soldier.]

P.2:**WILL OF ROBERT H.BUCKNER** :decd. Written 29 Dec.1845-Filed Hinds Co.,Ms.Dec.Term 1846-Recorded Wash.Co.,Ms.16 May 1894: Instructs exec.to pay his debts out of sale of his law library, reserving "Rents and Blackstones Commentaries" and "Stephens Pleadings" for my sons. Collect debts owed by Storm and Roberts, and from Stephen Jackson, and from Smith debt and the Bierne case. Asks exects.to sell Washington Co.Plantation and wild lands there and invest near T.FREELAND's place in La.so his hands may be transferred and overseen by MR.T.or MR.F.A.FREELAND for the benefit of"my family". Sell land in Yazoo Co., bought at the sheriff's sale from JAMES M.SMITH. All proceeds to go toward the education of his children, each child to receive his or her share as they reach their majority. Wife and children to share equally,with his wife taking her share when the youngest child is 21. Names servants WASHINGTON, LUCINDA, JULIET, LOUISA, AARON, CHARITY, HENRIETTA. WIFE:SARAH F.BUCKNER,grdn.of children,unless she remarries,then the Grdnp.switches immediately to AYLETTE BUCKNER of Natchez,or THOMAS FREELAND of Claib.Co.,Ms. He states that he has daughters,(unnamed); a son THOMAS FREELAND BUCKNER to get his gold watch + other things; son ROBERT H.,JR. to get his private library. Names as Exect.THOMAS FREELAND and wife-SARAH. Witnesses to authenticity of sd.Will:C.S.TARPLEY,W.F.SLOAN,A.L.DABNEY. (Clerk of Hinds Co.,Raymond,Ms.W.W.DOWNING,Dep.Clk.-W.H.SIMS.)Will recorded Hinds Co.Will Bk."1" p.195.[**Note**: Robert H.Buckner, Chancelor of State Chancery Court,was b.1802, marr.Sarah Fielding Freeland in 1830. Issue:Thos.Freeland; Emily Emma;Sarah Roberta;Robert H.,Jr. ;Kate;Nellie. Sarah (Freeland) Buckner,who decd.Claib.Co.,Ms.1892, was the dau.of Thomas and Emily (Willis)Freeland, and had 2 brothers-Thos. and Frisby Augusta Freeland.]

P.4:**WILL OF DOLLY HINES**; decd. Sister:Eliza Evans,resident of Port Gibson,Ms. Rev.Geo.W.Gaylor of Gagesville,Bolivar Co.,Ms.as Exect. Wit:N.C. TAYLOR,D.S.TAYLOR,O.L.GARRETT. Written 28 Jan.1893;Filed 20 Aug.1894.

WASHINGTON CO.,MISS.
WILL BOOK "2"

P.5: **WILL OF ALEXANDER M.JEWELL:** of Warren City,Trumbull Co.,Ohio. Asks that the Exects ROBERT H.JEWELL and SAML.L.KERR set aside $500 to erect a monument "at my grave". Wife:REBECCA C.JEWELL to keep their home in Warren,Ohio: Son-in-law:SAMUEL L.KERR; 2 sons JOHN D.JEWELL, WM.A. JEWELL to get the land in Wash.Co.,Ms. provided they pay the notes to Mary Hull,Rebecca Bell,John Cratsley. Son-ROBERT H.JEWELL who has already received proceeds from sale of Sanford Tyler Farm,which we sold to JESSE HALL. Daughters:SARAH J.KERR;LOUISA J.VEACH;MARY J.JEWELL (in feeble health). Grand children:ALBERT KERR,ALICE KERR,EMMA KERR,CHAUNCEY A.JEWELL. Written 6 Mar.1885-Filed Trumbull Co.,Ohio 18 Sept.1886.Wit: Albert Yearmans,T.W.Case who stated that A.M.Jewell decd.23 Feb.1886. Filed Wash.Co.,Ms. 4 Oct.1894.

P.12: **WILL OF MARY W.VAN NORMAN**:of Little Rock,Ark.,Pulaski Co.,living at #1202 Corner Izard and 12th Sts.-11 Nov.1882. "My 2 children living with me"-LULA WILSON VAN NORMAN and THOMAS BENJAMINE VAN NORMAN to get 2/3rd part of all holdings in Ark. Other 4 children: MRS.KATE E.GAN- AWAY and ELIZA E.VAN NORMAN of Fort Smith,Ark.;JAMES V.VAN NORMAN of Summitt,Miss.; ROBERT LESTER VAN NORMAN of Little Rock,Ark. Lula and Thos. Benj.must maintain and care for their father,CYRENUS C.VAN NORMAN. 1/3rd of Thos.Benj.'s inheritance to go toward 3 yrs.schooling.If he refuses to go,then the 1/3rd reverts to the youngest child of ISAIAH W.BRUCE,name - BIRDIE, of Fort Smith,Ark. Exects.: Husband, Cyrenus and Isaiah W.Bruce. Wit:John Ingram,Mrs.Fannie McDaniel,both of Little Rock, Ark.// CODICIL: 4 Mar.1884: Leaves Lot in Redfield,Ark.to Robert Lester Van Norman; other children-Kate,Eliza,James to get $10 unless James comes to visit her. Remainder of Est.to be divided between Thomas Benjamine and Lula,now Lula W.McLaughlin + 94 ac.in Bolivar Co.,Ms. Mary states in sd. Codidil that her husband Cyrenus is now decd.,and asks that W.F.Blackwood replace him as exect.//Filed 28 May 1891 in Ark.//Filed Wash.Co.,Ms.15 Nov.1894.

P.15:**WILL OF BELLE L.HARTMAN:** Written 21 Jan.1891-Filed 8 July 1895: Daughter:NETTIE not yet 21,to get "my diamond ring,ruby ring,my mother's watch";Husband LEE HARTMAN to be exect.;My baby NANCY to get necklace; Son MARSY 6 silver spoons + 1 dozen other spoons. (She refers to all my children,so there may be others.) Wit: E.G.Marshall,Louis &Joseph Waldauer.

P.16: **WILL OF HATTIE T.BALDWIN:** (OLOGRAPHIC WILL) New.Orleans,La. 4 May 1893. Exect.,husband,G.A.BALDWIN,property in La. and Miss.// There . is an application of MRS.MARTHA BALDWIN et als,before Fred D.King,Judge,

WASHINGTON CO., MISS.
WILL BOOK "2"

for admission of WILL. Wit:Charles C.Gilmore,Daniel Fulton,same date.//
Filed:15 July 1895 in New Orleans;14 Sept.1895 Wash.Co.,Ms.

P.18:WILL OF HELEN L.MORRIS :of Wash.Co. Written 14 June 1892.
Husband WM.M.MORRIS to get everything. Probated Mar.Term 1896. Wit:E.V. MORRIS,W.C.MORRIS who recognize the signature of their mother.
[Chanc.Clerk,Wash.Co.   Thos.H.Hood,Dep.Clk.W.W.Miller]

P.19:WILL OF RACHEL BRANDT: Written 26 Aug.1893
Husband:A.BRANDT; Daughter:JENNIE CARO wife of HENRY CARO, exect.
Son:ISADORE BRANDT; Wit:LOUIS D.HARRIS, LOUIS BRANDT
Recorded Shelby Co.,Tenn.,Memphis 17 Feb.1896
Recorded Wash.Co.,Ms. 24 Feb.1896

P.22: WILL OF KITTIE BOLDIER ,resident of Winterville,Wash.Co.,Ms.
Daughter:ROSE CORPAL - Son: WARREN BOLDIER; Kittie owned 10 ac.in
Bolivar Co.,Ms.known as "Boldier's Place"bought by her late husband ROBERT BOLDIER. Wit: O.L.GARRETT,PETER GREW,HENRY BROWN.
WRITTEN:14 MAR.1895: Recorded 20 Mar.1896.

P.24:WILL OF SEDDON AIKEN: Written 29 Apr.1893
Mother: MARTHA GILES AIKEN to get all property in Miss. & Va.
Wit: J.M.JAYNE,H.C.WATSON - Recorded 30 May 1896 in Wash.Co.,Ms.

P.26: WILL OF MAGGIE KENNEDY of Greenville (She owned Lots in towns of Greenville,Leland,Arcola-Wash.Co.,Ms.)¶To:WILLIAM KENNEDY of St.Louis, Mo.to get land in Wash.Co.;¶Late Husband: EDWARD KENNEDY,decd.;
¶Niece: FRANCES LEONARD of Chicago;¶Mother of late husband, MRS. MARGARET KENNEDY of Ireland to get town Lot 8,Block 3 in Leland and at Margaret's death it will revert to her(Margaret's)daughter,ALICE KENNEDY;
¶To:BRIDGET IGO,"the little girl who lives with me",a Lot in G'ville on Poplar St. bought by John Hanway &the late Edward Kennedy from Wm.Green;
¶Niece: MRS. JENNIE CHAFULL (CHAPELL ?) of W.Plains,Mo.;
¶Niece:MRS.CARRIE NEWSOM, dau.of JENNIE CHAFULL-the Fish Lake Place;
¶Gr.Niece:ADDIE NEWSOM,dau.of Carrie;
¶To:MARGARET KENNEDY,dau.of JOHN KENNEDY of G'ville;
¶To:My father FRANCIS BIGGINS of G'ville. Asks that a monument be placed on her grave in G'ville Cemetery beside her late husband,also one on the grave of her father when he dies. Written 20 Feb.1896 - Probated 20 Aug.1896. Wit:JAMES ROBERTSHAW,P.J.KORSTENBRACK [See Obit.this Vol.]

WASHINGTON CO., MISS.
WILL BOOK "2"

P.31: **WILL OF WM.H.BABTIST:** of Village of Belzoni, Wash.Co., Ms.
Wife: <u>ELLA BABTIST</u>, to get land in Sec.2, T15, R3W. Nephews: <u>JAMES WILLIAMS</u>
and <u>EDWARD POWHANTAN BUFORD</u> Written 21 Feb., 1895-Prob. 19 Sept. 1896
Wit: S.CASTLEMAN, A.R. TURNER.
[Note: Belzoni and the land described above, are now in Humphreys Co.]

P.32: **WILL OF ROBERT GRAY CAMPBELL:** Written: 29 Sept. 1888
Wife: <u>PATTIE ROFF CAMPBELL</u> to be Exect. and Grdn. of minor children
Son: <u>ROBERT GRANVILLE CAMPBELL</u>-Dau: <u>AMITE BAIER CAMPBELL</u>
Wit: CHARLES H.EVANS, DeWITT M.COLEMAN at Springfield, Greene Co., Mo.,
where WILL was filed 4 Apr. 1895: WILL filed Dallas Co., Mo. 15 Feb. 1896
WILL filed Wash.Co., Miss. 3 Oct. 1896.

P.38: **WILL OF MATTHEW F.HUGGINS:** of Wash.Co., "being sick and weak"...
Wife: <u>JENNIE HUGGINS</u>-2 children of said Jennie, "begotten by me"(unnamed)
"My dau.<u>LAURA HALL</u>", wife of <u>HENRY HALL</u> to get 1/4th of his estate
Exect.: MORRIS COHN of Belzoni, Ms. Written 25 Mar. 1896- Wit: CHARLES
H.MORRIS, WM.CRAVEN, seeking Probation of sd.WILL, appear before Justice
of Peace S.CASTLEMAN on 8 May 1896 - WILL recorded 22 Oct. 1896.

P.40: **WILL OF DAVE L.LEYSER:** " now lying ill at St.Joseph Hospital in
Memphis, but a resident of G'ville, Miss." Will written 11 Feb. 1897.
Wife: <u>HELEN LEYSER</u>, Exectx.
Wit: LEE HIRSCH, E.P.SALE, JOHN HENLEY-Recorded Wash.Co. 17 Feb. 1897

P.42: **WILL OF S.W.FOGO:** Written: 4 Nov. 1892, New Orleans, La.
To my cousins: <u>ELISE URGUHART, ALICE ROSALIE URGUHART, ISABEL WILKINS
URGUHART</u>, the money invested in their home at #1305 St.Charles Ave, New
Orleans. + 3/4ths interest in "Belzoni Plantation" in Wash.Co., Ms.
Aunt: <u>MISS M.A.WILKINS</u> - Cousin: <u>CHARLES T.URGUHART.</u>
Probated: 29 April 1897

P.43: **WILL OF JOHN D.JEWELL**, of Wash.Co., Ms. Written: 27 Jan. 1891
Wife: <u>JOSEPHINE H.JEWELL</u>-Wit: A.S.OLIN, W.A.POLLOCK-Recorded: July, 1897

P.43: **WILL OF JOSEPH WILCZINSKI:** of G'ville-Written: 11 July 1890
Wife: <u>JULIA</u> to get all real estate in G'ville; Brothers: <u>HERMAN, JAKE,
NATHAN WILCSINSKI</u>; Daughters: <u>SADIE JOSIE</u> and <u>ESTELLA</u> to get land on
Lake Washington and Swan Isle known as "The Arlington Plantation",
"The Emma Plt." and the "Cain" and "Hill" Plts. + 1/2 of "Marathon Plt."

WASHINGTON CO.,MISS.
WILL BOOK "2"

Sons:JOEL FRANK and PERCY to get land on Fish Lake known as "Wickliffe" and "Valliant Plts.", the "Clary Place", and land formerly belonging to Capt. Jack, the "Matilda Plt."- all to be kept in trust until Percy is 25 yrs.old. Sons also to get divided int. in merchantile business,'Wilcsinski & Reiser'. Sister:BERTHA FABIAN living in New York
Wit:B.F.LENGSFIELD,J.C.GOLDMAN,W.YERGER. Probated: 2 Aug.1897
[Note: There was no punctuation between names of daus. or of sons.]

P.47:WILL OF R.L.WRIGHT: Written:11 Aug.1897
Wife:MRS.G.G.(S.S.?)WRIGHT;Son:J.W.WRIGHT,Exect.,to get land on W.side of Murphy Bayou.;Daus:MAGGIE O.BAGGET and MARY R.EPPERSON
Sons:A.L.WRIGHT and RICHARD L.WRIGHT; Dau:FLORENCE E.WRIGHT-her property to be managed by J.W.WRIGHT as she "is incompetent".
Wit:DR.A.MILLER,B.T.WINTER - WILL Prob.23 Aug.1897

P.51: WILL OF MARTHA R.BLANTON of G'ville. Written 28 Apr.1896
Sister:FANNIE HARRIET SMITH;Dau: GEORGIE GREENWAY FINLAY
Gr.ch.:LAVINIA LANGHORN DABNEY, HARRIET LOUISE DABNEY, JOHN DABNEY
Husband:ORVILLE M.BLANTON; Gr.Ch.:ORVILLE PELHAM FINLAY, HELEN MARGARET FINLAY, SAML.D.FINLAY, LOLA BELLE FINLAY, SARAH STONE WALKER. Part of the property named in WILL was "Belle Air Plt." bounded on S.by Magnolia St.,extending W.to Miss.River,and E.by Poplar in G'ville.
Wit:MRS.MARY E.CAPERS,GEORGIANA KIRK, appeared before Morris Rosenstock,J.P. WILL Probated 18 Sept.1897.[Note: Buried "Old" G'ville Cem.
Martha Rebecca Blanton 1826-1897/Orville Martin Blanton 1828-1911/ Georgia Blanton Finlay 1857-1925/]

P.56:WILL OF F.P.MONTGOMERY: of Penn Valley,Nevado Co.,Calif.
Written 3 July 1893 - Recorded Wash.Co.,Ms.26 Aug.1897
Niece:SALLIE A.MONTGOMERY of same,sole Exectx.to get everything.
Wit:H.B.EVERETT,Kent,Sutter Co.,Calif.; C.L.BROWN,1002 Polk St.,San Francisco,Calif.

P.57:WILL OF NANNIE I.PERCY: ,lived on Broadway & Percy Ave.
4 ch;LEROY,WM.A.,WALKER,LADY who lives in Knoxville,Tn.(to get painting of her mother and sister)Written:18 June 1894 - Recorded: 29 Sept.1897

P.58:WILL OF JOHN HANWAY: Written 2 Feb.1894-Recorded 19 Oct.1897
4 Children:JULIA,MARY, JOHN, TIMOTHY; Trustees for children: JAMES E.NEGUS, H.C.WATSON; Wife:ANNIE to be Admx. and Grdn. for minor children

WASHINGTON CO.,MS.
WILL BOOK "2"
Sister:ANNIE CARRIGAN and her daus.,now residing 28th Fontenay St., Dublin,Ireland. Wit:T.W.McCAY,A.B.NANCE,H.C.WATSON

P.60:WILL OF SAMUEL NURSE: of G'ville, Written 16 Feb.1893
Wife:HARRIET NURSE,Exectx. Probated 10 Dec.1897

P.61:WILL OF BRIT FAIRCHILD: of Wash.Co.,Ms.,also owned real estate in Sharkey Co.,Ms. Son:CHARLES HENRY FAIRCHILD, Adm. Dau:SUSAN BANKS Wife:SALLIE (to get $5,they have been divorced 6 or 7 yrs.)
Written:22 Feb.1897 - Prob.:22 Dec.1897
Wit: P.M.ALEXANDER, JOHN T.CASEY.

P.62:WILL OF CHARLES G.WALKER , 607 Alexander St.,G'ville,Miss. Brother:GEORGE D.WALKER,of Mobile,to get my interest in patent of W.A.Ragsdale,now pending in Wash.,D.C.; Neice:ANNIE WALKER;Nephew:GEO. D.WALKER,JR.; Sister-in-law:MARCELITE. Refuses to acknowledge any other heirs. Written 3 July 1897 - Prob.:1 Jan.1898
Wit: JOHN H.MOORE, W.B.MEISNER

P.63:WILL OF MARY R.HORN Written 5 Feb.1898.¶Sister:MRS.BETTIE H.NELSON, of Dallas,Tx.,whose husband is now decd.,to get Lot #3,Block 10,Batchelors Bend Addition,G'ville,Miss.¶To:MRS.FANNY A.SEARS,*wife of REV.P.G.SEARS of Holly Springs,Ms.; ¶To:MASTER CLAUD SEARS*; ¶To:FRANCES SPEARS*;¶To:MRS.MARY M.M.THOMAS of Mayersville,Ms. and MRS.FLORENCE CHARLES of Clinton,Ms. -notes made out to Carrie C. and J.H.Fox of Clinton;¶To:MARY LINDERMAN of Fayette,Ala.;¶To:JESSE NELSON; ¶To:ROBERT PARISH of Greenwood,Ms.;¶To:RUTH DOUGLAS of 755 Government St.,Mobile,Ala.;¶To:EARL DOUGLAS of Mobile,Ala.¶The Exect.,Rev.P.G. SPEARS*, is to place a monument at mother's grave in Clinton,Miss.and a shaft-4 sided at the base,engraved with the names, dates,births,deaths of "my father,mother,brother and sister OSSIE and MAGGIE". My father is buried in Natchez,but I want his name on this stone. Also erect a stone over me to match my husband's and bury me beside him in Clinton. Wit:H.C. WALTERS, HUGH R.BROWN. Prob.:Marshall Co.,Miss.10 Feb.1898-Wash.Co.,17 Feb.1898. *Name spelled interchangeably SEARS-SPEARS
[NOTE: Cemetery Records,Clinton,Miss. *Mary R.Nash, wife of Dr.Robert Horn,b.Natchez,d.Holly Springs 22 Mar.1831-7 Feb.1898// Dr.J.R. Horn b.Edgecombe Co.,N.C. 3 Apr.1827-d.22 May 1881//Orsa Long son of Orsa L.and Maria L.Nash b Columbia,Miss.12 May 1835-d.6 Nov.1867//Rev.Orsamus Long Nash,buried Natchez, b.2 Dec.1802 d.8 Aug.1853//Maggie Nash Archer, dau.of Orsa L.and Maria*

WASHINGTON CO.,MS.
WILL BOOK "2"

L.Nash, b.Columbia,Miss 23 Feb.1846-d.28 Apr.1879//Maria Louisa, wife of Rev.Orsa L.Nash 3 Sept.1809-22 June 1871]

P.68:**WILL OF SARAH A.HAVEMEYER:** (Spelling of surname sometimes looks like Hoormeyer) of New York,N.Y.,widow of WM.F.HAVEMEYER,who lives on N.Easterly side of 14th St.,between 8th and 9th Ave.
¶Sons:JOHN C.; JAMES; WILLIAM; CHARLES and his children JULIA L. and LOOMIS by his wife JULIA IDA HAVEMEYER;¶and my decd.son HENRY who had daus.and sons.¶My Daus:SARAH C.ARMSTRONG; LAURA A.MaCLOY ;¶Son,James to get portraits of sister AMELIA, grandfather MR.H.CRAIG, SARAH and husband in HECTOR'S room,and also portrait of gr.father WM. HAVEMEYER.
¶Son to get certificate showing their father was once the Mayor of N.Y.
¶Gr.son:WILLIE ARMSTRONG;¶Gr.Dau:SARAH AGNES HAVEMEYER, dau.of JAMES.¶Exect.:JOHN C.HAVEMEYER-Written:New York 27 June 1891
Wit:WM.SCHNEIDER, LEMUEL SKIDMORE// CODICIL: 9 June 1894-rearranges gifts,no new heirs listed.Witnesses attest to authenticity of sd.WILL:25 Feb.1895-New York//Probate Court:(N.Y) Proof of WILL names the following heirs that appeared at the hearing: ¶JOHN C.HAVEMEYER,exect.and his attorney Lemuel Skidmore in support of proof of WILL;¶CHAS.W.HAVEMEYER "one of heirs and next of kin of sd.decd.";¶Gilbert M.Speir,Jr.-Special Grdn.of GORDON LEROY BURCHATIM,minor,one of the heirs and next of kin;
¶Almet F.Jenks, Special Grdn.to EDYTHE HAVEMEYER,WM.F.HAVEMEYER,JULIA HAVEMEYER,LOOMIS HAVEMEYER minors,gr.children and legatees. No others appeared.//WILL Probated Wash.Co.,Miss. 25 Mar.1898

P.86:**WILL OF JOHN M.FRANCIS:** of Troy,Rensselaer Co.,N.Y.,18 Nov.1896
Sis:ELEANOR J.CRIBB,wife of the late JOS.P.CRIBB,of Naples,Ontaria Co,N.Y.
¶To:Children of sd.Eleanor;¶To:Children of late sister AMMIE H.TUTHILL
¶Sis:MRS.MARTHA LAMPMAN,now residing with my niece MRS.HATTIE M. BROWN,wife of ALFRED BROWN in town of Pultney,Steuben Co.,N.Y.
¶Nephew:JOHN S.PARKER of Prattsburg,Steuben Co.,N.Y.;¶Nephew:EDGAR B.LAMHEIR of Union City,Pa.;¶To:WM.F.McLEAN of Prattsburg - Exect.
¶To:WM.B.WILSON of Troy,N.Y.;¶Gr.Children:JOHN M. and HARRIET-children of my son CHAS.S.FRANCIS;¶Gr.Ch.;JOHN FRANCIS HAVEMEYER and HARRIET FRANCIS HAVEMEYER children of my dau. ALICE A.HAVEMEYER;
¶Son:CHARLES S.FRANCIS to get the Francis Family sideboard, dated 1705.
¶Gr.Son:POMEROY T.FRANCIS;¶Gr.son:JOHN FRANCIS HAVEMEYER;¶The decd., John M.Francis,owned interest in "The Troy Daily Times" and "Troy Weekly Times". Wit:JOHN H.PECK,JAMES H.POTTS - Troy,N.Y.
Probated:Troy,N.Y. 22 Sept.18 - Wash.Co.,Miss. 9 Apr.1898

WASHINGTON CO.,MS.
WILL BOOK "2"

P.94:WILL OF ED EBERT; of Paducah,Ms.(Wash.Co.) Written 10 Mar.1898
"I will my place house horse and everything to my cook LIZZIE HARRIS"
Recorded:9 Apr.1898

P.95:WILL OF JOANNA P.HARSHE ,of G'ville-Written 11 Apr.1894
Dau:ANNIE H.LEE wife of J.M.LEE; Son:M.N.HARSHE
Wit:K.H.NELMS,LOUIS VORMUS,J.B.BELL. Probated:20 May 1898

P.96:WILL OF MARGARITE MANIFOLD of G'ville - Written 10 Apr.1898
Niece:MARGARITE ESTHER HUGHES-her mother LELIA B.HUGHES to be Exectx.
Proof of WILL:R.W.TILFORD,age 44,living G'ville,had known the decd.18
yrs.,attested to her signature. Probated:9 Jan.1899.

P.97:WILL OF JAMES A.DEATON, of G'ville-Written 12 Dec.1898
Wife:KATHERINE C.DEATON, land in Wash.Co., and "Point Chicot Plantation"
in Chicot Co.,Ark.Wit:J.D.SMYTHE,C.M.CURRELL,EMMA K.HYDE,FANNY V.GORDON
Probated:25 Jan.1899

P.98:WILL OF N.C.SKINNER ,of G'ville- Written 1 Jan.1898
Wife:ELIZA NEILSON SKINNER to be exectx. and to get everything as he has
already provided for his children by his 1st wife,now decd.,and knows that
Eliza N. will provide for their children. Wit:N.S.NELSON, L.PINK SMITH
Probated:27 Feb.1899

P.100:WILL OF T.B.COWAN, of "Esperanza",Issa Co.,Ms..7 June 1899
To all his 1st cousins who come forward and identify themselves to get
$25 each.Friend:WM.R.TAYLOR of"Esperanza",everything in Stocks-@$20,000
Friend:PAUL L.MANN who "now lives with me on 'Esperanza'" to get 4
Plantations in Issa.Co.-"Lakeside","Hopedale","Fairy Field", "Esperanza".
Exect.:P.L.MANN-Wit:W.G.ALLEN,E.M.JORDAN,J.T.DONAHOE
Probated: Issa.Co.,Ms.1 Aug.1899 - Wash.Co.,Ms.11 Aug.1899

P.103:WILL OF CLARISSA GRIFFIN , age 89, resident of G'ville
To my adopted dau: VIOLA YOUNG, the child of PAUL and FANNIE YOUNG, who
was born Aug.27,1890. Exect.:PAUL YOUNG and C.R.YOUNG of G'ville
Wit:NAT JOHNSON,MAJOR DAVIS;Written:6 July 1899-Probated 30 Aug.1899

P.105:WILL OF FRANK BECK,JR. - Parish of Orleans,La. 7 July 1886
This WILL was dictated to JOHN BENDMAGE,Notary Public: "My name is
Frank Beck,Jr. I am 34 yrs.old, mother and father both dead, never married,

WASHINGTON CO.,MS.
WILL BOOK "2"

no heirs"- leaves everything to JAMES ALEXANDER MAXWELL and HARRIET MARIAS MAXWELL, his wife.
Probated: New Orleans 23 May 1899 - Wash.Co.,Ms.27 June 1899

P.108: **WILL OF MARTHA JOHNSON** of Wash.,Co.Ms.
Son:CLINTON, after his death, the 11 ac.in town of G'ville to go to his children. He is to be exect.; Son:CHARLES,whose children get $10 each. Grandchildren: unnamed. Wit:J.C.GRENSBY,S.C.BELL,JR.
Written:15 Dec.1898 - Probated 14 Sept.1899

P.109:**WILL OF JOSEPH UHL:** of G'ville-Written 11 July 1899
¶Sis.-in-law:LEANNE KAPPS of G'ville;¶Exect.: JAMES E.NEGUS, to act as trustee for the bank Stock Dividends to be paid to Leanne Kapps.¶Sister in Chicago to receive Insurance Policy in Memphis;¶Sister:JOSEPHINE DIETRICH in Rattwriiter,Germany,who has a dau.¶To:THOMAS C.HOLMES -Masonic Jewels and watch + other items that belonged to Thomas's mother which Joseph states that he was holding + money and other things for Thomas from his mother;¶Nephew:ADOLPH;¶To: Wife of James E.Negus-$100 for "the purpose for which she knows";¶To:WILL E.NEGUS-stamp collection; ¶Sister:BONA NAST of Chicago. Wit:J.H.LEAVENWORTH,T.W.McCOY,A.B.NANCE
Probated:Wash.Co.,Ms.18 Oct.1899

P.112: **WILL OF MARY M.L.MORGAN,** of Wash.Co.,Ms.-Written 21 Mar.1895
Dau:M.L.HOOD,Exect.; Gr.Dau:O.L.MASSEY,should she reach age 12,to use money for her education. Wit:B.P.SHELBY,JAMES E.NEGUS,T.W.McCOY
Probated:4 Oct.1899

P.113:**WILL OF JOHN J.KENNEDY:** Written 11 Nov.1899,G'ville
Wife:ALICE RYAN KENNEDY- Exectx.& Grdn.; Dau:BYRL; Unborn child of Wife ALICE. Wit:P.J.KOSTENBROOK, DR.S.R.DUNN, J.D.SMYTHE

P.115:**WILL OF WILLIAM GWIN YERGER:** G'ville-Written 4 June 1896
¶Wife: JENNIE, dwelling house and Lots "we occupy"-3rd Addition, G'ville, Blanton Park Block, from Broadway to Wash.Ave., embracing Lots 1 and 2, deeded from Mrs. Theobald in 1886 to Mrs.Bernie Moore.¶Nephew and Namesake:WILLIAM GWIN YERGER,JR.;¶Namesake:WILLIAM GWIN RUCKS; ¶Sister-in-law:MISS ANNA HUNTER;¶My 3 children: MARY LOUISE WHEATLY, WILLIAM NUGENT YERGER, JENNIE YERGER;¶Son:JIMMIE who is deceased (very eloquent eulogy)//CODICIL:Written:13 Apr.1899, records gift to daughter JENNIE on her wedding day. No wit.listed. Filed 22 Nov.1899

WASHINGTON CO.,MS.
WILL BOOK "2"

[Note: From "Old"Greenville Cem. by Payne: *Wm.Gwin Yerger 1840-1899 Jennie Hunter Yerger 1842-1920/Mary Louise Yerger Wheatley 1868-1933/George Wheatley 1863-1937/Wm.Nugent Yerger 1869-1908/James A.Yerger 1872-1893 /Jennie Yerger Wilson 1875-1918/ Samuel Burton Wilson 1872-1937*]

P.118:WILL OF SALLIE J.SMYTHE , temporarily stopping at Rockbridge Alum Springs, Va., but living in G'ville,Ms.-Written 11 Sept.1899
¶3 children:JAMES S.SMYTHE, SADIE LOIS SMYTHE, ROSCOE SMYTHE
¶Husband:DR.J.D.SMYTHE,Exect.;¶Sister:MRS.E.C.GILLILAND (She and Sallie owned property jointly) There was property in Leake Co.,Ms., + Timberland in Wash.Co.,Ms. Her home address in G'ville-N.E.Corner of Broadway & Valliant Ave. Wit:WM.R.JONES,JR; ROBERT TALLEY;EDMOND WADDELL,JR.
Filed:30 Dec.1899

P.122:WILL OF FRANK S.ALDRIDGE : Written 13 Feb.1900
Wife:LUCY P.,Exect.and Grdn.; 3 ch.unnamed; WIT:A.J.PAXTON,JR., SAML.B.PAXTON, MATTIE D.WINGFIELD. Filed: 6 Apr.1900

P.123:WILL OF B.P.SHELBY : Written 8 June 1889, No witnesses
Everything to REBECCA W.BLACKBURN; GEORGE F.BLACKBURN - Exect.
Filed: 6 Apr.1900

P.124: WILL OF EDWIN H.FAY: signed at Stilleman Female Collegiate Institute- Written 1 May 1880-Owned 100 ac.of land called "Needmore" + 100 ac.known as "The Ranton Tract" + 80 ac opposite the city of Montgomery,Ala. Wife SARAH SHIELD,Exectx; Children-unnamed//
CODICIL: written 1 May 1880: Clinton,La. names Son:CHARLES SPENCER FAY
Wit:ELLA CARPENTER, LIZZIE FONGER of E.Feliciana Parish,La.
Filed: 5 Apr.1900,E.Felic.P.,La.- Wash.Co.,Ms.27 Apr.1900

P.125:WILL OF SAMUEL BAREFIELD: Written 19 Aug.1891
¶Dau:MRS.C.O.McKINNEY, land in Sec.8,T15,R6W;¶Son:ROBERT A.BAREFIELD, land in Sec.9,T15,R6W;¶Dau:MARIAH L.RYALS, land in Sec.9,T15,R6W
All land located in "Barefield Colony";¶Sons:SAMUEL MARION BAREFIELD, STEPHEN A.BAREFIELD to be exects.¶Wife of Son STEPHEN - ELLA
¶Children of Son, STEPHEN:MAY BIRD, LUCILE,SARAH JONES BAREFIELD.
¶Wife:CATHERINE H.BAREFIELD - Wit:J.V.CHURCH,J.A.STINSON,F.C.BRICKLEY
Filed:31 May 1900

WASHINGTON CO.,MS.
WILL BOOK "2"

P.129:**WILL OF G.A.LAMB**: of Wash.Co., written:7 May 1900
Wife:ELLA to be Exectx., land near Warsaw (Wash.Co.), also land in Sunflower and Tallahatchie Cos. (Ms.) Wit:J.M.JAYNE,JR; L.L.JAYNE; FRANK BINDER. Filed 21 July 1900.
(Note: From 'Old'Greenville Cem. by Payne: *GEORGE A.LAMB 1849-1900 ELLA LOWRY LAMB 1853-1941*]

P.130:**WILL OF ANDREW PAXTON**: of Wash.Co., Written 16 May 1900
Children:ANDREW,JR.; ELISHA, ALEXANDER G.; LUCY P.ALDRIDGE; HANNAH M. ALDRIDGE; CORNELIA B.CHAPMAN; SAMUEL B.PAXTON. Exect.- SAML.B. "who has been my agent and manager" of 3 plts.in Wash.Co. Wit:S.F.FINLAY, W.D. LOVE,S.B.WEEMS.// CODICIL: Written:11 June 1900:Divide the land on Deer Creek and on Bogue(Phalia) in T17,R6W and R7W, between the 7 children. Do not sell land at Wilmot station that he bought from J.D.HOPPER, but hold it for 5 yrs.// CODICIL#2: 9 Aug.1900: Extends Saml.B.'s employment from 1900-1901. Wit:WM.WOOD,J.H.HUTCHENS,A.P.WINGFIELD. Filed:15 Oct.1900

P.138:**WILL OF J.C.LUSBY**: of Wash.Co. Written:22 Oct.1900
To all blood kin in La.and Texas. To Mr.SPINKS children in Texas.
Exect.:DR.WM.M.PAYNE Wit:J.E.McCUTCHEON,PAT PEARSE,ROMY GRIFFIN, N.M.EVANS. Filed:29 Oct.1900.

P.139:**WILL OF B.P.FOSTER**: Huntington, Bolivar Co.,Ms.
¶Wife:GENA JENAKE, to beAdmx.; ¶Dau: ZULEE; ¶Son: RIGBY.
"OAKWOOD PLACE" in Wash.Co., house and Lot in G'ville
Wit: DR.C.P.SMITH,G.W.WILKINSON. Written:13 Nov.1900-Filed 6 Dec.1900

P.140:**WILL OF HARRY ST.L. CAPPEL**: Written 29 Apr.1889
Wife: MARY BELL MARSHALL, Exectx.
Sister:JULIA CLEWILL CAPPEL JENKINS or her son JAMES
Filed:16 May 1901

P.140:**WILL OF SOLOMAN ROMANSKY**: of G'ville, Written: 30 Jan.1901
¶Wife:BERTHA, ¶Dau:SARAH ROMANSKY, ¶Sons:JULIUS C. andJOSEPH L. ROMANSKY to be exects. Wit:NATHAN GOLDSTEIN, M.RABINOVITZ
(SOLOMAN was a partner in the Firm 'J.Romansky & Co.') Filed:13 June 1901

P.157:**WILL OF ISAIAH INMON JAMES**: of Wash.Co.,Written:28 Oct.1899
To:NANNIE MARTIN GLATHARY-'Forest Home Plt.', near James Station (Wash. Co.), + interest in 'Blue Ridge Plt.', also near James. (cont.)

WASHINGTON CO.,MS.
WILL BOOK "2"

Brother:THOMAS VICTOR JAMES, Exect.
Wit: GEORGE WILHELM, W.T.GLATHARY, H.C.WATSON-Filed:6 Aug.1901

P.158:**WILL OF MARK ROSENBERG**: of Avon,Wash.Co.,Ms. 31 July 1901 To:NANCY CLARY and her 5 children-CLARA BROWN,SAMUEL ROSENBERG, MARY ROSENBERG,MANN ROSENBERG,RACHEL ROSENBERG,,land in Sec.5,T16N, R8W + land in town of G'ville. Exect:MORRIS ROSENSTOCK also to be Grdn.of minors and Trustee for NANCY; Brothers and sisters: unnamed;
Wit: JAKE SCOTT, J.H.HELMS, NATHAN GOLDSTEIN//
19 Aug.1901:MORRIS ROSENSTOCK petitions for L\Grdnp.//
19 Oct.1901:PETITION by CLARA BROWN, SAML.ROSENBERG, along with NANCY CLAREY, asking the Court to allow MORRIS ROSENSTOCK to be their Grdn.and Trustee, stating that MARK ROSENBERG decd.11Aug.1901, testate, making bequests to NANCY and her 5 children: CLARA, now18;SAML.16; MARY 12; MANN 7; RACHEL 4. Two oldest children are over 14, and choose MORRIS as Grdn.// WILL filed:19 Aug.1901.

P.169:**WILL OF E.T.WORTHINGTON**: Wayside,Wash.co.,Ms. 29 Mar.1902
¶Mother:Unnamed: ¶Brother:WM.W.WORTHINGTON and wife LILLIE:
¶Brothers:THOMAS and CHARLES WORTHINGTON
¶Sis:SALLY W.SAMUEL and MARY W.NUTT. Instructs his mother to use his property to help any of the sisters or brothers who were unsuccessful in business. Wants WM.W. to have 500 ac.'The Homeplace' + residence,because "he has always been my best friend and nurse and helpmate in all my sickness for last 12 yrs with Muscular and Inflamatory Rheumatism".
¶Brother WM.W.'s children:FLOURNOY,WM.W.,JR. EDNA;¶Brother THOMAS P.'s children: ANNIE ,ARLENSE ¶Sister SALLIE's children:DR.WM.W.SAMUEL, JOEL, ED, BETTIE SAMUEL. The rest of his land,that bought from RICHARD TRACEY sale and from RICHARD HEART & wife, and from PATTIE R.CAMPBELL, known as 'The Robb Place',to be divided between other brothers and sisters, + part of "my father's Place".¶To Nurse:JANE HALEWAY,25 ac.of land by the negro schoolhouse. Filed: 29 May 1902.
[Note: FROM "AMANDA WORTHINGTON DIARY":Edw.T.and Wm.W. were twins]

P.171:**WILL OF IDA B.BENOIT**: Written:n/d-Filed:2 June 1902
¶RUTH BENOIT EDWARDS AND GEORGIA B.FINLAY,co-exectx.
¶Mother:GEORGIA KIRK; ¶To my 5 children:RUTH BENOIT EDWARDS, LOU ELLEN BENOIT, CELEST, ADELE, A.W.,JR.BENOIT. ¶Husband:A.W.BENOIT and Son:WM.BLANTON BENOIT have already received their inheritance. Written on margin of Will:"Mrs.J.L.Newhorn,Maggie Wright,Eleanor R.Hutchinson.

WASHINGTON CO.,MS.
WILL BOOK "2"

P.172:**WILL OF MARY F.HUNT**: Arkadelphia,Ark.-26 June 1888
¶Son:EDWARD T.HUNT: ¶Grandchildren:MARY T., SALLIE R., JOHN, HENRIETTA M.HUNT, the children of Son ALEX T.HUNT,decd. ¶Dau;ANNA F.HUNT,Exectx.
Wit:TEENIE W.VALLIANT,C.A.VAUGHAN. Filed:16 July 1902

P.173:**WILL OF STACY LORD**: Chattanooga,Tenn., 20 Aug.1894
¶Brother:FRED A.LORD,2/10-1/10th for himself,1/10th for Father,W.L.LORD
¶Sisters:MRS.ANNA LORD CARNES, MRS.NETTIE LORD COOPER-1/10 each
¶Sister:WILLIE LORD-6/10ths. Filed:Wash.Co.,Ms.22 Sept.1902

P.174:**WILL OF HOUSTON HOLMES**: of Wash.Co., Written:6 Dec.1902
Sister:JANE KING,Exectx., who is to support "my dear Mother"
Wit: DR.J.H.MILLER, ADDIE BROWN. Filed :20 Dec.1902

P.175:**WILL OF ANNA CATHERINE SALZIGER** of G'ville,15 Nov.1901
2 Children:WILLIE L.FREY and LOUISE T.HIGGS.
Wit:J.H.WYNN, JOHN H.MOORE, BEN F.WASSON. Filed; 1 Jan.1903

P.176:**WILL OF SAMUEL D.WINN**: of Wash.Co., Written:22 June 1900
Wife:MARTHA ORRI (?)WINN,Exectx. If wife decd.,all goes to young son SAMUEL HALDEN WINN. Wit:S.R.BERRY, S.H.B.HANNA. Filed:22 Jan.1903

P.177:**WILL OF CHARLES M.WILLIAMS**: of G'ville, Written 25 Mar 1897
¶Dau:LESSIE W.GEISE,Exectx. "who watched over me these last years."
¶Friend:MAJOR JAMES E.NEGUS and wife, to determine amount to be paid LESSIE and her husband S.R.GEISE for my care and expenses incurred. If they (the Negus's) are decd.,then the pastor of G'ville Presbyterian Church along with "one of my sisters"to decide. ¶Dau:LYDA W.SYKES. Wit: MATTIE S.THOMAS, R.D.BEDON. Filed 14 Feb.1903

P.179:**WILL OF JAMES ENGLE NEGUS**: of G'ville, Filed:23 Mar.1903
¶Wife:LOUISE McALLISTER NEGUS,Exectx. ¶Son:WADE H. ¶Sister:SUSAN NEGUS. Refers to his Grdnp.of 3 nieces and nephews,and also of THOS. C. HOLMES. Written:(20 Oct.1898-scratched through) 27 Feb.1902(written in)

P.180:**WILL OF LEWIS(LOUIS) CAFFALL**: of Wash.Co.,Written:11 Aug.1881
Wife:AGNES,Exectx.Wit:M.GENSBURGER,F.VALLIANT. Filed:28 Apr.1903

P.180:**WILL OF GEORGE MORTIMORE SWEEDEN**: Written: 22 Feb.1890
¶Wife:CAROLINE, Exectx. ¶Daus:MARY, EVEY, HARRIET, MARTHA SWEEDEN

WASHINGTON CO.,MS.
WILL BOOK "2"

¶"Boys":WILLIAM, GEORGE SWEEDEN Wit: CLIVE METCALFE, FREDX.METCALFE, JOHN A.MILLER METCALFE.//CODICIL:(no date)¶Son:JOHN A SWEEDEN. ¶Dau:ANOLIVIA SMITH Filed:22 June 1903

P.181:WILL OF HAMPTON COX: 27 Oct.1881,¶Wife:C.R.COX-'Forest House Plt.' + medical and literary libraries, all belongings to care for his wife. "I don't wish her to ever go out of the room we now occupy."// On 9 Oct.1886, Yazoo City,Ms.,J.N.GIERUTH, and J.K. HOLDER swear they know the handwriting of HAMPTON COX,decd. WILL attached to petition of MRS.C.R.COX for Probate. Filed Yaz.Co.,Ms.Bk."B",p.209,1 Sept.1903-Wash.Co.4 Sept.1903

P.183:WILL OF C.R.COX ,decd.Written:10 Dec.1888-¶Daus:MRS.M.E.BOWMAN, MRS.T.J.BRICKELL-$10 ea.¶Gr.dau:LUTIE COX-land in Yaz.Co.,silverware,etc.+ "my inheritance from Harlem Flats,N.Y." ¶Dau.-in-law:BETTIE COX,wife of son XAVIA COX,(Exect.) to be LUTIE's Trustee. Wit:N.P.S.CHEATHAM, J.W. CARTER, J.M.SMITH. Filed:Yaz.Co.June Term-1896: Wash.Co.4 Sept.1903

P.185:WILL OF MARY GILLIAMS :To:LUCINDA McLAUREN,exectx., and only heir living-'Daybreak'& 'Rose Plt.'as surveyed by HUGH J.FRILEY in Nov.1891

P.186:WILL OF WILLIAM EUGENE MONTGOMERY : Wash.Co., 6 June 1903 Wife:MARY ADELIA CLARK MONTGOMERY. Filed:5 Nov.1903

P.187:WILL OF PRICILLA MOORE:, 4 Oct.1900-Filed 19 Nov.1903 MRS.LOU McALLISTER NEGUS,wife of JAMES E.NEGUS,Esq.to receive everything,"She took care of me."Wit:NANNIE S.TRIGG, CATHERINE McCAULEY

P.187:WILL OF JESSIE K.MAGRUDER ,Vicksburg, 3 Nov.1895 Husband: L.W.MAGRUDER,Exect. Filed:3 Dec.1903

P.188:WILL OF KATIE BANKSTON: HOLLANDALE,Wash.Co., 16 Sept.1903 ¶Niece:WILLIE MAY JONES; ¶Nephew:JOHN WESLEY JONES. Wit: WM.H.S.BUSH, LOU BIRDIE BUSH. Filed: 30 Nov.1903

P.189:WILL OF JULIA GENSBURGER: Wash.Co.,Written:15 Nov.1897 ¶Husband:MARX GENSBURGER ¶Son-in-law:LOUIS ROTHCHILD,Exect. Wit:JACOB ALEXANDER, SOL BRILL. Filed 30 Dec.1903

P.190:WILL OF T.P.HOUSE: Written: Arcola(Ms.) 24 July 1900 ¶Wife:MATTIE. ¶BABY ¶Mother:MRS.M.E.HOUSE. Filed: 4 Jan.1904

WASHINGTON CO., MS.
WILL BOOK "2"

P.190:**WILL OF PHEABY BALLARD**: Written:7 Jan.1904-Filed:22 Jan.1904
¶Friend:SALLIE VAUGHAN-1/2 interest in land in city of G'ville
¶Husband:OFFICE BALLARD-1.2 interest in same
Wit:ELLA SMYTHE, ELVIRYA BROWN, BEN F.WASSON

P.192:**WILL OF COMFORT PAGE**: G'ville, Written: 31 Mar.1902
Son:ROBERT PAGE,sole Exect.; Wit: JAN COSHUN, A.S.HIDER. Filed:2 Feb.1904

P.193:**WILL OF HENRY MURPHY**: Wash.Co., Written: 8 June 1903
Exect.L.R.WILLIAMS to receive benefits from Masonic Benefit Ass.(MBA)
Wit:W.H.DOUGHTERY, S.R.ROBERSON Filed:5 Feb.1904

P.194:**WILL OF IMOGENE THOMAS**: Gonzales,Texas. 12 Oct.1903
¶Bros:JOE R.THOMAS,E.N.THOMAS to receive money loaned out around G'ville
¶ROSELLE NICHOLSON to have $100 COL.S.B.THOMAS owes me.
Instructs Exect.to "mark my father's grave in Brandon,Ms."
¶Niece:MARY THOMAS, dau.of E.N. and MATTIE THOMAS - property in G'ville.
Wit:MRS.A.W.HARMON, ROSELLE NICHOLSON. Filed:Gonzales,Tx. 30 Jan.1904
Filed:Wash.Co.,Ms. 17 Feb.1904-A.J.ROSE, witness.

P.195:**WILL OF H.M.BARNES**: ¶Living Children-unnamed. Admr.CHARLES
H.BARNES,J.E.KENDALL "whose actions shall be binding on all my other
children" Wit:L.WILZIN,MAUD E.KENDALL.Written:n/d-Filed:1 Mar.1904

P.196:**WILL OF J.D.JONES** , G'ville, Written:9 Dec.1902
¶To:ANNIE J.STARLING, the wife of friend CHAS.H.STARLING,Exect.
Wit:VAN B.BODDIE, WALTER SHIELDS. Filed: 21 Mar.1904

P.197:**WILL OF W.H.DRUMMOND**: G'ville, 18 Sept.1893
¶Children:CORRINNE H., SALLIE L., MARY A., FLORENCE A., W.H.JR.
¶SALLIE and MARY to be Exectxs.and Grdns.
Wit:J.M.JAYNES,L.C.WATSON, LAMAR WATSON Filed: 31 May 1904

P.198:**WILL OF HARRY RAYFORD**: (Also sp. RAIFORD)Written: 8 FEb.1904
¶Cousin:JENNIE COOPER,exectx.; ¶Son:WILLIE RAIFORD
Wit: JAS.J.CARRAWAY, JAS.H.MILLER Filed: 16 June 1904

P.199:**WILL OF LOUISE SCHMALHALZ**: G'ville, Written 12 Apr.1903
To MRS.ROSA M.VAUGHT "my best friend"
Wit:D.L.McLEON, A.GAYO, P.J.KORSTENBROK-Filed: 24 Aug.1904

WASHINGTON CO., MS.
WILL BOOK "2"

BEGINNING NOV.1904, MOST OF THE RECORDS ARE TYPEWRITTEN, SO ANY IRREGULARITIES WILL BE COPIED AS WRITTEN.

P.200: WILL OF MRS.MARIA P.SESSIONS, Natchez, 15 Oct.1887
¶Dau: SUSAN G.McCONNELL; ¶Sons: JOHN G. and RICHARD SESSIONS;
¶Dau: ANNA M.SESSIONS. Wit: E.B.BAKER, S.DUNCAN BAKER.//CODICIL #1: 2 JULY 1887, AND CODICIL #2: 26 FEB.1898 add no new information//CODICIL #3, July 1898, "Woodstock Plt." managed by 2 sons named above.
Wit.by T.OTIS BAKER, SIMON MAJOR.
Filed: Adams Co., Ms., 10 Oct.1904; Will Bk."5", p.502-Wash.Co. 12 Nov.1904

P.202: WILL OF HENRY HOLLAND of Hollandale, Ms.(Wash.Co.)
Mother: ANNIE LAWSON; To: LINNIE HOLLAND; Wife: ADLINE HOLLAND;
2 Ch: MARY TAYLOR, EUGENE HOLLAND; To: BELL BROWN
Wit: E.P.SIMMONS, GREEN DAVIS, P.R.JAMES - Filed 19 Nov.1904

P.202: WILL OF HENRY HARRIS: Written: 11 Dec.1903-Filed 24 Dec.1904
Wife: MATILDA HARRIS; Exect.GEORGE ROBERSON;
Wit: JOHN F.HARRIS, JULIA HARRISON

P.203: WILL OF HENRY T.IREYS, JR.: Written 27 Jan.1904
Wife: EVELYN HOGE IREYS; Filed 3 Jan.1905

P.204: WILL OF ALBERT GASTON WINEMAN: Written: 10 Jan.1905
Wife: MARY ANN WINEMAN; Children: LAWRENCE W., ALBERT V., ROBERT, JENNIE, SUSIE, OTTO WINEMAN, LELIA WINEMAN FERGUSON; Bro: PARKER WINEMAN. Wit. H.C.WATSON, A.S.WINFORD. Filed 7 Feb.1905

P.206: WILL OF J.T.CURRIE: of G'ville, Written 13 Aug.1903
Asks that a marble slab be placed over his grave. Niece: MRS.CATHERINE BRADY of Belton, Bell Co., Texas, to get the land in Bell Co.; The following are nieces, nephews, gr.nieces and g.nephews: MRS.ELLA SCOTT of Lexington, Okla.Territory; WESLEY HILL, near Blount Springs, Ala.; J.C.HOOTEN, W.W.HOOTEN, ALTHA CONDREY, ROSA CONDREY all of Tyranzo, Ark.
Wit: A.K.BURNETT, J.BURNETT. Filed: Wash.Co. 14 Feb.1905

P.207: WILL OF ADOLPH BLAND: of G'ville, Written: 24 Feb.1905
Wife: FANNY BLAND; Sister: NARCISSIS COLEMAN to be Exectx.;
Wit: P.W.DAVIDSON, REV.DAVID HARRIS.
Filed: 11 Apr.1905

WASHINGTON CO.,MS.
WILL BOOK "2"

P.207: WILL OF INEZ H.SHELTON : 3 Apr.1903, Written "my home known as Jennie Bagley home on 111 Poplar St." Husband:W.P.SHELTON; 2 Children: an infant girl, and dau.ALMEDA SHIPMAN. Mentions "furniture in Lady D's parlor, and furniture in Harry's room". Wit:MRS.J.A.SYLVESTER, MRS.J.E.JASEY Filed: 9 Mar.1905

P.208: WILL OF ALLEN MILLER: Jackson Bayou,Wash.Co. 22 Feb.1905 Wife:GEORGIANA MILLER; Dau:COLUMSA MILLER; Son:JACOB MILLER; Grdns.:PEMBERTON MILLER, WALTER LIVINGSTON.
Wit:ED GANT,G.W. CHEATHAM - Filed: 31 May 1905

P.208: WILL OF M.A.WILKINS : Written 13 Mar.1897-Filed 4 Apr.1899 3 nieces:ALICE ROSLIE URQUHART, ELICE URQUHART, ISABEL URQUHART

P.209: WILL OF DAN HUGHES: (Also sp.Hughs) Written: 4 Apr.1905 To:LIZZIE HUGHES and EMMA HUGHES,"house in which I am now lying sick. On NW corner of Hinds St.and Shirley Alley". To:CARRIE BROWN; LULA DOYLE; ELIZA PATTERSON; WALTER BIRD; JENNIE HUGHS; DAN HUGHS,JR.; AMELIA HUGHS. Wife:JENNIE HUGHS,Exectx.; 2 youngest ch.-DAN,JR. and AMELIA. Wit:CHAS.H.STARLING,SHEP HUGHES,IRENE WEBSTER. Filed: 1 May 1905

P.210: WILL OF ANNIE GOODLOE ROWLAND: of Madison So.,Ms.
Mother:ANNIE I.GOODLOE who is buried in New Cemetery in Canton,Ms.
To children of my sister:MRS.MARY G.LOVE who was wife of Col.WM.C.LOVE of Madison Co.,and who decd.Jan.1896. These nieces and nephews are: MRS.R.B.BRIDGES of Crystal Springs,Ms.; MISS W.D.LOVE,near Arcola (Ms); MRS.WM.C.RUTLAND near G'ville;WM.C.LOVE,JR. near Yazoo River at Cruger, Ms.; and D.GOODLOE LOVE,Canton,Ms.-to be Exect. Written:12 Mar.1896 Filed Wash.Co.,Ms.27 June 1905

P.211: WILL OF T.B.WARFIELD: G'ville, 6 May 1903
To: CHANEY MARSHALL, "she has taken care of me." Filed 14 July 1905

P.211: WILL OF JESSEE A.CROOK: "Honey Oak Plt."Wash.Co.,Ms.In T19N,R6W To:BETTIE HUNTER, who is residing on 'Honey Oak Plt.' and her children: JOHN HENRY CROOK, ALBERTA CROOK, JESSE CROOK, LUE JAMES CROOK, WM. McKINLEY CROOK, ARTHUR CROOK. Excluding any other children of BETTIE's. His 'Bogue Plt.'(North side of Bogue Phalia-T19,R6W) to be divided between his sisters and bros.as follows: 1/5th to bro.WM. HENRY CROOK of Victoria, Ala. and he is to be exect.; 1/5th to bro.JOHN MOORE CROOK of Bessemer,

WASHINGTON CO.,MS.
WILL BOOK "2"

Ala.;1/5th to JANEY CROOK,sis.-in-law, and wife of JOHN BENA CROOK, and her children of Victoria,Ala.; 1/5th to sis.VIOLET LOUISE CROOK DAVIS of Union Springs,Ala.; 1/5th to decd.sis.ANNA MARIA CROOK THRAIN,wife of DANIEL THRAIN,formerly of Braggs Store,Lowndes Co.,Ala. Written:3 Oct. 1905. Wit:J.A.LONG,S.E.FRIERSON,WM.GRIFFIN. Filed:Wash.Co.13 Oct.1905.

P.213:WILL OF POLLY ANN GREEN: Written: 5 Mar.1905
Husband:PLUMBER GREEN; Son:WM.LITTLE of Plumb St.,St.Louis,Mo.
Wit:MISS MARY L.GRIFFIN,NELLIE GRIFFIN - Filed: 9 Dec.1905

P.213:WILL OF VINCENT GREGO: Written: 26 Nov.1905-Filed 17 Jan.1906
To:M.GREGO of G'ville; MRS.MARY GREGO, Exectx.; Wit:MRS.F.GREGO,F.GREGO.

P.214:WILL OF H.B.ROBINSON: Written:5 Feb.1906-Filed 28 Feb.1906
Wife:LELIA SILLERS ROBINSON, Exectx.& Grdn.
Wit: LOUIS A WITNEY, JOS.A SHALL.

P.215:WILL OF EJ.D.GRAY: of G'ville,Written:15 Apr.1885
Nephew:GEORGE B.ALEXANDER son of beloved bro.AUSTIN F.ALEXANDER
Filed: 26 Mar.1906

P.215:WILL OF BENJ.SMITH; of Louisville,Ky. Written 24 July 1846
Dau:FRANCES E.SMITH to get 'Longwood Plt.'and 'Hill Place' + all slaves on it,etc.; Wife:IRENE SMITH, Plt.near Port Gibson called 'Ever May' + slaves on it,etc.;"My house and Lot on which I reside in sd.city of Louisville,on Jefferson St.and conveyed to me by GEORGE W.SMITH".."My BLACK Place in Wash.Co.,Ms."; Niece:SARAH F.JOHNSON, and after her death,legacy to go to her children; To:Family of my bro.G.W.SMITH and his 2 children-BENJ.and IRENE SMITH. Exect.:Wife and Dau. (WILL signed 'BEN SMITH') Wit:JOHN P. OLDHAM,WM.H.POPE. Filed:Jeff.Co.,Ky.-5 Oct.1846/ Claib.Co.,Ms. 31 Mar. 1906/ Wash.Co.,Ms.24 Apr.1906

P.217:WILL OF DR.JAMES HARRISON MOORE: Harrodsburg,Ky,Mercer Co.
¶Son:DANIEL LAWSON MOORE and gr.son:JAMES HARRISON MOORE,JR.-exects.
¶To:ANITA MOORE and MINNIE B.MOORE, children of my son DANIEL L.MOORE.
¶To:BELL PAYNE;OLIVIA ROCHESTER;MARY McCALEB,ESTHER MORSE; KATH-ERINE KEIGHER;BERTHA HEBB;LILLIE McCALEB.¶To: THOS.MOORE of Honduras, son of LAWSON and BETTIE MOORE;¶To:DANIEL L.MOORE,JR., my nephew and namesake,the distiller;¶2 Nephews:WM.D.MOORE,DR.J.H.MOORE (gets medical books); ¶Children of my son BACON MOORE:MARY BACON MOORE,VIRGINIA

WASHINGTON CO.,MS.
WILL BOOK "2"

MOORE,DANIEL MOORE,JOHN B.MOORE. ¶Gr.sons:BACON R.MOORE,MACK MOORE, HARRY MOORE. ¶To: MRS.WALLACE BARTLETT;¶To: McBRAYER MOORE; ¶Great gr.son:VINCENT R.BARTLETT. Written 21 Sept.1901. Wit:E.H.GAITHER,LOTTA LUNG//CODICIL: dated 22 Sept.1902,same wit.as WILL,adds names BOWMAN MOORE, and gr.dau.MARY MERSINGLE WHILDEN.//Filed:Mercer Co.,Ky. 2 Oct. 1905/Wash.Co.,Ms.17 Apr.1906/Sharkey Co.,Ms.4 Jan.1906 (W.Bk."A",p.47)

P.219:WILL OF J.J.PEYTON: of G'ville,Written:23 June 1906
Wife:MARY,Plt.in Sunflower Co. + residence in G'ville; Son:WM.PEYTON; To:MALINDA HENDERSON of G'ville; Son:JOHN PEYTON; Wit:L.F.KELLY,GEORGE PRYOR,MAGGIE ELLIOTT, L.BEASLEY,LELA SHARPE. Filed:5 July 1906

P.220:WILL OF MARY LOUISE WILLIAMS: Written: 2 Sept.1905
¶2 sisters:MRS.IRENE S.WILLIAMS, MRS.CAROLINE M.STRATTON-Exectxs.
¶To:ANNA E.WILLIAMS and her 5 daus:IRENE S.;KATE C.; CAROLINE; RUTH; FANNY B. ¶To: FLORENCE HARPER and her dau.MARY LOUISE HARPER.
¶Nephew:CHARLES DAHLGREEN BRUMLEY. ¶To:FANNY B.MARSHALL;CHARLES PEARCE WILLIAMS;PRICILLA KERN(colored);CHARLEY JOHNSON(colored); PENNY CLARK(colored). ¶Bro-in-law:MERRITT WILLIAMS. Filed:22 Aug.1906

P.221:WILL OF MARGARET JOHNSON: of St.Louis,Mo. 23 July 1906
¶Husband:SOLOMAN JOHNSON-$1.
¶Sons:SOLOMAN JOHNSON,JR.; WILLIAM JOHNSON-$1 each.
¶Dau:SARAH A.HUMPHREY,wife of RUFUS J.HUMPHREY to get the rest.
Wit:MRS.EDITH HICKS,EDWIN S.FISH. Filed:Wash.Co.,Ms. 15 Oct.1906

P.221: WILL OF WILLIAM A JEWELL: G'ville, Written: 26 Dec.,1902
Sis-in-law:MRS.JOSEPHINE A.JEWELL- to get his 1/2 of 'Silver Lake Plt.' "we own as tenants in common" + Lots in G'ville. To:MRS.LOUISA JEWELL VEACH-$5000, also, she is to hold an inheritance in Trust for MISS MARY A.JEWELL. $500 to each:ALBERT KERR,CHAUNCEY JEWELL,MRS.ALICE BURNETT,MRS.EMILY VANNESS. Leaves funds and arrangements for upkeep of JEWELL lots in Oakwood Cemetery,Warren Co.,Ohio.
Wit:ALFRED H.STONE,MARCELLUS HARTMAN,WM.GRIFFIN. Filed:26 Nov.1906

P.223:WILL OF HATTIE E.CASEY: of Wash.Co., Written:8 July 1903
¶Husband:JOHN T.CASEY,Exect.
¶Sons:R.L.CASEY,J.H.CASEY to each divide 2/3rd of Estate.
¶To: the children of decd.son CHARLES G.CASEY,get other 1/3rd.
Wit:JNO.S.JOOR,N.T.BAGGETT. Filed:Wash.Co.,12 Dec.1906

WASHINGTON CO.,MS.
WILL BOOK "2"

P.224:WILL OF JOHN EVANS,of G'ville, Filed:29 DEc.1906
To:SARAH GREEN, "my housekeeper".
Sister:SARAH C.LAFOE,who has children and gr.children to divide his estate as follows: LUCY E.TEMPLE-1/5th; HILLIARY BELL,LEE A.BELL,JOHN BELL-grand children-1/5th which would have been their decd.mother, SARAH BELL's share; JAMES LAFOE-1/5th;SUSAN TEMPLE-1/5th;WM.LAFOE,RAY LAFOE,EDWARD LAFOE-1/5th-their decd.father,T.E.LAFOE's share;
Exects.:LEE A.BELL,H.C.WATSON. Wit:J.J.RYAN,JOHN SAGER.

P.225:WILL OF WILLIAM R.HARVEY :of G'ville, Written 24 Sept.1906
Wife:ADDIE. Dau:ADALINE. Wit:THOMAS QUIGLEY. Filed:14 Jan.1907.

P.225:WILL OF WM.L.TILLMAN: Muscogee Co.,Ga. Written:19 Apr.1906
¶Trustees for Wife,HATTIE and exects.for estate-her bro. R.E.CLEMENTS of Buena Vista,Ga.; DR.C.T.DRENMAN-Hot Springs,Ark.;FRANK A. HEARD- Columbus,Ga.¶Decd.Sister:MRS.A.A.HEARD's children-except for DR.GEO.P.HEARD.
¶To:MINNIE DRENMAN,formerly RYAN.¶To:W.T. McCAY,son of T.T.McCAY of Al. ¶To:C.T.HELMS,son of W.S.HELMS.¶To:WM.THREATT,son of ROBERT T.THREATT
Wit:CHAS.H.HUMBER, B.L.BLANCHARD,F.BURRUS// CODICIL: Written 19 Apr. 1906. Gives a scholarship to State Normal College,Athens, Ga. to BESSIE OSBURN,dau. of GEORGE OSBURN of Stewart Co.,Ga. Wit:CHAS. R.HUMBER, P.M. DANIELS,J.L.LEANARD.//CODICIL:#2:$50 to HATTIE SHELTON -same date and wit.//CODICIL:#3:Sell the 'Humber Plt.'in Stewart Co.,Ga. about 1200 acs. + lands in Russell Co.,Ala. Lands in Miss.in Wash.Co.: on Murphy Bayou, to be rented-worth @$30 per ac.and land on Deer Creek worth @$65/70 an ac.//
Filed:Office of Ordinary,Musc. Co.,Ga. 6 June 1906-WAsh.Co.,Ms.13 Mar.1907

P.230:WILL OF MARX GENSBURGER : of G'ville,Written:16 Apr.1907
Children:EUGENIA,SARAH,HELEN,FLORA,AMELIA,ARTHUR,ESTHER,SEYMOUR.
Bro:DAVID GENSBURGER-Grdn.of EUGENIA's estate.
Wit:SOL BRILL,FERD L.MOYSE,MAURICE A BERGMAN. Filed:7 June 1907

P.231:WILL OF AMELIA C.PENNY: Written:7 June 1905
Friend:WADE H.NEGUS,son of JAS.E.and LOUISE M.NEGUS. To:WILL ENGLE NEGUS,CARRIE BELLE NEGUS,SUSIE E.NEGUS. To:RECTOR HALSEY WERLIEN,JR.
Wit:MRS.HENRY K.FISHER,LELIA B.JACKSON. Filed: 24 July 1907

P.231:WILL OF ANDREW SCHMITT :(Also sp.Schmidt) Yazoo City,Ms.
Bro:THEODORE SCHMIDT. Written:13 Mar.1888-Filed Yaz.Co.,Ms.WBk"B"p.230, May 1,1888 - Wit:D.R.BARNETT,JNO.J.SCHMIDTT. Filed Wash.Co.29 Aug.1907

WASHINGTON CO.,MS.
WILL BOOK "2"

P.233:WILL OF ALEY ANN TILLMAN: Muscogee Co.,Ga. Written:4 Aug.1890. "of advanced age",instructs Exect.to purchase stones for her grave and the graves of her mother and dau.BOBBIE,who are buried at Uchee,Russell Co., Ala. Advises the Exect.to sell the 'Hunt Place' in Russell Co.,Ala. Her decd. husband, WM.TILLMAN,owned 1/16th interest in lands in Wash.Co.,Ms. Exect. to sell 1/6th int.in these lands(Wash.Co.)[Note: believe 1/16 to be a typographical error,and should read 1/6th]¶Gr.dau:ALEY ANN SNIDER,dau.of WM.F SNIDER-appointed her Grdn.¶Gr.dau:ALEY HEARD,dau.of "my dau." A.A.HEARD, with GEO.P.HEARD,husband of sd.ALEY HEARD to be Grdn.of ALEY [Note: very confusing-copied as written]¶Gr.dau:ETHEL and MABEL HEARD, sisters of sd.ALLEY (also sp.Ailey).¶Gr.son:WILLIE P.SNIDER, bro.of ALEY ANN SNIDER. ¶All of the children of sd. WM.F.SNIDER - WILLIE P.;HENRY;ALEY ANN. ¶Daus.of my dau.A.A.HEARD - ETHEL,MABEL,AILIE HEARD. ¶Exect: son - WM.L.TILLMAN of Muscogee Co.,Ga.
Wit:J.M.THIGPEN,A.L.PALMER,JOEL BUCK,J.R.BRANNAN,J.A.CURRY-who testify on 7 Nov.1890-Filed Muscogee Co.,Ga.5 Jan.1891-Wash.Co.,Ms. 10 Sept.1907

P.235:WILL OF LANDIN CAIRO: Written 24 Oct.1906
Only son, SAM. Filed: 24 Oct.1907

P.237: WILL OF M.GEORGIE SMITH: in form of personal letter addressed to "Georgie"....promising to leave her everything. Written: 22 Aug.1905, G'ville,Ms. Filed 18 Jan.1908

P.237:WILL OF M.WHEELER: of Bourbon (Wash.Co.),age 59 on 6 Oct.1905 left an Insurance Policy with the Masonic Benefit Ass. to Wife:CLINTHA WHEELER; To:SPELLINGER WILLIAMS,GRANVIL WILLIAMS.

P.238: WILL OF LEE SKINNER: (Filed: 8 Apr.1908)of Hollandale, age 42 on 22 Aug.1905. Policy with Masonic Ben.Ass. to wife :ANGELINE;
Children:ANCY, HENRY, LEE, BEN, THOS, EMORY, OLIVER
Exect.:E.P.SIMMONS. Wit:ANDREW JACKSON, C.R.ROLLING, G.DAVIS.

P.239:WILL OF W.N.YERGER: Written 25 Mar.1908-Filed 13 May 1908
Mother:JENNIE YERGER Wit:MARY L. and GEORGE WHEATLEY

P.240:WILL OF CORINNE URQUHART GRIFFIN: Written:16 Jan.1908
Dau:SARAH LANE GRIFFIN; 2 sisters:ELOISE U.HAMPTON,SADIE W.FERGUSON; Servant:NANCY BURRELL; Children: unnamed; Husband:WM.GRIFFIN to be Exect.and Grdn. Filed 19 May 1908.

WASHINGTON CO.,MS.
WILL BOOK "2"

P.241: **WILL OF JOHN V.SMITH**: of McLennan Co.,Tx.,Written:11 Feb.1893.
Sis:FANNIE SMITH,Exectx.; Wit:O.A.WORSHAM, DEE COOK, MORTON J.SMITH, L.W.BAGLEY, H.L.TAYLOR, C.W.MORRISON, R.S.LUNSFORD.
Filed:McLennon Co.,Tx.5 Feb.1908- Wash.Co.,Ms.21 May 1908

P.242:**WILL OF D.M.SAYLE** of G'ville-June 1,1908-Filed 5 June 1908
Mother:MRS.LUCY ANN SAYLE; Bro:D.B.SAYLE, exect.

P.242:**WILL OF RAB FREEMAN**: Masonic Benefit Ass. Policy- age 59,5 May 1908. Niece:HASTY SLAY; Exect.:B.W.SMITH; Filed 7 Aug.1908

P.244:**WILL OF J.RANDOLPH CRAIG**: Masonic Benefit Ass.-age 29, 15 July 1905; wife: NIOLA CRAIG; children: LILLY, RUTH, DOGELON, MAGELINE CRAIG Filed:5 Oct.1908

P.245: **WILL OF MRS.ROSA JANE PACE**: Written:21 May 1907
Dau: IDA BRISCOE BAILEY-sole exectx. Wit:R.L.WASHINGTON, J.H.PARHAM
FILED:19 OCT.1908

P.246:**WILL OF NANCY SMITH**: of G'ville, Written:25 Nov.1907
To:MARY ESTHER COLEMAN, dau.of JERRY and LIZZIE WILLIAMS COLEMAN
Wit: A.J.ROSE, M.M.HARTMAN, EDNA BUTLER. Filed: 3 Dec.1908

P247: **WILL OF JAMES A.V.FELTUS**: "Born at Woodville,Ms. 22 Oct.1839, now residing at Leland,Ms." WILL written in Chicago, 6 July 1908. 1/3rd Estate to wife:KATE BERKLEY FELTUS; 2/3rds to Trustee,JAMES B.FRALEY of Chicago,Ill., to hold for children (unnamed); Wit:JULIAN C.RYER-Chicago; FLORENCE A.HARTWICK of Chicago; ARTHUR W.MAY of Oak Park,Ill. WILL filed Wash.Co.,Ms. 4 Jan.1909

P.250:**WILL OF DANIEL HARVEY**: Masonic Ben. Ass.-age 37,10 July 1905; Endorses certificate to KATIE and ROSETTE HARVEY. Filed:14 Jan.1909.

P.251:**WILL OF JOHN ALLISON**: Written: 5 May 1908-Filed:29 Jan.1909
To pay servant,MRS.GRACIE SMITH.

P.252:**WILL OF EVERETT C.TAYLOR**: Written: 1 Nov.1904
Wife:JESSIE C.TAYLOR, sole Exectx.,she should seek advice of WM.C.BURK of Thornton,Ind. Wit:GEO.M.SMITH, EDWARD T.COLLINGS, HENRY B.WILKERSON all of Phoenix,Ariz. Filed Boone Co.,Ind. 18 Jan.1905-Wash.Co.,Ms.:n/d

WASHINGTON CO.,MS.
WILL BOOK "2"

P.254: **WILL OF J.B.CONLY:** Written-n/d; Filed 26 Mar.1909
Exects.:THOMAS MORRISSEY, HARLEY METCALFE. Sister:MRS.MARGARET HAMMOND of Wash.,D.C.; Bro:LANDON CONLY and his 2 ch.; Nephew:MACK SCARBOROUGH; Wit: GEO.B.HUNT, D.E.BEAMS.

P.255: **WILL OF VIOLET UNDERWOOD**: Written:2 Jan.1909
4 Gr.ch:TERESA GIPSON; BENNIE UNDERWOOD; CHARLIE UNDERWOOD,SAMMIE UNDERWOOD- Lots in G'ville. 2(other) Gr.ch: VIOLET GIPSON, CARRIE GIPSON. Exectx: TERESA GIPSON with N.S.TAYLOR as legal advisor.
Wit:J.W.BROWN,J.C.CHAPPLE, R.J.DIXON. Filed: 3 Mar.1909

P.256: **WILL OF MARY SWISHER:** of Belzoni (Wash.Co.,Ms.), 3 Mar.1909
Dau:ANNIE A SWISHER- the 'Swisher Place',North of Tchula Lake in Holmes Co.,Ms. [Note: Mr.Swisher apparently left this land to his wife and dau. with the stipulation that it could never be sold, but could be given away.]
To: VANNIE; Wit: JOHN DAVIS, ROBT.McDILL. Filed 19 Apr.1909.

P.257:**WILL OF CARRIE S.BRANDON:** Helena,Ark. 21 July 1907
¶Sisters:MRS. ANNIE S.MONTGOMERY,MRS.ELIZABETH S.DOUGHTIE,CHARLOTTE BRANDON;¶Niece:FANNIE MAURY STANTON-money to be invested by MR.WM. T. McCOY;¶Husband:GERARD P.BRANDON;¶Mother and father:FANNIE MAURY STANTON and SAML.W.STANTON who are buried in Natchez.¶To:DAVID STANTON, J.M.STANTON, AARON STANTON¶WIT:none.Filed:Wash.Co.,Ms.3 May 1909

P.258: **WILL OF MARTHA GILES AKIN:** (Also sp.AlKIN) G'ville
Decd.son:SEDDEN AKIN left land to me known as 'Seddin Akin Estate' on the Counties' Books, which was mine during my lifetime,and at my death to go to my children. Exectx;MATTIE G.AKIN, dau., who is to care for her father, SEDDIN P.AKIN; 2 sons:ALBERT and SPENCER B.AKIN; Wit:J.W.JOYNER, W.S.ANDREW. Written 27 Apr.1906-Filed: 10 May 1909

P.259:**WILL OF ALLEN SUTTON:** Masonic Benefit Ass.-age 60, 20 Aug. 1906. Exectx:MATTIE SUTTON; To: VICKY SUTTON,PETE SUTTON,AMY SUTTON;[Written in:"*Amy is dead,died Dec.21,1906-Widow W.Burns*"]
Wit: W.BURNS, C.WINSLOW, D.J.HARVEY. Filed 20 Apr.1909

P.260: **WILL OF J.A.SHACKLEFORD:** of G'ville, Written 24 Mar.1908
Bro.-in-law:FELIX ASKEW-$1000; Servants: ANDREW and wife ALICE TUGGLES. Nephew:JOHN W.SHACKLEFORD, Exect.of Carroll Co.Ms.
"*I revoke WILL made on 23 Aug.1905*". Wit:J.H.WYNN,BEN F.WASSON//

WASHINGTON CO.,MS.
WILL BOOK "2"

CODICIL: 18 Mar.1909:revokes the $1000 to FELIX and gives it to JOHN W. SHACKLEFORD. Wit:J.H.WYNN, H.A.GAMBLE,M.D; M.H.TRIGG. Filed:21 July,1909

P.261:**WILL OF LYMAN D.ALDRICH:** of Natchez,Adams Co.,Ms.
In his Will, LYMAN D. said that he was in the process of building a tomb for the ALDRICH Family in the Natchez Cemetery. He requests that the body of BENJAMIN G.DAVENPORT be removed from New Orleans,and brought to the 'Aldrich Tomb'. Into this tomb, "also place remains of my late wife, a casket representing the remains of my 1st wife,and eldest son and dau.by 1st wife, and infant child by 2nd wife."
Son:LYMAN GODFREY ALDRICH and wife BETTIE A.ALDRICH and their children now living-LYMAN D.and SARAH DAVENPORT ALDRICH, and the 3 children of BETTIE A.'s by her 1st husband, namely MARY, ANNA ,BETTIE WILSON- All ch.to receive interest in plantations 'Whitehall' and 'London',in Wash.Co.,Ms. My late wife,MARY NEIBERT ALDRICH, died intestate, but I know she would want to leave her beloved nephew,WM.LEWIS NEIBERT something. She was LYMAN GODFREY's step-mother, but she loved him dearly, and I will trust him to set aside WM.LEWIS NEIBERT's inheritance. To my sisters-in-law, widows of my late brothers CHARLES and EBERNEZER ALDRICH. To my brother BENJAMIN,now living. Written: 1 Oct.1875
Filed:Adams Co.,Ms. 27 Nov.1877-Wash.Co.,Ms.6 July 1909

P.266:**EST.OF W.H.TRIBBETT:** of Hinds Co.,Ms.
Petition of R.W.MILLSAPS,SAML.S.CARTER,EUGENE SIMPSON, residents of Hds.Co.,shows that W.H.TRIBBETT decd.13 Nov.1897 in State of New York, having gone there for medical treatment. He lived in Terry,Ms.,left a large estate + a WILL which petitioners offer for probate. WILL is wit. by JAMES E.NEGUS,DAN HEAD, JAMES D.SMITH. The petitioners are named in sd.WILL as Exectrs. Pet.filed 30 Nov.1897// **WILL OF W.H.TRIBBETT** :
He instructs the exectrs.named above, to sell property and divide the proceeds between the following:
¶Niece:FLORENCE E.TATE and her ch.ISAAC F.TATE,EUGENE SIMPSON TATE, WILLIE J.,HOWARD C. ,CHAUNCEY G.,FLORENCE F.,GRACIE J.TATE.
¶Nephew:GEORGE TRABUE and his dau.RAUZA FAY TRABUE.
¶Nephew:OTTO TRABUE and his ch.MARION REX TRABUE, MAUD TRABUE.
¶Niece:MEECA LOU ANNION and her son FRED LEON ANNION.
¶Niece:DAISY TRABUE.
¶Nephew:ORRIN SIMPSON and his ch.ERNEST LYLE SIMPSON,OTHO SIMPSON, ESTELLE SIMPSON,CEIL SIMPSON,WARD SIMPSON,KERN SIMPSON.
¶Nephew:LAWRENCE SIMPSON and his ch.STELLA and ROXA SIMPSON.

WASHINGTON CO.,MS.
WILL BOOK "2"

¶Niece:ESIE INGELS and her ch.BERT LEE INGELS, CLARENCE (OR CLARIESE), INGELS, RAY and EFFIE INGELS. ¶Nephew:NORMAN SIMPSON. ¶Niece:CARRIE COLEMAN,¶Niece:HENRIETTA BUSBY and her son PAUL LANDON BUSBY.
All the above are residents of State of Indiana.
¶Nephew:THEODORE LANDON and his ch.JESSEE,CLIDE,EUGENE.
¶Gr.nephew:HARRY COLLINS. ¶Gr.niece:FANNIE COLLINS.
¶Niece:MINNIE E.TATE and her dau.SIBYL TATE. ¶Nephew:ERNEST LANDON.
The above are residents of State of Illinois.
¶Nephew:ELLIS LANDON and his dau.MYRTLE of Penn.
¶Sister:L.E.LANDON of Ill. ¶Sister:M.M.SIMPSON of Ind. ¶Nephew:EUGENE SIMPSON and ch.RUTH,WM.,DENTON,EUGENE HOOKER SIMPSON of Miss.
¶To:WM.H.FITZHUGH, IDA BONNER FITZHUGH,ANNIE HESTER of Miss. ¶*All of the above I denominate as Class #1 for conveinent reference. Class #2: any children or grandchildren of each above, except the FITZHUGHS and ANNIE HESTER.* TRIBBETT then sets up a very elaborate program of payments to the heirs, with provisions made for increase of generations, covering the next 50 yrs.!
WILL written 16 Feb.1895-Filed Wash.Co.26 Nov.1897
[Note: From Terry,Miss.Cem.Records: *Wm.H.Tribbett e b.2 Apr.1828-d.13 Nov.1897*]

P.276:WILL OF MRS.AGNES CAFFALL: of G'ville, 9 Dec.1904
Decd.husband: unnamed; WILL states that Mrs.CAFFALL made her home with dau.AGNES SAGER and her husband JOHN SAGER. Their homestead was on the SE corner of intersection of Shelby and Percy Streets,"property purchased by my husband for me 28 Dec.1891, from THEO POHL" + furniture,etc.she leaves to Agnes. The rest to all my children:ROBT.CAFFALL,now living in Vicksburg; LOUISE AYDELL,living in Houston,Tx.;LENA RING of Shaw,Ms.and son-in-law JOE RING,who is to be exect.; to children of my decd.son CHARLES CAFFALL-his 1/4th to be divided among them. Wit:ALEXANDER ANDERSON,JOHN GEORGE ANDERSON,EUGENE J.BOGEN. Filed:21 Aug.1909.
[Note: From 'Old'Greenville Cem., by Payne: *Louis Caffall 1828-1903/ Agnes Caffall 1832-1909/Agnes Sager 1860-1924/John Sager 1845-1925/Joseph N.Ring 1864-1930/Lena Caffall Ring 1874-1968/Robert Caffall 1856-1920 I 3 Ch.of L.A.Caffall -N.Willie, Lewis W.,Edward A.died 1878* in the Yellow Fever Epidemic.]

P.278:WILL OF PRINCE WILLIAMS: of Wash.Co.,Written 19 Aug.1909
Dau:LOUISE CARR,Exectx. Wit:JEFF GRANVILLE,J.C.CARTER,R.F.DIXON, AMANDA HARDY. Filed: 31 Aug.1909.

WASHINGTON CO.,MS.
WILL BOOK "2"

P.279: WILL OF CAROLINE WASHINGTON: of G'ville, Written: 26 Mar.1900
To: CAROLINE REBECCA LLOYD; Late husband: GREEN WASHINGTON
Part of her property previously given to ISAIAH EMSON. Wit: J.H.WYNN,
EUGENE J.BOGEN, JOSHUA SKINNER, W.R.TRIGG. Filed: 18 Oct.1909

P.280: WILL OF WILLIAM GRIFFIN: of G'ville, Written: 22 July 1908
Sisters: MARY L.GRIFFIN and KATE K.GRIFFIN- Exectxs.& Grdns.
Wit: R.B.McMAHON, BEN F.WASSON. Filed: 29 Oct.1909

P.281: WILL OF H.C.WALLACE : 8 June 1905-Masonic Benefit Ass.Policy
Wife: LILLIE O.WALLACE, Exectx. Wit: JNO.W.STRAUTHER, BEN WALTON.
Filed: 2 Nov.1909

P.282: WILL OF DAVID WELLS, of Leland (Ms.)MBA-age 53, 29 Dec.1905
Exectx.: ALICE WELLS; Wit: J.P.WARD, E.N.GARDNER, RANDOLPH CRAIG.
Filed: 3 Nov.1909

P.283: WILL OF WILLIAM BACON: Written: 14 Sept. 1839
¶Wife: SOPHIA BACON, to get Plt.in Warren co.,Ms. ¶Mother: LYDIA FELLOWS
money in the hands of DANIEL MESSINGER of Egremont,Mass.¶2 sisters:
CHARITY HARMON, LAURA WARNER. ¶Nephew: DANIEL BACON MESSINGER.
¶2 sisters: MARY MESSINGER, LYDIA ANN ELIZA MESSINGER of New York.
¶Exectx: Wife, SOPHIA and nephew, DANL.B.MESSINGER. Wit: E.D.WALCOTT,
FRANKLIN WHITE, S.W.PERKINS, IGNATIUS FLOWERS.
Filed: Order admitting WILL for Probate in Warren Co.,Ms., in Prob.Minute
Bk."P"p.49. WILL filed Wash.Co.,Ms. 22 Nov.1909

P.286: WILL OF WILLIAM SUMMERS : of Wash.Co.,Ms., Written 9 Mar.1907
¶Niece: MRS.MOLLIE SAGE, Jefferson, Ind. ¶Niece: MRS.ALICE M.NELSON and her
son ROBERT. ¶Servant: PHOEBY McCOY. ¶Niece: MRS.HELEN FRANCIS CUMLEY.
¶Exect: EMMET Y.NELSON of Hedges,Ky. Wit: T.D.JOHNSON, BEN F.WASSON.
FILED: 30 OCT.1909

P.288: WILL OF GEORGE LEWIS: 31 Mar.1909
"All my property to FLEMING MILES and his wife ANNA MILES. Wit: THOS.S.
REDD, GEORGE V.WARD-Glen Allan (Ms.) Filed: 29 Dec.1909

P.288: WILL OF SALLIE CLARK: formerly known as SALLIE ROWLAND of
G'ville.¶Mother: JANE THOMPSON . ¶Niece: QUINTINA DAVIS of G'ville to be
exectx. Written: 19 Dec.1908. Wit: A.G.PAYNE, M.O.SHIVER. Filed 28 Dec.1909

WASHINGTON CO.,MS.
WILL BOOK "2"

P.289:WILL OF JERRY DOUGHTERY : Masonic Benefit Ass.Policy of Goodwater Lodge of Winterville-age 63, 14 May 1909. He signs policy over to; ALFRED, HENRY, LUCINDA, MINARVY, JOHN, ANDREW DOUGHTERY. Exect.:CLAIBON BYARS. Wit:CHARLES WILLIAMS, CHARLES STERLING, REV.J.H.HAWKINS, HANNAH FOWLER, ADDIE DERTIE, JULIA T.NAMED, LUCINDA DOUGHTERY. [written in:"My wife due $1, we are parted and not living together."] Filed:7 Jan.1910

P.290:WILL OF E.J.BRYAN :Walnut Ridge,Ms.-20 June 1903 ¶Daus:MAUDE H., PEARL,DAISEY ¶Bro:GEORGE D.TURNER. ¶Sister:AMANDA DUN.¶ Decd.wife:JOSEPHINE BRYAN bury me beside her in G'ville Cemetery. Filed 12 Jan.1910. [Note: FROM 'OLD'G'VILLE CEM. by Payne: *Josephine Owen Bryan 1847-1902/ Eratus Jones Bryan 1837-1910*]

P.290:WILL OF DUKE ROBINSON: M.B.A.of Arcola Lodge,age 73,2 July 1908 Certificate to;J.D.ROBINSON. Wit:E.W.WILLIAMS,W.M.;M.A.JOHNSON,S.W.; ALLEN PERKINS,J.W. Filed:10 Mar.1910

P.291:WILL OF WILLIS HARPER: M.B.A. of Hollandale-age 43 ,22 Aug. 1905.¶Wife:LUCY.¶Children:LEMPA,WILLIS,EDDIE,JERRY, HARRISON, ALFRED, ROSA. Wit:E.P.SIMMONS, ANDREW JACKSON,C.R.ROLLINS. Filed 9 Mar.1910

P.292:WILL OF E.G.MARSHALL: of G'ville,Written 25 May 1901-Filed:4Mar. 1910. Wife:BERTHA MARSHALL. Wit:ABE WALDAUER, SIMON SCHWARTZ

P.293:WILL OF SONNY ERVIN: of Winterville,Ms. [Written above-"Died 1 Feby.1910, Address J.E.Williams,Wilczinsky,Ms."] Wife:LIZZIE ERVINS. Exect:C.H.WILLIAMS. Written:22 Jan.1910-Filed 4 Apr.1910

P.294;WILL OF FRANK GRAY: M.B.A., of Refuse-20 Feb.1910 Wife:MAGGIE GRAY. Exect.:S.G.THOMAS Wit:W.W.WOODFORK,JOS.MOORE, ALEX WARD. Filed 24 May 1910.

P.295:WILL OF JOHN HOLMES: of Swiftwater(Ms)M.B.A.,age 65,13Apr.1908 Wife:OPHELIA,to be exectx. To:ZADIA,LOTTIE,JOHN HOLMES. Wit:A.J.RATBERRY, WM.GLASCOW, R.L.BROWN. Filed 25 May 1910.

P.296:WILL OF MRS.REBECCA S.STREAM: written Jan.1906 Foster dau:SADIE GILLIAM TURNER to have everything. Wit:JAS.ROBERTSHAW, S.C.BULL,JR.. Filed 26 May 1910.

WASHINGTON CO.,MS.
WILL BOOK "2"

P.297:WILL OF SADIE SPINGARN: wife of SIGMOND SPINGARN of Leland (Ms.) who is to be Exectr. Written:12 Aug.1909-Filed:31 May 1910 Wit:A.SCHWAB,JOS.B.LEVY,GEO.E.LEVY

P.297:WILL OF I.J.CALENDER :M.B.A.,age 39,16 Sept.1909-Filed:13 Jun 1910.Wife:ADA C. to be exectx. Wit:B.T.LEWIS,W.G.MAYFIELD,JOHN MONROE

P.298:WILL OF MRS.HANNAH SCOTT: G'ville,Written:13 Aug.1889 Husband:HENRY SCOTT,exect. Dau:MAMIE RACHELMAN. Son:JACOB SCOTT. Henry and Jacob to be Trustees for children: HENRIETTA,ADOLINE,LOUIS, ISADORE,ESTHER,SOLOMAN SCOTT. Wit:C.M.CURRELL, WM.CROSS. Filed: 27 Junly 1910.

P.300:WILL OF JAMES C.ESTILL : of Wash.Co.,Written 15 Apr.1905 Exect.:M.A.ESTILL who gets 'Florida Plt.'on Deer Creek,Estill,Ms. Dau:M.R.WICKS and her heirs. Wit:J.B.DUKE, T.L.ELY, W.J.DORAN FILED:4 AUG.1910

P.301:WILL OF EDWARD W.LAMPTON ,G'ville,Written:8 Apr.1907 Children:Dau.EDDIE DELIAH LAMPTON-Exectx.; PEARL GERTRUDE LAMPTON; ETHEL EMMA LAMPTON; CORNELIA DEIRICK LAMPTON. Wit:LAWRENCE H.LEWIS,MARY KELLUM,MATTIE M.WASHINGTON. Filed:10 Aug.1910

P.301:WILL OF HERBERT ESKRIGGE: G'ville and Marple Co,of Chester, England. Wife:LOUISE VALLIANT ESKRIGGE; sister:ELLEN BERTHA ESKRIGGE of Marple,England. Wit:A.N.BENACHI of Biloxi,Ms., W.H.ARCHER of G'ville. Filed:22 Aug.1910.

P.302:WILL OF EMMA V.WELLS: of Louisville,Ky. Written:15 Feb.1903 4 children:MAMIE WELLS SMITH, MAGGIE W.OFFUTT, JOHN H.WELLS, OSCAR WELLS. ZACK OFFUTT and MILTON SMITH to settle estate. Filed:26 Aug.1910

P.302:WILL OF SIMON WALKER: ,Masonic Benefit Ass.Policy-age 65, Arcola, 26 Feb.1908: ¶Wife:EADDIE WALKER: Exect:E.W.WILLIAMS Filed:13 Oct.1910

P.303:WILL OF W.M.MATTHEW ,Arcola, M.B.A.Policy; age 60, 16 July 1908 ¶"My children": MARRIE MATTHEWS, EDDIE M.WILLERBERTHE, JOHN MATTHEWS, WALTER MATTHEWS, LUIESER MAGIC. Wit:E.W.WILLIAMS, M.A.JOHNSON, ALLEN PERKINS. Filed: 24 Oct.1910

WASHINGTON CO.,MS.
WILL BOOK "2"

P.305:**WILL OF JULIA J.WILSON**: G'ville,
¶To:JULIA WILSON,dau.of FLOYD WILSON ¶MISS JENNIE WHALEN of Wash. D.C.
¶WILLIAM WILSON, son of S.D.WILSON; ¶ROBERT LUCKETT son of LOUELLA LUCKETT of G'ville- a watch that formerly belonged to RUBEN WILSON.
¶SALLIE LUCKETT of Canton. ¶CLINTON LUCKETT,son of LOUELLA LUCKETT.
Exect:J.H.WYNN. She requests to be buried at Sulphur Springs,Madison Co.Ms.
Wit:V.S.McLELLAN,MD; J.H.WYNN; BEATRICE LUCKETT. Filed: 21 Nov.1910

P.306:**WILL OF E.BANKNIGHT**: of Belzoni (Ms.)MBA Policy-14 June 1910
¶To:LULA BANKNIGHT. Wit: C.W.RATLIFF, A.D.YATES, COLEMAN SIMMONS
Filed: 21 Nov.1910

P.307:**WILL OF MRS.HENRIETTA WALDAUER** : widow, of G'ville
¶Sons:LOUIS WALDAUER of G'ville &JOSEPH WALDAUER of Vicksburg-$1ea.
¶Daus:MRS.RACHEL BLOCK,Galveston,Tx.&MRS.BERTHA MARSHALL G'ville,$1
¶Dau:MRS.MARY ERHLICH, G'ville-$1-to be Exectx.
WILL provides for permanent upkeep of lot in Jewish Cemetery, G'ville
¶Dau:MRS.EMMA WINSTON, Memphis, all real Estate.
Wit:M.M.HARTMAN,SAM HARTMAN. Written:27 Oct.1910-Filed:13 Dec.1910

P.309:**WILL OF MORRIS COHN**: of Belzoni, Written:27 June 1910
¶Dau:MRS.FREDA DAVIDOW ¶5 children:ABE COHN, JAKE COHN, FREDA DAVIDOW, MRS.PAULINE CASTLEMAN, MAURICE JULIAN COHN.
¶Wife:HANNAH. He owned 'Fisk Plt.',(aka 'Belzoni Plt.') with MORRIS LEVY.
¶Gr.daus;ESTHER, HENRIETTA and SYLVIA DAVIDOW. Wit: O.WINN,
C.A.MAHONEY,M.DUNN. Filed: 2 Jan.1911

P.311:**WILL OF ANGUS FIELDS**: MBA Policy,age 65,5 May 1908,Heads Lodge
¶Wife: PHOEBE FIELDS ¶ Daus.PHOEBIE DORSEY & JANE YOUNG.
Wit:HENRY WILLIAMS, T.W.WRIGHT, T.J.WILLIAMS. Filed: 6 Feb.1911

P.312:**WILL OF DOCK PORTER**: MBA Policy,Written:2 Aug.1910
Wife:JERLEAN PORTER. Exect.R.SLEDGE Filed:14 Feb.1911

P.313:**WILL OF EMMA THORNTON**: 12 Mar.1910- Filed: 21 Feb.1911
¶Daus:MATILLDA STRAUGHTER, SUSIE STRAUGHTER, LUCINDA DAVIS, LUCY STRAUGHTER. ¶Husband:CHARLES THORNTON,Admr. ¶Baby son:CHAS. THRONTON,JR. ¶ Sons:SANDY STRAUTHER, JACOB LANGLEY, ALBERT STRAUTHER to get $5 apiece... "they having left me and the girls to do the best we could by ourselves." [Note: Spelling of daus.& sons name as copied]

WASHINGTON CO.,MS.
WILL BOOK "2"

P.314:WILL OF HORACE HOLLINS: "a very old man", having raised a large family and spent most of my property in trying to keep them up...they have all neglected me. Written:1 Apr.1910-Filed:22 Feb.1911
¶Son:ABE HOLLINS. ¶Daus:ADELINE,SARRAH. ¶ Gr.son:JAKE HOLLINS
¶SON:GASTON HOLLINS - all get $1 ea. "I don't even know if GASTON is alive". ¶Admrx.:Cousin BELL WILLIAMS,"She has been to me as a dau., and she is to receive all my worldly goods". He requests to be buried in Greenway Park "where my wife is buried." Wit:B.C.TRIGG,GEO.E.RIGNEY

P.316:WILL OF JERRY COLEMAN: MBA Policy, age 50, 20 May 1909. Policy is signed over to LIZZIE W.COLEMAN. Exect.:A.BOWLES. Filed:23 May 1911

P.317:WILL OF JOHN COWAN: Chattanooga,Tn.Written: 27 Apr.1906
¶To:LETTIE VICK DOWNS, dau.of A.C. and CLARA B.DOWN of Chattanooga to get land in Wash.co.,Ms.-@209 ac. Exectx:MRS. CLARA B.DOWNS
Wit:FRANCIS MARTIN, J.P.P.PEMBERTON.// CODICIL:Written:19 Dec.1907-no new information.//All filed Wash.Co.,Ms. 9 Mar.1911.

P.318:WILL OF ALEX WARD: MBA Policy, Refuge Plt. Written:7 Apr.1910
¶Wife:WILLIE ANN WARD ¶ Exect:WILLIE WOODFORK Wit:WALTER MOORE, WILLIE WOODFORK, WM.COOPER. Filed 10 Apr.1910.

P.319:WILL OF REUBEN RANDOLPH TANN: MBA Policy, Arcola, age 61.
¶Dau:BERTHA A.TANN-Written:23 Aug.1905 - filed: 13 Apr.1911
Wit:JOHN CARTER, HENDERSON HARRIS, SAM TURNER.

P.320:WILL OF N.J.McFARLAND: MBA Policy, Swiftwater,age 43.¶Wife: MARY McFARLAND. ¶Others,with no punctuation between names: HAGGER SUSAN ALBERTER JAMES A.McFARLAND and ANER CONTAWAY. Wit:A.J. RASBERRY,WM.GLASGOW,T.L.BROWN. Written:13Apr.1908-Filed:18 May 1911

P.321:WILL OF SALLIE GREEN: Written:31 July 1908-Filed:31 May 1911
¶Sister:MARY EARLY. ¶Brothers:NORMAN GREEN, JACOB GREEN, SOLOMAN GREEN. Exects:LEE A BELL, H.C.WATSON Wit:W.S.WATDON, F.N.ROBERTSON.

P.322:WILL OFGEORGE T.ANDERSON: G'ville,1 June1911-Filed:1 July1911
¶Wife: EDNA JOSETTA ANDERSON; Wit:A.S.HIDER,W.P.HIDER,FLORENCE DAVIS.

P.322:WILL OF NED DEZAVION ,MBAPolicy,26 Mar.1911-Filed:31July 1911
Wife:ELLEN.,Exectx.Seeks a Grdn for NED,age 17-and MARY JOHNSON, age 21

WASHINGTON CO.,MS.
WILL BOOK "2"

P.324:WILL OF G.W.FOLEY: Wash.Co., Written:28 May 1907.
¶Brother:FENTON M.FOLEY. ¶SUSAN VIRGINIA FOLEY, MARTHA A MATTHEW to be Exect.with FENTON. ¶ Servant:ELIZABETH ELLIOTT Wit:S.S.COSENS,PERCY BURRES,CLIVE METCALFE (names copied as typwritten) Filed:22 Aug.1911

P.325:WILL OF WILLIAM ANDERSON: MBA Policy,Swiftwater,11 Mar.1911
Wife:MARY,Exectx. Filed 9 Sept.1911

P.326:WILL OF G.W.NOSS:of G'ville,Written:28 Mar.1907-Filed:5 Oct.1911
¶Servant:SUSAN HAMILTON. ¶Dau:MRS.AMELIA CAFFALL. Exectx.
Wit:J.H.WYNN,JOS.N.RING, BEN F.WASSON.
[NOTE: From 'Old'G'ville Cem. by Payne: *GEORGE W.NOEE 1820-1911*]

P.327:WILL OF W.H.HOWE: MBA Policy, Glen Allan, 13 Feb.1911
¶Wife:MARTHA HOWE; ¶Exects:JERRY HOWE,JOSH LEWIS Appoints JERRY HOWE Grdn.to minor children: BENJAMIN-7, ANNIE-2, KATHERINE-4
Filed: 14 Nov.1911

P.338:WILL OF HENRY BUCKNER: Wash.Co., Written:14 July 1902
¶Wife:LOUISE BUCKNER. ¶Children by LOUISE: ELLEN McDAVIS nee BUCKNER; RANDALL; EUGENE; REASON; PAULINE; COLONEL; FLORIDA BUCKNER.
¶Son: SOLOMAN BUCKNER. Filed: 5 Aug.1912

P.347:WILL OF LITTLETON MUNDY: of Franklin Co.,Ms., Written:8 Feb.1854
¶Wife:LUCINDA MUNDY ¶Daus:LOUISANA B.BALDWIN; MINERVA J.CALVIT-a note I hold on WM.CALVIT,JR; ANGELINE CAMERON; ROWENA C.SELLERS-land in Wash.Co.; HELENA MUNDY-the youngest; HELEN IONE KINNISON.
¶To: ABNER F.KINNISON, ¶Sons-in-law:WM.H.BALDWIN, GEORGE H.SELLERS to be exects. Wit:SAM M.HARRISELL, C.C.CAMPBELL, JOHN KEY.
Filed: Frank.Co.,Ms.Bk."A"p.34/38-19 May 1911
Filed:Wash.co.,Ms. 24 Jan.1913

P.352:WILL OF JOHN T.CASEY: Written:9 Mar.1909
¶Wife:MARIE L.CASEY, exectx. Filed:13 Feb.1913

P.353:WILL OF MARY W.NUTT: Wash.Co.(#4899 Chanc.Dkt.)
¶Father:W.W.WORTHINGTON,SR.who left me part of 'Maryland Plt.'
¶Bros:EDWARD T.; CHARLES T. to be Trustees of Plt.named above.
¶Husband:JOHN K.NUTT,Exect. Written:24 Mar.1905-Filed:24 Feb.1913
Wit:SAM WORTHINGTON; B.W.INMAN, MD; D.M.BUCKNER

WASHINGTON CO.,MS.CIRCUIT CLERK'S OFFICE
Book entitled "Naturalization"

Date	NAME	AT AGE	CAME TO U.S.A. YRS.AGO	RES./MS. YRS.	FROM
12 Dec.1891	Ferdinand Strauss	18	15	15	Austria
12 Dec.1890	Mendell Wachsman	24	24	23	Austria
12 Dec.1890	Julius Mendell	25	27	26	Austria
17 Dec.1892	Dave B.Spekter	Preliminary declaration			Russia
13 Dec.1892	Thomas Friel	"			England
23 Dec.1892	Samuel Nurse	37	12		England
26 Jan.1893	Jacob Schwab	18	21	G'ville 11	France
-- Dec.1891	Louis Vormus	20	18	12	France
20 May 1891	Charles Jordan	Preliminary declaration			Eng.or Ire.
1 Feb.1894	Fred W.Gambal	24	8	6	Germany
4 June 1896	Charles Carter	22	28	23	Denmark
21 Aug.1897	Frank Giardina	28	21	12	Italy
6 Jan.1898	J.H.Friedrichsen	48	5	2	Germany
29 Jan.1898	Joseph Mibletsch	34	6	6	Austria
5 Feb.1898	George Robert Nurse	27	7	7	England
8 Feb.1899	Charles Muffoletto	15	7	7	Italy
27 June 1899	E.A.Mommen	18	15	4	Germany
22 May 1900	Louis Nepoto	37	14	9	Italy
18 July 1900	Oscar Rubmetren	16	6	5	Russia
22 Aug.1900	B.Mafreds	29	11	4	Greece
22 Aug.1900	N.Galenos	28	5	5	Greece
31 Aug.1900	Max Weinberg	19	8	5	Russia
13 Sept.1900	Stephen Chas.Psichalenopulos	27	--	2	Greece
11 Sept.1900	Nicholas Christoduler	28	5	3	Greece
13 Mar.1901	Benn Tee	20	15	10	Russia
8 May 1901	Frank Binder	23	16	13	Germany
29 May 1903	Louis Feinstein	18	5	2	Germany
3 June 1903	J.Feinstein	22	5	3	Russia
4 June 1903	George D.Weaver	21	11	2	Gr.Britain
15 June 1903	Joe Jeselnik	25	8	3	Austria
17 Nov.1903	Stephen Psychalinopulos	35	5	4	Greece
7 July 1904	Isreal Rubenstein	44	4	4	Russia
21 Nov.1905	Max Meyer	18	5	4	Russia
12 Feb.1906	Harry Finklestein	52	5	5	Romania
4 June 1906	Sam F.Khoury	18	6	5	Turkey

END OF RECORDS

RECORD BOOK FROM SOMMERS FUNERAL HOME, GREENVILLE, MS.

REMAINS OF	ORDERED BY	AGE	D/BUR.	CAUSE	CEMETERY
ISAC TURNER	Rev.Turner	9	Jan.8,1892	Shot	City
BOB STINSON	W.P.Richardson(Refuge)	26	" 9	---	Shipped to Canton
MATILDA WEST	---	---	" 12	---	City
VERDINA HINES	Elder Hines	---	" 14	(Security on Sewing Machine)
JIM ROSS	Pauper - City	---	" 20	---	City
HAIRE	Lizzie Haire	---	" 19	---	Leota,Ms.
WM. BROWN	Chas.Rivers	---	" 21	---	Lake Village,Ark.
MRS. HOGDKINS	---	---	" 24/25	---	---
MARY RANSON	Levy Richardson	---	" 28	---	---
HATTIE JEFFSON	J.T.Currie	---	" 28	---	---
INFANT NEERUM	City	---	" 28	---	City
CHILD/JONES	Tom Jones	---	" 30	---	---
INFANT	Wm.Diamond	---	" 31	---	---
ISAM ROCKHILL	---	---	Feb.1	---	---
DELIA COOPER	---	---	" 3	---	City
STEVEN HENDERSON	Pauper- City	---	" 3/4	---	County
ELICK HUGHES	Parker Neal	---	---	Shot	County
SAM SMITH	H.Willzinski	19	" 8	---	City
GIRL of Sol Richardson	"	---	" 9/13	Shot(Metallic Casket)
SAM BROWN	Pauper - City	---	" 9/13	Pneu.	City
JONAS GOODMAN	Nathan Willzinski	17	" 12/13	Consumpt.	City
JAMES CARSON	W.H.Carson	9	" 11	---	City
GRANT COTTON	---	---	" 12	---	Meningitus County
HARRIET WASHINGTON	---	20	" 14/15	---	---
WILLIE ROBINSON	Bazzele Moore	5	" 15/16	---	Woodstock Plt.
HORTENCE WILLZINSKI	N.Willzinski	35	" 16/17	---	City
JIM EVANS	N.D.Johnson	---	" 19	---	City
EMMA SIMS	J.T.Currie	---	" 19/20	---	City
LUCY JOHNSON	Pauper - City	52	" 19/20	---	City
PLUMMER RUSS	Monroe	36	---	Pneu.	City
JULIA KIRKSKEY	Thos.Kirksey	---	---	---	City
JOHN ROBISON	City	18mo.	" 25	---	City
LEWIS CLEM WILSON	Clem Wilson	28	" 26/27	Congest.	City
ANNIE GAY	Fannie Smith	40	" 27/28	LaGrippe	City
MRS.L.ATIER	Nat Robison	25	" 27/28	Gun shot	County
WILLIAM GOODMAN	L.&N.Willzinski	---	---	---	County
GRANT BLUE	Robison	24	Mar.1	---	City
MRS. CARTER	J.B.Barnes	---	" 4	---	County
MARY JACKSON	Rollie Williams	3	" 8/9	---	City

FUNERAL HOME, Cont.

REMAINS OF	ORDERED BY	AGE	D/BUR.	CAUSE	CEMETERY
WILLIAM KATELY	J.S.McDonald	---	---1892	---	Greenwood
THOS.WOODS	Ike Early	46	Mar.10/11	Heart Dis.	City
STELLA BARG	Pauper-City	24	" 10	---	City
CHARLIE MARTIN	B.Church	---	" 18	---	City
AMANDA WILLIAMS	Her Husb.	---	" 20/21	---	---
INFANT	R.J.Ralph - Sol Cahn	---	" 23	---	---
MARY CHAINEY	Jno.T.Currie	---	" 27	---	Grand Lake, Ark.
JOSEPH W.MURPHY	Henry Lengsfield	---	" 27/28	---	City
LYDIA J.STEVENS	J.Stevens	---	" 28/29	---	City
JACOB LEVEY	Weis & Goldstein	---	Apr. 1	---	City
MATILDA ROSS	Dr.Blanton	---	" 1/3	---	From Indianola
HORTENSE GIBBS	Lee Gibbs	---	" 4	---	City
MR.JOHN SKIPPER	Mrs.Skipper	---	" 5/6	---	City
ED HIGGINS	Pauper - City	---	" 8	Shot	City
DODD (Metallic Cask.)	G.W.Dodd	---	" 11	---	City
ROBT.NEAL	J.H.Leavensworth	---	" 12	---	Grand Lake, Ark.
--- (Metallic Cask.)	G.R.Reed	---	" 13	---	City
SPENCER MOTEN	J.H.Levensworth	---	" 18	---	Lake Village, Ark.
DICK NEWMAN	Pauper - City	---	May 4/5	---	City
HORTENSE COOK	P.Lewis	18	Apr.18/19	---	City
MRS.T.HILLIARD - (Heathman Store)	Ehrlich	---	Apr. 23	---	Grand Lake, Ark.
McDONALD BROWN	I.& N.Willzinski	---	" 24	---	---
WOODS	E.P.Bailey	---	May 1	---	---
NICK SHAW	Alfred H.Stone	---	" 3	---	---
PETER MARTIN	Mr.Lewis	---	" 6	---	---
ROBERT PRINCE	Chas.Smith (Metallic Cask)	---	" -/8	---	---
JULIA HOWARD	Steamer"Mary Houston"	---	" 8/9	---	---
WILLIS JOHNSON (From Cincinnati,Ohio)	City	---	" 12	---	(Metallic Cask.)
CAPT.FARRIS'S CHILD	L.C.Dulaney by W.A.Pollock	7	Nov.26/27,1894	Hem.of Bow.	City
HOPPER	City	---	Dec.12/14	---	Grand Lake, Ark.
DR.MARK ALLEN	Mrs.N.Allen	---	" 15/16	---	Jewish Cem.
NORVELL LEMLER	Marx Lemler	16mo.	" 30/31	---	City
McBRIDE	City	---	Jan.13/14,1895	Sent/Pickins,Ms.	
McAtee	McAtee	---	" 22	Gun Shot	Jewish Cem.
WM.BURH	John Griffin	21	" 22	---	Grand Lake, Ark.
CHILD of	C.Meyers	---	" 22	From Grand	Lake, Ark.
MAX COHEN	M.Cohen	---	" 22	Shot	Jewish Cem.

FUNERAL HOME, cont.

REMAINS OF	ORDERED BY	AGE	D/BUR.	CAUSE	CEMETERY
CARRIE ADA WALSH	Walsh	--	Jan.25/26,1895	--	Catholic Cem.
SAMUEL HALE	Music	68	Feb.12	Eryisphilis	Shpd./Carrollton
INFANT/WEST	C.H.West	--	--	--	Grand Lake,Ark.
A.B.BARTLETT	C.M.Johnson	--	Mar.24/25	--	G'ville Cem.
EDWARD ENOS	Masonic Lodge	--	Apr.20	--	Jewish Cem.
HATTIE ISENBERG	J.Isenberg	--	May 4/5	--	G'ville Cem.
TWIN INF.	Perkins	3hrs.	" 25/26	--	City
THOS.LAZERS	Capt.Hides-Gov.Fleet	35	June 4/9	Drowned	Shpd./Cincinnati,Ohio
W.H.TAYLOR	Dr.Winchester	--	" 14	--	Dudley Station
INF./McGHEE	T.D.McGhee	--	" 26	--	Stoneville,Ms.
MARY MULLEN	Kings Daus.	30	" 25	Consump.	G'ville Cem.
EMANUEL ROSE	Mrs.E.Rose,Leland	57	" 27	Dysentery	Shpd./Vicksburg
CHAS.AXMAN	Eli McDaniels	76	" 29	--	G'ville Cem.
JOSEPH MEDDER	J.Skinner	80	July 5	--	Catholic Cem.
WHITTLE	Pauper - County	50	" 20	--	City
DANIEL LEMLE	Mrs.D.Lemle	78	" 30/31	--	Jewish Cem.
ROBT.A.ROACH	C.W.Roach	7	Aug.5/6	--	G'ville Cem.
MR.CLARKSON	Crane Bros.& Jordan	19	" 8/9	--	Catholic Cem.
GAETANO GIARDINO	F.Giardino	16mo.	" 8/9	--	G'ville Cem.
INFANT of	Leanthall(Buelah,Ms.)	7mo.	" 10/11	--	Fish Lake
WM.BENNETT ROCHE	C.W.Roche	5	" 15/16	Hematura	G'ville Cem.
JOSEPH HENDEL	W.B.Hendel(Itta Bena)	2	Sept.1	--	Jewish Cem.
MISS SALLIE HUGHES	J.A.Deaton	87	Sept.8	--	Shpd./Florence,Ala.
INFANT of	W.L.Hay	2	" 9	--	Sent to Leland
C.A.SANDERS	R.C.Howison	--	" 11	--	to country
CORA LACEY	Robt.Lacey	--	" 13/14	--	G'ville Cem.
FRED TEAMON	Pauper - City	--	" 15	--	City
INFANT/Chas.Jordan	Thos.Smith	--	" 29/30	--	G'ville Cem.
GRACIE AGNES HEARY	I.E.Hevey	--	Oct.2/3	--	Catholic Cem.
SAM PERRIN	John Kennedy	--	" 2/3	--	G'ville Cem.
MRS.STAUT	J.Staut	--	" -/3	--	Hollandale

WASHINGTON CO., MS.
GUARDIANSHIP BOOK "1", 1873-1913

MINOR	HEIR OF	GUARDIAN - DATE
(Rachel Alexander	Clara Alexander	Jacob Alexander/23 Aug.1874
(Esther Alexander	"	" "
Lucy Moseley	John A.Moseley,decd.	W.H.Bunn/7 Jan.1875
Bettie Erwin	E.P.& Bettie Johnson	Geo.V.Ward/22 June 1875
(Harriet B.Ireys	Volney S.Ireys,decd	Henry T.Ireys/11 June 1885
(Charles G.Ireys	"	" "
(Beatrice Ireys	"	" "
(Marion Ireys	"	" "
Heddens Montgomery/son of Saml.Montgomery,decd.		J.M.Montgomery/1Dec.1886
(Etta Orgler	-------Orgler	I.Isenberg/27 June,1890
(Dora Orgler	"	" "
Arthur Lisbony	Fannie A.& W.A.Lisbony	R.S.Golden/Oct.1889
Katie Dodo Hampsey	Jas.Hampsey,decd.	Kate Hampsey/6 Aug.1896
Carrie Chapin	dau.of W.A.Chapin with surety of Jennie Chapin	W.A.Chapin/1 Sept.1896
Joe Cleaton	J.E.Cleaton,decd	T.H.Hood/11Sept.1896
(Ida Richardson	----------------	W.O.Aldridge/25 Sept.1896
(Lottie Richardson	both of Fluvana Co.,Va.	" "
Annie A.Clouston	----------------	W.G.Clouston/6Mar.1896
(Frank Chas.Keesecker	------	E.N.Thomas/May 1896
(Clara Keesecker	both of Dubuque,Iowa/sur.by Imogen Thomas and Mattie S.Thomas	
Adelia Newsom, of New Madrid Co.,Mo.	----	W.C.Newsom.26 Nov.1896
(Mason Hill	Coleman Hill,decd.	May Hill/14 Jan.1897
(Effie Hill	"	" "
(Nannie Hill	"	" "
Frank M.Pierce)	F.G.Pierce,decd.	Annie O.Pierce/11 Feb.1897
Edgar Pierce)	"	" "
Willie Lipscomb	W.M.Lipscomb	Chas.H.Starling/7 June,'97
Richard Brown	James Brown,decd.	T.H.Hood/(Clerk)8Jul'97
Torry Wood)	Mrs.Annie Wood,decd	Wm.Wood/10 Nov.'97
Wm.Minter Wood)	"	" "
(Ida Ruth Aldridge	W.O.& Mary Aldridge	W.O.Aldridge/12Nov.'97
(Robert Newton Aldridge	"	" "
(Jno.Atterbury Aldridge	"	" "
(Joseph Holliday Aldridge	"	" "
George Taylor)	Spencer Taylor,decd.	Amanda Robinson/5Apr.'98
Spencer Taylor)		
Cyrus Taylor)	(Amanda states that these ch.are hers by her	
Louisa Taylor)	1st marriage)	
Mary Taylor		
D.C.Montgomery	D.C.Montgomery	Mary N.Montgomery/Ap.'98
Lizzie Crow	Geo.& Abbie Crow,decd.	Warren Crow/24 May,'98
Margarite Esther Hughs/child of Lelia B. Hughs		Lelia B.Hughs/28Jan.'99
Ivy G.Kitchens	J.W.Kitchens,decd	Fannie M.Kitchens/28,Feb.'99
(Mabel Wheatley	Robt.S.Wheatley	same Apr.'99
(Hazel "	"	"
(Dudley,S. "	"	"
(Sara Lee "	"	"
(Wm.Forsyth"	"	"

WASHINGTON CO.,MS.
GUARDIANSHIP BOOK "1", 1873-1913

MINOR	HEIR OF	GUARDIAN - DATE
Geo.R.Akin	- non compus mentis	James A.Aikin - June '99
Lydia Lofton	Silas Lofton	Hattie Gray - Sept."99
(Annie Aldridge Paxton	Mrs.Mary Noland Paxton	A.G.Paxton - S.'99
(Jennie Ruth "	"	"
(Mary Noland "	"	"
Hattie Belle Plumber)	Wilford & Amanda	R.E.MONTGOMERY Oct.'99
Adeline ")	Plumber	
Amanda ")	"	"
(Frank Aldridge	F.S.Aldridge,decd.	Lucy P.Aldridge Apr.1900
(Cornelia "	"	sur:Saml.B.Paxton
(Jackson "	"	" :A.J.Paxton
Edwin Vasser Parker)	R.R.Parker &	R.B.Parker-----May "
Bessie Blanche Holland)	Nancy E.Parker,dec.	R.O.Parker,sur.
Parker		
Oliver Lee Parker)		
(Delia Brown	Laura & Eli Brown	Thos.Brown,Sr. June "
(Thos. "		
(Mary "		
Alex Suggs)	Alex Suggs,decd.	Robt.Hinds Aug. "
Reuben ")	"	"
(Hugh E.Slater	V.C.Slater,Sr.,decd	T.H.Hood,Clerk Oct. "
(Renna May "	"	"
Clare Epperson)	--------------	" Nov. "
Wessie ")	--------------	"
(Rufus Peters	--------------	Sarah Wheatley Dec. "
(Walter "	--------------	"
John Shields Hood	Mary Shields Hood,decd.	T.H.Hood Jan.1901
Mary Young	Alex Young	John Strouther " "
		sur:Louis Young
		Louis Williams
(Irma Brown	--------------	Joseph Brown,Jr. Jan. "
(Roserder" (?)		"
(Nash "		"
Ella Stone)	------------	W.W.Stone Feb. "
Annie ")		sur:Alfred Stone
		E.P.Odende
Andrew Robinson	------------	Jake Shaw Mar. "
(Joseph S.Smythe	Sallie J.Smythe	J.D.Smythe " "
(Sadie Lois "	"	"
(Roscoe "	"	"
Ethel Brandon	Danl.Brandon	Mildred Hawkins Mar. "
Mary Young	Alex Young	Corinne Young Sprinkle APR.
(Hattie Crump	Ella & Bob Crump	Phil Phillips Apr. "
(Lula "	"	sur:L.D.Hebron
		J.L.Hebron,Jr.
Nelson Billingsley	non comp.mentis	Charley Shaw Mar. "
Nathaniel Mars	Aaron Mars	Ned Mars Sept."
(Wm.Henry Owens	Wm.Owens,decd.	Stephen Castleman Oct."
(Leander "		
(Anna Belle "		
(Eddy "		
(Rebecca "		
(James "		
(Isreal "		
(Laura Ann "		

WASHINGTON CO.,MS
GUARDIANSHIP BK."1873 - 1913"

MINOR	HEIR OF	GUARDIAN	- DATE
OWENS, Lucy Ann	Wm.Owens,decd.	Stephen Castleman,	Oct.'01
" ,Irene		of Belzoni	
" ,Insomia			
HEAD, Daniel B.	----------	M.O.Head -	Oct.'01
SMITH, Lillie	----------	E.L.Smith	Dec.1901
" ,Ruth	----------	sur:Lillie Smith	
" ,Nellie	----------	" J.B.Smith	
		" H.C.WATSON	
AKIN, Albert	----------	MarthaGAikin	Dec.'01
" ,Spencer B.		" Mattie Aikin	
COOPER, Leana	Geo.Cooper	S.E.J.Watson	" "
" ,Eugene	"	" :Wash Burns	
" ,Viola	"	:A.Jones	
" ,Ellen	"	:J.T.Dean	
		:E.Pickle	
IGO, Bridget	Maggie Kennedy,decd.	L.G.Wineman	Jan.1902
CROWELL, Daisey	----------	James Crowell	" "
" ,Nina	"	"	" "
SMITH, Mary	Alice Smith,decd.	Mary Huffman	May,'02
		sur:C.C.Dean	
		Clan Huffman	
HOBBS, Beatrice	Mary Hobbs,decd	Rebecca Price	Sept.'02
CROUCH, Mary A.	----------	John H.Crouch	Nov.'02
JACKSON, George	David & Emma Jackson	Adam Jackson	" '
WILE, Meyer	Louis Wile	Louis Wile	Dec.'02
" ,Isodore	"	sur:Emily Wile	"
" ,Isabel	"	Isodore Gross	"
" ,Mary T.	"		
GOFF, Lealia	Chas.R.Goff	Jas.A.Waring	Nov.'02
" ,Chas.	"	"	"
,Thos.	"	"	"
BAREFIELD, Sam Jones/	S.A.Barefield,dec.	Mary Ella Barefield/	Jan.'03
" ,Rivers	"	sur:R.A.Barefield	
" ,Maybird			
" ,Lucile			
PARKER, Eddie V.	R.B.Parker	T.H.Hood	Jan.'03
" ,Bessie B.H.			
POHL, Grace	The.Pohl,decd.	Marie Pohl	Feb.'03
" ,Elise			
" ,James			
PETERS, Walter	----------	Sarah Wheatley	Mar.'03
		sur: Perry Wheatley	
		T.S.Red	
JOHNSON, Robt.E.	----------	Lou Ella Johnson	May'03
" ,Percy D.			
LUSBY, Grundy C./of Lecainte,La./heirs of J.C.LUsby,decd./children			
" ,Pilgrim C. of Patten Lusby,Grdn.			June'03
" ,Smith M.			
HENDERSON, Alden	----------	N.G.Augustus	June '03
CHADDICK, Patten G.	J.C.Lusby,decd.	T.H.Hood,Clk.	" "
" ,Kelly R.			

WASHINGTON CO.,MS.
GUARDIANSHIP BK. 1873-1913

MINOR	HEIR OF	GUARDIAN - DATE
WORTHINGTON, Annie	/Rosina Worthington/	Thos.W.Worthington/July '03
" , Henrietta		
" , Thomas		
" , Mathilda		
" , Robert		
" , Theodosia or Tenie		
HUNT, Rebecca	Henry & Emma Hunt	Ed.Hunt Nov.1903
" , Gertrude		
JONES, Johnnie (alias John Wesly Jones)	----	Chas.Barton "
SPIERS, Bettie Olin	R.H.Spiers	Bettie S.Olin Dec.'03
" , Marie Shelby		
DYER, Eddie	Lottie Dyer	Lamar Watson Feb.1904
HEIDT, Mary Mildred	Thos.Heidt	Emma Ida Heidt "
" , Dorothy Thos.		
BARNES, Fred W.	--------------	Chas.H.Barnes Mar.'04
" , Edna		
DUNCAN, Robt.Lee	--------------	Jos.Duncan Mar.'04
GOFF, Thos.	Chas.R.Goff,decd.	Jas.A.Waring Mar.'04
" , Lealie		
" , Chas.		
HINDS, Evelyn	--------------	Lavinia Hinds Apr.'04
" , Thos.		
" , Lizzie		
" , Harry		
" , Robt.		
" , Quitman		
DRUMMOND, W.H.Jr.	W.H.Drummond,Sr.	Mary Anna Watson & May 04 Sarah Drummond Hill
SIMS, Annie Kate	John T.Sims,decd.	J.T.Atterbury June 04
" , Ruth Eugene		
HURST, Vernlon alias Walter	/Lena Hurst	G.E.Hossinger June '04
COWAN, Nancy	James Cowan	Noah Cowan July 04
CROSBY, Geo.	EMMIE & ANGELINE Crosby	Lula Tenant Aug.'04
DAWSON, Dock	Burton Dawson	Louisa Dawson Oct.'04
" , Sylvia		
FOWLER, Blanche	--------------	E.A.Fowler Nov.'04
" , Frances Dawn		
WETHERBEE, Ethel	H.E.Wetherbee	Dora Wetherbee Jan.1905
GRIGSBY, Herbert H.	Henry Grigsby	Henry Grigsby Mar.'05
" , Lula May		
HICKS, Henry	Willie Ann Hicks	W.A.Hicks Mar.'05
TAYLOR, Edmund	--------------	Edm.Taylor "
" , Eloise		
" , Wm.J.		
BRIDGES, Wealthy	David & Mrs.Mary Jane	J.M.Maxwell Apr.'05
" , Amanda Jane	/ Bridges	
" , Docia		
" , Lou Ella	All children from HOLMES CO.,MS.	
" , Mary Tom		
" , David Allen		
" , Mary Lee		
BYNUM, Sterling	Sterling Bynum	A.B.Bynum Mar.'05
" , Alonzo		

WASHINGTON CO., MS.
GUARDIANSHIP BK. 1873-1913

MINOR	HEIR OF	GUARDIAN - DATE
WILE, Meyer " , Isadore " , Isabel " , Mary T. " , Sadie F.	Louis Wile	Louis Wile Apr. 1905
(JONES, Sadie (" , Willie	----------	Chas. Barton-June '05
WADE, George S. " , Lawrence T. " , Chas. C.	W.W. Rife	Kate Wade July '05
ALEXANDER, Percy	Ida Alexander	Estella Moore July '05 sur: Henry Briggs Robt. Moore Leon Moyse
GOODEN, Sy. Jr.	Sy Gooden	Mattie Goodin Sept. '05
GIST, Yeba M./legatee of John Conn(Cain), decd/Lena Gist Oct. '05 sur: Harry L. Wetherbee W.N. Gist		
HUGHES, Dan Jr. " , Amelia " , Ina	Dan Hughes, decd.	Shep Hughes Oct. '05 sur: Eliza Pattison Ada Scott
MOORE, Lizzie HUGHES, Emma	Dan Hughes, decd. " "	Eliza Pattison Oct. '05 sur: Carrie Brown Lula Doyle
WHITE, Lawrence (of Ala.)/Eliza Ann Jackson, decd./Jas. E. Baker/De. '05		
CROOK, Ernest " , Arthur " , Douglas " , Pauline " , Paul	J.A. Crook, decd All children from Lowndes Co., Ala.	Wm. H. Crook Dec. '05
CHILTON, Florence	H.R. Chilton	Chas. M. Chilton Nov. 1904
REED, Willie	--------------	Nancy Reed Jan. '06
LITTLE, Wm. " , Margurite	Lucy A. Little	Lucy A. Little " " SUR: Cornelia Sessions W.L. Wright
JACKSON, Wm.	Wm. Jackson, decd. & Elizabeth Jackson	Jas. E. Baker Jan. '06
COOPER, Leana " , Eugene " , Viola " , Ellen	Geo. Cooper, dec. All minor children of Geo. Cooper	J.T.D. Kinnison Feb. '06
ALLEN, LEE, Jr. " , Essie	Josephine Allen, decd.	Lee Allen Apr. '06
BAREFIELD, Sam Jones/S.A. Barefield, decd. " , Rivers		M.E. Barefield Hollings- worth Apr. '06
PARKER, Mary	Birdie Searcy	Will Searcy Apr. '06
CAPSHAW, Elijah " , Joanna " , Ella " , Lizzie " , Alonzo	F.C. Capshaw	Frank J. Capshaw " "

WASHINGTON CO.,MS.
GUARDIANSHIP BK.1873-1913

MINOR	HEIR OF	GUARDIAN	DATE
SUGGS, Alex " , Reuben	----------	Lavinia Hinds	Apr. 1906
WRIGHT, Walker " , Dudley	J.A. Walker	Mrs. J.A. Walker	May '06
TENANT, Lydia CURTIS, Lillie S.	Martha Tenant Martha Tenant	Willis Tenant Willis Tenant	May '06 " '
FISHER, Ann R. " , Wm. H. " , Alfred L. " , P.H.	P.H. Fisher, decd.	Mattie L. Fisher	June '06
THOMPSON, Thos. - non compus mentis		Hiram Young	Aug. '06
REED, Burrell Ellis/Malissa Snowden		Burrell Reed	Sept. '06
FORD, Stella " , Willie " , Charlie	Henry & Sarah Ford Henry Ford Henry Ford	Easter Davis Stella Dennis Robt. Davis	" " " " Oct. '06
COLLINS, Rachel	Wm. Collins, decd.	Fannie Tripp	" "
SMITH, Maggie " , Sallie	S.S. Wells, decd.	M.B. Smith	" "
SALMON, Mamie " , Gertrude	Maurice Salmon, dec.	Zachie H. Salmon	Dec. '06
JOHNSON, Geo. Henry	----------	Carroll Johnson	Fe. 1907
JACKSON, Fannie " , Andrew " , Cornelius " , Viola " , Wm. " , Henry " , Lionel " , Leona Taylor - nee Jackson	Sandy Jackson	Saloman White	" "
WRIGHT, Charlott " , Mamie " , Viola " , Anna " , James " , Benj.	Ella Wright	J.S. Bowles	Feb. '07
LAFOE, Paul R. " , Edward A. " , Willis S.	----------------	Nettie Arthur Bell	Feb.
BASS, Irene " , Elizabeth	Mrs. Annie Farris	E.E. Bass	Feb. 1907
BERKLEY, Jennie " , Mary " , Elizabeth	Houton Berkley	P.P. McIntyre	Fe. '07
ORR, Mary Catherine/Olah Hurd Orr, Decd. ", Jeff Redd		Elsie Orr Sur: Sam D. Winn Stephen Castleman Wm. Owen A.R. Turner	Nov. 1900
LONG, Johnnie A. " , Wm. A. " , W.C.	Minor children of J.A. LONG	J.A. Long Sur: Idela E. Thompson Birdie A. Long Virginia Adeline Long	Apr. '07

WASHINGTON CO., MS.
GUARDIANSHIP BK. 1873 - 1913

MINOR	HEIR OF	GUARDIAN - DATE
(JACKSON, Malvina	Simon Jackson	Ellen Jackson Apr.1907
" , Carrie		
" , Amanda		
" , Turner		
" , Orvile		
" , Simon		
" , Euroy		
HUGHES, Emanuel	Moses Hughes	Moses Hughes Apr.'07
(COLLINS, J.R.	David Collins, decd.	Courtney Ann Collins Apr.
" , Ophelia		1907
" , Maud		
" , Chester W.		
GENSBERGER, Eugenia/Dave Gensberger		Dave Gensberger/June '07
McCORTNEY, Mary ch. of Frank McCortney, decd.		T.H.Hood, Clk. July'07
PRESTON, Lorenzo	)Patience E. Preston decd./N.B.Preston	" "
" , Columbia	)	
" , Essie D.	)All ch. of Patience E. Preston, decd.	
" , Patience E.	)	
JACKSON, George, minor ch. of Amanda Beckwith, decd./L.F.Winston/Jul.'07		
		sur:N.S.Taylor
GENSBERGER, Seymour/ch. of Max Gensberger		E.N.Thomas Aug.'07
DAVIS, Andrew/age 15/ --------------		Annie White Sept.'07
FLEUALL, Edward	)Martin Fleuall(sp.?)decd./Lula Fleuall	"
" , Aaron	)	
" , Virginia	)	
" , Joseph	)	
" , Elas	)	
" , Session	)	
" , Mattie	)	
" , James	)	
" , Fannie	)	
" , Betsy	)	
BROWN, Mattie	Manuel Brown	Geo.W.Williams Sept.'07
" , Myra		
FERGUSON, John Wm. Leonard - non compus mentis - Malvina F. Collum		
		R. Collum
		Jennie Stinson
DAVIS, Walter	---------	Annie White Oct.'07
HERNDON, Elvin	Elvira Herndon	Peggy Bailey "
BROWN, Mattie	)Manuel Brown, decd.	Julia Brown Nov.'07
" , Myra	)	
" , Callie	)All the minor ch. of Manuel Brown, decd.	
" , Eddie	)	
BUNTIN, Arlington	D.B.Buntin	Cary Buntin Nov.'07
CROOK, Eugene	J.A.Crook, decd	Bettie Hunter Dec.'07
" , Arthur		
" , Jessie A.		
" , Alberta		
" , Wm.McKinly		
JAMISON, Clarence	B.H.Hill, decd.	Thos.Guice Nov.'07
ASH, HENRY	)CHILDREN of Mattie Ash., decd.	Henry Ash Jan.1908
" , Sam	)	

WASHINGTON CO., MS
GUARDIANSHIP BK. 1873 - 1913

MINOR	HEIR OF	GUARDIAN - DATE
ROSENTHAL, Maude	----------	Sam Selliger Feb.1908
		Sur: Nellie Rosenthal
		Sal Sellinger
SPRIGGS, Carrie Bell	----	Frank Wise Feb.'08
" , Genera	-----	Frank Wise "
GREEN, Juanita	----	Frank Wise "
FONDER, Rosa)	----------	Louvinia Cambridge "
" , Jas.R.)		
FLETCHER, Leon, Jr.		Leon Fletcher Mar.'08
HALLETT, Robt.)	----------	Robt. Hallett "
" , Madyline)		
(WHEATLY, Georgia	----------	Robt. Seth Wheatly Mar.
" , Parker		
BATTS, B.F. - lunatic	--	Addie Emma Batts Apr.'08
(ROSENBERG, Rachel/minor ch. of Ma(r)x Rosenberg, decd./Walton Sheilds
C(L)ARY, Nancy/heir of Max Rosenberg/ Apr.'08
(BROWN, Clara   "   "   "
(ROSENBERG, Saml."   "   "   "   Walton Shields, Grdn. to all
" , Mann "   "   "   "   (Note: Did not specify any child
" , Mary "   "   "   "   except Rachel)
WRIGHT, Walker)	Mrs.J.A.Wright Eddleman, decd./O.T.Eddelman/May'08
" , Dudley)		
REED, Lela)	Bettie Reed	John Reed May '08
" , Marian)		
" , John)		
COOPER, Frank	S.E.Cooper, decd.	Lugenia Cooper June'08
(WILLIAMS, Granville	------------	Abraham Luicalus Williams "
(" , Spelliney		sur: James Gray
		H. Kaplan
WILLIAMS, Shep., Jr.)	----------	Jake Williams July '08
" , Adam Preston)		sur: P.L. Mann
" , Jozabee		R.H. Fishburn
LEE, Clara	Quitman Lee, decd.	Edward Marshall Aug.'08
(BRISCOE, Elias	Cornelius Briscoe, decd	Louis Thomas "
(" , Derutha		
(" , Clarence		
(" , Cecil		
(" , Cornelius		
FAGGINS, Geo.	Geo. Faggins, decd.	Mary Faggins Aug.'08
(MILLER, Marion/ /	Harvey Miller, decd./	Aunt -Louise V. Eskrigge Se.'08
(" , Robt. Valliant	"	Sur: Thos. Worthington
(" , Harvey	"	T.W. McCOY
(" , Eliz. Louisa	"	Gr. mother: Marian R. Valliant
		Sur: Morris Rosenstock
COLLIER, Abe	Abe Collier, Sr.	John Jenkins Sept.'08
POLLARD, Willie	Hattie Mitchell	M.A. Johnson "
REID, Elizabeth W.	Sherman Reid	J.L. Reid Oct.'08
CLARK, Henry, Jr.	--------------	Nannie Clark "
STEELE, Herbert	--------------	Carrie Steele "

WASHINGTON CO.,MS.
GUARDIANSHIP BK. 1873-1913

MINOR	HEIR OF	GUARDIAN - DATE
(JONES,Geo.M.	Maggie Jones,decd.	J.E.Jones Nov.1908
" ,Arrabella		
" ,Minnie		
" ,Philanders		
" ,J.E.,Jr.		
SMITH,John	Thos.Smith	F.M.Lonsman Nov.'08
" ,Felix		Sur: Reber Collum
" ,Adam		Torry Wood
" ,Dudley		
" ,Amanda		
" ,Leana		
BAREFIELD,Rivers	----------	W.W.MILLER,Clk. Dec.'08
HALLETT,Robt.A.	Robt.Hallett,decd.	Matilda Hallett "
RAINEY,GEO.	Wm.& Maggie Rainey	Maggie Rainey "
JONES,Susie	Aaron Jones	Savanah Jones "
" ,Emma		
NATHAN,Edward	Geo.Nathan	Viola Billingsly Jan.'09
ROHILLIARD,Addie	Josephine Goldstein	Fred D.Dixon Jan.1909
		Sur:J.Albert Lake
		R.P.Dunn
(FELTUS,Katharine	Berkly/J.A.Feltus,decd./	Jas.B.Fraley Jan.'09
" ,Martha Ryan		Sur:Kate N.Feltus
" ,Annie Fraley		M.L.Griffin
GREEN,Vivian	Henry Green	Margaret Eastland/Jan.
	(also signed Marg.Taylor)	
HARTMAN,Lester	---------Sur:M.M.Hartman/Grd.Lee Hartman/Jan.'09	
PATTON,Levi	Lena Brown	Frances Hinton "
PERKINS,Hallett	James Perkins,decd.	Elnora Sutton Feb.
" ,John Franklin		Sur: H.B.Sutton
		W.P.Bell
HARRIS,Sandy	Leanna & Thos.Harris	Leanna Harris Feb.'09
" ,Richard		
KEYS,Bennie	Gabriel Keys	Cela Keys "
(JONES,Annie	I.S.Jones	India Watkins Mar.'09
" ,Rufus		Sur:J.T.Atterbury
" ,Ollie		J.H.Shall
" ,Willie Mai		
BALOR,John	Geo.Balor	Richard F.Elder Mar.'09
" ,Johnnie Lee		Sur: T.E.Mortimer
		Walter Levingston
		Joanna Sims
		Sarah Balor
		Emma Brown
		Georgana Miller
CLAYTON,Jas.Edward	W.H.Harris,decd.	Edw.Clayton Apr.'09
CAPP,Leana	Lizzie D.Miles	Geo.Ballard May '09
WRIGHT,John	Rosa (Wright)Hampton	Westly Wright "
" ,Lillie		
(CRAIG,Lillie	Randolph Craig	Nalia Craig May '09
" ,Ruth		
" ,Daylon		
" ,Magelien		
" ,Randolph		
" ,Albert		

WASHINGTON CO., MS.
GUARDIANSHIP BK. 1873 - 1913

MINOR	HEIR OF	GUARDIAN - DATE
HUNTER, Anderson	G.A.Hunter & Caledonia Hiah (or Kiah)	G.A.Hunter May 1909
THORNTON, Joseph " , Mariah " , Eliza	Lem Thornton, decd.	Lewis B.Harris June '09
WILSON, Ruben " , Izetta " , Ruth	Columbus Wilson	Louvenia Wilson June '09
LEE, Chas.H.Jr.	P.D.Lee	M.D.Henderson June '09
PULLUM, Angeline " , Chas.	John Pullum	James Pullum "
McKINNEY, Clara " , Willie " , Mary E. " , Louis	Thos.McKinney	Grant McKinney July '09
WEDDINGTON, Rodgers, et al (No other heirs listed)	James Weddington	Pricilla Weddington Aug. '09
GRIFFIN, Wm.N. " , Sarah Lane " , Geo.	Wm.Griffin	Mary L.& Helen Griffin Nov. '09
CAMPBELL, Daisey/children of Collins Campbell/Kye Campbell Nov. '09 " , Caroline " " " "		
JOURDAN, Lawrence " , Wilhemenia " , Richard " , Wm.H. " , Emily " , Alice	W.H.Jourdan, decd All the minor children of W.H.Jourdan	Mamie Jourdan "
STINSON, Robt.E. " , Mabel	--------------	Mrs.J.E.Stinson Dec. '09
CAFFALL, Lena	--------------	John Sager " Sur: Agnes Sager Jos.N.Ring
MOORE, Geo.	John Moore	Celia Moore Jan.1910
SCOTT, Valley " , Charley " , Bessie " , Lilly " , Callie " , Laura	Sam Scott	Ollie Scott Feb. '10
LEE, Tribbett ", Ruby ", Corrie Bell ", Britt ", Martha ", Margaret (also written as Mary A.)	B.L.Lee	Jennie O.Lee Feb.1910 Sur: W.B.Swain W.L.Hay
WRIGHT, Walker " , Dudley	Mrs.M.T.Wright	B.A.Wright Mar. '10
FRANKLIN, James	Wm.Franklin	Charles Clemens Apr. '10
RUSSELL, Claude Evan/ch.of Wm.J.Russell, decd./Dora Woods "		
WEATHERS, Sylvia " , Jonas	---------	Horace Weathers May '10
BROWN, A.B.	Matilda Turner	A.H.Brown June '10
WADE, Mabel	Agnes & Thos.Wade Sur: Jas.Brittan;H.Kittle	Thos.Wade July '10

WASHINGTON CO., MS
GUARDIANSHIP BK. 1873 - 1913

MINOR	HEIR OF	GUARDIAN	- DATE
DANIEL, Martha	Wm. Daniel, decd.	Ella Daniel	Aug. 1910
PATTERSON, Maria, et al*	Mahala Patterson	A.S. Patterson	Sept."
*(No other children listed)			
(TRISBON, Tom V.)	---------	W.W. MILLER, Clk.	Oct."
(" , Earles)		"	"
(HOBSON, Rosa Lou)	---------	"	"
HOWARD, Dave)	Rosa Howard	Anna Page	Nov. '10
" , Anna)	"	Sur: J.C. Chapple	
		H.C. Pounds	
MASSEY, Julia	---------	Anna Page	Nov. '10
LUCKETT, Clinton	------	Louella Luckett	De. '10
(COTTON, Monah	Mary E. Cotton	Eugene Gerald	Jan. 1911
" , Lane			
" , Gertrude			
" , Delthena			
COHN, Maurice	Julian/M. Cohn	Mrs. Hannah Cohn	Jan. '11
		Sur: A.M. Levy	
		J.S. Jackson	
JONES, Evelyn	Geo. Jones	J.C. Armstrong	"
TUCKER, Mary	Laura B. Tucker	J.T. Tucker	"
" , John T., Jr.	"	"	
BELL, Archie C.	- non compus mentis -	J.B. Bell	"
(HOWARD, Dave	Rosa Howard, decd.	J.M. Page	"
(" , Anna			
(MASSEY, Julia	All three children of Rosa Howard, decd.		
CATCHINGS, Lee)	C.L. Catchings	C.L. Catchings	Feb. '11
" , Neal)	"	Sur: Eugenia Catchings	
		Ben F. Wasson	
COLEMAN, Rebecca	Anne Coleman	John Coleman	Mar. '11
(ARCHER, Worthington	S./J.P. Archer /Mary	Worthington Archer	Apr. '11
(" , Bettie Stone	"	"	
BROWN, Bertha	Frances Shackleford	L.B. Harris	"
(GREEN, Lillie Belle	Eli Green	Sadie Mallet	"
(" , Emma			
(" , Hattie			
SIMS, Bertha)	---------	David Sims	May '11
" , Lee)			
(ZEIGLER, Gertrude	Henry Zeigler	Hattie Zeigler	"
" , Henrietta			
WALKER, Eula)	Emma Walker	John Walker	"
" , Jeff)			
" , Willie)			
MOORE, Geo.	Celia Moore Strand	Adeline Corpery/	Apr. '11
RITCHIE, Rose Alena/Esma Ritchie		F.L. Harbison	May '11
" , Walter Lewis			
HIGGS, Cyrus	Cyrus Higgs	Louisa T. Higgs	June '11
" , Catherine E.			
JONES, Sidney	J.E. Jones	J.C. Holmes	"
" , Thelma			
(PORTER, Shirley	---------------	Matilda Clark	Sept. '11
" , Etoy		Sur: Lamar Watson	
" , Gerlean		Hugh C. Watson	
" , Idenia			

WASHINGTON CO., MS.
GUARDIANSHIP BK. 1873 - 1913

MINOR	HEIR OF	GUARDIAN - DATE
(SOMMER, Louis H.	Louis P. Sommer	Mrs. Margaret Sommer
" , Mary Gertrude		Oct. 1911
" , Margaret Mary		
" , Herman B.		
HARPER, Jno. Edward)	Willis & Lucy Harper	Green Davis Nov. '11
" , Harrison)		
" , Jerry)		
" , Alfred)		
" , Rosa)		
(SMITH, Clarence	children of MALINDA SMITH	Wm. Lawson Nov. '11
" , Joseph		
ALLEN, Laura A.	James Allen, decd.	Mary Allen "
(TAYLOR, Anthony	Lewis Taylor	Alice Taylor "
" , Ellen		Sur: W.L. & J.C. Murphey
JACKSON, Willie)	Madie Kyart	Pollie Harris "
" , Morie)		Sur: B.A. Wright
		H.M. Wiggens
WETHERBEE, Ethel	Mrs. Dora Wetherbee	H.L. Wetherbee Jan. 1912
(HUGHES, Shepherd, Jr.	Lucy Hughes	Shepherd Hughes Dec. '11
" , Ada (Hughes) Ellis		
CATCHINGS, Marie)	Laura Catchings	Walter Livingston Nov. '11
" , Saml.)		
, Will)		
" , Ella)		
" , Emma)		
" , Flora)		
(WHITEANS, Lula	Asberry Whiteans	Emma Whiteans Dec. '11
" , James		
MILLER, Calency	Allen Miller	Georgia Ann Miller "
" , Jacob	"	"
BRYANT, Bennie	Harriet Whitley	Edith Bryant Jan. 1912
McDANIELS, Albert C. / Josephine McDaniels / Mildred McDaniels "
(HOLMES, David	Willie Ann Holmes	John Holmes Feb. '12
" , Hamton		
" , Frankie		
JONES, Jos.	Maggie Jones	Sarah Russell Feb. '12
HOPKINS, A.G.	G.A. Hopkins, decd.	Helen G. Hopkins "
(BARNEY, Essie	Nancy Baker	Jas. E. Baker "
(BAKER, Sallie J.		Sur: Percy Bell
		C.G. Bell
COTTON, P.H. - habitual user of morphine -		Wm. Ray Toombs May '12
BURKS, LeRoy	Fannie Jacobs	Jack Williams Aug. '12
FOWLER, Sam, Jr.	Annie Fowler, Decd.	Sam Fowler "
BAILEY, Thelma	Wm. & Lucy Bailey	Wm. Bailey "
(PATRICK, Tony	Margaret Mack	America Butler "
(JEWITT, Jno. Edward		
CORNELIUS, Georgia / Clarisy Carter		Geo. Massey Oct. '12
(MITCHELL, Oliver	B.J. Grigsby	Charlotte Grigsby / Nov.
" , Flora (now Broadnax)		
" , McKinley		
(GRIGSBY, B.G.		

WASHINGTON CO., MS.
GUARDIANSHIP BK. 1873-1913

MINOR	HEIR OF	GUARDIAN - DATE
LACY, Celia " , Etter " , Lee Bertha " , Ora " , Willie " , Bettie " , Mosella	Wm. Lacy	Ella Lacy Nov. 1912
GRIFFIN, Louisa	Jacob Griffin	S.A. Griffin Nov. '12
GREEN, Reverand " , Johnnie	Paul & Line Green	Wm. Scott "
VASILICO, Christian " , Angelica	Geo. Vasilico	Christo Vasilico Jan. '13
GOLDEN, Mattie	Mollie B. Golden	A.R. Golden Nov. 1912
WALTON, Ella " , Gertrude	------------	John T. Walton Feb. 1913
ALMA, Rose RICHIE, Walker L.	------------ "	Dr. L.M. Shankel Mar. '13 " "
HOWE, Benjamin " , Annie " , Willie	Wm. H. Howe, decd.	W.W. MILLER "
ERWIN, Willie " , Viola	Henry Erwin "	Henrietta Erwin " " "
FISHER, Annie " , Wm. " , Alfred " , Pleasant	Mary Addie Fisher	Mattie L. Farrar "
OWENS, Laura " , Lucy " , Susie " , Irene	Wm. Owens, decd.	Wm. Henry Owens Apr. '13 Sur: Lee Andrew Owens
ALDRIDGE, Wm. Ousley " , Catherine Warren	A.J. Aldridge "	Frank P. Aldridge " "
CROSBY, Lucy M. " , Willie B. " , Henry " , Ruth " , Julia	------------	Mrs. Ruth B. Crosby/June Sur: B.O. McGee Eugene Gerald
WORD, Rosa Bell " , Princella	Emeline Jackson	Wm. Wood June 1913 Sur: Louvinia L. Carter Lillie O. Wallace
THOMAS, Mary " , Joe, Jr.	---------	Joe Thomas June '13
DAVIS, C.C. " , St. Francis " , Fred " , Anna Bell	---------	Wm. Yerger July '13
SMITH, Mary Stewart, Willie B. MOORE, Mattie E.	------------ "	Annie Reed & Ann Robinson Jul. '13 " " " "
CALLAHAN, Shed.; Sam; Mation; Edward	----------	Rose Callahan Aug. 1913
JONES, Vivian; Lilly; Daisey	R.H. Jones, decd.	Norma Jones Leech Oct.
BOONE, M. Ida	------------	Mrs. Lizzie Guar Oct. 13

END OF THIS BOOK

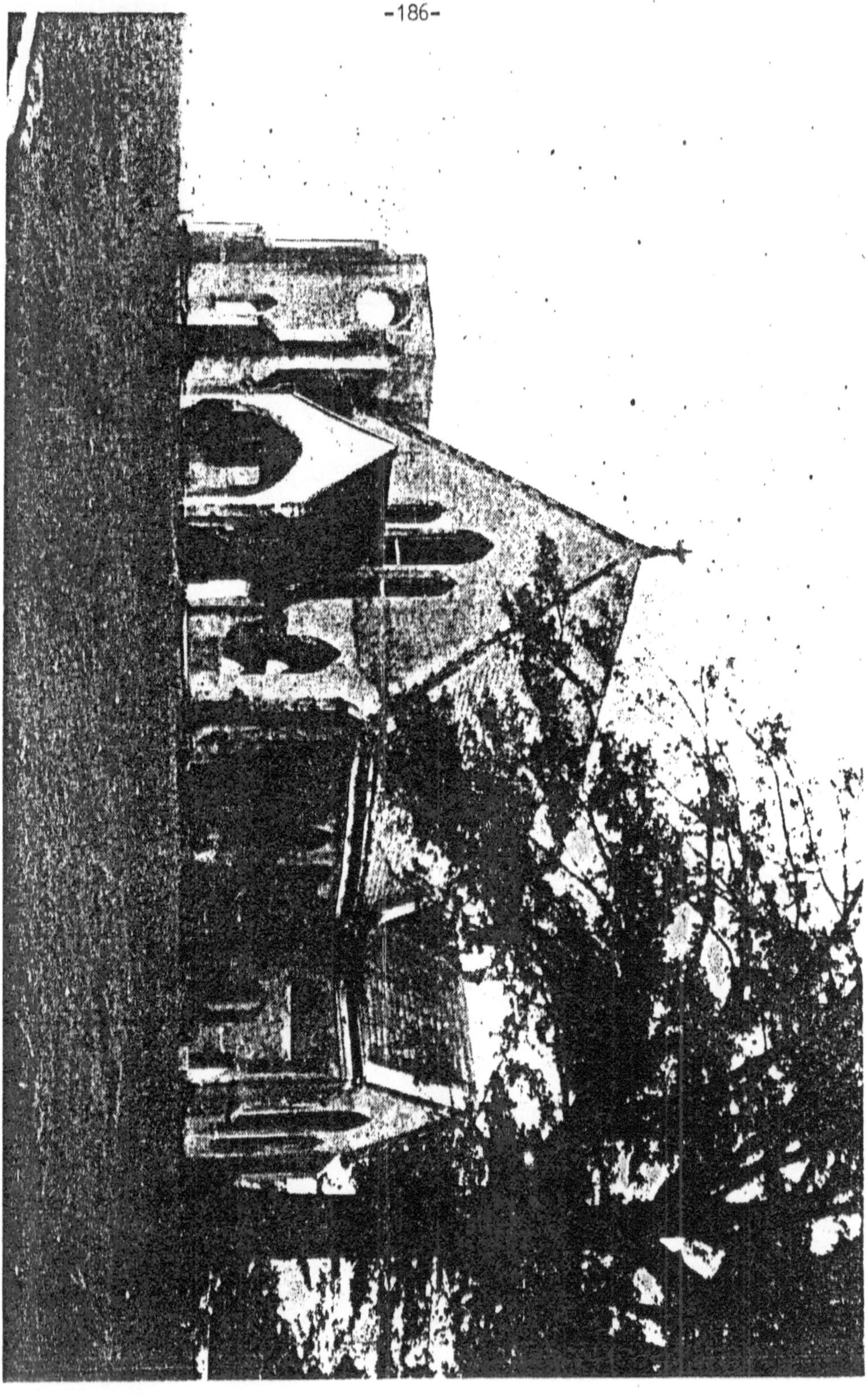

Photo opposite page taken 1904   Photos this page by H.Branton,1982

"ST.JOHN'S PROTESTANT EPISCOPAL CHURCH"

Here stood St.John's Protestant Episcopal Church, erected 1854-56, consecrated April 5,1857, by Bishop William Mercer Green.Sr., exposed to wind and water when lead from its windows was made into bullets during the war between the states and finally destroyed by a cyclone in 1904.

Greenfield Cemetery has been hallowed ground since 1852 when Jonathan McCaleb deeded this site to St.John's Parish, whose warden then was Robert J.Turnbull and Christopher F.Hampton and whose vestrymen included Wade Hampton,Wade Hampton,Jr.,John T Chapman, Henry P.Duncan, John Butts,C.F.Hamil,Thomas J.Likens, and Abram F. Smith.

This Centennial Marker was placed here in 1952 by Francis Stuart Harmon in loving tribute to relatives and friends asleep here.

TILL THE DAY BREAKS AND SHADOWS FLEE AWAY

WASHINGTON COUNTY, MS. CEMETERIES

CEMETERY RECORDS:
- GREENFIELD -Lake Washington-Pictures---------------------186
- MT.CARMEL - MAUD BRYAN PARK----------------------------201
- ERWIN, LAMMERMOOR, COLDSPRINGS, COUNTY PAUPERS,-------202
- LINDEN, KEYSTONE, GREENVILLE GOLF COURSE---------------203
- MONTGOMERY FAMILY -AUBURN PLT.,----------------------204
- FERGUSON FAMILY, MOUND CEM. At STONEVILLE --------------204
- YELLOW-FEVER CEMETERY----------------------------------205
- McKEONE FAMILY-- 206
- LOUGHBOROUGH PLT., WILKERSON FAMILY --------------------207
- METCALFE FAMILY, PETERS-PETTIT FAMILY------------------208
- LELAND-STONEVILLE--------------------------------------210
- LOCUST, MULBERRY PLT.----------------------------------220
- PAXTON FAMILY, ARCOLA BAPTIST CHURCHYARD-------------221
- ALDRIDGE-ROBERTSHAW PLOT-G'VILLE CEM.,----------------222
- RIVES FAMILY ---222
- ARCOLA CEMETERY,--------------------------------------223
- WINGFIELD FAMILY--------------------------------------226
- HOLLANDALE CITY--------------------------- -----------227
- ALEXANDER-DREW-BAREFIELD FAMILY ---------------------235
- CLETONIA---236
- ALDRIDGE FAMILY-ESTILL, ------------------------------237
- SMITH FAMILY-ARCOLA/CASEY FAMILY-HOLLANDALE/DUPUY-MURPHY-238
- HUDDLESTON/ESTILL FAMILY/COLLIER FAMILY--------------239
- INDEX--240 - 257

WASHINGTON CO.,MS.CEMETERIES

GREENFIELD CEMETERY
Located South of Lake Washington, below Glen Allan,Ms. Ruins of St.John's Episcopal Church on the North side, graves in tranquil, shady grove.Copied by MRS.JOHN CRAFT-1984-'85

DON L.NORRIS/Oct.23,1950/Dec.23,1976
FLORA LEE MAGNESS LUMBLEY/Jan.8,1930/Aug.9,1965/MOTHER
(Dbl.Stone)MARY PEARL NORRIS/Aug.8,1903/Jan.23,1962
       SEABORN FRANKLIN NORRIS/Jan.5,1898/ no other date
(Dbl.Stone)LAURA D.BENNETT/ Sept.30,1891/Apr.25,1959
       THOMAS J.BENNETT/Aug.16,1880/Oct.9,1958
CHARLES E.McGREW/Feb.25,1949/May 31,1975/Sgt.US Air Force
MRS.MARY J.MARTIN/1898/Mar.19,1978/age 80 yrs.,2 mo.,9 da.
MARY ELLEN McGREW/Feb.1,1919/Oct.22,1951
PIO PEDRETTI/Nato 1,Marzo1910 /Morto, 30 Settembre 1910
MARIA PEDRETTI/Nata 10 Aprile 1902/Morta 18 Agosto 1910
CELESTE MANGIALARDI/Feb.7,1847/June 25,1910
CHARLIE W.ROBERTS/June 17,1920/Feb.20,1952/Miss CPL 371 Field Arty
       BN/World War II
GEORGE E.ROBERTS/Aug.2,1925/Feb.20,1952
(Dbl.Stone)EFFIE L.JAMES/ 1906-1967: CLINTON T.JAMES/ 1907 - ?
JERRY FLOYD JAMES/June 25,1938/Jan.2,1942
JIMMY L.JENNINGS/DEc.5,1939/Apr.14,1944
ROBERT J.JENNINGS/Feb.16,1898/Jan.15,1969
(Dbl.Stone)CLARENCE BRIGGS/1875-1963: ALICE E.BRIGGS/1870-1948
MRS.MYRTLE LEE CREWS/Mar.16,1910/Sept.12,1977
ELBERT SPURGEON/Oct.24,1895/May 14,1944/Miss PVT US Army
ODICE SPURGEON/Feb.8,1905/Aug.16.1944
WILLIAM WATSON SPURGEON/b.and d.1948
MARY E.SPURGEON/ 1879-1966
VERNON LAMAR EVANS/Feb.14,1927/Sept.13,1947/Miss USNR WW II
W.W.SPURGEON/ 1864-1950
MYRTLE G.SCUDDER/d.Aug.5,1955/wife of/WALTER H.SCUDDER (no age)
WALTER H.SCUDDER/ JULY 8,1892/NOV.12,1953/SGT.340 CO MTG WWI
GERTRUDE PEYTON SCUDDER/1866-1919.wife of DR.W.H.SCUDDER
MURRAY M/PEYTON/1st Lt./Co.A 3 Miss Inf.CSA (no dates)
ETOILE PETERS/1912-1917, adopted dau.of DR.& MRS.W.H.SCUDDER
E.A.PEYTON/Lt.Col 3 Miss Inf. CSA (no dates)
JAMES LEWIS CRISWELL/1877-1932
DOVIE MAE BENNETT/Sept.14,1937/June 27,1939
(Dbl.Stone)CORA MAE POTEET/Sept.7,1893/Aug.23,1964
       JOHN LEE POTEET/Jan.7,1878/Apr.29,1942

WASHINGTON CO., MS. CEMETERIES

GREENFIELD CEMETERY

Crumbling brick top, concrete inside-2 graves or a cistern?
INFANT dau. of MR. AND MRS. W.W. GAINEY/June 27, 1944 (only date)
Grave-base of stone, no writing
JOHN E. NORRIS/Mar. 6, 1870/Feb. 23, 1947
FOOTSTONE: P.P.
2 graves- brick vault, crumbling, no names or dates
MARJORIE POWELL/Apr. 5, 1924/Feb. 23, 1949
CLAUDIE S. HOUSTON/July 28, 1887/Apr. 20, 1958
GEORGE A. LOGGINS/July 13, 1939 (only date) Ala Corp 167 Inf 42 Div
L.E. HOUSTON/ Oct. 29, 1887/Nov. 28, 1931
AUSTIN H. BINGHAM/1861-1927/ FATHER
MAGGIE R. BINGHAM/Apr. 22, 1871/May 23, 1948
Grave- brick vault, crumbling
Grave-unreadable-(BENNETT?)
VIRGIL MILTON MARKS, 1853-1937
NELLIE JANETTE MASSEY/July 16, 1934/Nov. 3, 1934
Grave-concrete headstone and footstone-no names or dates
REVA KAY BLADE/Apr. 7, 1959/June 11, 1966
BENNIE R. SINGLETON/Oct. 20, 1928/Nov. 18, 1964
(Dbl.Stone)ROSE COOLEY COCHRAN/1890-1982
      WILLIAM A. COCHRAN/1888-1967
(Dbl.Stone)LOUVENIA COCHRAN/Jan. 7, 1919/no other date
      JACK COCHRAN/Oct. 14, 1913/Jan. 26, 1979/ FATHER
BONNIE JERRY FILLIAND/June 8, 1937/Jan. 4, 1980
LOUIS DeLAINE MOSLEY/July 13, 1937/Aug. 29, 1937/son of/
      MR. & MRS. LOUIS A. MOSLEY
CATHERINE N. BROWN/Dec. 10, 1907/May 15, 1967
WILLIAM H. BROWN/SR./1870-1945
ADDIE R. BROWN/Aug. 29, 1880/May 29, 1969
CORNELIA ROOT/1850-1943
JOHNNIE F. ROOT/Dec. 29, 1875/June 4, 1933
LEROY FRANK BROWN/Dec. 24, 1918/Apr. 4, 1924
ADDIE FLORENCE BROWN/Ap. 3, 1908/Oct. 3, 1912/dau. of/W.H. & ADDIE BROWN
JOHN PIERRE "PETE" BROWN/Oct. 15, 1903/Feb. 7, 1982
VENNIE ROOT BROWN/Nov. 13, 1874/July 28, 1897/wife of/W.H. BROWN
FRANCES IRENE THOMAS/1922-1923
Y.K. LIGHT, SR./Mar. 5, 1909/Sept. 9, 1955
MRS. FRANCES BROWN LIGHT/Sept. 22, 1905/Mar. 17, 1984
CHASTEEN MOORE/Aug. 4, 1853/Feb. 20, 1896
HERMINE LEE LACHS/d. July 17, 1907/age 49 yrs./wife of WILLIAM LACHS

WASHINGTON CO.,MS.CEMETERIES

GREENFIELD CEMETERY
LULA B.HASIE/1882-1966
C.L.HASIE/1874-1948
CHARLES STANLEY HASIE/1916-1970
JOHN SAMUEL BALDRIDGE/Mar.17,1847/ d.-----/Co.K Miss L.Arty
ROBERT HOWARD COOPER/Sept.22,1908/Jan.14,1960
MRS.MILDRED H.COOPER/Nov.29,1908/Oct.28,1984
(Dbl.Stone)JOSEPH S.COOPER/Oct.19,1876/Mar.15,1958
       ARTIE E.COOPER/Oct.22,1882/Aug.21,1971
JAMES WILLIAM KIKER,JR./Jan.10,1956/July 15,1981
(Dbl.Stone)T.B.COWAN/July 20,1826/July 16,1899/ BROTHER
       MARIAH L.PIERCE/Mar.25,1836-July 1,1897/ SISTER
(Dbl.Stone)PAUL LARUE MANN/June 20,1869/Jan.28,1946
       NANCY BANKS MANN/Apr.19,1867/Feb.16,1962
CHARLES LYNWOOD MANN/,Dec.18,1914/Aug.21,1955/Miss Capt US Army
       WWII
BELLE IRENE BANKS/Sept.5,1865/Oct.22,1958
G.M.HERRINGTON/Mar.6,1832/Jan.7,1898
Grave-marble base with top missing
MARIA FAVA/Nata 1905/Morta 1909
CAROLINA LUISA FAVA/b.and d.MAR.2,921/ dau.of/ERNEST & ANGELA FAVA
L. MARGHETTI /no dates
SARTI DOMENICA FAVA/ Nata 1840/Morta Dicembre 1907
3 graves-no marker, metal cross, no marker
SRA TIMOTEA ADE/ Rivas Nacio 1892/Ymurio 1942/8 Do Nortebfre
VANITA McCOOL JORDAN/Sept.12,1902/Jan.17,1922
(Dbl.Stone) STELLA GILDER McCOOL/1875-1935
       BENJAMIN V.McCOOL/1873-1965
ALICE I.WISE/1894-1934/ MOTHER
ROBERT LAMAR KING/1934-1948
WILLIAM DAVIS KING/Nov.23,1926/July 31,1937/son of/MR.& MRS.LEWIS &
       GERTRUDE KING
(Dbl.Stone) LEWIS F.KING/May 2,1895/Aug.15,1970
       GERTRUDE D.KING/Sept.8,1896/May 14,1979
ERNEST BROWN PACE/Dec.17,1939/Jan.4,1961/Miss A3C US Air Force
(Dbl.Stone)W.J.C.DAVIS/1889-1932:
       LAURA HARDY DAVIS/Apr.13,1896/June 4,1983
BOBBIE LYNNE COUSINS/Dec.15,1946/Sept.14,1969
VERNON C."BROWNIE" WEST/Sept.1,1941/Jan.25,1974/Husband and Father
At this point, the old iron fence opens into a newer section of the Cemetery, that runs east and north across the southern side.

WASHINGTON CO.,MS.CEMETERIES

GREENFIELD CEMETERY

The following readings continue around in the old section of the cemetery, north of the iron fence.

PETER RANDALL ROBINSON/Mar.5,1927/Mar.10,1927/inf.son of/
    MR.& MRS.O.S.ROBINSON
(Dbl.Stone)JESSIE BOUNDS WILLIAMS/Sept.10,1906/ no other date
    WILLIE EMMA WILLIAMS/Mar.24,1910/Apr.5,1980
(Dbl.Stone)JAMES F.BRATTON/Oct.24,1901/Aug.12,1975
    CLYDE BRATTON/Dec.13,1902/ no other date
(Dbl.Stone)HORACE WILKIENSON/Aug.25,1891/ no other date/Daddy
    DEALIE WILKIENSON/June 10,1901/May 25,1975/ Mama
(Dbl.Stone)WILLIAM EVERETTE WALKER/Jan.2,1903/Mar.7,1976
    NEVIA M.WALKER/May 8,1919/no other date.
(Dbl.Stone)JAMES B.STEVENSON/Sept.14,1919/Mar.5,1976/Pvt.US Army
WWII
    THELMA E.STEVENSON/Sept.11,1923/no other date
NANCY DEXTER CARLISLE/Aug.22,1853/May 1,1925/wife of/J.A.CARLISLE
J.A.CARLISLE/Apr.1,1862/Jan.29,1930
HENRY COOPER/Feb.5,1914/Oct.30,1984
Footstone: L.B.
(Dbl.Stone)LILLIE MAE MILLER/ 1884-1932/ Mama
    MORHUN W.MILLER/ 1873-1929/Papa
AUSTIN J.MILLER/Oct.26,1905/Sept.22,1945
DARVILLE BROWN McLEMORE/Oct.26,1886/July 26,1921
CHARLES Q.McLEMORE/Aug.7,1906/Dec.1,1967/Miss Cpl US Army WWII
McLEMORE/no names or dates
(Dbl.Stone)GAINES E.CAVENDER/Mar.13,1918/May 13,1981
    NORA M.CAVENDER/Nov.25,1919/June 11,1980
BERYL L. REYNOLDS/May 22,1904/Feb.3,1978
___NCELIA RIOS,Nacio fn 1912/Fallecio en 1924/(broken)
EDWARD W.CROZIER,JR./ 1909-1931
GRACE M.SMITH CROZIER/ 1882-1914/wife of EDWARD W.CROZIER
EDWARD W.CROZIER// 1871-1927
FRANCIS F.WHITE/Nov.14,1844/Oct.1,1922
KATIE McGRAW WHITE/Apr.22,1854/Mar.7,1930
EDNA W.BROWN/Oct.23,1884/June 22,1947
JOSEPH E.McGRAW/Aug.23,1864/July 2,1944
A.O.STANTON/June 15,1849/Aug.27,1931
Grave- broken stone - unreadable
MARSHALL McGRAW WHITE/ 1890/Nov.15,1977/US Army (partially buried)
KATIE W.HARMON/June 9,1893/Nov.8,1955

WASHINGTON CO.,MS.CEMETERIES

GREENFIELD CEMETERY
FRANCIS W.HARMON/Dec.30,1925/only date
(Dbl.Stone)IRA HAWKINS/Sept.25,1892/May 10,1967
       SADIE V.HAWKINS/Nov.1,1893/Mar.7,1975
(Dbl.Stone)FELTON LOUIS BINGHAM/Sept.26,1907/Jan.28,1978
       WINIFRED WELLS BINGHAM/Jan.14,1903/Feb.17,1980
LUTHER EDWEARD FLEMING/(Partially buried)
SARAH E.FLEMING/Feb.16,1895/Nov.2,1945/ Mother
SAMUEL RUSH FLEMING/June 13,1894/Apr.8,1976/Father
SAMUEL D/FLEMING/Feb.2,1933/Dec.29,1945/ Son
Grave-rusty funeral home marker-unreadable
(Dbl.stone)MARGARETT J.JOHNSTON/Mar.26,1869/Oct.3,1949
       JOSEPH E.JOHNSTON/June 28,1872/Dec.31,1938
WALTER W.ELLIOTT/1875-1937
CHARLES S.ELLOITT/1878-1959
GENEVIEVE ELLIOTT/1878-1954
FRANCIS P.HOLCOMB/1928-1941
SANDRA LEE HOLCOMB/June 24,1951/Sept.9,1952/dau.of/JEWELL &
       WM.E.HOLCOMB
(Dbl.Stone)WILLIAM E.HOLCOMB,SR./1905-1964
       NORA LEE HOLCOMB/1909-no other date
ELLA JANE PAYNE/Aug.21,1890/Nov.4,1983
CHARLES ELLIOTT PAYNE/1927-1942
ROBERT A.PAYNE/Sept.1,1876/June 17,1969
MRS.JULIA G.McCOOL/Apr.6,1847/July 10,1943/wife of/G.W.McCOOL
REBECCA McCOOL DILL/Jan.24,1870/Apr.11,1949
BROWNSON REEVES BANKS/July 16,1892/Feb.7,1947/Miss PVT 47 Field
       Arty 16 Div WWI
DANIEL L.DUVAL/July 4,1941/ only date/Missouri PVT 164 Depot Brig
JANE D.BINGHAM/May 21,1899/Feb.2,1979
NORA B.DILL/Nov.27,1909/Dec.29,1981
NANCY IRENE KENDALL/Nov.18,1953/Nov.22,1953/dau.of MR.&
       MRS.W.D.KENDALL
HOMER WILLIAM "BILLY" DILL/Mar.14,1939/Oct.5,1952
HOMER W.DILL,SR./Feb.2,1901/July 6,1969
ROBERT F.McCOOL/Nov.18,1884.July 15,1948/Father
EFFIE McCOOL BOATRIGHT/Oct.27,1893/Nov.26,1969/ Mother
JAMES BERT MOSELEY/Nov.28,1928/Feb.14,1944
SE CORNER INSIDE IRON FENCE
JOE C.JOHNSON/Mar.20,1880/Jan.21,1946
INFANT son of /MARGARET & WILLIAM SHUTT/Jan.9-11,1944

WASHINGTON CO.,MS.CEMETERIES

GREENFIELD CEMETERY

CHARLES McGINNIS/Apr.10,1857/May 18,1945
CHARLOTTE BLACKBURN McGINNIS/Jan.21,1868/Oct.31,1953
CHARLOTTE McGINNIS McKAMY/Apr.11,1896/Feb.5,1978
WILLIAM CLINTON McKAMY/Feb.9,1893/Dec.30,1974
(Dbl.Stone)ALICE LILLIAN HAMMERS LAW/Jan.22,1917/Dec.28,1976
      ALBERT LEE LAW/Sept.26,1915/ no other dates
(Dbl.Stone)SUSIE BUSICK LAW/ no dates
      SIDNEY IVASON LAW/Nov.14,1866/Nov.30,1945
ANNIE LAW COCHEO/Jan.16,1909/June 27,1965
BLAISE COCHEO/Feb.13,1891/Aug.24,1959
ETHEL EARL TRIPLETT/July 18,1886/Jan.8,1961
MYRTIE HARRISON TRIPLETT/ June 17,1888/May 26,1980
WILLIAM HESTER BROWN,III/June 16,1920/June 7,1943/Ensign USNR
WILLIAM H.BROWN,JR./ Oct.13,1896/Feb.1,1963
HUGH LAWRENCE WADE/1921-1976/ Sgt US Army WWII
LURLYNE STOVALL MANN/Aug.5,1916/Dec.7,1981
JOHN HERBERT FLEMING/Nov.5,1884/Oct.10,1970
FLORENCE ALLEN FLEMING/Aug.14,1890/Apr.20,1977
MARY K.CRAIG/Apr.10,1888/Apr.24,1967
FELIX E.NICHOLSON/Apr.26,1882/Nov.3,1943
MINNIE B.NICHOLSON/Jan.2,1886/Apr.8,1958
MARY JEFFREYS CHERRY/Feb.14,1895/Feb.11,1972
LINDROSE ADDINGTON LEEDOM/Aug.22,1981/Dec.20,1968
WILLIAM "BULL"ADDINGTON/Apr.9,1918/Feb.2,1982
ROBERT LYNN JORDAN/1882-1943/Dad
MAUDE B.JORDAN/1880-1961/Mama
ROBERT LYNN JORDAN,JR./July 20,1908/June 10,1973
JOHN MADDEN JEFFREYS/June 5,1881/Sept.26,1943
ELIZABETH LOWREY JEFFREYS/Apr.3,1893/Jan.30,1981
JOHN MADDEN JEFFREYS,JR./Sept.9,1922/Oct.29,1941
ELIZABETH JEFFREYS HARRISON/May 2,1920/May 23,1983
(Dbl.Stone)JOHN COX/1871-1938: CLARA C.COX/1874-1948
HAROLD E.COX/July 18,1900/Feb.15,1966
MRS.NELL COX PERKINS/Oct.16,1902/Aug.16,1984
CHARLES A.PERKINS/Oct.10,1893/Nov.15,1965
(Dbl.Stone)ALLEE McEACHERN YOUNGBLOOD/no dates/ MOTHER
      CHARLES GARFIELD YOUNGBLOOD/1878-1951/FATHER
FRANCES V.BROWN PERKINS/May 14,1924/Jan.7,1951
CHARLES E.PERKINS/Aug.13,1922/June 1,1977/ US Army
SIDNEY HAYDEN PERKINS/June 7,1889/Oct.28,1969

WASHINGTON CO.,MS.CEMETERIES

GREENFIELD CEMETERY
LAURA WEAVER PERKINS/Oct.22,1890/June 22,1961
BERTRAM N.DARNELL/Mar.13,1889/Jan.11,1945
ROBERT GILBERT CARR/Oct.2,1895/Jan.29,1969
LILLIAN KLYCE CARR/Oct.20,1897/June 25,1953/wife of ROBERT G.CARR
HENRY CHRISTIAN LETH ESPENSEN/June 12,1952/Inf.son of/LILLIAN &
      KENNETH ESPENSEN
JOHN R.KLYCE/Aug.15,1873/Feb.5,1951
BESS F.WILKES/1900-1960
FRANK C.WILKES/1898-1949
CYRUS KNAPP MEGGETT/Apr.1,1871/Mar.22,1949/1st Lt.8 Calif Inf/
      Sp Am War
LEO R.STEVENS,SR./July 27,1881/Feb.20,1949
NADINE P.STEVENS/Mar.18,1897/June 17,1971
REV.W.D.BENNETT,1887-1948
ORMA W.BENNETT/1895-1977
ORVILLE K.BENNETT/Jan.2,1931/Feb.17,1959/Miss S.Sgt US Air Force
GEORGE HAMPTON UZZELLE/Aug.12,1896/Dec.27.1960
LOUIS HABER HAUFF/Oct.26,1895/Feb.21,1952
EVELYN HEAD HAUFF/June 21,1901/Dec.25,1952
CLARENCE BYRON SMITH/Feb.24,1907/Dec.11,1981
(Dbl.Stone)GEORGIA BURNETT HAUFF/Oct.4,1892/no other date
      GEORGE VICTOR HAUFF/Dec.16,1888/Sept.15,1983

Have returned to the entrance of the old cemetery, enclosed by fence. All of the above inscriptions are located on the outside of the circular drive.i The following graves are located inside the circular drive of the old cemetery.

(Dbl.Stone)CLARENCE CLARKE/Mar.2,1870/July 29,1910/son of/
      J.P.& M.R.CLARKE
      MIRIAM R.CLARKE/Sept.4,1832/Dec.9,1911/wife of J.P.CLARKE
JAMES CAMERON CLARKE/Jan.10,1907/July 9,1909/son of/
      W.A.& L.O.CLARKE
LOUIS DURWOOD REED/May 18,1924/Mar.18,1945/Miss PFC 26 Marines 5
      Marine Div WWII
(Dbl.Stone)ZORA LACKEY/1857-1920: J.FRANK LACKEY/1858-1930
ENLORA McCHEARLEY DAVIDSON/June 8,1881/Aug.17,1907/
      wife of Y.E.DAVIDSON
WILLIAM RENO FLEMING/1879-1937
BABY FLEMING/Sept.24,1905

WASHINGTON CO.,MS.CEMETERIES

GREENFIELD CEMETERY
RUSSELL LESSLEY FLEMING/June 17,1908/June 12,1909
EDDIE McNAIR PORTER/Jan.2,1880/Aug.27,1960
ALBERT J.PORTER/Aug.13,1872/July 29,1948
MABEL MAY PORTER/Nov.29,1916/Nov.18,1921/dau.of/MR.& MRS.A.J.PORTER
N.B.MORRIS/Oct.17,1854/Nov.18,1909/son of/J.J.& M.M.MORRIS
LUCIAN A.YOUNGBLOOD/Sept.3,1880/Dec.24,1911
WILLIAM ALEXANDER YOUNGBLOOD/June 11,1845/Dec.26,1916
ELLEN NOBLIN YOUNGBLOOD/Oct.29,1853/Feb.7,1942
GERTRUDE HENRY/Nov.22,1892/Dec.28,1919/wife of A.HENRY
AMZIE HENRY/Feb.29,1876/Nov.18,1935
HATTIE HENRY/July28,1868/Aug.15,1940
BYRON CADMUS SHIPP/Sept.27,1898/Aug.10,1965/MISS PVT US Army WW I
FRANK W.WYNN/Jan.9,1903/Sept.15,1969
WAYNE WYNN/1937-1964
WAYNE ADAMS/Apr.4,1934/Aug.4,1965
WILLIAM ADAMS/Oct.15,1910/Dec.24,1978
SADIE LEE JONES/1897-1932
PERCY JONES/Feb.1901/Dec.1923
FLOSSIE MAYE JONES/Dec.13,1895/May 17,1896/dau.of/J.F.& ANNA E.JONES
ALLEN REED JONES/Feb.18,1907/May 6,1908/son of/J.F.& ANNA E.JONES
JULIUS FRANKLIN JONES/Dec.31,1909/Apr.9,1911
MARIAN LEE JONES/Sept.7,1906/Apr.27,1908/dau.of M.L.& OLIVE R.JONES
J.F.JONES/Feb.14,1867/Nov.19,1939/ DAD
ANNA REED JONES/May 27,1877/July 1,1968/wife of J.F.JONES
OLIVE REED JONES/Apr.1,1884/Oct.13,1973
MARIAN LEE JONES/Dec.6,1879/Oct.14,1930
MARTHA E.JONES/Sept.14,1911/Sept.29,1965
BETTY CANTRELL REED/Dec.18,1860/Oct.11,1936
ELMO GRAVES NELSON,SR./1891-1972
ELMO GRAVES NELSON,II/Apr.24,1927/Mar.22,1956/ SON
MABEL HAUFF KNIGHT/1890-1976
JAMES B.KNIGHT/1884-1946
J. EDWARD HAUFF/Apr.25,1845/Oct.22,1896
NANNIE DICKEN BOYD/Dec.16,1869/Nov.28,1937
JOHN WILLIAM BOYD/1868-1912
MARGARET BOYD/Dec.28,1904/age 6 mos. dau.of/ J.W.& N.D.BOYD
SIR PETER BARWICK/Sept.27,1898/July 16,1899/son of H.K.& M.BARWICK
THOMAS C.SHIELDS/July 19,1917/June 8,1944/MISS CAPT 22 INF 4 DIV WWII
THOMAS HOUSTON SHIELDS/1884-1926
JAMES FRANKLIN SIMMONS/Sept.25,1883/Mar.27,1952

WASHINGTON CO.,MS.CEMETERIES

GREENFIELD CEMETERY
JAMES CECIL BARWICK/Nov.16,1902/Apr.1,1982
CLAYTON HOWARD BARWICK/1872-1956
R.J.E.BARWICK/1864-1938
CLEMMIE S.BARWICK/1903-1930
BABY BARWICK/1929
LUTHER M.FARMER/Aug.20,1895/July5,1948/MISS PVT 150INF 38 DIV.WWI
NANCY M.FARMER/1866-1946
JAMES EDWARD FARMER/Sept.20,1924/June 11,1945/Flight Officer,
	#420Bomber Sqdn. #382 Bomber Group, USA Army Air Force
(Dbl.Stone)SARAH E.FARMER/July 27,1901/May 5,1977
	CHARLES E.FARMER/Apr.11,1892/July 24,1960
(Dbl.Stone)GEORGE ELISHA HAYDEN/Dec.24,1883/Sept.29,1969
	BETTY W.HAYDEN/Nov.13,1892/Mar.22,1979
GEORGE PATRICK BOYD/DEc.9,1939/Feb.13,1940/son ofJOHN & ERLINE BOYD
MRS. ERLINE HAYDEN BOYD/Jan.27,1911/Nov.12,1983
JOHN WILLIAM BOYD/Sept.7,1909/Dec.18,1966
BETTY BOYD MATHIS/Jan.28,1931/June 27,1962
LUCY FLORA HAMLETT/1893-1934
OLICER CYLDE HEAD/1883-1944
JOHN C.HEAD/Feb.21,1899/Jan.18,1976/S1 US NAVY WW I
MARION WILLIAMS PHILHOWER/Apr.28,1905/May 13,1966
LUCIAN GREEN WILLIAMS/Apr.12,1906/Dec.28,1977/son of MARION & MARY
	WILLIAMS
MARIANNE WILLIAMS/Sept.21,1929/Feb.14,1930
MARION RAWLINGS WILLIAMS/June 26,1878/July 28,1926
MARY HEAD WILLIAMS/Feb.15,1879/May 12,1962/wife ofMARION WILLIAMS
WILLIAM T.TOUCHBERRY,JR./Mar.12,1942/July 15,1966
KATHERINE TOUCHBERRY BALLARD/June 1,1935/Apr.9,1978
MARY EVELYN ANTHONY/June 14,1930/July 26,1972/dau.of WILLIAM &
	CLARA TOUCHBERRY
NEAL OTTWAY WELLER/June 3,1909/Nov.29,1956
ROBERT CLAYTON SMITH/Sept.16,1961/Oct.10,1961
ROBERT JOSEPH SMITH,JR./Aug.30,1963/May 22,1980
MARTHA WINIFRED JONES/Aug.12,1898/Sept.11,1912/dau.of McA.&
	M.S.JONES
MURRAY E.NEAL/Apr.15,1906/July 10,1930
ANNIE LAURIE HOBART/1941 (only date)
ALVIN A.NEAL/Dec.3,1882/Feb.19,1934
STELLA HAMILTON NEAL/Nov.11,1888/Jan.11,1973
RICHARD B.PHIPPS/1848-1912/UNCLE

WASHINGTON CO., MS. CEMETERIES

GREENFIELD CEMETERY
R.T. CARTER/1879-1913
JULIA HENDRICKS OGLESBY/Dec.16,1898/Apr.21,1959/wife of JOSEPH A.
    OGLESBY
JOSEPH A./OGLESBY,SR./Apr.8,1900/Oct.1,1971
EVA H. OGLESBY/1876-1942/MOTHER
J.H. OGLESBY/1850-1929/FATHER
WILLIAM RUDY SIMMONS/Sept.30,1912/son of W.D. & FLORENCE SIMMONS
BARTON JONES FARR/July 27,1872/May 1,1940/MISS 1 Lieut Med Corps
MINNIE F. VANDEVENDER/June 10,1881/July 29,1943
PURVIS H. VANDEVENDER/Oct.4,1879/Dec.1,1944
LEONARD G. VANDEVENDER,JR./Sept.8,1937/FEb.18,1938
ROSE S. NESMITH/1874-1938
NANCY E. SHIELDS/1850-1941
CAROLYN R. BOYKIN/Nov.4,1849/May 17,1934
KRISS HANSEN/d.Jan.1932
EMILYN CANNIE FOSTER/Dec.3,1870/June 1,1937
ZACHRIAH FLYNN FOSTER/Apr.19,1880/Sept.5,1960
WALTER R. BOYKIN/Dec.6,1872/Jan.5,1973
HANNIE V. BOYKIN/Aug.8,1875/Jan.19,1942
STENNIS L. BOYKIN/Dec.26,1903/Sept.29,1974/GM2 US Navy WW II
    [NOTE:Ft.Stone has date of b.1902]
EARLY NESMITH SPIARS/Sept.8,1911/Nov.24,1978/LT US NAVY WW II
LYDIA M. SPIARS/1840-1922
ELIZABETH SPIARS/1859-1927
MARSHALL LEWIS SPIARS/Feb.14,1907/Feb.5,1970
MARSHALL M. SPIARS/1875-1940
MARIE SHIELDS SPIARS/1880-1967
ISRAEL S. LEE,JR./Nov.21,1885/Jan.11,1961
ISRAEL S. LEE/ Mar.29,1844/Feb.21,1924/Corp.Co.D 6 La Inf CSA
JOHN S. McNEILY/Aug.12,1941/MISS 1 Lieut Inf (only date)
(Dbl.Stone)JOHN SEYMOUR McNEILY/Nov.20,1841/July 16,1924/
    Co A 21st MISS Vol CSA
    MARY BERKELEY McNEILY/June 2,1855/July 18,1942
KATE SEYMOUR McNEILY/Jan.6,1892/Apr.21,1907
KATE SEYMOUR ERWIN/(no dates)
FRANCES PERCY ERWIN/Dec.29,1884/May 22,1982
DUNCAN V. HAZLIP/May 20,1870/Oct.29,1945
IMOGENE ROBINSON/1864-1963
CHARLOTTE L. HART/Jan.27,1874/May 18,1962
DAVID HART/Jan.24,1859/Sept.22,1937

WASHINGTON CO.,MS.CEMETERIES

GREENFIELD CEMETERY

MARGARET PRESTON McNEILY ERWIN/Feb.9,1887/Aug.22,1982
VICTOR FLOURNOY ERWIN/Oct.6,1878/Nov.23,1936
W.D.ERWIN/Dec.9,1881/Aug.23,1925
MATTIE WARD ERWIN/Feb.9,1849/May 31,1940
JOHNSON ERWIN/Mar.10,1850/Mar.7,1923
BESSIE ERWIN/Dec.10,1879/June 16,1922
LETHA BOYKIN ERWIN/July 1,1886/July 27,1970
J.W.ERWIN/June 2,1876/July 14,1952
(Dbl.Stone)AMBROSE FOSTER ESTES/Aug.23,1891/Mar.7,1934/ Father
        MAY SPENCER ESTES/Nov.20,1897/incomplete/ Mother
ANNIE WORTHINGTON SPENCER/Nov.14,1875/Sept.30,1963
S.MARSHALL SPENCER/Feb.27,1874/Apr.27,1920
LINNIE W.SPENCER/Nov/.29,1906/Mar.10,1923
SUSAN BANKS ALLEN/July 5,1857/Feb.2,1953
WILLIAM GEORGE ALLEN,MD/ Apr.12,1846/Jan.12,1922
(Dbl.Stone)GILLIAM M.SMITH/Dec.25,1880/Aug.5,1937
        MABELLE K.SMITH/May 13,1888/July 29,1978
MARSHALL R.SMITH/Co F 3 SC Light Arty (CSA?)(practically buried)
VIRGINIA GRACE/Oct.28,1858/Oct.28,1897/wife of T.E.GRACE
JAS.R.GRACE/Dec.27,1883/July 11,1899/son of T.E.& VIRGINIA GRACE
JOHN MAX KILLIAN/Oct.13,1874/Aug.5,1892/age 17 yrs.
MARY YOUNG/Jan.1,1865/July 28,1896/wife of Dr.J.L.YOUNG
MAX KILLIAN/May 4,1834/Mar.14,1899
MARGARET KILLIAN/June 29,1836/Aug.21,1924
JEHU LEWIS YOUNG/Mar.25,1837/Sept.2,1911
VALENTINE A.KILLIAN/May 7,1869/Oct.13,1917/2nd son of MAX &
        MARGARET KILLIAN
CHARLIE M.KILLIAN/Oct.6,1862/Dec.21,1911
MARGARET A.HARWELL/June 28,1859/Apr.29,1909
GRANT HOOKS/Aug.30,1874/May 4,1929
EDWARD THOMPSON/Mar.17,1877/Mar.29,1934
GRAHAM THOMPSON/July 25-26,1923/ son of MR.& MRS.EDWARD THOMPSON
JOHN JULIUS ALFORD/ 1883-1925
INF.dau.of NELLIE & FLOYD ALFORD,11/1920
INF.Twins of BETTY & CINC ALFORD,11/1949
ELLEN MARTIN TAYLOR/ 1846-1937
MARGARET CONNELL BIGGS/June 18,1867/Nov.22,1961
ELISE "BETTY"HOVIS ALFORD/May 3,1920/Sept.10,1976
C.E.ALFORD/Jan.18,1875/Nov.2,1918
WILLIAM WALLACE/d.Dec.22,1881/ (broken stone)

WASHINGTON CO., MS. CEMETERIES

GREENFIELD CEMETERY

NELLIE BIGGS ALFORD/May 6,1887/June 11,1967/wife of FLOYD ALFORD II
STEWART FLOYD ALFORD,II/ 1873-1940
FLOYD ALFORD HEALY/May 19,1935/Aug.6,1945
(Dbl.Stone)BEE WEBB/Jan.17,1914/Jan.18,1969
    MARGUERITE C.WEBB/ incomplete
CHARLES CHRISTIAN KLEINSCHMIDT,JR./Dec.30,1948/Nov.5,1967
MAUDE BIGGS FINLAY/June 20,1890/Aug.4,1973
ROBERT C.FINLAY,MD./Dec.7,1885/Oct.15,1947
(Dbl.Stone)FANNY C.CRAWFORD/Jan.11,1870/Oct.18,1956
    JOHN S.CRAWFORD/June 8,1866/Dec.16,1930
CLARENCE OGE' COUVILLON/July 14,1895/June 13,1938
NANCY AUGUSTA COUVILLON/Mar.26,1931/May 14,1932
MILDRED DUKE SPENCE/July 31,1917/Oct.4,1972
TILLMAN DUKE/Jan.28,1912/Dec.4,1930
DR.W.T.DUKE/Oct.6,1889/July 23,1931
LOTTIE DUKE MINYARD/Nov.7,1890/Jan.26,1975
JERRY LEON SHIELDS/Aug.10,1933/Mar.13,1970/MISS A3C US AIR FORCE
    KOREA
WILLIAM K.DUKE/Jan.1,1920/July 16,1962/Miss Cpl339 Bomb.Sq.AAF WW II
JOHN H.PERKINS/ 1869-1939
WILLIAM A.JORDAN/ 1861-1922
LINWARD JENNINGS/Feb.8,1897/Mar.28,1954/Miss Pvt.Inf.WW I
J.LEWIS JENNINGS/ 1868-1945
MARY ELIZABETH LOVE SAAD/ 1942-1964
ALPHEUS N.SMILEY/Apr.9,1834/Sept.24,1972
MARY VIRGINIA EIFLING/Feb.22,1933/incomplete
WILLIAM THOMAS EIFLING/May 11,1931/Jan.26,1982
(Dbl.Stone)C."MIKE"GARNER/Sept.2,1910/ incomplete/ Husband
    EILEEN L.GARNER/Jan.14,1912/Apr.22,1979/ Wife
(Dbl.Stone)MARTHA TAYLOR/July 31,1838/Oct.28,1893
    W.J.TAYLOR/Jan.31,1833/ June 14,1895
Two inf.children of M.J.& W.J.TAYLOR/d.July 24,1875 and May 5,1878
MYRTICE ESTHER BACON/Aug.27,1888/July 31,1893/dau.of W.O.& J.L.BACON
(Dbl.Stone)FRANK HAMMONS/Aug.9,1916/July 14,1965
    LOUISE HAMMONS/Jan.2,1916/incomplete
MORRIS E.MORGAN/Mar.20,1873/Dec.22,1930
EDGAR ROYAL/ 1883-1953
ROY HARVEY/ 1911-1954
CLYDE LAVEL NICHOLS/Dec.10,1923/Oct.4,1981
FRANK EUGENE WARREN/Jan.28,1903/Feb.8,1963

WASHINGTON CO.,MS.CEMETERIES

GREENFIELD CEMETERY

IDA CAROLINE GILKEY/Dec.19,1869/Mar.24,1890/dau.of A.J.& ADIE L.GILKEY
EVA GILKEY SCOTT/May 18,1864/Dec.26,1930
ADA LOGAN GILKEY/Jan.11,1838/May 29,1879/wife of A.J.GILKEY
ANDREW J.GILKEY/Sept.28,1827/June 13,1910
MARY E.GILKEY/June 8,1850/Nov.1,1910/wife of A.J.GILKEY
(Dbl.Stone)LORRAINE CATCHINGS DULANEY/Dec.29,1862/Nov.30,1945
       CALLIE HARRIS DULANEY/June 13,1869/Aug.20,1960
GEORGE ANTHONY GRAVOIS/1865-1922
(Dbl.Stone)JOSEPH GRAVOIS/1867-1950
       ROSA GRIFFIN GRAVOIS/1883-1949
JACK GRAVOIS/1909-1909
JOSEPH LORAINE GRAVOIS/1902-1919
MARY DORIS KING STONE/Aug.23,1914/Jan.2,1980
LOTTIE L.STORM/Feb.17,1927/May 19,1980,US Air Force/Wife
(Dbl.Stone)HERBERT P.CLEVELAND/Apr.28,1892/Jan.20,1973/ Father
       MARY F.CLEVELAND/Apr.30,1898/Aug.25,1965/ Mother
(Dbl.Stone)SARAH H.RICH/Sept.29,1901/ incomplete
       MEL H.RICH,SR./Nov.21,1895/Oct.6,1972
WILLIAM MERCER HARRIS/Mar.19,1841/Aug.1,1917 (Capt)
SUE HARRIS/Aug.17,1842/Mar.10,1929
JOSEPH H.PRESTON/1870-1929
MARGARET Z.DINKINS/Apr.30,1881/Jan.15,1887
SAMANTHA McMAHON/June 28,1879/Nov.22,1963
JOSEPH A.WALKER,SR./ Aug.26,1905/Apr.10,1946
WM.DAVID WALKER/June 28,1879/Oct.27,1954
MAGGIE S.WALKER/ Nov.30,1878/Apr.1,1959
ROBERT DANDRIDGE LANCASTER/Feb.28,1864/Sept.28,1891/
       b.Henry Co.,Ga.,d.Glen Allan,Miss.
MARY A.BLACKLEY/1884-1971
FRANK BLACKLEY/Aug.18,1915/Nov.21,1955
BEN BLACKLEY/June 30,1920/Sept.22,1944/Miss PFC 167 Inf.31 Inf.Div.
       WW II
ANDREW TURNBULL/d.Mar.20,1870/age 69 yrs.,1 mo,20 da.
CHARLES FREDERICK TURNBULL/d.July 27,1870/aged 29 yrs.,11 mo,9 da./
       Erected by his Mother
MARSHALL S.WAKEFIELD/d.Nov.1,1873/aged 43 yrs.
MELISSA SLATER/Aug.27,1844/May 19,1885/wife of J.D.SLATER
JOHN DANIEL SLATER/1851-1886
MARY SETTLER SLATER/1826-1886/ Mother
CHARLES TURNBULL SLATER/1853-1887

WASHINGTON CO.,MS.CEMETERY RECORDS

GREENFIELD CEMETERY
JOEL SLATER MYRES/Mar.21,1889/Sept.23,1965
JOEL MYRES/Apr.3,1860/July 28,1943
EMMA SLATER MYRES/June 3,1862/Feb.7,1945
CLARIBEL DAVIS MYRES/July 8,1904/Nov.16,1955
HARPER RIVERS MYRES/May 21,1896/Feb.3,1959
MARIE MYRES MARTIN/Sept.13,1903/Oct.14,1970
JOHN KIRKLAND/d.Dec.7,1866/aged 59 yrs.

Copied Nov.1984, by Mrs. John R.Craft, assisted by Mrs. Caledonia J.Payne, and Mr.Joe Reilly.

∞∞∞∞∞∞∞∞∞∞∞∞∞∞∞∞∞∞∞∞∞∞∞∞∞∞∞

MT.CARMEL CEMETERY; Location Sec.21,T18N,R8W. Copied by Mr.& Mrs. Hafter,1977,this list has appeared in Cem.& Bible Records, Vol.XVII. The property had been converted into a City playground, later called Maud Bryant Park. In June of 1985, the city moved the existing stones to the city section of Greenville Cemetery. Those that made the transition are marked by **, and were copied by C.Payne,shortly after the last move.

JOE DIN/d.Mar.7,1898
SOLOMON BLACKWELL /d.May 15,1888/erected by his wife
"G.A.R."/George WASHINGTON /age 60/d.Sept.16,1894
**LON TSONG /d.July 1,1899
**JOE HEE/1899
**JULIA/ dau.of SARAH & J.A.WILLIAMS /Mar.11,1875/Mar.4,1898
LOTTIE/wife of JERRY COLEMAN /1848/Mar.7,1898/ *Joining Mt.Olive Lodge No.87 of the I.O.ofS.&D.ofJ.of A./1898*
MINNIE MERCY BROWN/d.June 7,1892
REV.H.N.VALLARD /Oct.26,1856/Dec.1,1895
**ISAAC/son of A.& D.HILL /d.Jan.14,1889/aged 19 yrs.
**ELIZA/dau.of P.H.& M.DIXON /DEC.13,1886/JULY 6,1889
**B.D.STEELE /b.May 4,1850
EMMA/wife of F.T.STEVENS /D.Feb.24,1899/"IDSD of J.A."
**JAMES G.MARSHALL /1851/Sept.14,1891
**ANNER DESAVIEU /d.Jan.5,1897/aged 26 yrs.
**J.T.ROHELIA /Feb.22,1863/Sept.22,1897
**CORPL.NELSON BLACKWELL /Co.3, 53 USC 1
CORN ---- HE-----/Co.F. 50 USC
**WINSDON COOPER /Co.A. USCHA
BEATT /Co.D. 51st USCT
**NATHAN DIXON /Co.D., 84 USCI
**REBECCA HOLT /Aug.4,1872/Oct.8,1909
**ANN HOLLMAN/ *Asleep in Jesus* [not on the Hafter's list]

∞∞∞∞∞∞∞∞∞∞∞∞∞∞∞∞∞∞∞∞∞

WASHINGTON CO.,MS.CEMETERY RECORDS

ERWIN:Single stone in front of the SHUTE HOUSE, on banks of Lake Washington, at Erwin,Ms. Grave of the son of MARGARET JOHNSON **ERWIN** and JAMES **ERWIN**, it was formerly in a vault,now with a headstone. MRS.SHUTE remembers a large graveyard on E. banks of the Lake that washed into the water during the 1927 flood. There is no documentation of those graves.

    VICTOR FLOURNOY **ERWIN** /b.Lexington,Ky/Oct.18,1846/
       d.New Orleans,La./Jan.29,1885.

LAMMERMOOR PLT.:Sec.17,T14N.R9W; On North end of Lake Washington. The METCALFE FAMILY vault has been repeatedly vandalized. Names and dates supplied by MRS.JANE METCALFE **WEATHERS**.

EVELINA MATILDA MACALEB METCALFE **HAMMET** /dau.of DAVID **MACALEB**
   and MATILDA **FARRAR** /b.Pendleton,S.C. Fev.15,1802/d.Jan.7,1865
   (at her son's home on Newstead Plt.,Wash.Co.,Ms.)
DR.WILLIAM HENRY **HAMMET** /b.Mar.25,1799 Donmanway,Cork.Co.,Ireland/
   d.Lammermoor Plt.June 9,1861

[Note: Further information from Mrs. WEATHERS: EVELINA MACALEB'S 1st husband was ALBERT GALLATIN **METCALFE**, who d.constructing a house on Lammermoor Jan.28,1833, and is buried in Cold Springs Cemetery, Claib. Co.,Ms. He was the son of CHRISTOPHER METCALFE. ALBERT and EVELINA METCALFE had one son-FREDERICK AUGUSTUS METCALFE, who is buried in METCALFE CEMETERY.EVELINA and her 2nd husband,Dr.Hammet had no issue.]

COLDSPRINGS PLT. Was located on present site of the Old G'ville Airbase. Once the property of the JACKSONS, the widow,MARY J.ASKEW **JACKSON** married into the **HORD** family. When the base was constructed, the stones were moved to the City section of the G'ville Cemetery.

T.H.JACKSON /Feb.3,1810/May 25,1852
J.B.JACKSON /FEB.20,1854/aged 47 YRS. *"Erected in loving memory"*
DAVID F.ASKEW / *who departed this life*/Apr.10,1849/ *only son of his*
   widowed mother.

COUNTY PAUPERS CEMETERY -South of Reed Rd.,Greenville, near intersection of Reed and Hyway #1, large graveyard,with a few stones.

J.H.TUCKER /Apr.4,1860/July 29,1917
C.W.BURNELY /Apr.10,1863/Aug.31,1917
GLADYS ROBINSON /June 8,1905/Sept.18,1919

LINDEN PLANTATION CEMETERY

Location:S5,T14N,R8W:Linden Plantation, Lake Washington. Property owned by Mrs. Nancy Mann Dinkins.
Copied by:Mr.and Mrs.Jerome C.Hafter,Feb.27,1977

Note:The remaining portion of the Turnbull Cemetery is located in the extreme northeast corner of the house lot,behind the main house,beneath a small group of holly trees,completely overgrown with cane.(JCH)

JOHN TURNBULL/who departed this life on the 26th day of Aug.,1840 in the 34th yr.of his age.
MARY McLIN BRYAN/d.Jan.11,1870,aged 20 yrs.1mo.12 days
McLIN EVANS/Dec.10,1806/Apr.5,1849

KEYSTONE PLANTATION CEMETERY

Location:Sec.7,T16N,R8W,Avon,Ms.Property now owned by Anson Sheldon,Avon,Ms.
Copied by: Mr.and Mrs.Jerome C.Hafter,Apr.10,1977

Note: This cemetery has been almost completely destroyed by tenant farmers on Mr.Sheldon's property. There is no way to locate the site of each grave due to the moving of markers and destruction from farming. Fragments of markers are in evidence,with the majority of those markers found being broken.

SUSIE/dau.of JAMES &NANETTE ABEL/Nov.4,1857/Aug.29,1865 (broken)
MINNIE D.SWITZER/wife of W.B.POWELL/No.7,1866/Dec.16,1888
JOHN T.SWITZER/d.May 23,1871,aged 38 yrs.
JAMES ABELL/d.May 21,1861,aged 38 yrs.
T.W.POWELL/d.Apr.27,1882/aged 4 yrs.1 mo.3 days
JAMES WM.ABELL/Apr.16,1852/June 30,1897 (Ft.stone J.Wm.A.)
EDGAR/son of JAMES & NANETTE ABELL/d.Nov.1,1861,aged 5 days
GEORGE ANNA/dau.of J.S.& B.J.NELSON/Dec.7,18--/Aug.7,187(3?)
Fragments included:ft.stone" G.A.M."; broken marker "Sept.Died Oct.1883";broken marker "Born 4,182-,Died Nov.---"

GREENVILLE GOLF COURSE CEMETERY

Location East bank of Deer Creek,north of first green of the Greenville Municipal Golf Course,Sec.14,T19N,R8W (On the Old Air Force Base)
Copied by:Jo Cille Hafter,Jan.16,1977

NORMAN GREEN/Apr.16,1849/Mar.9,1912
ISAAC TAYLOR,JR./ Apr.15,1905/Apr.9,1927

GOLF COURSE, cont.
FRED THOMAS,JR.Mar.15,1904/aged 19 yrs.,10 mos.
GEORGE M.SWEDEN/Maryland,Nov.30,1821/Miss.,May 17,1903/81 yrs.5 mos.17 days.

MONTGOMERY FAMILY CEMETERY
Location:Auburn Plantation,James, Ms.Sec.6,T16N,R8W
Copied by:Mr.and Mrs. Jerome C.Hafter,Feb.20,1977

HOWELL MONTGOMERY/son of DAVIS & ELIZABETH MONTGOMERY/
    d.Sept.119,1837/in his 10th yr.
DAVIS MONTGOMERY/Feb.7,1798/May 29,1844
THOMAS HOWELL/son of THOMAS H. & LOUISE BUCKNER/
    June 20,1847/May 7,1850
INFANT dau.of T.W.& B.A.WILSON/b.d.Jan.13,1852
INFANT son of T.W.& B.A.WILSON/b.d.July 5,1855

FERGUSON FAMILY CEMETERY
Located: In the alley just back of the old Lee home,later owned by Mrs. Gracia Walton at 211 South Hinds Street,Greenville,Ms.
Copied by:Jo Cille Hafter.

Note:This cemetery list was found in the WPA Source Material for Mississippi History for Washington Co. "In it are buried GEN.FERGUSON's FATHER and his infant daughter ELEANOR,MAJ.WILLIAM HENRY LEE, and his 2nd wife,formerly a MISS KNIGHT,of Louisville,Ken. and SAMUEL,little son of HARRY PERCY LEE." The property extended from the alley to Central Ave.and from the cnter of present Hinds Street to what is now Theobald St. (JCH)

Ed.Note: The Cemeteries copied by Mrs. Hafter have appeared previously in various volumns of the BIBLE AND CEMETERY RECORDS,AS PUBLISHED BY THE MS.ST.HISTORICAL SOC.

MOUND CEMETERY
Location:Due West of the Stoneville Experiment Station,on top of an Indian Mound.Sec.10,T18N,R7W. When the Boy Scouts camped on top of this mound 20 years ago,they remembered "lots of tombstones".
Copied by:Katherine Branton and Caledonia Payne,1983

JAMES HENRY YERGER/b.Jany.9,1827/d.May 13,1858/"He was greatly beloved"
1 large stone face down
1 small broken piece of white marbel "----ys"

WASH.CO.CEMETERY RECORDS

YELLOW FEVER CEMETERY

LOCATION:Greenville,Ms., between Nelson and Union, opposite the Courthouse Square (existing in 1876). Divided in three parts - the Catholic on the South,Jewish in the center, and the General Cemetery to the North end of the block. This cemetery became crowded in 1878, and negotiations were underway for a new cemetery, when the Yellow Fever Epidemic struck in the late summer of that year. During two months over 33% of the city's population died and many were buried in the new Greenville Cemetery,called "Greenway". Those graves left in the old cemetery were mostly of families who had been wiped out in the epidemic or who had moved away leaving the dead behind them. Most graves were removed to the new cemetery. (COPIED FROM A PAPER BY NINA PEPPER,LOUISE,MS. DEC. 1969) Cemetery copied by EUNICE STOCKWELL,1934. [Note: Since 1969, the former cemetery has been turned into a playground for the neighborhood. The few stones that were left are isolated in one corner.K.B.]

ANNA,dau.of WM.& ANN YOUNG/Jan.14,1859/ Aug.8,1876
THOMAS L.TAYLOR/Jan.7,1852/Aug.18,1874
HOWELL HINDS/ n\d
MRS.M.L.HEATH/Nov.20,1849/Sept.1,1874
LOU/wife of/JOHN KIRKLAND/Sept.4,1837/Jan.7,1875.
T.J.MAGNUM/Sept.6,1832/June 16,1889/ Mason
CAMERON/son of I.S.& C.C.ROBINSON/Dec.20,1865/----1876
NICHOLAS B.JOHNSON/Feb.29,1832/Sept.5,1876.
MARY A./wife of J.G.BECK/d.July 15,1875/aged 34 yrs.
-----/son of J.G.& MARY BECK/d.Apr.15,1874/age 2 yrs.
W.O.WETHERBEE/May 8,1846/d.Sept.30,1878.
MABLE/dau.of W.O.& B.V.WETHERBEE/Apr.1,1873/Oct.7,1878
ELIZABETH A.SEARS/adopted dau.of --W.& ---.
A.ELLIOTT/Feb.19,1865/Oct.2,1873
THEODORE/son of J.&C.HARICHT/Oct.3,1858/Sept.12,1878.
M.W.JOHNSON/d.Oct.4,1878/aged 23 yrs.
F.M.JOHNSON/d/Oct.12,1878/aged 9 yrs.
B.JOHNSON/d.Oct.15,1878/age 11 yrs.
3 Children of J.I.& AUGUSTA LENGSFIELD:INFANT DAU./n\d
      INFANT DAU./Feb.18,1868// AUGUSTA/Nov.10,1871/Jan.16,1872
NAOMI/dau.of W.H.& LAURA SMITH/Mar.4,1888/Aug.22,1890.
PALLERFEN KEENE/son of WILFORD H.& LAURA SMITH/Oct.22,1886/
      d.Sept.14,1887.

WASHINGTON CO.,MS.CEMETERY RECORDS

"YELLOW-FEVER CEMETERY", was used prior to 1878, and long after the NEW Greenville Cemetery was opened. It has fallen into sad condition. In 1971, Carol Ray found the following stones piled in a corner. They appear to be from the Jewish Section of the old cemetery, with a few exceptions. We don't know where they were moved. These names are in addition to those on the previous page.

JACOB BARNETT /1822/Oct.1902
MORITZ BROH /b.at Lekno,Prussia /n\d
DAVID COHN /9 June 1863/14 Aug.1902/39 yrs. W.O.W.
JACOB A.GOLDMAN /d.1 July 1873/52 yrs.
JONAS GOODMAN /17 Jan.1861/9 Feb.1892
WILLIAM GOODMAN /27 Nov.1868/27 Feb.1892
JOSEPH JOHN /son of MEYER &ADA HENDEL /D.31 AUG.1895/7 MOS.9DAYS
SARAH/dau.of M.&.F.HENDEL d.5 Feb.1896/21 yrs
JACOB HIRSCH / n\d
MICHIAL IMMERGLUCK /b.Krakan,Austria/14 Aug.1869/11 Oct.1890
CLEMENCE JACOB /b.St.Avolo,Lebannon/ n\d
ROSA GOLDFARB/wife of JOSEF KLINGER /b.Tarnpo,Austria/10 Feb.1866/
   d.28 Oct.188-
T.J.MANGHAM /6 Sept.,1832/16 June 1889/Mason
CARRIE ORGLER MARKS /d.7 June 1880
DAVID/son of A.& C.MEYER /of Grand Lake,Ark./9 Sept.1879/July 1883
ANNIE G./wife of WILLIAM MULLER /18 May 1820 (no other date)
JACOB ORGLER /b.Krakan,Austria 1838/d.11 Oct.1889/51 yrs.
JULIA DREYFUS/wife of M.SALMON /d.26 Nov.1886/26 yrs.11 mos. 1 da.
Children of S.& E.SILBERBERG /15 Oct.1879-26 Nov.1879
   and 15 Oct.1879 - 25 July 1880
SILVERBERG /1866-1881
HARRY N.SNOWBERGER /b.in Philadelphia/26 Jan.1847/20 Nov.1888
EDWARD STEINBERG /4 Jan.1847/18 Sept.1878/Mason
CORNELIUS F.SULLIVAN/ d.30 Mar.1903/age 65 yrs.
ESTER TEMA/ INFANT/28 DEC.1879/8 JULY 1880
ALBERT VORMUS ,B.IN Delme Lorraine,France/15 May,1851/14 June 1899
CORA A.WARD /dau.of JAMES B.& DOLLIE WARD /23 Jan.1884/20 May 1888
JULIUS WERNER /d.2 Sept.1891/30 yrs.

∞∞∞∞∞∞∞∞∞∞∞∞∞∞∞∞∞∞∞∞∞∞∞∞∞∞∞∞

McKEONE : located North of Greenville, West of Highway #1, on back edge of the CARSON Place, on road to the WINN Place. Sec.18,T19N,R9W. On N.side of drainage ditch, in a clump of trees. Copied by Tut and C. Payne,1986.

PATRICK McKEONE /b.in Roscommon Co.,Ire./d.Sept.29,1878/age 44 yrs.
JANE BERGIN /d.Apr.1911/age 56 yrs.

∞∞∞∞∞∞∞∞∞∞∞∞∞∞∞∞∞∞∞∞∞∞∞∞∞∞∞∞

WASH.CO.CEMETERY RECORDS

LOUGHBOROUGH CEMETERY

Location:LOUGHBOROUGH PLANTATION, Winterville,Ms.
Copied by MARY ALICE WILLIS, Summer 1976
[Note:Fragment of a marker believed to be at the gravesite of BENJAMIN HUMPHRIES SUTTON, known to be buried in LOUGHBOROUGH CEMETERY. These parts of a marker are now (1976) partially in the ground, near the group of SUTTON family stones. B.H.SUTTON was the son of JAMES M.SUTTON and his first wife,ELIZA VAN NORMAN SUTTON. Born in Port Gibson,Ms. in 1834, he was a member of Co.D.,28th Ms.Volunteer Cavalry, CSA. M.A.W.]

Dble Stone:JAMES M.SUTTON/b.Elizabethtown,Pa./Dec.25,1806/
    d.Greenville,Ms. Sept.24,1883/ 77 yrs.,8 mos.,27 days.
       LAURA CROSS SUTTON/b.Ballstown Springs, N.Y./died on Island 83
       near Greenville,Ms. Oct.15,1875/ 62 yrs. 2 mos., 5 days.
Dble Stone:SARAH/wife of THOMAS J.SUTTON/Feb.8,1849/Nov.6,1869
    ANNA F./dau.of THOMAS J.& S.L.SUTTON/Mar.14,1868/ Aug.21,1875
CAPT.JOHN MALCOLM MONTGOMERY/ Nov.7,1841/Mar.13,1910
A.F.ALEXANDER/d.Sept.1865
Dbl.Stone:J.B.MOSBY/Dec.11,1876/aged 23 yrs., 1 mo.
    L.H.MOSBY/d.July11,1878/aged 21 yrs. 4 mos.
    [Sons of G.E.& ELIZA MOSBY]
ELIZA G.MOSBY/d.Sept.18,1862/ aged 32 yrs., 8 mos.,29 days.
GERVAS BURKS/ son of A.W.& G.W.McALLISTER/Sept.8,1854/Dec.16,1874
CAROLINE L.McALLISTER/d.Sept.26,1878/aged 62 yrs. 21 days.
CHARLES KEITH/ son of A.M.& C.L.McALLISTER/ b.at WILDWOOD (Plt.)
    May 31,1852/d.Sept.19,1878
Dbl.St.:WILBERT J.THOMPSON/Nov.7,1878/Oct.16,1882
    GRACE E.THOMPSON/Oct.20,1882/Dec.10,1890
MRS. L.C.MARTIN/Jan.23,1829/Nov.7,1891/aged 62 yrs. 9 mos.,14 days.
NANNIE G.DAVIS/Aug.8,1865/Mar.20,1890
EARLE HARDY/Feb.7,1896/May 15,1896

WILKERSON CEMETERY

Location:On Black Bayou Plt.,Tupelo Gum Swamp,Bolivar Co.,Ms., on a mound surrounded by an iron fence. Across the levee, about 1/4 mile from the Ms.River.Copied by CATHERINE WILKERSON BRYAN, Nov.1952. [Note: By1986, this cemetery has almost disappeared,due to high water and vandalism. }
THOMAS J.WILKERSON/d.June 17,1875/age 22 yrs.
IRENE/ dau.of J.& ELIZABETH/b.Oct.31,1855/d.Aug.10,1856
JEFFERSON WILKERSON/b.June 1,1807/d.Feb.13,1868/
ELIZABETH SHELBY/d.Jan.12,1897/age 63 yrs.
PETER WILKERSON/d.Nov.11,1859/age 77 yrs.

METCALFE CEMETERY:

Located in SW 1/4 of Sec.36,T16N,R8W. Adjoining the house and yard of the old METCALFE house, on the West banks of Deer Creek, East of the village of Metcalfe. Inclosed in a brick and wrought iron fence, it is well kept and serene. In the center is large monument METCALFE. Copied by KATHERINE BRANTON and CALEDONIA PAYNE, 1983.

F.A.METCALFE/b.July 5,1830/d.Jany.15,1883
PRICILLA EVALINA METCALFE/wife of MAJOR THOMAS COLLINS/ CSA/
    Aug.3,1856/Jany.28,1932
ALBERT HAMMET/son of F.A.& M.P.METCALFE/ b.Mar.10,1855/d.Aug.3,1877.
HARLEY METCALFE,JR./Mar.27,1897/Jan.27,1979/ with a Ft./Stone -
    HARLEY METCALFE, JR./Pvt.U.S.Marine Corps/WWI 1897-1979
FREDERICK AUGUSTUS/ son of HARLEY & SALLY J.METCALFE/b.Mar.10,1901/
    d.Apr.30,1915/ "*Beloved*"
HARLEY METCALFE/ Mar.5,1865/July 24,1946
SARAH JEFFRIES METCALFE/ "SALLIE"/ wife of HARLEY METCALFE/
    Nov.24,1875/Feb.11,1975
INFANT/ son of HARLEY & SALLIE METCALFE/ (couldn't read date)
INFANT/ son of GEORGE & MAUDE METCALFE/ b & d. Nov. ----
JEFFRIES/ infant son of SALLIE & HARLEY METCALFE/
    May 27,1899/June 8,1900
WALTER THORNTON WEATHERS/"BOOTS"/ Jan.12,1907/June 3,1974/
    Ft.Stone:WALTER T.WEATHERS/Capt.U.S.Army

PETERS - PETTIT CEMETERY

Location:Avon,Ms.-West side of Highway #1, in a grove of trees.Copied by JO CILLE HAFTER, Jan.8,1977.[Note:The original list of people buried in this cemetery was found in the WPA Source Material for Miss.History for Wash. Co. This list was taken in 1977 and compared with existing cemetery. The names indicated by an*were found. An unmarked vault had been vandalized.]

*DR.MATTHEW L.PETERS/Dec.25,1821/DEc.11,1875
  ANN GARLAND HOOE/1800/ d.Dec.16,1876
*JOHN PETITT/Dec.16,1844/Mar.2,1899
*HALLIE HOOE/wife of M.L.PETERS/ Apr.6,1836/Feb.18,1905/ MOTHER
*CLARA LOUISE/infant dau.of MORRIS & MINNIE PETERS ROSENSTOCK/
    Apr.12,1887/June 18,1887/ (Monument broken)
BETTIE T.(PETERS)/wife of DANIEL G.PEPPER/Feb.15,1859/Apr.4,1879/
    and her Babe
*In Memory of MINNIE PETERS ROSENSTOCK/ 1867/1899

WASHINGTON CO., MS. CEMETERY RECORDS
Leland-Stoneville Cemetery

Chartered in 1921, this cemetery was used prior to that time. Some stones were obviously moved from other locations, and some placed as memorials for earlier deaths. Located on "Old Leland Road", West of Stoneville. In cataloging this cemetery, we adopted a flexible system of copying the older graves, those b. before 1885 or who d. before 1912, unless a whole family plot brought in other family ties. Babies decd. after 1912 were not enumerated in this list, as this was the date when the State initiated the death and birth certificates. [ ] denotes family plots. Beginning in Section #1, 1st road on the East side. Catalogued by C. Payne and K. Branton, 1986.

[Dbl.St.: Mother-LOU ELLA DAY JOHNSON / Apr.4, 1867 / Oct.1, 1956
    Son-ROBERT EDWARD JOHNSON / Nov.27, 1894 / July 13, 1953
EDWARD NOAH DAY / Aug.25, 1871 / Dec.17, 1949
Dbl.St.: Father-ELBERT R. DAY / Nov.29, 1833 / July 19, 1920
    Mother-MARTHA J. DAY / His wife / Aug.25, 1833 / Oct.6, 1916
DELLA DAY REINHOLD / 1877-1948   FRANK O. REINHOLD / 1865-1941]
[Dbl.St.: ISAIAH W. READ / 1848-1920 >>>> His wife / EFFA CHASE / 1864-1920
E.E. VAUGHAN : 1861-1936]
[JAMES HAMPTON, JR. / son of J.H. & MARY L. COLLIER / May 10, 1910 /
    Nov.21, 1910
JAMES HAMPTON COLLIER / July 28m 1870 / Oct.1, 1910
AVA WATKINS COLLIER DAVID / Aug.20, 1892 / Jan.15, 1964
JOHN ALLEN COLLIER .Sr. / June 19, 1890 / Mar.27, 1945
OLIVIA WEILENMAN COLLIER / Feb.2, 1858 / Oct.14, 1944
J.B. COLLIER / 1840-1916]
[GEORGE T. PATTERSON, SR. / 1899-1967
GEORGE T. PATTERSON, JR. / Miss AET M3 USNR / WW II / Feb.28, 1926 /
    July 30, 1955   GEORGE R. PATTERSON / 1874-1954
LUCY M. PATTERSON / 1872-1952   CHARLES M. PATTERSON / 1902-1913
DONALD McLEAN PATTERSON / 1906-1980]
[CLEMMIE T. KLINGMAN / Nov.16, 1874 / Apr.29, 1947
WILLIAM KLINGMAN / Mar./ 15, 1869 / Apr.5, 1942
CLEMENTINE KLINGMAN CLOWER / JULY 4, 1900 / Sept.3, 1979
    Beloved wife of CHARLES McGEE CLOWER]
[Dbl.St.: GEORGE WILLIAM PIGG / June 30, 1884 / July 13, 1953
    KATE WITHERSPOON PIGG / July 20, 1885 / Oct.10, 1970
GEORGE HUGH PIGG / SSGT U.S. ARMY / WW II / Oct.17, 1913 / July 11, 1982
MATTIE O. WITHERSPOON: Jan.8, 1869 / June 8, 1943]
[WILLIAM MERCER RICH / 1905-1981   LUCY WHEELER RICH / 1872-1951
WILLIAM ARTHUR RICH: / 1867-1942   ROWENA RICH BEARD / 1897-1982
WALTER LEE BEARD, Sr. / 1890-1960   ANNIE COLLIER BEARD / 1890-1914
    WALTER LEE BEARD, JR. / 1914-1930]

WASHINGTON CO.,MS.CEMETERY RECORDS
Leland-Stoneville Cemetery

[WILLIAM HOWARD HORTON /W.O.W./1874-1917
MADIE JOYCE JOHNSON /1856-1942]
[CURTIS HENRY MOORE /Aug.29,1884/Dec.9,1946/ *Beloved Teacher*
ALLIE WHITE MOORE /Dec.28,1883/Feb.23,1973/ *Devoted wife &mother*
ELLINE MOORE /Mar.29,1910/May 1,1935/ (Carving of a piano on stone)]
LILLIE THOMPSON /age 21,d.Nov.11,1936/(Stone is a round post.)
[Dbl.St.:JAMES C.CARVER /1871-1938>>>>>MELISSA CARVER /1869-1945
FREDRIC H.IVY /1859-1915/Ft.St. *His Trust Was In God*]
[MELISSA MALOY HALL /Sept.17,1883/July 4,1938
JOHN THOMAS HALL /OCT.16,1881/Jan.19,1940
CHARLES JAMES HALL,Sr./Mar.21,1910/July 10,1968
RUTH MANSELL HALL /Apr.4,1891/Jan.7,1968
ARCHIE B.LANCASTER,SR. /Dec.8,1885/Jan.9,1958
RUBY MANSELL LANCASTER /Apr.4,1891/May 18,1965]
[Dbl.St.:Father:WALLACE B.CASON,SR./July 7,1884/Dec.25,1935
    Mother:MABEL STINSON CASON /Nov.24,1895/Aug.14,1977]
MARY BARTON JONES /1892-19--/Memorializing my son/ROBERT SELDEN
    INGRAM II/1918-1924
NETTIE M. ZEIGLER PERRY /Nov.19,1903/June 4,1985
ALVIE LAWRENCE ZEIGLER /Sept.28,1890/Mar.15,1945/Father
NETTIE HEFFNER /NOV.21,1979/JAN.24,1920
CHARLES J.SEABROOK /OCT.30,1875/FEB.2,1920
CHARLES J.SEABROOK /June 17,1920/Nov.5,1922
KATE S.WOOD /May 23,1880/Jan.23,1965
Dbl.St.:ROSIE ANNA OVERTON/ 1872-1944>>JOHN A.OVERTON /1871-1942
Dbl.St.:CHARLEY B.THOMPSON /Sept.5,1874/May 24,1921
    AMELIA, His wife/Sept.6,1870/Oct.31,1946
Dbl.St.:JOHN FINLEY McKENZIE /Sept.27,1867/Dec.20,1963
    MARY JANE/Wife of J.F.McKENZIE /Mar.4,1861/Feb.7,1946
Dbl.St.:ALVIE MILAM /Oct.2,1895/Sept.9,1969
    JARRETT CARROLL MILAM /May 17,1881/Jan.11,1931
JACK SALES ALEXANDER /Jan.31,1885/May 21,1963
[HARRY PRATT /Apr.10,1879/Apr.9,1926
BEULAH N. PRATT /July 4,1881/Nov.9,1956]
[BESSIE APPLEWHITE/Wife of E.ALTON BATES /Sept.11,1897/June 13,1926
LILLIE McGEE BATES/ Oct.9,1902/ n/d
EMMETT ALTON BATES /Oct.28,1894/May 17,1971]
<u>Section #2 adjoins #1 on the East side. Working south and eastward.</u>
[FAMILY OF I.W.KITTLE:
IRA WYCHE KITTLE /1878-1964 << IRA W.KITTLE /1929-1946
REAVIS KITTLE /1881-1942 >>>>>>SAM W. KITTLE/ 1878-1921

WASHINGTON CO.,MS. CEMETERY RECORDS
Leland-Stoneville Cemetery

AGNES E.KITTLE /1855-1898 >>> GEORGE I.KITTLE /1849-1913
EUGENE KITTLE /1892-1957 >>> KATE S.KITTLE /1904-1969]
[ELISE MARBLE /1911-1913 >>> DONALD MARBLE /1917-1919
RUTH LYNN ABERNATHY / n/d >>> LUCY MARBLE /1886-1943
FRISBY GRIFFING MARBLE /1883-1965 >> W.G.MARBLE /1856-1934
SADIE B.MARBLE /1861-1945 >>> REGINALD L.MARBLE /1886-1955
AVA ANNETTE MARBLE /1890-1971<<EVELYN BELLE GRIFFING /1888-1966
DR.Z.B.GRIFFING /1822-1914 >>>> J.A.MARBLE /1859-1932
CLEMMIE MARBLE /1894-1936 >>>> EMMETT G.MARBLE /1884-1954]
[FANNIE H.DAVIS /June 28,1828/Nov.10,1914
SARAH/dau.of JOHN S.& F.H.DAVIS /Jan.10,1854/Apr.3,1907
JOHN SHAW DAVIS /Oct.20,1855/Oct.29,1920
N.E.WILSON /Feb.28,1830/Aug.5,1905/Mother
JOHN W.DAVIS /D.Sept.22,1903/Aged 60 yrs.]
ANDREW T. GRAVES /1862-1914 >>>>CYNTHIA ANN GRAVES /1862-1936
F.L.BUTTS /Dec.4,1852/Sept.22,1914/ *Brother is Home*
JOSEPH LEE JOHNSON /Nov.24,1866/Feb.23,1899
CELESTIA T.McGEE /1831-1899
[ONE STONE: KATE - DAISIE - CORINNE - WALTER
        Infant children of/W.W.& ELLA HOLT STONE /1877-1884
DAVID L.STONE /SEPT.28,1846/SEPT.25,1878/HUSBAND]
[SAMMIE RAY/son of B.L.&J.O.LEE/Jan.22,1889/Oct.17,1901
JIM LEE/Jan.16,1910/June 28,1910
MARGARET/ dau.of B.L.& J.O.LEE/June 19,1897/June 27,1897
Infant dau.of B.L.& J.O.LEE /1886
WILLIAM T.LEE/Jan.26,1893/Dec.26,1962
FRED W.BARNES,JR. /Sept.8,1911/Aug.21,1969
HATTIE LEE HUGHES/ Aug.12,1891/May 26,1976]
[Dbl.St.:HAZEL/Infant son of T.D.& V.B.MAGEE /Dec.3,1894/June 26,1895
        ROBERT P./d.Oct.16,1896/age 3 mos.,19 days]
ALTON V.MASON/ July 11,1911/Oct.23,1933
TOM HURL --/1870-1936 (BROKEN STONE)
[Dbl.St.:MONTFORT J.RILEY /1871-1937/Father
        ROCHESTER E.RILEY/ 1879-1962/Mother]
Dbl.St.:BESSIE LAWS /1879-1948 >>>>> CHARLES O.LAWS /1877-1939
[W.H.McGOWEN /1866-1933 >>>>>>>>> C.O.BELL /1876-1940
Dbl.St.:SARAH JANE BELL /1871-1937>>>>CHARLES W.BELL /1868-1943]
Dbl.St.:MARTHA BURK GIARDINA /June 6,1877/Mar.14,1948
        F.J.GIARDINA /Jan.20,1855/Nov.26,1928
Dbl.St.:EUGENIA L.MOSLEY /Mar.3,1872/Aug.28,1954
        J.S.MOSLEY Dec.28,1864/Apr.19,1941

WASHINGTON CO., MS. RECORDS
Leland-Stoneville Cemetery

E.BENJAMIN TRIM /Sept.29,1868/Dec.14,1940
BUELAH TERRY LEE /May 3,1892/Mar.1,1930
MRS.J.GREER / 1857-1933
MARTHA JONES /Mother of Sam'l JONES /Apr.3,1838/Sept.22,1910
WM.RICHARD ROBERTS /Sept.18,1870/Mar.10,1952
FLORENCE NELL ROBERTS /Oct.16,1895/Aug.31,1924
LILY SMITH PATRICK / 1884-1964   R.CLAY PATRICK / 1882-1963
<u>Middle section, working South to North</u>
ELIZABETH HALL SANDERS /JULU 2,1878/OCT.18,1954
DR.J.S.SANDERS /May 3,1872/Apr.9,1952
WM.B.ETHRIDGE /July 4,1876/May 30,1929
LILLIE V.ETHRIDGE /NOV.20,1883/OCT.,17,1980
Dbl.St.:RUFUS RIPEE / 1871-1945>>>>>> LOTTIE RIPEE / 1882-n\d
Dbl.St.:JESSE F.CASWELL /July 31,1881/Mar.30,1946
         LENA F.CASWELL /Nov.15,1879/n\d
Father:MARION F.CASWELL /Aug.25,1856/Aug.17.1950
Mother:MARY L.CASWELL /AUG.1,1862/APR.12,1947
ANNIE O.RIVERS /Dec.14,1870/Mar.19,1926
J.M.RIVERS / 1858-1940
HANS EDWARD DEENER /Aug.25,1887/Oct.9,1948
RICHIE S.DEENER /Apr.13,1897/Feb.20,1966
C.B.WILLIAMSON,SR. / 1888-1949/Father
LETHA V.WILLIAMSON/ 1889-1956/Mother
Dbl.St.: S.LaSALES SHELTON /July 21,1884/June 5,1946
         BESS DAVENPORT SHELTON /Mar.1,1894/Sept.30,1983
DAVID S. FLANAGAN /Mar.29,1874/Feb.11,1955
Dbl.St.:SAMUEL S.BARR / 1859-1949/Father
         WILLIAM A.BARR /Dec.22,1882/Dec.9,1959
ROBERT WYATT McKEOWN /Jan.7,1881/Oct.26,1911
[Dbl.St.:JAMES EDWARD RATHER /Oct.5,1854/Dec.9,1911/W.O.W.
         FANNIE WILLIS RATHER / His wife/ Sept.7,1863/May 27,1939
TOLBERT ALEXANDER BURFORD /Aug,17,1870/FEb.6,1927
KATE WILLIS BURFORD /Nov.15,1868/Nov.4,1930
WILLIS A.BURFORD /Ms.SGT Med Corps/Mar.11,1939
ROSA VIRGINIA LOCKE WILLIS /Aug.17,1895/Oct.22,1960
ROBERT LESTER WILLIS /Apr.16,1859/June 16,1940
MARTHA WEILENMAN WILLIS /Sept.19,1869/July 17,1954
                <u>Triple Memorial Stone:</u>
ARTHUR CROSS WILLIS /son of ALFRED & EMELINE WILLIS / 1855-1910
ALFRED WILLIS / 1816-1868>>>> EMELINE SUTTON/ 1834-1913/wife of
         ALFRED WILLIS 1854-1868/wife of H.H.MELCHOR 1872-1876

WASHINGTON CO.,MS.RECORDS
Leland-Stoneville Cemetery

HARRY SUTTON MELCHOR /son of H.H.& EMELINE MELCHOR /1872-1884]
[CLARA W.HAMMETT /Apr.19,1853/Mar.20,1936
Dbl.St.:MARGARET F.WEILENMAN /1832-1917/Mother
    JOHN WESLEY WEILENMAN /1812-1869/Father
Dbl.St.:WILLIE E.WEILENMAN/ Dec.26,1866/DEc.18,1931
    MAYDELL LATHAM WEILENMAN /Nov.28,1873/Apr.10,1945
Dbl.St.:BENJAMIN F.BATTS /Aug.8,1848/Oct.29,1913
    ADDIE WEILENMAN BATTS /Sept.17,1863/Jan.11,1962]
GEORGE H.McRAVEN /1856-1929>>>>>> LILLIE F.McRAVEN /1870-1950
FLORA HOSKINS /Sept.7,1875/July 22,1956
[JOHN ,WILLIAM ALDRIDGE /US ARMY KOREA/Aug.3,1929/May 28,1976
KATHLEEN J.ALDRIDGE /June 6,1892/Mar.28,1968
GILBERT DUMAS PITT /Tenn. 2nd Lt.MPC/WW II/Sept.16,1914/Dec.7,1962
JOSEPH THOMAS MATHIS /Sept.10,1876/Nov.9,1950
RUTH ALDRIDGE MATHIS /Nov.18,1885/June 29,1968
JOSEPH HOLLIDAY ALDRIDGE /May 2,1886/July 24,1948
Infant son of JOSEPH HOLLIDAY & HELEN FRAZIER ALDRIDGE /Dec.1924]
[ABRAHAM L.LENHART /1865-1946>>>CLARINDA W.LENHART /1869-1936
[KATIE F.JOHNSON /Nov.4,1887/Dec.30,1939
JOHN C.JOHNSON /Sept.19,1853/Sept.7,1916/ Father
ALICE E.JOHNSON /June 17,1855/Apr.10,1941
ROBERT ABNER IRELAND /Mar.25,1887/Nov.10,1944
CLARA LEE JOHNSON IRELAND /MAR.10,1892/OCT.28,1968
"BOBBY" ROBERT A.IRELAND,III /June 19,1946/Aug.3,1954]
[DEEB K.HAIK /Feb.15,1876/Mar.11,1943
ROSA K.HAIK /July 12,1889/Nov.15,1962]
[SADA A.ABDO /May 21,1873/Jan.27,1964
ELIAS N.ABDO /Mar.29,1872/DEc.24,1862
GABRIEL N.ABDO /Miss PFC 364 CO MTC/WW I/Apr.29,1887/Jan.24,1952
AGEIE ABDO /1841-1935/Mother>>>>>A.ABDO /1886-1935/ Brother]
[CORNELIA ALDRIDGE INGRAM /Apr.14,1887/Mar.7,1977
ROBERT LEE INGRAM /Nov.11,1886/Feb.1,1960
MARY BOWEN HELM /1857-1931
NEVILLE ALLIN HELM /DEc.1,1882/DEc.25,1970]
[JOHN A.BAGLEY /June 11,1862/Mar.30,1934
M.E./ wife of JOHN A.BAGLEY /Sept.7,1866/Mar.24,1928]
[MIMIA HORTON/ 1872-1948
THOMAS L.HORTON /May 12,1850/Jan.8,1942
CLARA F.HORTON /Aug.11,1870/Dec.2,1939]
[Dbl.St.:ERNEST GREER /OCT.22,1882/JAN.4,1955>>>> ETTA ROBERTA
    MASON/ wife of ERNEST GREER /Sept.10,1888/O ct.10,1937]

WASHINGTON CO., MS. RECORDS
Leland-Stoneville Cemetery

[MURIEL WOOD SHORTREED /May 24,1848/July 17,1928
 JAMES WALTER SPROTT /Dec.15,1885/Apr.6,1953/Husband
 GLADYS SHORTREED SPROTT /Nov.1,1885/Nov.21 1976/Wife]
[PINKNEY WATT LANIER /July 6,1848/July 3,1920
 CLIFFORD GUNN LANIER /Sept.22,1856/Apr.15,1933
 ARTHUR JOHN HILL /June 13,1867/Mar.6,1936
 MARY WILBOURN LANIER HILL /Oct.23,1882/Dec.30,1963
 BURTON D.HILL /May 1,1896/Apr.29,1972]
[DAN WELK ALLEN /Mar.17,1876/Dec.15,1944
 EVIE McMILLAN ALLEN /Apr.26,1885/Apr.20,1959]
[WILLIAM NELSON INGRAM /1889-1938
 GARLAND BARTON INGRAM /Nov.30,1931/Nov.18,1979
 Dbl.St..ROBERT SELDEN INGRAM /1854-1921
         JENNY WATSON INGRAM /1858-1891/Wife
 MARY SELDEN HELM /1913-1955]
[JOHN ANDERSON WAITS /Sept.19,1867/Nov.27,1931
 JULIA MAY TURNER WAITS /Nov.4,1877/Feb.27,1968]
[WILLIAM H.GRIMES /Dec.12,1878/Dec.3,1943
 LONA R.GRIMES /Oct.26,1894/Oct.3,1976
 EUGENIA/ Wife of W.H.GRIMES /Dec.20,1878/July 19,1921
 ORELLA GRIMES TURNER /July 8,1881/June 24,1943
 THOMAS JOSEPH TURNER /Nov.13,1876/May 24,1956]
 NOMIE/ Wife of J.B.FINKLEA /Oct.31,1880/July 13,1921
[OBIE FRANKLIN McLEROY /Jan.1,1898/Nov.11,1935
 HATTIE SKINNER McLEROY /Sept.11,1886/Apr.28,1968
 TRISTRIM L.SKINNER /Feb.22,1858/May 19,1930
 ELIZABETH SKINNER /Sept.13,1862/June 30,1944]
[WALTER EDWARD FALOON,JR. /1910-1953
 WALTER EDWARD FALOON /1885-1921
 PRICILLA OAKMAN FALOON /Dec.13,1884/Aug.19,1973
 WALTER E.FALOON /T.SGT.US AIR FORCE/Mar.26,1910/Aug.18,1953
 GEORGE OAKMAN /Feb.1,1882/Jan.25,1929
 LELIA P.OAKMAN /June 25,1883/Aug.12,1963]
[THOMAS E.TANNER /Cpl.5 U.S.VOL.INF./SP.AM.WAR/n\d
 MATTIE COOK TANNER /Sept.2,1874/June 3,1969
 T.F.COOK /Aug.23,1871/Dec.27,1913/W.O.W.
 ESTELLE COOK /Aug.25,1897/Oct.18,1918]
[JOHN PIPPIN /Dec.22,1862/Nov.16,1928
 ANNIE RINER PIPPIN /Jan.11,1871/May 10,1944
 CYRUS C.JOHNSON /Sept.14,1888/Nov.25,1918/Mason
 MARY PIPPIN JOHNSON /Aug.11,1891/Aug.16,1972]

WASHINGTON CO.,MS.CEMETERY RECORDS
Leland-Stoneville Cemetery ,cont. - Older graves only.

ROBERT H.McKEY /1849-1936
[ROBERT N.BLAKEMORE /1833-1916
GEORGE M.HELM /Major CSA/Oct.4,1837/Feb.23,1930/Father
GAY COLEMAN HELM /1910-1970/Husband of BESSIE MAE SHIELDS]
[ENOCH FRANKLIN TURNER ,MD/Mar.19,1852/Mar.7,1918/ Mason
HELEN HOWARD TURNER /Feb.6,1871/Nov.26,1954
INA TURNER /Aug.9,1908/Sept.29,1920]
[ORSAMUS PERRY BEST /Mar.19,1876/Oct.13,1915
JENNINGS OBANNON BEST /Aug.10,1871/Dec.23,1917]
[MARY SWAIN HAY /Oct.9,1862/Feb.28,1941
WALTER LESLIE HAY /Sept.29,1861/Apr.13,1915
WALTER L./son of W.L.& M.R.HAY /Jan.20,1893/Sept.9,1895
WARREN HAY /May 20,1891/Nov.20,1891
Infant son of W.L.& M.R.HAY /Aug.18,1889]
[REBECCA J.SALE /FEb.25,1821/Dec.7,1891
JANE AMANDA/ Wife of JAMES ANDREW COWAN /Oct.17,1828/Mar.6,1900
THOMAS L.DOBSON ,MD/Dec.6,1871/Mar.29,1957
BELLE HAY DOBSON /Sept.20,1887/Dec.5,1969]
Start back at the front fenceline: Working W. and S., between the 2 roads.
[VIVIAN STANDEFER /1906-1922
BERTHA LORENZEN STANDEFER /1883-1950
CECIL STANDEFER /1878-1953
EDNA COOLEY STANDEFER /1894-1970
ANN ELIZABETH STANDEFER /1920-1922
SEATON SKELTON STANDEFER /1888-1936
VERNA PALMER STANDEFER /1913-1973]
[GLEN COPELAND /3 NOV.1912/JUNE 17,1979
ROBERT T.HARRIS /MISS 2d LT. ADJ GEN DEPT/ WW I/July 1,1890
    Jan.6,1967
JOSEPH W.COPELAND /Aug.23,1901/Sept.21,1925
SALLIE POOL COPELAND /28 July 1877/22 Aug.1966
JOSEPH W.COPELAND /MD/ 15 Aug.1871/7Jan.1954]
[DEAN HEBRON /1897-1958 >>>   CORA HEBRON MOORE /1900-1928
JOHN LAWRENCE HEBRON /1864-1945>>>LULA DEAN HEBRON /1870-1945]
[INA McGEE HOPKINS /1873-1929
CLARENCE Mc.HOPKINS /28 Dec.1870/Oct.12,1952]
[KATHERINE JACOBS /1845-1926
JOHN JACOBS /1 Jan.1887/29 Dec.1965
MARY WEBER JACOBS /15 Oct.1903/20 May 1974]
[SWEET ANNETTE McGEE /Mar.2,1903/Aug.28,1903
ADDIE STOVALL McGEE /JAN.17,1867/Apr.6,1931

WASHINGTON CO., MS. CEMETERY RECORDS
Leland-Stoneville Cemetery, cont. - Older graves only.

BURREL OTHO McGEE /Nov.18,1857/Dec.3,1936
RALPH WALDO McGEE /MAY 25,1892/MAY 31,1935
WAYNE McGEE /SEPT.12,1896/DEC.15,1900
INFANT dau.of B.O.& CORA McGEE /1898]
[CAPITOLA McGEE DEAN /Nov.11,1870/June 17,1968
CHARLES C.DEAN /Jan.28,1858/DEc.20,1925
CHARLES OTHO DEAN /Mar.31,1899/Apr.30,1976]
[SARAH McGEE /Mar.13,1911/Aug.9,1923
JEAN McGEE JOHNSON /Dec.9,1924/Oct.1,1951
CLYDE McGEE,SR. /Jan.23,1880/Apr.13,1958
SARAH SEABROOK McGEE /Mar.18,1882/Feb.20,1959
ADAM C.CRAWFORD /MS MAJ.U.S.ARMY/WW II/June 22,1907/July 24,1968]
[ROSA JONES DARDEN /Feb.28,1861/July 29,1935
GEORGE M.DARDEN /Aug.2,1891/May 9,1941]
[WILLIAMSON T.FREEMAN /Aug.3,1866/July 17,1922
MARY BELLE FREEMAN /Oct.11,1870/Jan.26,1930]
SANTO S.CATALDI /1888-1928
[MARY BRUCE MOORE MILAM /Jan.31,1898/Feb.11,1976
BEN STOVALL MILAM /June 17,1892/July 8,1932
CYNTHIA REBECCA STOVALL /Mar.11,1861/Mar.9,1943]
[SOLOMON ABRAHAM /Miss QM SGT/ 312 FIRE TRK.& HOSE CO. QMC/WW I/
    May 10,1895/Feb.20,1953
ISAAC ABRAHAM /1856-1931
KAREEMY J.ABRAHAM /1877-1954]
[EUGENE GERALD /JUly 30,1882/Apr.6,1957
MAY HANEY GERALD /24 Oct.1894/June 13,1979]
[ETHEL BAKER DEAN /wife of HOMER EUGENE DEAN /Ja.17,1884/1 Apr.1956
HOMER EUGENE DEAN /26 Dec.1880/31 July 1960
ROBERT EUGENE/ son of HOMER & ETHEL B.DEAN /30 Apr.1909/12 May 1911
LITTLE HOMER BAKER/ son of HOMER & ETHEL B.DEAN /Apr.30,1906/
    May 21,1908]
[MATTIE LEA WEAVER /Nov.9,1865/Oct.11,1950
NONA WILLIAMSON WOOD /17 Nov.1878/Mar.25 1961
EDWARD WALTHAL WOOD /Nov.15,1876/Nov.8,1940]
[Dbl.St.WILLIAM P.WEIMER /June 1,1861/Jan.2,1923
    MARY E.WEIMER /JULY 4,1864/NOV.11,1956
HELEN WEIMER THOMPSON /1901-1966
ROBERT CUNNINGHAM THOMPSON /May 20,1895/Apr.17,1976]
[EDWARD H.BERRY /July 3,1881/June 26,1925
ELEANOR McBRIDE BERRY /Aug.2,1882/June 21,1958]
[DELLA TILL NETTLES /Oct.3,1885/Oct.7,1936

WASHINGTON CO.,MS.CEMETERY RECORDS
Leland-Stoneville Cemetery ,cont. - Older graves only.

CHARLES EARL ROBBS /Jan.20,1887/June 30,1965
BETTY ROBBS SHELTON /1924-1966]
[MARY GORMAN HUTCHINSON /July 28,1903/Mar.4,1942
LOIS STOVALL GORMAN /Oct.31,1895/Nov.22,1939
THOMAS WALTER GORMAN,SR. /1895-1976
LENA BURNETTE GORMAN /1913-1975
THOMAS J.GORMAN /1915-1940
JAMES THOMAS GORMAN /Oct.27,1868/July 9,1929
AMELIA HENN GORMAN /June 5,1871/Sept.30,1951]
[JAMES B.GIBBS /Sept.29,1884/Sept.30,1939
ROSA THOMAS GIBBS /Nov.13,1880/Sept.17,1958]
[JOHN McGRAW /22 Sept.1869/9 Nov.1941
SLOANE RYALS McGRAW /1 Jan.1890/3 Oct.1970]
[EUGENIA BRANTON ALLEN /15 Oct.1894/June 21,1979
LEROY BARRY ALLEN /2nd LT. ARMY/ WW I/Dec.5,1892/May 2,1977]
[DANIEL THOMAS WILKINS /Aug.16,1884/Apr.6,1949
ADA BARRY BRANTON WILKINS /17 June 1872/Jan.29,1957]
[GEORGE BREISCH /28 Mar.1885/23 Apr.1971
LUCILLE M.BREISCH /21 MAY 1891/SEPT.18,1967]
[SAMUEL ARTHUR BROWN /Dec.10,1879/Nov.4,1965
BLANCHE McGEE BROWN /Mar.18,1882/Nov.14,1961]
ROBERT L.OAKMAN /Sept.7,1889/July 11,1953
[HARRIET GEORGIANA CALLIHAN/1869-1960/wife of GEORGE W.SMITH and
        CHARLES M. MOORE - CSA
CLAYTON QUINTON HOLLOWELL /Sept.3,1893/Jan.3,1980]
[Dbl.St.:ROBERT G.JONES /1865-1949>>>MARY T.JONES /1879-1954
Father:BEN R.JONES /1877-1956>Mother:DELILAH TOLERJONES /1886-1958
[JAMES H.BROOKS /MISS CORP TRANS.CORP/Dec.7,1892/Dec.10,1940
JAMES L.BROOK /1865-1940]
CHARLIE F.PARKER /July 19,1894/Mar.21,1963
[DR.SMITH C.TANNER /"Sugar"/Nov.21,1882/Oct.9,1957
CATHERINE B.TANNER /"Catherine Dear"/Nov.10,1898/July 5,1976]
[HENRY L.FLAKE ,MD./1857-1940
HARRY FLAKE /1904-1962
LEILA DAY FLAKE /1872-1927
JESSIE BERRY NEWMAN /1891-1931]
BERTHA WOLFE BECKER /Nov.3,1881/June 9,1969
[FLORA ABDOR GAZELLE /1864-1951
ALEX GAZELLE /1880-1956]
[MIKE KAZAN /JAN.5,1886/Nov.5,1969
ADELE K.KAZAN /Sept.12,1895/May 20,1961]

WASHINGTON CO.,MS.CEMETERY RECORDS
Leland-Stoneville Cemetery, cont. - Older graves only.

[J.W.ELLOITT /1873-1964>>>>MARY DOTSON ELLIOTT /1885-1970]
EDWARD R.BANKS /Jan.9,1872/Feb.12,1962
[LILLIE MAE GORMAN /Mar.2,1886/Feb.19,1931
JOSEPH H.GORMAN /Mar.15,1880/Aug.2,1963]
[JOHN W.TOLER,SR./Oct.27,1889/July 16,1967
MYRTIS TOLER /FEB.1,1913/n\d]
[ROBERT A.HOLLAND /Dec.25,1887/Feb.22,1966
BURMAH D.HOLLAND/ July 6,1888/Sept.28,1967]
[JOHN ANDREW MORSON /Apr.21,1886/AApr.11,1962
RUTH ELDRIDGE MORSON /Oct.4,1892/Nov.28,1983]
[NELL V.KIRKLAND /Aug.18,1888/Mar.8,1945
ELLA S.KIRKLAND /1861-1935>>>>JOHN R.KIRKLAND /1846-1929]
[FLOYD D.HUDDLESTON /Aug.21,1892/Mar.4,1946
ADDIE COLLIER HUDDLESTON /Oct.4,1887/Oct.9,1970
ARTHUR O.HUDDLESTON /Apr.21,1882/Apr.30,1956]
[JOHN HORACE O'QUINN /Jan.6,1884/Nov.18,1953
MARGARET COLLIER O'QUINN /Oct.4,1887/Jan.23,1978]
ALFRED BURTON HICKS /Jan.13,1875/Oct.22,1952
[EUGENE H.FISHER /MS.PVT.U.A.MARINE CORPS/WW I PH/Mar.22,1894/
    Aug.21,1967
ALLENE WRIGHT FISHER /Aug.22,1904/Feb.25,1971
EMMA C.FISHER /Sept.11,1871/Dec.15,1942
E.S.FISHER /Feb15,1874/July 17,1932]
[ABRAHAM J.KOURY /Feb.1890/Sept.8,1936
ALBERT J.KOURY /Dec.1886/Nov.9,1970
EUGENIA C.KOURY /Jan.9,1901/Oct.30,1966]
JOHN L.GARRETT /1899-1941
[MARY A GREENE BLOCKER /1901-1982
LILLIE E.WILLIAMS /1907-1984
MELVIN WILLIAMS /1898-1941
KATE BERKELEY FELTUS /1867-1948
HENRY T.AARDWEG /July 5,1899/Jan.29.1979
THELMA C.AARDWEG /Sept.22,1897/June 23,1974
JOHN AARDWEG /Dec.13,1874/July 24,1949
MARY JANE WARD AARDWEG /1878-1959]
[WILLIAM H.HARDIE /Dec.9,1882/May 19,1949
AIMEE HARDIE BUTLER /May 13,1904/Dec.11,1969
ANDREW JACKSON ALDRIDGE ,III/May 23,1918/Mar.22,1930
FRANK PAXTON ALDRIDGE /1885-1959/son of A.J.&H.P.ALDRIDGE]
New Back Section
[MINNIE GRAVES BOUNDS /DEc.22,1887/June 30,1961

WASHINGTON CO.,MS.CEMETERY RECORDS
Leland-Stoneville Cemetery, cont. - Older graves only.

GROVER C.BOUNDS / 1888-1964]
WILLIAM J.HAMILTON / 1893-1964
LOYD E.TABOR /Feb.15,1895/Jan.6,1957
[JESSIE EUGENE SWANNER /Oct.11,1894/May 3,1972
IDA MAY ROTHER SWANNER /Jan.7,1897/May 11,1977]
[VERNON MOORE /Jan.31,1884/Dec.5,1969
OLNEY O.MOORE /Aug.14,1883/May 23,1978]
[JOE OWENS / 1895-1967
MARY DELLA OWENS / 1895-1963]
CARL W.CONLEE /May 25,1888/July 11,1959
[WILLIAM D.RAY /Apr.3,1894/May 12,1959
LUNA H.RAY /APR.20,1885/NOV.6,1962]
[PARIS NATHANIEL BALLARD /Sept.9,1884/Jan.6,1959
EMMA STRINGER BALLARD /July 17,1882/Mar.25,1979]
[JOHN MOON LEE / 1889-1954
LUCY HARRIS LEE / 1889-1970]
OSCAR HOMER JONES /Dec.15,1879/June 28,1953
[SAMUEL FERGUSON MARSH / 1880-1964
FLORA MARTI MARSH / 1884-1956]
JOSEPH N.DILLEY /Aug.25,1881/Apr.27,1972
WALTER LEE WREN /May 5,1884/n\d>>>ROSE ELLA WREN / 1885-1955
[JOSEPH RAYMOND BROWN /July 29,1886/Feb.1,1965
MINNIE MAE WOODS BROWN /Sept.10,1897/May 1,1954]
[HARVEY A.YORK /Aug.8,1884/Jan.22,1954
BERTIE M.YORK /Nov.9,1889/Apr.5,1971]
[W.A.CRIPPEN /June 25,1882/Mar.2,1963
SUSIE CRIPPEN /Dec.2,1883/Dec.18,1967]
ANNA R.McCLINTOCK /Apr.13,1872/Jan.2,1973
ALICE HUDSON RIVERS /May 8,1882/May 16,1966
[LOUIS FRATESI /May 20,1889/Sept.12,1961
CLAUDINA FRATESI /Sept.2,1893/Mar.23,1972]
[ROBERT REX WINTER /May 15,1888/Oct.17,1959
MARY BROWN WINTER /Feb.17,1897/Mar.6,1979]
ALBERT F.COPELAND /MISS 1st LT. U.A.ARMY/WW I/Apr.14,1888/
    June 19,1967
[SAMUEL L.PEEPLES /Feb.8,1890/May 17,1963
BEUNA V. PEEPLES /Aug.9,1896/Feb.16,1982]
[MIKE PALOMBA COLUMBUS / 1864-1957
VINCE P.COLUMBUS /Nov.18,1899/Sept.10,1980]
[BASILIO FRATESI /Mar.22,1887/Nov.2,1971
ELIZABETH C.FRATESI /Dec.8,1893/Oct.12,1980]

WASHINGTON CO.,MS CEMETERY RECORDS
Leland-Stoneville cemetery,cont.

[EZRA TUNE /Se.17,1878/May 12,1957>ZOE TUNE /Jun.8,1887/Mar.28,1971]
WILLIAM H.McCARTY /Apr.18,1889/Oct.12,1956
[FRANK BRAME TUCKER /1888-1956
HELON MELISA SHIELDS/ wife of FRANK BRAME TUCKER /1897-1976]
[LUCY KIMBROUGH VAUGHAN /June 5,1887/Mar.1,1963
LUCY VAUGHAN KEARNEY /Dec.26,1910/Dec.9,1955
NOBEL S.KEARNEY, SR./Oct.12,1908/Feb.21,1967]
CLAKREY G.SHAPLEY /Apr.2,1888/May 19,1955
WALTER BEAUREGARD SWAIN,SR./Aug.12,1905/Dec.17,1975
[JOE L.HILL /1894-1960>>>>>GRACE D.HILL /1904-1983
CHARLES WILBUR FULLER /Sept.29,1887/Oct.14,1957
LOIS HINSON FULLER /Sept.12,1891/May 11,1973]
[KINNEY L.WITTE,MD/Jan.29,1882/Aug.17,1954
JOHNIE LONG WITTE /Jan.7,1888/Sept.22,1960]
[GEORGE BERKELEY WALKER /hus.of BESSIE RAE WALKER /
      Feb.17,1883/Mar.2,1971
BESSIE RAE WALKER /wife of GEO.B.WALKER /Dec.12,1885/May 21,1964

LOCUST CEMETERY

Located in Sec,33,T18 N,R8W; Former homesite of the late WM.P.
MONTGOMERY, near the present (1986) Bayou Road,South of Greenville.
Catalogued by Kitty Wilkerson Bryan of West Point,Ms. in 1952.

CATHERINE/wife of W.P.MONTGOMERY /d.Dec.4,1848/age 37yrs.2 mo.26 da.
CHARLES C.P./b.Jan.21,1838/d.Mar.20,1843>>>>PINCKNEY/b.May 8,1844/
      d.Feb.13,1848/ sons of W.P.& C.C.MONTGOMERY
LAURA/dau. of W.P.&E.C.MONTGOMERY /Dec.15,1850/Oct.23,1851
[Note:Mrs.Bryen believes that W.P.MONTGOMERY was also buried in LOCUST
but his marker is no longer there. He was b.Nov.27,1799/d.Oct.4,1876]

MULBERRY PLANTATION CEMETERY

On East side of Deer Creek,@3 miles S.of Leland, located on Plantation of
Mr.& Mrs. E.E.COOPER. Copied by K.Branton,Spring 1986. Two plots-one
inclosed in a wrought iron fence, with a tall marble marker:

WILLIE CARTER /Aug.24,1894/Oct.28,1918
  THE OTHER PLOT IS INCLOSED IN A CHAIN LINK FENCE
ALEASE J.CARTER /Sept.22,1917/Apr.25,1941
PATSY LEACH /May 9,1869/May 17,1937

WASHINGTON CO.,MS. CEMETERY RECORDS

PAXTON FAMILY CEMETERY

Location: Kinlock Plantation, between Wilmot and Arcola, on old Highway #61, in a cedar grove, West side of Deer Creek. Sec.26,T17N,R7W. Wrought iron fence inclosure. Copied by C.Payne and K.Branton - 1983.

DBL.ST.:FRANK SAUNDERS ALDRIDGE /July 17,1848/Apr.3,1900/Father
        LUCY PAXTON ALDRIDGE /Jan.20,1855/Jan.30,1942/Mother
CATHERINE WALKER/dau.of JACK & SUE FOOTE ALDRIDGE /FEB.-MAR.1931
NANNIE PORTER/dau.of A.J.&H.M.PAXTON /d.Feb.27,1879/aged 11 yrs.5 mos.
ALEXANDER GALLATIN PAXTON /Jan.15,1853/DEc.2,1917
A.G.McNUTT/son of A.J.&H.M.PAXTON /d.Oct.15,1860/age 3 yrs.
HANNAH/dau.of A.J.&H.M.PAXTON /d.July 3,1859/aged 2 yrs.8 mos.
ELISHA/son of A.J.&H.M.PAXTONP/ d.Sept.15,1868/age 14 yrs.
HANNAH M./wife of A.J.PAXTON /Jan.1830/d.1890
MARGARET SUSAN/dau.of A.J.& H.M.PAXTON /------
ANDREW PAXTON /Mar.18,1816/Oct.3,1900
HANNAH/dau.of A.J.& H.M.PAXTON /1859-1911
WILLIAM FRANK/son of A.J.& H.M.PAXTON /Mar.27,1860/July 14,1884
HANNAH/Infant dau.of F./S.&L.P.ALDRIDGE /Apr.1880/Apr.1885
ANDREW/son of F.S.& L.P.ALDRIDGE /1884-1886
GILES MOBLEY/son of J.N.& S.C.COLLIER /d.May 22,1870/aged 14 yrs.
Brok.Stone-could not read
-ATTON KNOX (broken) [Note: Believe this to be PATTON KNOX COLLIER /
    Eldest son of Col.J.N.&S.C.COLLIER /d.1875,age 23/Obit in "Democrat
IN Memory of EMILY MACLENNAN /Sept.29,1850/Dec.14,1884
JAMES A./son of R.(B.?)L.& ANNA M.PAXTON /Feb.18,1874/Aug.28,1875
COLIN BUCKNER /son of J.W.E.& R.E.M.BUCKNER /May 26,1851/DEc.10,1854
WILLIE/b. and d.Nov.1859/son of J.W.E.& R.E.M.BUCKNER
LUCY ALDRIDGE/dau of A.G.&M.N.PAXTON /b.1887 (infant)

        ∞∞∞∞∞∞∞∞∞∞∞∞∞∞∞∞∞∞∞∞∞∞∞∞∞∞∞∞∞∞∞∞∞

[Note: Hinds Co.Ms.Marriage Records:
ANDREW J. PAXTON to HANNAH M.BEASLEY /Oct.28,1847/Bdsm.JOHN
    H. HARRELSON
Warren Co.Ms.Cemetery Records: NOLAN FAMILY GRAVEYARD located on Anderson Tully Farm @14 miles S.E.of Vicksburg.
MARY NOLAN/wife of A.G.PAXTON /Mar.13,1862/Feb.23,1890]

        ∞∞∞∞∞∞∞∞∞∞∞∞∞∞∞∞∞∞∞∞∞∞∞∞∞∞∞∞∞∞∞∞∞

ARCOLA BAPTIST CHURCHYARD :Located in rear of Church Lot,under a tree. Found with the aid of J.E.MATTHEWS. One stone with these names:
MATTIE/dau.of R.C.& M.H.SOUTHALL /Sept.12,1889/Oct.18,1889
CARRIE EMMA/dau.of R.C.& M.H.SOUTHALL July 17,1887/July 18,1887
MATTIE H./wife of Dr.R.C.SOUTHALL /June 19,1863/Sept.22,1889

WASHINGTON CO.,MS. CEMETERY RECORDS

GREENVILLE CEMETERY: ALDRIDGE-ROBERTSHAW LOT:

Sometime in the late 1940's, the ALDRIDGE Plantation, located East of Deer Creek at Arcola, was sold and the Family Graveyard was removed to the GREENVILLE CEMETERY. The family representative at the time of removal was JAMES ROBERTSHAW, grandson of of A.J. and H.M.P. ALDRIDGE. The graves were placed with other existing family graves. Only the older existing graves, and those moved are listed here. (K.B.)

Dbl.St.:ANDREW J.ALDRIDGE /Mar.21,1851/Aug.8,1911
    HANNAH MARY PAXTON/wife of A.J.ALDRIDGE / Dec.3,1865/
    Aug.10,1907/ *A Devoted Wife and Loving Mother*
ANDREW J.ALDRIDGE ,JR./June 25,1888/July 3,1959
WILLIAM LOGAN WEBB ,Sr./Oct.23,1894/AApr.5,1979
CATHERINE ALDRIDGE WEBB /Jan.1,1904/Jan.22,1979
INFANT/son of A.J.&H.M.ALDRIDGE /b.d.July 10,1907
THOMAS R./son of A.J.& H.M.ALDRIDGE /Jan.25,1900/May 26,1901
LUCY/dau.of A.J.& H.M.ALDRIDGE /Dec.14,1886/July 10,1887
MARGARET McNUTT/dau.of A.J.&H.M.ALDRIDGE /b.d.Nov.20,1885
FRANK N.ROBERTSHAW /Aug.14,1883/Nov.19,1944
MARY A.ROBERTSHAW /July 31,1890/Mar.31,1974
WILLIAM OWSLEY ALDRIDGE /Aug.31,1897/Jan.20,1969
BERNICE DAY ALDRIDGE /Oct,9,1903/Mar.6,1975

RIVES FAMILY CEMETERY

Location: Old Highway #61, 1 mile North of Arcola; in a cultivated field; fenced in; on the West side of the road. Sec.36,R17N,R7W. Copied by Payne, Branton 1983,with additions by CAROL RAY who documented it in 1971.

EMMA/wife of REV.F.G.HOGUTT /d.Oct.25,1873/age 21 yrs. 6 mos.
MARY W.RIVES wife of O.C.RIVES /Jan.9,1804/Oct.9,1883
ORVILLE C.RIVES ,Sr./ Mar.8,1802/Nov.22,1878
LEONE/wife of O.C.RIVES ,JR./d.Aor.12,1878/aged ---
O.C.RIVES ,JR./d.June 1888
ORVILLE N./son of REV.J.D.&MATTIE A.MURFF /Apr.7,1872/Nov.2,1872
CHARLES DUDLEY /eldest son of REV.J.D.&M.A.MURFF /
    Dec.31,1870/Oct.21,1884
Dbl.St.:JOHNNIE/b.d.Apr.1856>>>>>>>> SUE STILES,b.d.June 15,1852
    Children of J.T.& R.S.MORSON
JAMES M./son of O.C.& MARY W.RIVES /Mar.28,1837/Sept.30,1862
ANNIE M./wife of J.W.RIVES /d.-----1881/aged 39 yrs.3mos.3days
    [Note:Wash.Co.Pkt.#598 states that NANNIE M.RIVES d.17 Apr.1880]

ARCOLA CEMETERY

Located 1 mile N.of Arcola,Ms.City limits;beside old Highway 61,West bank of Deer Creek;in a cedar grove.S.36,T17N,R7W. Many stones are broken - destroyed by a tornado and time.Ronnie Yarbrough,who lives next door,has tried to clean it up and keep trespassers away.Several individual plots are encircled by wrought iron fences.The outer perimeter is not fenced.
Copied by Alice Wade,Caledonia Payne,Katherine Branton - Apr.7,1984

Starting from front.(East side)outside of existing fences:
BEATRICE/dau.of J.R.& BLANCHE HENDERSON/Feb.3,1903/June 20,1903
FATHER/BENJAMIN S.KENT/Jan.13,1873/Aug.10,1916
4 little flat stones::"LITTLE"LEE NICHOLS/1887-1891.FRANK NICHOLS/1890-1904.CHRISTINE NICHOLS/1903-1911.MAUDE NICHOLS/1892-1912
W.E.BRYANT/at rest/1861-1910(Another BRYANT stone lying face down)
On second row-fenced in a block-3 stones marked INFANTS -
Large Center stone - W.D.LOVE/Aug.9,1858/Oct.21,1903/Erected by Woodmen of the World.
LODISKA LOVE/1 Sept.1898/7 Feb.1899
W.D.LOVE,JR./APR.17,1900/OCT.21,1900
MARY C.LOVE/30 Oct.1861/4 May 1954(Note:*Small funeral home marker reads CAROLYN LOVE)*
'MAMIE':MARY GOODLOE SACKSE/dau.of W.D.& M.C.LOVE/1893-1924
WM.C.LOVE/1873-1940
D.G.LOVE/25 Jan.1877/July 7,1904
Middle of Row 2:HOLMES: *1 stone* -DANIEL ROBERT/1864-1923
  (Was his name DANIEL ROBERT HOLMES?)
Section 3:Stones piled up and broken:
HARTWELL HOLMES/June 4,1824/Aug.20,1890/age 68 yrs.2 mo.16 days (?)
EMMA A.HOLMES/June 15,1832/Feb.8,1895
Next graves inclosed in low brick wall that must have had an iron fence on top at one time.
MARY B.WEEMS/Aug.18,1848/Oct.22,1891
JULIA WEEMS/July 14,1873/July 29,1897
JOHN CLIFFORD FRANKS/May 9,1875/June 4,1905
INFANT/dau.of J.B.& A.J.WILLIAMS/Sept.19,1893
North end of Sec.#2:Fenced in plot with many small markers,one large Obelisk with names on all sides: North side :
BETTIE JOHNSON/wife of H.D.HILL/Apr.17,1855/Jan.16,1882
JOHN SEDDON/son of H.D.& B.HILL/Jan.8,1882/May 30,188-:"With Mother in heaven"
JAMES STEWART/son of H.D.& BETTIE HILL/Jan.3,1882/Nov.10,1886(Note: Date rechecked,and both John S.and James S.read as copied)

ARCOLA, cont.

West side of Obelisk:
MABEL/dau.of J.S.JR..& E.JOHNSON/Oct.18,1883/June 26,1883
South side of Obelisk:
FRANCES M./wife of J.S.JOHNSON/Aug.11,1833/Sept.28,1885/MOTHER.
JAMES SANDSBERRY JOHNSON/Mar.11,1823/Mar.17,1906
East side of Obelisk;
SUSIE/dau.of J.S.& F.M.JOHNSON/Nov.3,1868/Aug.3,1872
JAMES SEDDON JOHNSON/1856-1925/Ft.stone J.S.J.
A row of small stones, names & dates on1 central stone..:
JAMES JOHNSON/infant son of W.H.& SUSIE H.HORTON/d.Sept 22,1901
JOHN SEDDON HILL/no date
JAMES STEWART HILL/no date
Headstone buried - unreadable - Ft.stone -SMJ
MABLE JOHNSON/no date
JAMES VERNON JOHNSON/Mar.14,1882/Sept.4,1887
FRANCES ESKELINE JOHNSON/July 2,1885/Feb.5,1887
In middle of same lot as above:
FRANCES THOMAS JOHNSON/no dates
Broken buried ft.stone -J.S.J.
BETTIE JOHNSON HILL/no dates
GENIE JOHNSON CARSON/no dates
*Top broken off stone:*B.F.MORGAN/Aug.12,1856/Sept.3,1887
Row #3:Inclosed in iron fence:
MAMIE IDA MURPHEY/Nov.28,1877/Aug.20,1883
"HOLY BIBLE"/THOMAS J.WILLIAMS/Jan.3,1884/aged 27 yrs.9 mo.27 days
NEWTON WEST/son of J.T.& IDA ATTERBURY/July 28,1883/Mar.12,1884
ANNA SLOAN/wife of DR.W.A.GILLASPIE/May 4,1880/Mar.19,1899
Fenced area next to the Williams':Broken shaft decorated with flowers, North end:
MOTHER/wife of GEORGE D.BUTLER/Feb.14,1839/June 12,1900
North side of Sec.#3:Large stone -CATO -
W.R.CATO/Sept.30,1848/Oct.28,1916
Broken stone lying face down
STEWART A./son of J.W.& L.H.CATO/Mar.31,1878/Mar.8,1909
DAVID GUTELIUS/Sept.9,1915/Aug.1,1916 (broken stone)
JOHN CATO/May 23,1852/June 3,1904
"Holy Bible"/L.E./wife of W.B.CATO/May 29,1848/June 29,1905
*2 ft.stones without headstones:*D.R. - L.S. no dates
LEON/son of B.N.& KATIE SHEFFIELD/Sept.28,1887/Oct.18,1887/"Erected by his Grandmother""Budded on earth, Bloomed in Heaven."
ARTHUR W./son of W.M.& A.M.PINFIELD/Mar.28,1887/Sept.12,1888

ARCOLA, cont.

LUCY/ Erected by her Sister/S.E.C./no dates
Several broken ft.stones, nothing readable

Sec. #4: behind the Cato Plot:
LIZZIE/infant dau.of G.W.& S.E.COOK/May 8,1881/July 29,1882
In Memory of CHARLES MATHEWS,SR./who d.Sept.11,1891/age 63 yrs.11 mo.2 days/Erected by his wife.

Sec. #4: Inclosed in iron fence:
GEORGE RAGARDO FALL/July 7,1808/Nov.29,1869
ELIZABETH A.FALL/d.May 26,1893/age 80 yrs.(broken stone)
JENNIE H./beloved dau.of S.I.& S.F.PHILLIPS/Nov.3,1877/May 30,1893
SELDON F.PHILLIPS/Jan.2,1849/Feb.25,1902/WOW
KATIE NEWSOM/d.Sept.1,1895/age 35 yrs.
INFANT dau of J.T.& A.D.SIMMS/no date Ft.stone - I.S.
ANNIE D.OLIVER/wife of J.T.SIMMS/July 9,1869/Aug.17,1894

Behind this plot: Fenced area with 4 graves, on N.side of Cem.
EDWARD/first son of ROBERT & MARY THOMAS/b.at Cowbridge,England/Feb.3,1849/d.Nov.8,1883/"Gone to Rest"
INFANT son of M.E.& C.C.HARRISON/d.Mar1899
LUCY/small stone, no dates

On backline of Cem. is a large group of blooming jonquils: the following graves are within this planting.
LIZZIE(written of face)DORSEY(on rear)(double stone - broken at base)
LIZZIE M./dau of J.E.& F.C.NIXON/Jan.25,1882/Oct.8,1908
DORSEY A./son of E.A.& J.A.STINSON/Oct.31,1880/July 17,1906
Ft.stone - E.T.

In back NW corner - buried in ground - we dug it up and propped it against another stone:
ROBERT ROSS/Aug.24,1898/Oct.7,1899
Large Marker - BUCKLEY- *only one ft.stone* - R.E. or R.B.

Near West corner of Cem. is the COLEMAN PLOT:
LULA ELIZA COLEMAN WOOD/Aug.3,1882/Sept.18,1903/Tall Monument
West side of same stone:
JAMES HENRY COLEMAN/Apr.1,1892/May 12,1924
Footstones around Coleman marker:O.W.C./L.E.C.W/J.H.C./
OSCAR WARREN COLEMAN/FEB.28,1884/AUG.27,1899
SW side:WILLIAMS
THOMAS M.WILLIAMS/My husband/June 4,1828/Nov.2,1889
GEORGIA MARIA WILLIAMS/Aug.23,1836/Sept.18,1906
AMELIA J.WILLIAMS/Sept.29,1868/Jan.15.1900
CLAYTON OLIVER WILLIAMS/Oct.28,1896/Mar.5,1897
IRMA SLOAN/dau.of J.B.& A.J.WILLIAMS/1888-1889/"Sweet Irma's now at rest"

WASHINGTON CO.,MS. CEMETERY RECORDS

ARCOLA CEMETERY, cont.

LUCIE LENORIA LEE BRYANT /Dec.3,1868/d.Feb.16,1910
South side of Row #5. HOUSE Plot:Beautiful,elaborite stones:
FANNIE M./dau.of J.P.& E.HOUSE /Dec.28,1886/Sept.14,1895
MAMIE LEE HOUSE /Mar.23,1884/Dec.26,1898
W.R.SEALES /Oct.18,1865/Jan.15,1890/ (broken stone)
J.S./son of J.P.& ELIZABETH HOUSE /Sept.14,1875/May 20,1893
J.B.HOUSE /Nov.12,1877/Jan.4,1916/ W.O.W.
In the rear of Cemetery, the graves are in no apparent order. Believe many more should be here.
ELMOD/son of W.M.& A.E.MANN /July 17,1887/age 12 yrs.,6 mos.,28 days
ROY ARKELL/son of V.C.& M.W.GOLDING /Sept.4,1883/Sept.22,1888
BAXTER/son of W.E.DAVIS & S.J.DAVIS /Dec.10,1888/May 7,1890
BENJAMIN WILLIAMSON /killed at Arcola/Oct.20,1883/age 21 yrs.**

**NOTE :GREENVILLE TIMES:OCT.27,1883:GRAFTON BAKER shot and killed BENJAMIN WILLIAMSON...(the case was)investigated by COL.A.J.PAXTON,(who)sent a note to the G'ville Times/"The case of the St.of Miss.vs GRAFTON BAKER for the killing of BENJAMIN WILLIAMSON on 20th instant,came on this day to be heard before Justices HILL and FERRIS,...who concurred that the homicide was justifiable as having been committed in necessary defence of his younger brother PERCY BAKER, and they discharged the defendant." GREENVILLE TIMES:Nov.13,1883: (Letter to the Editor)ARCOLA,Ms.-"In a late issue of your paper...an article in relation to the murder of my brother by GRAFTON BAKER,saying he was wholly justified in the act to save his brother's life...would have been just as easy to have knocked my brother down. Myself and my brother came to this county,children and by honest labor have succeeded in making a living and raising 2 younger sisters. If it is right to kill a man because he is drunk...then A.J.PAXTON was right. Otherwise I am right".(signed)ARCHER WILLIAMSON.

WINGFIELD CEMETERY : Located on SLIGO PLANTATION,1/2 mile North of Wilmot(Ms.)on West side of Deer Creek, just off Old Highway #61. In middle of plowed field,fence inclosure,overgrown with honeysuckle vines. Beautiful, small carved marble stones. T17N.R8W. K.Branton,C.Payne-1984.

LIZZIE/no further information
FRANCIS G.WINGFIELD /23 Sept.1816/6 Mar.1871/ *Separation is our
    lot,Meeting our hope/(carving of wooden cross with vines)*
MATTIE E.WINGFIELD /JUNE 3,1834/DEC.4,1867/ *Blessed are the pure in
    heart for they shall see God.*
MARY/n\d
WALTER M.WINGFIELD /Aug.21,1867/Oct.23,1878/ *GONE HOME*
WILLIE J.WINGFIELD /Mar.21,1843/Oct.5,1878/
BOWDRIE WINGFIELD /Oct.2,1861/Jan.28,1879/AT REST

HOLLANDALE CEMETERY (City)
Location:East side of Deer Creek,NE of Hollandale.
Copied by:Caledonia Payne,Katherine Branton - 1984,85

Beginning SW Corner:
WM.N.HANNAH/Sept.3,1857/Apr.28,1916 "With a steadfast faith in the promises of God he has gone to his reward"
OUR MOTHER:L.ANNIE HANNAH.May 24,1848/Nov.1,1926(broken stone)
F.M.FULCHER/b.Jan.20,1852/d.Dec.6,1890 "There is a bright region above..."
INFANT dau.of J.E.& ELVA HOLLAND/Feb.24,1905
McGEE /infant/no dates
KATE/dau.of JULIE & LOUIS DAMERON/Aug.19,1898/Aug.8,1899/"At rest"
J.A.MORSON/28 Mar.1839/Feb.5,1898 "Gone Home"
      DOUBLE STONE ---------MENDROP
BUELAH G/1888-1932   ELDON R./1882-1938
Ft.stone/BUELAH G.MENDROP/D.MAY 20/1932
R.S.GOLDEN/Apr.4,1853/June 7,1906/W.O.W./Mason
A series of small rectang.,flat stones,appearing to be ft.stones,no hd.st.
MRS.OSBORN/d.25 July 19--
LIZZIE A.GOLDEN/b.10 July 1908/d.19 Nov.1908
M.F.HARRI-(S?)/5 Sept.1884/1902
E----- S----/20 Aug.1827/28 Dec.1893
E.-. A.GRAY/no dates
DAVIS/nothing else
MOTHER/MARY SANDIDGE LOWE/20 Dec.1851/31 Oct.1934
MARGARET/Apr.13,1912/Dec.7,1912//MARIE/Apr.13,1912/Nov.12,1912
    Children of E.T.& A.L.SPIVEY
VICTOR H./son of G.A.& VICTORIA SPIVEY/Sept.23,1900/Mar.24,1902
CLARENCE EUGENE/son of E.T.& A.L.SPIVEY/June 16,1916/Nov.13,1916
WINSTON W.WEST/May 10,1845/Sept.14,1895
Row of 5 stones on end of Row #1 as follows:
SGT.J.C.WINDHAM/Co.H/4 Ms.INF/CSA
BILLIE WINDHAM/1871-1899
CLEVELAND WINDHAM/1886-1896
GERALD WINDHAM/1879-1897
PATTERSON/Aug.1866/July 11,1892
Row #2 - South to North:
LUCY MOSELEY SCOTT/Apr.24,1865/Jan.12,1943
E.W.SCOTT/Dec.12,1848/June 28,1907
LORICE/dau.of E.W.& LUCY SCOTT/July 27,1897/Mar.16,1900
BENNIE/son of E.W.& L.J.SCOTT/Nov.3,1887/Mar.24,1890

HOLLANDALE CEM., cont.

JOSEPH W.HAMMONS/1880-1907
WM.H.H.HAMMONS/Co.B/48 Va.Inf./CSA
Tall stone - both sides:MARY A.HAMMONS/June 9,1846/Oct.7,1899
Reverse:LUCINDY NAIL/d.Apr.27,1898/age 66 yrs.
WM.ALBERT/son of W.B.& M.A.HAMMONS/Feb.22,1890/Apr.5,1890
MARTHA A.KEETH/wife of W.B.HAMMONS/Jan.15,1864/Oct.18,1899
J.N.KEETH/Dec.30,1827/May 20,1902/(broken and leaning on tree)
MRS. BESSIE KEITH/Ft.stone - no dates
Row #3:
MATTIE ANNA GRIFFIN/Jan.9,1888/Aug.24,1895
OUR FATHER/J.D.GRIFFIN/Aug.28,1819/Sept.6,1891
OUR MOTHER/MARTHA ANN/wife of J.D.GRIFFIN/Dec.5,1833/Aug.5,1906
ENOS/son of G.J.&M.J.TOAL/Dec.19,1878/July 29,1886
VESTINE C./husband of I.M.SLATER/Mar.21,1854/Sept.25,1900
LAURA A./wife of V.C.SLATER/Sept.3,1861/July 14,1884
GEORGIA/wife of J.R.NIXON/d.Jan.30 1888/aged 28 yrs.
T.JEFFERSON BAREFIELD/June 3,1844/Aug.12,1893
KATIE E./wife of J.STOUT/d.Nov.21,1895/age 19 yrs.11 mo.24 da.
W.F.STOUT/Nov.22,1879/Oct.31,1910
JACOB STOUT/Mar.16,1845/Mar.13,1905
CAMARINE/wife of JACOB STOUT/d.Oct.3,1895/aged 46 yrs.
INFANT son of J.& C.STOUT/b.d.Aug.27,1874
EDDIE/son of J.& C.STOUT/b.Sept.16,1870/d.July 7,1874
Row 4,headed South
SARAH E./wife of ALFRED FERGUSON/Mar.4,1831/Nov.8,1887/age 56
1 large tombstone,lying face down
MAGRUDER/son of A.& SARAH E.FERGUSON/July 2,1852/July 17,1872
ANNIE A./dau.of F.C.& J.E.NIXON/Oct.25,1874/Aug.21,1875
JAMES A.NIXON/May 12,1877/Apr.6,1883
'LITTLE'FRANKIE/son of F.C.& J.E.NIXON/Oct.17,1886/Nov.16,1886
'LITTLE'WILLIE/son of F.C.& J.E.NIXON/Sept.12,1879/Oct.12,1887
F.C.NIXON/d.Feb.15,1890/aged 47 yrs./Mason
Ft.stone:STINSON/Sept.29,1893/Aug.17,1894
ROBERT E.STINSON/Aug.4,1892/Nov.22,1961 - ft.st.S2-USNRF-WWI
JENNIE F.STINSON/1854-1939
Row #5_ Heading North-5 children - same tb.stone,as follows:
REBER LEROY/son of R.& M.F.COLLUM/Nov.30,1896/Feb.19,1897
EVERET/son of R.&M.F.COLLUM/Aug.6,1881/Nov.20,1885
EFFIE/dau.of R.& M.F.COLLUM/July 26,1879/Sept.4,1885
CLARA/dau.of R.& M.F.COLLUM/Jan.7,1877/Sept.23,1878 /
INFANT son of R.& M.F.COLLUM/b.d.Nov.15,1899

WASHINGTON CO.CEMETERIES

HOLLANDALE CEMETERY, cont.
Row #6: THOMAS J.SMITH/d.May 13,1875/aged About 75 yrs.
BASIL L.HOGUE/Sept.12,1834/Mar.12,1876

....

4 sided shaft: *[Note:death date on S.V.HIGHTOWER copied as written]
S.V./wife of/J.M.HIGHTOWER/ b.1853/d.1874*
MAUD EDNIE/dau.of/J.M.&S.V.HIGHTOWER/Mar.11,1881/Oct.22,1882
GUSSIE/dau.of/J.M.& S.V.HIGHTOWER/Dec.1,1883/Dec.14,1883
ANNIE LEE/dau.of/J.M.& S.V.HIGHTOWER/Dec.22,1878/Jan.4,1884

....

SEV---E/son of/E.& C.F.F.COLLUM/ Dec.3,1870/Feb.27,1873
Broken stone: JESSIE L.CARTER/n/d
PERMELIA STINSON/Jan.25,1845/Mar.8,1879
JENNIE,infant dau.of/W.A.& P.J.STINSON/July 23,1873/Nov.6,1873
ELIZA MORGAN/wife of/F.M.TILLMAN/July 10,1835/Apr.14,1873
WM.MINTER MORGAN/Feb.11,1839/Sept.29,1875
FANNIE A./wife of/W.A.LISBONY/Aug.2,1847/ Bottom of stone buried

....

4 sided shaft: C.H.PARKER/May 11,1867/Sept.15,1884
SUSAN P./wife of/R.B.PARKER/Mar.3,1838/Sept.7,1882
LIDIA S.PARKER/Nov.3,1873/Dec.10,1885
VIRGINIA A.PARKER/Dec.2,1869/Nov.22,1884

....

C.W.HOLLINGSWORTH/Pvt.33 Miss Inf.CSA/Mar.25,1912
MINNIE LEE HOLLINGSWORTH/ 1878-1897
LEVI W./son of/JAMES & NANCY J.HOLLINGSWORTH/Oct.4,1857/Nov.11,1874

....

4 sided shaft; LAURA/wife of/L.G.KEETH,June 10,1852/May 4,1887
L.G.KEETH/Oct,14,1847/Nov.30,1886
J.C.KEETH/ Apr.23,1859/Nov.25,1885
H.N.KEETH/Mar.18,1861/Dec.2,1887

....

A.M.KEETH/Apr.5,1849/Oct.19,1895
Row #7: M.A./wife of/R.S.GOLDEN/Apr.1,1860/Sept.13,1883
JIMMIE T./wife of/C.W.GOLDEN/Feb.7,1861/Sept.26,1878
HARRISON F.GOLDEN/ OCT.31,1879/ ------/ Ft.st. H.F.G.
M.M.PENDER/Nov.23,1854/Apr.1,1890
ARTHUR ARCHIBALD/son of /D.P.& M.E.FARLEY/Aprt.26,1874/Sept.6,1882
JAMES PINKNEY/son of/D.P.& M.E.FARLEY/Nov.7,1875/Aug.3,1883
HYMRICK E./son of/KENETH & SARAH O. FLOYD/Sept.17,1871/Mar.25,1872
Footstone: A.Z.S.

WASHINGTON CO.CEMETERIES

HOLLANDALE CEMETERY,cont.
Shaft, with writing on 3 sides:
Side 1:GEORGE R.FARMER/Apr.24,1833/Mar.20,1864
    CLARENCE B.FARMER/May 30,1875/July 24,1880
Side 2:HENRY O.REDDEN/July 23,1860/Oct.29,1869
    HARVEY H.FARMER/May 22,1865/Aug.12,1868
Side 3:LITTLE JOSEPH H./ Jan.2,1884/Jan.9,1884
ROW #8
ALICE ZELMA/dau.of/STEPHEN & LAURA B.STANDARD/June 23,1872/d.-----
UNICE LOVENA BRITT/Feb.18,1919/Sept.1,1924/Dau.of/Ed &MARY BRITT
    WILLIAMS
ROW #9:LOU GEIVELL/dau.of/W.R.& NANNIE CANNON/Nov.27,1873/ Aug.23,
    1889/ *Erected by her step-father JOSEPH A.HOLLINGSWORTH*
WM.R.CANNON/d.July 13,1874/aged 33 yrs.,9 days
CAPITOLA/dau.of/I.T.& N.L.RATHER/Apr.15,1869/Mar.1,1873
IVEY C./son of/I.T.& N.L.RATHER/Nov.9,1861/Feb.14,1873
WM.T./son of/I.T.& N.L.RATHER/ Broken stone with these dates leaning on
    broken stone of Wm.T.: Aug.12,1850/Feb.21,1873
ELIZABETH/wife of/WM.RATHER/Br.stone,leaning on Eliz.'s: Nov.29,1782/
    d.--- 7,1873
SMITH: WM.A./1834-1876: MARY ANN/1845-1875
PHILIP W.HOLLEY/Sept.1822/June 30,1881
Area Inclosed With Wrought Iron Fence:
Our Mother:KATIE BAREFIELD/d.13 May 1915/aged 83
SAMUEL BAREFIELD/Mar.11,1818/27 May 1900
LEONARD A./son of/SAML.& KATIE BEARFIELD/July 22,1854/Sept.2,1873
ALIENA A./dau.of/SAML.& KATIE BAREFIELD/ Oct.12,1868/Oct.5,1886
LUCINDA McKINNEY/Apr.10,1855/Aug.12,1948
LENARD ALMA/dau.of/S.M.& M.Z.BAREFIELD/Aug.15,1878/Feb.21,1883
CORA A./dau.of/S.M.& M.Z. BAREFIELD//Sept.24,1889/6 yr.4 mo.2 da.
SAMUEL MARION BAREFIELD/20 Mar.1867/3 Nov.1925 (Mason)
MOLLIE ZELMAR BUCKLEY/wife of/SAML.M.BAREFIELD/19Apr.1850/
    Jan.16,1918
BERNARD McKINNEY RUSSELL/Feb.5,1907/Feb.7,1908
ALENA LUCY/ dau.of/E.V.& C.O.McKINNEY/d.Oct.19,1888/ 1 yr.5 mo.24 da.
LOIS EVELYN/dau.of D.F.& M.O.RUSSELL/30 Dec.1901/14 Nov.1902
JAMES C.RYALS/25 Dec.1851/18 Apr.1888
Loose Footstone: B.McK.
LARGE HEADSTONE: FURNESS - McKINNEY
EUGENE M.FURNESS/1904-1939: EUGENE V.McKINNEY/1845-1918: CARRIE
B.McKINNEY/1856-1928

WASHINGTON CO. CEMETERIES

HOLLANDALE CEMETERY, cont.

ELLA BAREFIELD/wife of/J.A.HOLLINGSWORTH/1863-1909
STEPHEN A.BAREFIELD/17 Jan.1863/27 Dec.1902 (Mason)
RIVERS BAREFIELD/Miss. Cook 43 Inf./15th Div/Sept.30,1936
McALPIN: JOHN A./1867-1919:(Mason) MARIA LOU/1857-1938(E.Star)
RYALS: SAM COLLINS/1880-1851: MARGIE FIELDS/1880-1937
NEPPIE BAREFIELD RYALS/MOTHER OF/OLANO,EUROY,& R.A.BAREFIELD,JR./
    1876-1954
ROBERT A.BAREFIELD,SR./1866-1932/ (Mason)
CARRIE BELL/dau.of/EARNEST & MARY McKINNEY/Dec.17,1909/Dec.17,1910
McKINNEY: ERNEST EUGENE/DADDY/28 Oct.1882/10 Aug.1959
        MARY SLEDGE/MAMA/2 July 1884/16 Nov.1962
KATIE OPHELIA/wife of/HARRIS COWAN/28 Dec.1876/21 Feb.1904
HARRY EUGENE/son of/H.& KATIE O.COWAN/31 July 1902/15 Aug.1903
ADDIE/dau.of/S.A.& Z.?. STELL/8 May 1888/20 June 1902
Outside of fence, on Creek side.
Dbl.stone:ARTHUR N./son of/G.W.& M.E.FIELDING/2 Apr.1868/25 Aug.1874
        JOHN A./son of W.M.& LOUISA FIELDING/Oct.8,1869/June 28,1874
O.M.FIELDING/ *broken stone, dates unreadable*
NATHAN S.CRENSHAW/ *broken stone, n/d*
ANNIE M./dau.of/N.S.& S.D.CRENSHAW/d.June 1881/aged 18
ROBERT N./ son of/N.S.& S.D.CRENSHAW/d.July 1883/aged 8
NANNETTA/dau.of/N.S.& S.D.CRENSHAW/d.June 1882/age 11
Outside of fence, working East along Creek road
EZRA O.COLLUM/1857-1902
MARY A.COLLUM/1861-1909
PAUL H.COLLUM/1893-1913
THOMAS AUBREY LANDRUM/5 Mar.1879/21 June 1954
MARY COLLUM LANDRUM/23 Mar.1888/3 Oct.1976
VAN NAMEN-BAKER: *Group of stones together*
    JOHN WYNAND VAN NAMEN/5 May 1905/4 July 1947
    ROBERT E.VAN NAMEN/2 June 1864/29 July 1947
    C.A./wife of L.HENLY/Mother of the Van Namens/28 Mar.1840/
        20 Sept.1904
    MATTIE/wife of/R.E.VAN NAMEN/1871-1934
    STRADER KINGSLEY BAKER/4 June 1896/16 Dec.1979
BAREFIELD: MERCER D./1888-1936: EFFIE R./1888-1972
RUSSELL: FRANKLIN H.RUSSELL/Dec.8,1863/Oct.19,1957
    EMMA HENRY VAUGHAN RUSSELL/1870-1911
On East side of Fence:
WILLIE M.McCAMMON/ 30 Dec.1891/20 June 1946

WASHINGTON CO. CEMETERIES

HOLLANDALE CEMETERY, cont.
W.N. MOORE/Dec. 5, 1860/18 Sept. 1896
ALICE C. BROWN/5 Mar. 1868/21 Dec. 1945
H.B. BROWN/1864-1936
SCULL: JOHN DRAKE/1882-1968: MATTYE MOORE/1889-1952
South of Fence:
BEULAH TIFFEE BURNETT BUFORD/8 Sept. 1883/13 Dec. 1972
WM. McKEE BURNETT/28 Nov. 1877/22 Nov. 1918
ALLENE H. BURNETT/14 Dec. 1907/12 Aug. 1943
CLYDE LAMAR WEEKS/28 Apr. 1897/14 Jan. 1919
WEEKS: EVA B. - WILL W. n/dates
WM. DEAN WEEKS/10 Sept. 1900/29 July 1971
MARION/ beloved Mother of/FLOYD & MARION GRAHAM/n/d-Ft.St."Our Mita"
SIMEON M. CARNES/21 May 1875/7 Jan. 1954
MOTHER/ALICE/wife of/S.M. CARNES/15 Sept. 1878/19 July 1932
WILLIAM FENNELL/son of/A.& S.M. CARNES/9 Oct. 1904/3 Mar. 1918
WOW stone, fallen face down, with 2 small flat stones on either side: PERMELIA LITTLETON/1836-1912: S. HEZEKIAH NICHOLS/1840-1900
MARTHA/wife of/N.B. HULL/July 4, 1863/May 4, 1897
JOHN HULL/ no dates
TOM ROBERSON/d. July 13, 1914
WILLIE E. HORNE/13 Sept. 1861/23 Feb. 1884
INFANT son of/T.C.& W.E. HORNE/23 Feb. 1884
Double stone: MARTHA E./29 Mar. 1882/28 June 1883: JOHN M./4 Aug. 1880/18 Aug. 1882/ Children of T.C.& W.E. HORNE
EVERETT F. HARDY/27 Feb. 1869/1 Sept. 1883
MARTHA J. HARDY/12 Mar. 1878/26 Oct. 1878
Loose Footstone: MEADOW DEAN-n/d
Small Fenced area on Creek Road:
WALCOTT: MARY H./1869-1929: CHARLES D./1864-1935
SUSAN HILL/wife of W.W. JOHNSTON/Sept. 10, 1846/Mar. 2, 1920
W.W. JOHNSTON/Mar. 23, 1834/June 7, 1908
Ouside of fence:
JOHN HARDY/son of/J.H.& M.A. PIERCE/Nov. 30, 1910/July 30, 1911
MAGRUDER PLOT: CELIA MAGRUDER EGAN/Apr. 4, 1930/May 14, 1979
JAMES E. MAGRUDER/Mississippi/PFC U.S. Air Force/KOREA/ JAN. 28, 1932/JULY 29, 1971
Big Ft.st.on Lot: FATHER, MOTHER, JAMES
J.W. MAGRUDER/1854-1917: GEORGIA L. MAGRUDER/1864-1940
MAGRUDER: (Dbl. Stone) ELIZABETH RACHAL HUTCHINSON/June 23, 1891/Mar. 1, 1973: JAMES WILLIAM/Dec. 29, 1888/July 16, 1973

WASHINGTON CO. CEMETERIES

HOLLANDALE CEMETERY, cont.

One Large Stone: T.H.THAMES/FEB.8,1868/JAN.21,1921
    ARCHIE H.THAMES/July 23,1898/d.1919
    MARY C.THAMES/Apr.3,1900/Oct.10,1918
JOHN AUBREY WADE/June 8,1905/Feb.12,1979
JOHN D.WADE/Nov.25,1859/May 10,1918
COLENE WADE/Dec.10,1898/Nov.25,1947
SHANKLE: (Dbl.St.)DR.SEABORN M./1861-1936: LAURA M./1866-1951
(Double Stone adorned with American Flag)
    BYRD SHANKEL CARTWRIGHT/Apr.26,1891/Oct.10,1918
    ARCHIE T.SHANKLE/Jan.19,1896/Oct.10,1918

THOMAS M.BOZZA/Mar.26,1871/Dec.6,1942
MOTHER/OLA TREADWAY BOZZA/Sept.30,1881/Feb.2,1949/68yrs.4mo.2da.
HUSBAND/CHARLES S.TREADWAY/June 3,1871/Oct.11,1914
McCLEARY PLOT:WILLIAM T.McCLEARY/Miss.Pvt Troop M 301 Calvary/
    W.W.I/Dec.22,1891/Feb.18,1957
    BROTHER/GEORGE W.McCLEARY/Nov.5,1875/Aug.9,1929
    MOTHER/ROSA ADA McCLEARY/Dec.10,1866/Apr.17,1946
    FATHER/WILLIAM McCLEARY/Aug.11,1839/June 27,1915
MOLLIE EVANS RYALS/d.Oct.,10,1917/aged 45 yrs.
NORMAN M.EVANS/1868-1931
JORDAN:JOHN WESLEY JORDAN,JR./Nov.1,1920/Mar.20.1945
    MARY EVANS JORDAN/Mar.3,1892/July 8,1967
    JOHN WESLEY JORDAN,SR./Dec.19,1888/Jan.9,1959
MATTIE RYAN CARTER/Jan.6,1880/Jan.18,1918
SMITH:(Dbl.Stone)WILLIAM A./1834-1876: MARY ANN/1845-1875
   END OF THE OLD SECTION OF HOLLANDALE CITY CEMETERY
RANDOM SELECTIONS OF STONES WITH BIRTH DATES BEFORE 1885
Dbl.St.:SAML.M.**HORTON**/Oct.19,1874/May 11,1969
    EDNA K.**HORTON**/Sept.15,1876/Dec.27,1961
Dbl.St.:WILL S.**McDONALD**/1879/1971
    VIOLA H.**McDOANLD**/1878-1959
Dbl.St.:ELIE JAMES **GANIER**/Nov.15,1878/Aug.6,1975
    ETHEL RANDOLPH GILL **(GANIER)**/Feb.22,1888/Mar 5,1917
Dbl.St.:MARION C.**CARNES**/1868-1959
    LOUETTA C.**CARNES**/1885-1974
JOHN HENRY **KEITH**/23 June 1870/Dec.22,1944
Dbl.St.CHARLES LOUIS **KEITH**/Oct.30,1877/Dec.5,1947
    MINNIE ELLECE **KEITH**/Feb.17,1887/Mar.3,1964
HARRIET CROSS **RICKETS**/1878-1942

WASHINGTON CO. CEMETERIES
HOLLANDALE CITY CEMETERY, cont.
PAUL HOLLAND, JR. / 23 Dec. 1908 / 28 Apr. 1944
VIRGINIA HOLLAND PETERS 1905-1976
PAUL HOLLAND, SR. / 12 Feb. 1877 / 15 July 1959
MAYBIRD B. HOLLAND / Jan. 5, 1885 / May 17, 1961
WALTER HOLLAND, SR. / 1907-1953
KATHRYN M. HOLLAND / 1907-1985
E. MINYARD / Mar. 26, 1846 / Nov. 1, 1925
CLARENCE EUGENE SPIVEY / Aug. 27, 1855 / Apr. 9, 1937
MARGARET THOMPSON SPIVEY / 1861-1949
MARGARET GROOME JONES / 1874-1940
EDWARD VIRGIL JONES / 1876-1938
MARY HOLLAND / wife of L.C. HAYS / Jan. 19, 1874 / Nov. 2, 1943
LUTHER CLAY HAYS / 18 Mar. 1866 / July 1, 1938
ASA THOMAS RYALS / b. Wilmington, Va. Feb. 2, 1851 / d. Estill, Ms. Feb. 6, 1933
ALICE LOUISE RYALS / b. Ringold, La. (n\d) / d. Arcola, Ms. 20 Jan. 1936
Dbl.St.: FRANK P. BARRETT / 1855-1935 >>> ANNIE E. BARRETT / 1868-1937
J.M. CREEL / 16 Apr. 1869 / 21 Apr. 1942
Dbl.St.: ROBERT L. BRELAND / 1870-1939 >>> ROSA L. BRELAND / 1876-1940
INA P. WILLIAMS / 1880-1941 >>>>>>> C.A. WILLIAMS / 1876-1941
T.H. GRAY / Sept. 8, 1859 / Feb. 21, 1938
T.M. HERITAGE / 1864-1933 >>>>>> MINNIE TAYLOR HERITAGE / 1875-1953
Dbl.St.: BENJAMIN C. STUART / 1875-1930
LULA STOWERS (STUART) / Sept. 7, 1879 / 1937
JOEL FLETCHER SCULL / 1878-1940 >>>> ANNA CRISLER SCULL / 1880-1955
C.A. CLOWER / 1854-1932 >>>>>>>>> ANNIE H. CLOWER / 1866-1962
GEORGE WASHINGTON ALEXANDER / 23 July 1849 / 2 Oct. 1936
MATTIE HOPPER ALEXANDER / Apr. 21, 1855 / Dec. 8, 1927
JESSE BAREFIELD DREW / 8 Oct. 1860 / 8 Feb. 1930
BEATRICE DREW / June 26, 1882 / Oct. 25, 1945
MOLLIE GROWER BOGY / 1865-1928
EMMA MALONE QUILLIN / 1861-1934
GEORGE C. DISINGER / 1 Feb. 1865 / 11 Jan 1922
MARY N. PIERCE / June 18, 1866 / Dec. 10, 1948
R.C. TREADWAY / Ala. Pvt. Co. C 46 / Regt. GA INF CSA / Nov. 23, 1828 /
    July 25, 1923
CLARA E. HARRIS / DEC/25, 1860 / 28 FEB. 1927 / MOTHER
ROSA SMITH PETERS / 1872-1961 >> J.D. PETERS / 30 AUG. 1868 / 27 FEB. 1926
ADDIE DYSON STEVENS / 5 June 1870 / 14 Feb. 1957
J.F. STEVENS / 20 Sept. 1870 / 9 Apr. 1929
WILLIAM D. JAMISON / 1868-1932 / PAPA
MINNIE IRIS JAMISON / 1871-1968 / MAMA
ESTELLE C. TUCKER / 1873-1924 >>>>> BARTLEY H. TUCKER / 1869-1934

WASHINGTON CO. CEMETERIES

HOLLANDALE CITY CEMETERY, cont.-Random Early Graves

Dbl.St.: MAJ. ANDREW TREADWAY /Feb.14,1869/Feb.10,1954/son of RICHARD C.TREADWAY and ANNIE ELIZA SPIER OF RUSSELL Co.,Ala./FATHER
ANNIE LEE BELL TREADWAY /27 Nov.1884/2 June 1952/dau.of ALF-FRED C.BELL and ARABELLA D.LUNSFORD of Webster Co.,Ga./MOTHER
"CREAT"/ LOUCRESHIE W.WEAVER /1877-1957
ROXE LYLE MEADOW /1878-1936>>>>>>>JOHN M.MEADOW /1864-1949
ULTON MORRIS CALDWELL /1874-1960
CLARA PITTS CALDWELL /1878-1957
MARY HUTCHINSON /1872-1940
ANDREW W.BURCH /1867-1950>>>>>>>>MAGGIE STUART BURCH /1869-1953
Dbl.St,JEFF L.COCHRAN/ 1872-1931>>>>WILLIE P.COCHRAN /1886-1936
Dbl.St.:WALTER L.BOULER /1879-1946>>>> SARAH E.BOULER /1888-1946
MAGGIE EVANS SIMMS /31 July 1853/Nov.20,1939
PATTIE MALLETTE DUPUY /1880-1956
HOWELL ELDRIDGE DUPUY /1879-1956

ALEXANDER-DREW-BAREFIELD FAMILY CEM.

Located on North end of Hollandale City. The land for the Hollandale Cem. was given to the City by the ALEXANDER Family. Fence inclosure, old cedar trees., under City maintenance. Barefield Landing.

ELON O./son of J.B.&M.L.DREW/June 4,1881/1 Dec.1900
SARAH JANE DREW /Jan.20,1837/July 1,1910
MARTHA L.DREW /wife of J.B.DREW /DEc.12,1862/Sept.6,1881
NEWIT ELLIS/son of EDWARD T. and AMERINTHA THERESA DREW/
June 30,11874/Jan.24,1900
ANNIE LOU ALEXANDER /Nov.1874/Mar.1951
2 foot stones: S.T.B. - L.A.B.
Dbl.St.:LAURA /July 27,1872/Oct.31,1873
INFANT son of/ Aug.3,1867/Children of S.T.& A.B.BAREFIELD
NEWITT BAREFIELD /son of FRANCIS A.& STEPHEN BAREFIELD /
Aug.18,1875/July 5,1889/ Ft.St.N.B.
PINKEY/dau.of P.M.& E.E.ALEXANDER /July 12,1877/July 16,1883
JESSE N.ALEXANDER /dau.of P.M.&
E.E.ALEXANDER /Aug.16,1880/Aug.8,1895
P.M.ALEXANDER /Dec.14,1846/Dec.15,1927/FATHER
EUGENIA BAREFIELD ALEXANDER /May 24,1846/Sept.9,1910
Broken Stone: b.Ap&6,1839/d.Dec.4,1875 [Note: Must be STEPHEN T.BAREFIELD]

WASHINGTON CO.,MS CEMETERIES
CLETONIA CEMETERY, CLETONIA LANDING, S.E. OF HOLLANDALE

Located in Sec.17,T15N,R6W, on bank of Deer Creek. A disaster covered with dewberry vines, and johnson grass stalks. Many stones are broken, and possibly many others buried out of sight. Copied Jan.1986:Branton/Payne.

Starting on the N.W. corner: The **WOOD** plot is well kept.
PINKBOWLES WOOD / 1853-1925
JAMES W. ARINGTON / Nov.1,1878/Nov.26,1891
S.H. WOOD / Aug.24,1840/Apr.9,1893
WM. WOOD / Mar.4,1842/June 27,1912
Moving Eastward on outer perimeter:
ANNA LOU/ dau.of J.R.& A.L. WINPEGLER /Jan.17,1892/June 4,1893
JOHN CHEW HAWKINS /Native of Frankfort,Ky/d.Dec.17,1876/aged 52 yrs.
CARRIE/wife of/W.B.GO----/ *stone broken -dates on small piece leaning on this stone:* 4 Dec.183-/28 Nov.1887
Small Stone: ORA
On West side, moving south:
 LULA CLARKE WRIGHT/Nov.20,1857/Jan.29,1949
JOHN WESLEY WRIGHT/ 10 Apr.1852/21 May 1917/ W.O.W.
(Dbl.Stone)DAUGHTER: MARY ROBERTA/ dau.of/EUG.S.& ALPHA ROBERTA
          CLARKE/Sept.29,1903/Apr.19,1904
            WIFE:ALPHA ROBERTA WRIGHT/wife of/EUG.S.CLARKE/
            June 14,1881/Oct.14,1903
R.L.WRIGHT/Oct.16,1829/Aug.16,1897
MOTHER:SYDNEY S.WRIGHT/Oct.29,1833/Aug.27,1913
W.H.BRUMFIELD/Sept.15,1869/Dec.5,1924/**Mason
KATE HUNTER SIMMS/wife of/GEO.W.WHEELER/Mar.9,1858/Aug.9,1897
GEO.HUNTER/ inf. son of/G.W.& KATE H.WHEELER/July 31,1897/ Aug.31,1897
GEO.WILLIAM/son of/G.W.& F.M.WHEELER/Oct.8,1901/Nov.7,1901
Footstone: GWW- *In center of Cemetery, a large flat stone-*
JESS/The devoted dau.of /J.A.& NANNIE HOLLINGSWORTH/passed away
          Feb.2,1943
Large Matching stone, lying face down, marked- HOLLINGSWORTH
**JOSEPH ANDREW HOLLINGSWORTH/Col.Joe/29 Nov.1847/3 Oct.1941
NANNIE/wife of/J.A.HOLLINGSWORTH/Sept.20,1851/Oct.22,1894
JAMES HENRY/son of T.K.& R.BENSON/Jan.1,1878/Sept.10,1883
Fenced in area., 3 large stones, covered with vines.
SIMEON WHITE/b.1827/d.1873
MARY FRILEY/wife of **DAVID FRILEY/1820- ?/** 1835-1923
HENRY W.HOLLOMAN/1846-1917
Leaning against the lone cedar tree.:
        MOTHER:MRS.S.A.WRIGHT/Mar.27,1859/Dec.28,1922

**Additions from Carol Ray's list, compiled 1971

WASHINGTON CO., MS CEMETERIES

CLETONIA CEM., cont.

WARD LaFAYETTE JONES/July 27, 1907/Nov. 12, 1923
MOLLIE D./ wife of **A.B.GOLDEN/Jan.6, 1871/Aug.28, 1899
REBECCA J.-------/wife of R.T.O------/ *broken stone*
GEORGE TATE GRAY/Nov.5, 1854/Jan. 10, 1923
**DICKIE M.GRAVITT/11 Sept. 1869/12 Sept. 1882
**MATTIE A.GRAVITT/Apr.3, 1872/15 Sept. 1882
J.P.MITCHELL/son of J.H.& SUSAN MITCHELL/b.Apr.1, 1861/ n\d
WAUNET JONES/Oct.12, 1887/July 23, 1888
J.L.JONES/Oct.30, 1858/Sept.8, 1898
**MARTHA W.E./dau.of J.L.&S.A.JONES/Jan. 1883
NANCY/wife of F.SANDLING/d.1890/19 yrs. **d.12 Aug.1890/age 65
Broken stone: FANNIE BAKER/ no dates.
NANCY SMITH/b.Oct.3, 1881/ ----/ **d.Oct.3, 1888
LESLIE/son of S.M.& A.E.MURPHREE/b.May 6, 1894/Aug.20, 1894
ALEXANDER WEBER/Apr.1, 1869/Jan. 13, 1919/ **W.O.W.
Broken Stone: ENDORA. wife of ------
**ENORA/wife of HUGH SLATER/21 Aug. 1821/4 May 1897
**EARLY C./son of V.T.&M.C.I.SLATER/6 May 1881/8 May 1881
**ERNEST M./son of V.T.&M.C.I.SLATER/3 Feb. 1875/19 Oct. 1878
**LENARD/son of L.N.& L.S.SLATER/25 Oct. 1886/8 Oct. 1890
**MARGARETT C.I./wife of V.T.SLATER/1 July 1850/17 May 1881
GEORGE CADWELL/ "Known as COONEY"/Dec.27, 1923/72 yrs.old.
**JOHN M.BARRETT/13 Sept. 1882/3 yrs.
**Additions from CAROL RAY's list, compiled 1971

∞∞∞∞∞∞∞∞∞∞∞∞∞∞∞∞∞∞∞∞∞∞

ALDRIDGE FAMILY CEMETERY: Sec.24,T16N,R7W: North side of the R.N. ALDRIDGE Home, West side of Old Highway 61, Estill, Ms. Beautiful little cemetery, contained in a wrought iron fence, well kept, serene. 1986, by K.B.

Small stone leaning against fence - HATTIE LEE/dau.of/M.& F.M. WILMOT /
    b.Aug.9, 1875/d.Sept.14, 1875
Large Center Marker: ALDRIDGE - with 3 graves.
ROBERT N.ALDRIDGE /b.Nov.20, 1890/d.Aug. 19, 1960
WILLIAM O. ALDRIDGE /b.Sept.22, 1853/d.Dec.5, 1920
POLLY ATTERBURY ALDRIDGE /Oct.18, 1851/July 30, 1941
Out side of this fenced in plot, are a few stones leaning against a cedar tree, - "they've always been there". One small marker "WEST"/ Another: OUR BABY/ 1873/ ALDRIDGE Family lore recounts that "CAPT. HILL" is buried in an unmarked grave, next to the present day pump house.

WASHINGTON CO.,MS CEMETERIES

SMITH FAMILY CEMETERY: Located in South Arcola,Ms., next to the railroad track, now part of a gin lot. Family burying ground of the WM.F.SMITH Family, surrounded by a chain link fence, stones abused and knocked over. Copied by Caledonia Payne and Katherine Branton - Jan.1986

MALINDA L./wife of/J.S. MYERS /July 31,1833/Sept.4,1863
2 Footstones: G.(OR C)W.S. - J.E.S.
A broken stone,buried: JOHN E. SMITH/ b.Dec.3,1809/ d. Oct.10,1857
Buried stone:WM.F. SMITH /died Nov.3,1877/age (broken here)51(?) yrs.
Mrs. Mercer Rich had cataloged this little cemetery several yrs.ago, and had found 2 other stones, and another footstone:
    CLARK W. SMITH /son of/W.F.& LATTE SMITH /Dec.26,1853/ Oct.1885
    MARY/b.June 16,1855/d.June 23,1855/ dau.of/W.F.& L. SMITH
    Footstone: W.F.S.
The Church Records of the Methodist Church in Arcola gave MRS.RICH the following death dates: MR.E.L. SMITH /(son of W.F.& L.SMITH) d.1921
    MRS.E.L.(MATILDA) SMITH/ d.May 1940
    ADA SMITH(wife of JOSEPH SMITH -son of Wm.F.& L.)d.1901

CASEY FAMILY CEMETERY: Warsaw Landing, on Deer Creek, 2 miles north of Hollandale, on Old Highway 61. Casey home built ⊚1890 sat on North end of pecan grove, now cleared. One tall stone, four sided, with Masonic Emblems on all four sides, but only one name. According to obit in DAILY DEMOCRAT-Apr.14,1915, there should also have been grave of JACK CASEY / youngest son of/ J.T.CASEY / b.Hinds Co.,Ms.45 yrs ago.
Copied by Caledonia Payne and Katherine Branton - Jan.1986.

My Husband/CHARLES C./son of/J.T.& H.E. CASEY /Aug.3,1861/Sept.24,1895

DUPUY CEMETERY: Located near Murphy (Ms.) Destroyed by construction. A list of those interred given by MRS.ADELAIDE HUNTER, of Anguilla,Ms., granddaughter of Mr.and Mrs. Joel W. Dupuy - Jan.1986.

ALICE LOUISE HUNTER /b.Jan.30,1911/d.Nov.13,1911
BEULAH SMITH DUPUY / d.Oct.1913/(1st.wife of HOWELL ELDRIDGE DUPUY)
A JORDAN infant and 2 Infant ch. of BEULAH & HOWELL E.DUPUY
PHILLIP LESLIE DUPUY /b.Aug.15,1905/d.May 1917
JOEL WATKINS DUPUY /b.Feb.2,1848/d.Oct.11,1917
MARTHA RYALS DUPUY /(wife of Joel W.) b.June 19,1854/d.13 Nov.1940
CALLISE MALLET / no dates
An Inf. of HOWELL E. JR.& HELEN PINK MATTHEWS DUPUY / d.1932/3

WASHINGTON CO., MS CEMETERIES

Huddleston Cemetery
Located 1 mi. south of Cletonia Cemetery, on same side of Deer Creek.
Copied by CAROL RAY, 1971.

BERTHA **BATTLES** /Dec.24,1887/July 24,1923
WASHINGTON **BOYD** /C.O.I. 110 U.S.INF./d.Feb.22,1919
REV.L.W.**BRYANT** /Aug.6,1842/Mar.20,1919
JERRY **DANIELS** /June 24,1884/Oct.8,1911
CAROLINE **DAVIS** /Apr.18,1856/July 25,1908
THOMAS **DAVIS** /d.Sept.29,1913/CUO of OF. Lodge 4535
WALLACE **DIGGS**, Jr./MISS.WAGONER/803 Pioneer Inf./d.30 Sept.1918
THOMAS **DRYAN** /b.1837/d.Apr.11,1905/ Mason
WILLIS **HARPER** /1864/d.Oct.22,1909/Lodge #4535
HENRY **HOLLAND** /July 4,1850/Nov.1,1904/54 yrs.3 mo./Mason
MONA/ wife of ISAAC **JACKSON** /1846-1916
JOSEPHINE **MOORE** /D.JAN.23,1914/AGE 44 YRS.
PRESTON **SNOWDEN** /Jan.2,1878/Jan.10,1954
WINFIELDS **TAYLOR** /Apr.10,1873/Mar.16,1907/ Lodge #4535
ANNIE/wife of B.**WATSON** /b.1853/d.Nov.11,1906
ANNETTE/dau.of ANNIE & B.**WATSON** /July 5,1860/June 24,1906

ESTILL FAMILY CEMETERY
Sec.30,T16 N,R6W: Between Old Highway 61 and West bank of Deer Creek, just below Estill,Ms., in the middle of a plowed field. Originally surrounded by a wrought iron fence, now in a delapidated condition. Copied Jan.1,1986 by K.Branton, C.Payne.

Dbl.St.:JAS.C./Sept.17,1871/Sept.21,1871 -Infant son/ b.& d.Sept.11,1872/
        Children of J.C.& R.C.ESTILL
Small stone lying flat-JCE: and a ft.st..B.O.E.
Large Marble Stone, broken - names on 2 sides:
    NELLIE V./dau.of J.C.& R.C.ESTILL /Nov.5,1873/----1875
    REBECCA C./wife of J.C.ESTILL /Apr.26,1847/Dec.10,1875
Large Pink Marble Stone:JAMES CAMPBELL ESTILL /b.Mar.14,1823/
    d.May 18,1910/ *An Honest man is the noblest work of God*

COLLIER FAMILY CEMETERY
On East side of Deer Creek, @ 1 1/2 mi. below Arcola. 2 Stones under a tree. Copied by Carol Ray, 1971.

J.M.**COLLIER** /son of ROBERT & MARGARET COLLIER /b.Worchester Co.,Md./
    Oct.2,1824/d.July 22,1901
GEORGE **COLLIER** /Aug.13,1861/May 17,1903

AARDWEG:*218
ABAT,J.R.7
ABEL(L):Edgar 106;Fanny 106;
 James 106;Mary E.106;Mollie
 106;Nannette 106;Saml.J.106
 Susan 106;Wm.106,124.*203
ABDO:*213
ABERNATHY:*211
ABRAHAM:*216
ADAMS:Jno.D.10;Julia 137;
 *195
ADE:*190
ADEL:Harry 80
ADDINGTON:*193
ADDISON:Caleb 42;Jacob 52;
 Susan 42.
AKIN(AIKEN):Albert 160;
 Carrie P.99,132;Martha G.140,
 160(w);Sedden P.160;Seddon
 140,160;Spencer B.160;W.B.99
 132;Wm.B.99.*174,175
ALCORN:Geo.R.34
ALDRICH:A.D.41;Benj.161;Bettie
 A.73,161;Chas.161;Ebernezer
 161;Lyman D.161(w);Lyman G.
 29,161;Mrs.Lyman G.119;Mary
 N.161;Sarah D.161
ALDRIDGE:Frank S.147(w);
 Hannah M.148;Lucy P.147;
 *173,174,185,213,218,
 221,222,237.
ALEXANDER:Amos 12;Austin
 F.155;Geo.B.155;Jacob 63,105,
 161;Mattie 133;D.M.76,143;
 V.F.P.12,59,81,83;*173,177,
 207,210,234,235.
ALLEN:Jno.35,36;Jno.F.108;
 Jno.T.109;Mrs.P.C.108;Mrs.
 Sarah B.119;Dr.W.G.71,98,145.
 *171,177,184,198,214,217.
ALFORD:*198,199.
ALLISON:Jno.159(w).
ALMA:*185
ALVERSON,Wm.131;
AMERINE,M.H.133.
ANDREW(S):Jas.T.3;W.S.160
ANDERSON:A.118;A.E.66;Alex.
 104,162;Cecile 118;Christop.
 49;C.W.49;D.D.66;Doc 95;Edna
 J.167;Ella 104;Ellen F.57;Frank
 128;Geo.T.167(w);Jerry 82;
 Jno.F.8;Jno.G.162;Lomax 57,
 103;Martin 67;Mary 168;Mary
 M.8; Robt.3;T.A.14;Wm.168(w).
ANNION:FRED L.161;M.L.161.
ANTHONY:*196
ARCHER:Abram 41;Alice 133;
 Annie M.134;Eliz.41,62;Fanny V.
 W.62;Geo.F.69;Harriet 14;Jas.,
 Jr. 62;Jennie 41;Maggie N.143;

ARCHER(CONT):Margie 61;
 Mary 41;R.T.41;STEV.48,
 58,62,88,132,133,134;
 DR.:127;*183
ARMSTRONG:Burrell 67;
 Hugh 131;Julia 131;Matilda
 Sarah 67;Sarah C.144;
 Willie 144;*183.
ARRINGTON:*236
ASH:A.16;Morris 16;
 Michael 16;*179.
ASKEW:Felix 160;*202.
ATKINSON:Mrs. 87;
ATLER:170
ATTERBURY:J.T.110;*176,
 181,224.
AUGUSTUS:*175
AUSTIN,Char.81;Nat.82;
AXMAN:Chas.121;*172
AYDELL:Louise 162

BABB:Emily 107,108;L.H.
 108
BABTIST:Wm.H.141;Ella 141.
BACON:Wm.163(w);Sophia
 163;*199.
BAER:Rosalie 105;Bernard 105
BAGGETT:Maggie O.142;N.T.156
BAGLEY:Dr.Wm.122;Jennie 154;
 L.W.159;*213
BAILEY:Ida B.159;Sarah 2;S.P.
 2;*179,184.
BAIRD:T.Q.132;
BAKER:E.B.153;Edgar W.129;
 Grafton 66,74;H.L.42,85,94,
 108;Jas.25;Mary J.94;T.Otis
 153;S.Duncan 153;*177,184,
 226,231,237
BALDRIDGE:*190
BALDWIN:Hattie 139(w);G.A.139;
 Louisana B.168;Martha 139;
 Wm.168.
BALFOUR:Dr.51.
BALL:L.M.52,69;Dr.Spencer 81.
BALLARD:Office 152;Pheaby
 152(w);*187,196,219
BALOR:*181
BANKNIGHT:E.166(w);Lula166
BANKS:Bedford 25;King 116;
 Susan 143;*190,192,218
BANKSTON:Katie 151(w)
BARBOUR:Jno.53;
BAREFIELD:Cath.147;Ella 147;
 Fannie A.76;'Jesse H.45;Jno.
 41,45,63;J.W.63;Lucile 147;
 Marion 76;Mary J.45;May Bird
 147;Saml.63,76,127,147(w);
 Saml.M.147;Sarah J.147;Steph.
 A.147;Steph.T.63,75,76;(cont.)

BAREFIELD:Robt.A.147;*175
 177,181,228,230,231,235
BARG:*171
BARKER:Edw.12;Eliz.11,12;
 Jacob 11,12.
BARKES:*176,211.
BARKSDALE:F.47;
BARLOW:HENRY 52
BARNARD:Lizzie 41;Wm.B.
 41;Wm.T.41.
BARNES:Chas.H.152;ESTELLE
 127;J.F.127;H.M.130,152(w)
 Mrs.Harry M.122;*170
BARNETT:D.R.157;*206
BARNEY:*184
BARR:Rev.136;*212.
BARRETT:Lucien 137;*234,
 237.
BARRINGTON:E.H.125
BARROWS:Nancy 100,101;
 Bennett H.101;Ann E.101;
 Martha A.101;
BARRY:Ada Q.134;
BARTINO:Marcus 124
BARTLETT:Ludie 119;Vince
 R.156;*172.
BARTON:*176,177
BARWICK:W.B.77;*195,196
BASS:Council 20;C.R.93,94,
 100;Ella 20,21,94,100;
 Eugenia 94;*178.
BASSETT:Jane 111;
BATE(S):Ann F.100;Henry
 C.21;Jas.H.20,21;Mrs.
 A.C.131;Tunis L.132;*210
BATTLES:*239
BATTS:*180,213
BAUGH:Archie 27,29
BEAMS:D.E.160
BEARD:C.M.63; *209
BEARDSLEY:Mita 135.
BEASLEY:Amanda 46;John
 Collier 46,47;L.156;Mary
 A.46;Martha E,46,47;
 Minerva 47;Rich.46;Rosa
 Ann 46;R.R.(w)46,47;
 Susan S.47;*221.
BEATT:*201
BEATTY:Mrs.80
BECK:Cora May 74;Davis B.
 74;Frank,Jr.145(w);J.G.74;
 Mary A.74;*205
BECKER:*217
BECKWITH:*179
BEDON:Dr.101;Leonella 132;
 R.D.150;Willie 121;
BELL:Alice 135;Alice F.127;
 Caroline D.107;Chas.H.65,
 66;David B.25;D.Dickinson
 107;Hillary 157;Jas.107;

*Naturalization,Guardianship,CemeteryRecords   – Surname Indexed.

BELL (cont)J.B.145;John 157; John Jr.67;Jno.V.119;J.W.127; Lee A.157,167;Rebecca 139; Sarah 136,157;S.C.146; Swartz 98;Wilson 39;*178, 181,183,184,211,235.
BENACHI:A.N.165
BENDAGE:Jno.145
BENJAMIN:E.V.133
BENNETT:J.A.63; *186,194.
BENOIT:Adele 149;A.W.149; A.W.Jr.149;Celest 149;Ida B.149(w)129;Lou Ellen 149; Ruth 149;Wm.B.149;
BENSON:*236
BEREL:Rino 16.
BERGIN:*206
BERGMAN:Lillian 137; Maurice 157.
BERKLEY:*178
BERRY:Claudia 136;S.R. 150;Thos.H.59; *216
BERTINATTI:EUGENIA P.20, 21,94,100;JOS.20;
BEST:Willie F.132;*215
BIDDLE:Mrs.Frances 118;
BIGELOW:Amelia 73
BIGGINS:F.122,140;Jane 122;
BIGGS:*189,192;
BILLINGSLEY:Geo.91, 127;*174,181.
BILLUPS:Polly J.116;
BINDER:Frank 148;*169.
BINGHAM: *189,192.
BIRD:Walter 154;
BIRKHEAD:Jno.H.12,13, 14,15;
BISHOP:Elsey 82;
BIVENS:Louise 132
BLACK:Chas.104;Mrs.Jno. 117;Thos.63;Wm.C.59.
BLACKBURN:A.F.101;Dr.E.C. 133;E.Julia 101;Geo.F.147; Geo.T.101; Henry J.101; Lou 101;Mary B.6;Rebecca W.147;Pru H.101;
BLACKLEY:*200
BLACKWELL:*201
BLACKWOOD:W.F.139
BLADE:*189
BLAKEMORE: *215
BLANCHARD:Jno.R.7;B.L.157.
BLAND:A.153(w);Fanny 153.
BLANTON:Dr.119;Martha 142(w);Mrs.O.M.119;O.M. 142;Wm.C.129
BLOCK:Rachel 166
BLOCKER: *218

BLOCKETT:Bettie E.117;
BLOOMENSTEIL:B.136.
BLUE: *170
BOATRIGHT: *192
BODDIE:Mamie S.124; Van B.135,152
BOGEN:Rabbi 133,162, 163.
BOGEY:*234
BONHERT:F.C.89
BOIS:Phil 77
BOLDIER:Kittie 140; Robt.140;Warren 140.
BOLTON:Col.72;Wm.H.50, 66,72,83.
BOWMART:Rev.F.C.90.
BOONE: *185
BORODOFSKY:J.S.137.
BORUM:Edith K.130; Rev.W.A.130.
BOULER: *235
BOUNDS: *218,219
BOURGES:Camille G.130; Ernest 130.
BOWEN:Allen 122;Grant A.2;Jno.H.94,122; Mamie 104.
BOWERS:E.J.30
BOWLES:A.167
BOWMAN:Mrs.M.E.151
BOWMAR:J.H.D.34,35;
BOYD:---61; *195,196, 239.
BOYKIN: *197
BOYLE:Lucy 35
BOZZA: *233
BRADY:Cath 153.
BRADFORD:Amanda 35
BRANDON:Carrie S.160(w) Char.160;Ger.P.132,160; *174.
BRANDT:A.140;ISA.140; LOUIS 140;RACHEL 140.
BRANNON:J.R.158
BRANTON:J.E.121,134; Robt.P.121;Peter R.134.
BRATTON:*191
BRAWNER:L.T.127
BRAZELTON:A.J.133
BREISCH:*217
BRELAND: *234
BRENTLEAGER:R.H.71.
BRICKEL:Mrs. T.J.151
BRICKLEY:F.C.147
BRIDGES:Mrs.R.B.154 *176.
BRIGGS: *177,188.
BRILL:Sol 69,105,151, 157.

BRINKLEY:R.C.100
BRISCO(E):Allen 25;Emily 25;Hezk.25; *160
BRITT:Maggie 111;P.M. 111:
BRITTAN:*182
BROADUS:Rev.135.
BRODHEAD:J.Davis 35
BROECK:R.T.8;Patsy D.8.
BROH:Cecelia 102;Frances 102; Gab.H.102;Isa.102;Moritz102; Paulina 102;Rachel 102;Sarah 102;Yetta 102;*206.
BROOKS:David E.90;Fanny C.90; Mrs.131; *217
BROWN:Addie 150;A.E.68;Alfred 144;Amos 2;Bell 153;C.A.10; Carrie 154;C.75;C.L.142; Clara 149;Eliz.19;Elvira 152; Dr.Preston 19;Geo.74;Hannah 56;Hattie M.144;Henry 140; Jimmie E.69;Jno.T.68;J.W.160 Mary 71;Mattie McK.130;Milly 25;Orlando 19;R.L.164;R.M., Jr.71;Sam 74,97;Shepherd 20 Thos.L.71,167; *170,174, 177,179,180,181, 182, 183,189,191,193,201, 217,219,232.
BROWNELL:F.E.132.
BRUCE:Birdie 139;Isaiah 139
BRUMFIELD: *236
BRUMLEY:Chas.D.156
BRYAN:Daisey 129,164;E.J.98, 164(w);Josephine 129,164; J.Harey 127;Mrs. E.J.129; Maude 129,164;Pearl 164. *203,207.
BRYANT:*184,223,226,239.
BUCHANAN:Lula L.119;W.H.119;
BUCK:Joel 158
BUCKLEY:J.W.75; *225,230.
BUCKNER:Amanda W.40;Aylette 138;Betty A.29;Col.168;Davis 40,73,74;D.M.344,168;Ellen 168;Ellen F.57,138;Eliza M.55 Emily E.57;Eugene 168; Florida 168;Henry 66,168(w), 84,85;James H.73;H.L.42;Jesse 73,74Jno.W. 55;Katie 55,57(w); Louise 130,168;Louisa 73;Malinda 66;Mary V.55;Mrs.P.M.55;Pauline 168;Phillip 73;Phil T.73;Randall 168;Reason 168;Robt.H.57,138; Sarah 57,138;Solomon 168;Thos. .29,57,73,74,138.;P.C.55. *204, 221.
BUFORD:Edw.P.141.*232

*Naturalization,Guardianship,CemeteryRecords   - Surname Indexed.

BULL:Saml.B.Jr.133;S.C.
Jr.164.
BUNTIN:*179
BURCH:*235
BURCHATIM:Gordon L.144
BURDETTE:Emma 103;Fanny
103;Marsh.41,89,116,123;
Minerva 103,104;Nannie
103; Rich.41,89,103,123;
Willie M.103.
BURFORD:*212
BURGESS:Ernest 26;
BURK:Sarah 80;Wm.C.
159;*171.
BURKS:Eliza G.21;Saml.
21;*184
BURNETT:A.K.153;Alice
156;J.153; *232.
BURNLEY:*202
BURN(E)S:Kate 106,107;
James 106;W.160;*175.
BURR:Rev.137
BURRELL:Nancy 158.
BURRES:Percy 168.
BURRUS:F.157;
BURT:Lorenzo 51;
BURTON:Jos.50
BUSBY:Henry 162;Paul
L.162;
BUSH:Lou Birdie 151;
Wm.H.S.151;
BUTLER:Edna 159;*184,
218,224.
BUTTS:Mary B.65;W.R.
118;*187,211.
BYARS:Claib.164
BYNUM:*176
BYRNE(S):Dr.B.S.69;
E.P.7

CABBOTT:Jos.1
CADENHEAD:Maggie 137;
Mrs.W.H.137.
CADWELL:*237.
CAFFALL:Agnes 85,150,
160(w);Amelia 168;
Chas.85,162;Edw.162;L.81,
85,86,150(w)162;Lena 85;
Lewis 162;Louisa 85;Robt.
162;Willie 162;*182.
CAHN:B.43,60,64.
CAIN:*177
CAIRO:Landin 158(w);
Sam 158;
CALDWELL:Jno.T.1; *235
CALENDER:Ada C.165;I.J.
165(w);
CALHOUN:Alb.C.134;
P.C.16
CALLAHAN:*217,185.

CALVERT:Minerva J.168;
Wm.J.168.
CAMBRIDGE:*180
CAMERON:Angeline 168;
C.C.69;
CAMPBELL:Amite B.141;
B.M.81;C.C.168;Louise
122,135;Robt.G.141(w);
Patti R.141,149;Walter
81,131;*182.
CANNADA Thos.J.133
CANNON:*230
CAPERS:Mary E.142;
CAPERTON:Alex C.8;
J.C.117.
CAPP:*187
CAPPEL:Harry S.148;
Mary B.M.148.
CAPSHAW:*177
CARLETON,Sue 136
CARLISLE:*191
CARNES:Anna L.150;
*232,233
CARNEY:J.L.97
CARO:Jennie 140,Henry
140
CARPENTER:Ella 147;
H.27,41
CARRAWAY;Jas.J.152
CARR:*194
CARRICO:R.T.38
CARRIGAN:Annie 143;
Jno. 60
CARROLL:Mother 29
CARSON:A.B.21,60,73,
101,120;Andrew 9,12,
21,22,121,170;Eliz.J.
121;Mrs.M.B.77,101.
CARTER:Alf.B.10;A.G.26,
50;Alf.G.26,50;Ann B.
26;Crockett 45;Eliz.H.
10;Eliz.L.26,49(w),50;
Eleanor S.26,49;Jesse
L.45;Jno.167;J.C.162;
J.W.151;Mary E. 26;
Mittie 50;Robt.H.26,49,
50,128;R.M.49;Saml.S.161;
Sarah 45;Will 26;W.G.49,
50,116;*169,184,185,
197,220,229,233.
CARTWRIGHT:*233.
CARVER:*210
CASE:J.W.139
CASEY:Chas.G.12,156;
Hattie E.156(w);J.H.156;
Jno.J.143,156,168 (w);
Marie L.168;R.L.156; *238
CASON:*210,224.
CASTLEMAN:Pauline 166;
Steph.141;*174,175,178.

CASWELL:*212
CATALDI:*216
CATCHINGS:*183,184
CATO:*224,225.
CAVENDER*191
CHADDICK:*175
CHAMBERS:Mrs.P.M.55
CHA(I)NEY:Thos.Y.51; *171.
CHAPIN:*173
CHAPMAN:Cornelia 148;*187
CHAPPEL:Carter 128;Henry J.
128;J.C.160;Jennie 140;*183
CHARLES:Florence 143
CHEATHAM:G.W.154;Jno.L.14;
N.P.S.151;
CHERRY:*193
CHESNEY:Jas.F.74;
CHEW:Aug.41,57,59,114.
CHIASA:Alice 91,92;
CHICKLE:Patsy 2;Alf.2;
CHILDRESS:C.S.137.
CHILTON:*177
CHINN:Ned 25;Terrell 25;
Viney 56.
CHIPMAN:AAlma 129;T.J.129;
CHRISTODULAR:*169
CHURCH:Fanny P.92;Jno.91,92;
J.V.147.
CLACK:W.S.133
CLAPP:Emily 109;Emory 108,
109;Lily 109;Pamela 109.
CLARK(E):Ann118;C.W.99,108;
D.W. 118; E.D.50;FRANCES
118;Lewis 25;Penny 156;
Rich.25;Robt.29;Sally 163(w);
*180,183,194,236.
CLARKSON:*172
CLARY:A.W.66,68;Kate B.68;
Nancy 149;*180
CLAY:Green 122,135;Henry 117
CLAYTON:*181
CLEATON:Amanda 109,112;
Andrew 109;Asenath 109,111,
112;Chas.109,112;Edward
109,112;Jos.109,112;Mary
109,112 ;W.A.77,109,111,
112;*173.
CLEMENS:Plenty 98;*182
CLEMENTS:R.E. 157.
CLEVELAND:*200
CLIFTON:Caswell R.23
CLOCK:Fannie S.132
CLOUSTON:*173
CLOWER:*209,234
COBER:PRICILLA 40
COBB:Jno.D.31
COCHEO:*193
COCHRAN:*189,235
COHN:Abe 166;D.129;Freda 166;
Hannah 166;Jake 166;Maurice

COHN:(cont)J.166;Morris 144,166(w). *171,183, 206.
COHEN:Dave 133;*171.
COLE:Aaron 67.
COLEMAN:Carrie 162; Dewitt M.141;Dr.Frank 44; Jerry 159,167(w);Lizzie W. 159,167;Mary E.159;Matt 25;Moses 25;Narcissis 153; Rich.25;*183,201,225.
COLESCOTT:Thos.W.7
COLLIER:Caroline 95;J.W.63; Lem 95;*180,209,221, 239.
COLLINGS:Edw.T.159
COLLINS:Fannie 162;Harry 162;*178,179,208
COLLUM:Elbert 45,77;E.P. 76;Katy 45;*179,181, 228,229,231.
COLUMBUS: *219
COMEGYS:Jno.P.100
COMPTON:Jno.111;Y.J.42
COMSTOCK:E.J.4,30,40, 72;EVELINA 4.
CONDRAY:Althea 153; Rosa 153;
CONGER:W.B.44.
CONLEE: *219
CONLEY:J.B.160(W); Landon 160.
CONN:*177
CONNELL:Jas.89,90;
CONNERS:H.W.112
CONTAWAY:Aner 167
COOK:E.G.18;De.159; Henry F.15;McK.L.110; *117,214,225.
COOPER:Eliz.J.56,64; Jennie 152;Nettle L.150; Robt.S.56,64;Wm.167; *170,175,177,180, 190,191,201,220.
COOVERT:Jno.C.133
COPELAND;*215,219
COPPEE:H.L.St.128
CORNELIUS:ELIZ.123;*184.
CORNISH:Jeff 137
CORPAL:Rose 140
CORPERY: *183
COSENS:S.S.168
COSHUN:Jan 152
COTTON:Wm.66;*170, 183,184.
COURTNEY:Jno.T.4,8; Jane W.8,104;
COUSINS: *190
COUVILLON:*199

COWAN:Jno.167(w);T.B.145; *176,190,215,231.
COX:Bettie 151;C.R.151(w); Hampton 151(w);Jack 117; Lutie 151;Mack 117;Xavia 151;*193.
CRAFT: *201
CRAVEN:WM.141
CRAIG:Dogelon 159;F.J.85,94, 108;H.144;J.R.159(w);Lilly 159;Mageline 159;Niola 159; M.W.132;Randolph 163;Ruth 159;*181,193.
CRATSLEY:Jno.139
CRAWFORD: *199,216,
CREEL: *234
CRENSHAW:*231
CREWS:*188
CRIBB:Eleanor J.144; Jos.P.144.
CRIPPEN: *219
CRISWELL: *188
CROOK:Alberta 154;Arthur 154; Janey155;Jesse 154;Jesse A. (w)154;Jno.B.155;Jno.H.154; Lue J.154;Wm.McK.154; *177, 179.
CROSBY:Julia B.132;Henry T. 132;*176,185.
CROSS:Jerome 34;Rev.Wm.134, 165.
CROUCH: *175
CROW:A.J.H.79,85,94. *173.
CROWELL:Lily 137;*175
CROZIER: *191
CRUMP: *174
CUMLEY:Helen F.163
CUNNINGHAM:Jno.P.16,17;
CURRIE:J.T.153(w); *170.
CURRELL:C.M.145,165; Dr.119.
CURRY:J.A.158;Julia A.38; Sally Ann 38;
CURTIS: *178

DABNEY:A.L.138;HARRIET L.142;JNO.142;MRS.LOLA B.119;LAV.L.142;
DAILEY:Tim 82
DAMERON:Lewis T.51;*227
DAMSON:Thos.135;
DAND:Jane v;
DANIEL(S):Frank 5;Lee 5; P.M.157;Sarah 4,5;Wade 5;W.E.4; *182,239.
DARDEN: *216
DARETT:Adrian 125
DARLING:Eliz.127;Ella 127; Dr.Jos.121;Miss 121;

DARNELL: *194
DAVENPORT:Benj.G.161
DAVID: *209
DAVIDOW:Esther 166;Freda 166; Henrietta 166;Sylvia 166.
DAVIDSON:P.W.153;*194
DAVIES:Eliz.75;Evan 75;Jno.75
DAVIS:Ben 77;Cora 133;Eliza 34, 35;Eliza C.119;Florence 167;G. 158;Green 153;Hugh R.34,35; Jas.L.133;Jeff.34,35;Jno.160; Jos.2;Jos.E.34,35(w);Lulu 133; Lucinda 166;Maj.145;Marg.35; Mary 120;Mary M.35;Rebecca 2; Quintina 163;Sarah 111,120; Varina 35;Violet L.155;Warren 112,113;Wm.35,120. *178, 179,184,185,190,207, 211,226,227,239.
DAWSEY:Jno.42;Rachel 42.
DAWSON:Mrs.L.A.128; *176
DAY:Emory C.109;Sallie C.109; *209
DEAN:Lula 133;Thomp.10;*175, 216,232.
DEATON:Maj.Jas.A.121,126,145 145(w);Kath.145; *172.
DeCAMERANNA:Albert 100;Ella I.100;
DEENER: *212
DENNETT:Frances 107;
DENNIS: *178
DERTIE:Addie 164;
DeLAUREAL:G.R.138
DeSAVIEU:*201
DeSOUTER:Jno.39,105;Peter 105.
DETERLY:M.S.137
DeZAVION:Ellen 167;Ned 167(w)
DIAMOND: *170
DIETRICH:Jos.146
DIGGS:*239
DILL: *192
DILLEY:*219
DILLINGHAM:Jno.P.11,12,32,33, 50;W.A.P.33,50;
DIN:*201
DINGY:Emma E.51;Henry C.50,51; Martha 50,51;Minnie O.51.
DINKINS: *200,203.
DISINGER: *234
DIXON:R.L.22,31;R.J.160,162; *181,201
DOBSON:Rev.132 *215
DODD: *171
DODSON:Eddie 83
DONAHOE:J.T.145
DONLEY:Pat 116;
DORAN:W.J.165
DORSEY:Phoebe 166;*225

*Naturalization,Guardianship,Cemetery   Records - Surname Indexed

DOUGHTERY:Alfred 164;
 Andrew 164;Henry 164;
 Jerry 164(w);Jno.164;
 Lucinda 164;Minarvy 164;
 W.H.152;
DOUGHTIE:Eliz.160
DOUGLAS:Earl 143;Ruth
 143;
DOWNING:W.W.138
DOWNS:A.C.167;Clara B.
 167;Letty V.167;
DOYLE:Lula 154;Madge 132;
 *177.
DRENMAN:Dr.C.T.157;
 Minnie 157.
DREW:*234,235.
DREYFUS:Bertha 116;*206
DRONE:Rich.S.4
DRUMMOND:Corinne H.152;
 Florence A.152;Mary A.152;
 Sallie L.152;W.H.130,152(w);
 W.H.Jr.152;*176
DRYAN:*239
DUCHMON:F.90
DUDLEY:Anna 137;Chas.W.Jr.
 61,65,87;Chas.W.Sr.61,65;
 Mrs.Lou J.130;Mrs.M.A.65;
DUFFY:Mike 95;Pat 95,119;
DUGGER:Mrs.J.A.131
DUKE:A.R.132;J.B.165;J.W.
 132;MAMIE 132.*199.
DULANEY:Dr.126;*200
DUNBAR:A.W.59
DUNCAN:*176,187
DUNN:Amanda 164;Dr.S.R.
 117,146;Edna B.119;Fanny
 107;Francis L.107;Jno.N.119;
 M.116;Mary A.135;Mary F.
 131;Mrs.Mary Dee 119;
 Orville B.117;Pat 107;
 Willie T.107;*181.
DUPUY: *235,238
DUVAL:*192
DYER:*176

EARNEST:Jennie 83;
EASTERBROOK:Ellen 111;
EASTLAND:*181
EASTON:C.C.42;Emma 42.
EBERT:Ed.(w)145
ECKART:E.A.86
ECKSTONE:Louis 129
EDDLEMAN:*180
EDWARDS:Anna 60;Ruth 149;
EGAN:*232
EHLERS:Wm.85
EIFLING:*199
ELKAS:Carl 113;Isaac 113;
 Kittie 113;Louis 113;
ELDER:Mr.33; *181

ELLITE:Henry T.100
ELLIOTT:A.Foster 23;Eliz.
 168;G.W.70,74,79;H.H.79;
 Maggie 156;Marie A.O.23;
 *192,205,218.
ELLET:Gen.9
ELY:T.L.165
EMSON:Isaiah 163
ENOS:ED.73,121; *172
EPPERSON:Mary R.142;
 *174.
EQUEN:Jonte 79
ERHLICH:Mary 166
ERVIN:Sonny 164(w);
 Lizzie 164
ERWIN:Bettie 117;Eliz.J.65;
 Emma 65;Emily 65;Jas.65;
 Johnson 59,61,65,87;J.W.
 87,117;Lillie J.65;Tony 98;
 V.F.48,65;WM.65; *173,
 185,197,198,202.
ESKRIDGE:Ellen B.165;E.V.
 128;Herbert 137,165(w);
 Louise B.165;*180
ESTES: *198
ESTERLING,F.S.55
ESTILL:C.R.24,25,27,28;
 Jas.C.44,77,81,83,165(w);
 J.H.25,28;M.A.165; *239.
ESPENSEN:*194
ETHRIDGE:*212
EUBANKS:E.F.62,91
EUSTIS:Jno.G.48
EVANS:Chas.141;Eliza 138;
 Emily 57;Frank 86;Jno.
 157(w);Lewis DeN.57;
 N.M.148; *170,188,
 203,233.
EVERETT:H.B.142
EVERMAN:Mere.D.131;W.A.
 37,47,66,78,112,131.
EWING:Rev.135.

FABIAN:Bertha 142;
FAGGINS*180
FAIRCHILD:Britt 143(w);
 Chas.H.143;Sallie 143:
FALL:Eliza A.17;Geo.R.17.
 *225
FALOON:*214
FARLEY:Harry W.1*229
FARMER:Geo.41,45; *196,
 230
FARR:E.J.48;W.B.48; *197.
FARRAR:*185,202
FARRIS:*171
FASS:Nathan 137
FAVA:*190
FAWN:Chas.E.68;Jno.40,68.

FAY:Chas.S.147;Edw.H.147(w);
FEINSTEIN:*169
FERGUSON:Alf.63;Ann 63;Cath.
 52,53;Jas.P.27;Lelia W.153;
 Mrs.129;Mrs.Harry 130;Sadie
 W.158;Saml.W.31,44,47,52,
 53,57,58,65,66,68,72,78,88,
 97,115; *179,204,228.
FELLOWS:Corn.1,20;Lydia 163;
FELTUS:J.A.V.82,102,159(w);
 Kate B.159.*181,218.
FIELDING:Wm.77; *231
FIELDS:Angus 166(w);Phoebe 166
FILLILAND: *189
FINKLEA:*214
FINKLESTEIN: *169
FINLAY:A.B.69;Ann B.21;Dr.Jno.
 L.21;Ga.B.149;Ga.G.142;Helen
 M.142;Jno.P.64,93,109,114;
 Lola B.142;Orv.P.142;Saml.D.
 142;S.D.88;S.F.148; *199.
FINN:Ger.75;Robt.R.75;
FISH:Edw.S.156;
FISHBURN: *180
FISHER:Ellen 61;Henry 56;Mrs.
 Henry K.157;Jno.S.60,61;Jno.
 W.119;*178,185,218.
FISK:Stewart 4.
FITZHUGH:Ida B.162;Lewis T.
 69;Wm.H.162;
FLAKE:*217
FLANAGAN:*212
FLANDERS:A.80
FLANNERY:Marg.59
FLEISCHER:Simon 89;
FLEMING:Mary H.31;Mrs.Jno.
 113;W.R.31; *192,193,
 194,195.
FLETCHER:Amelia 133;Bob
 25;Sarah 137;*180.
FLUEALL:*179
FLOURNOY:E.J.26;Mrs.E.J.
 119;V.M.26,105;
FLOWERS:I. 163;
FLOYD:K.75; *229.
FOGO:S.W.141(w);
FOLEY:Fenton 168;G.W.
 168(w);Susan V.168;
FOOTE:H.W.114;Jno.T.30;
FONDER:*180
FONGER:Lizzie 147;
FORBUSH:E.16
FORD:Benj.B. v;Mary E.v;
 *178.
FORTNER:Doug.124;Josie
 H.129;Sed 124;
FOSS:Mrs.E.T.127;
FOSTER:B.P.148(w);Gena
 J.148;Rigby 148;T.J.22;
 Wm.98;Zulee 148;

*Naturalization,Guardianship,Cemetery   Records - Surname Indexed

FOWLER:Hannah 164;*176, 184.
FOX:Carrie C.143;J.H.143.
FRACTION:Pleas.77;
FRALEY:Jas.B.159; *181
FRANCE(I)S:Chas.S.144; Fred.62;Harriet 144;Jno.M. 144(w);Pomeroy 144;
FRANKEL:Ruby 122;
FRANKLIN:*182
FRANKS:*223
FRASER:Alex.G.111;Ann 111; Cath.111;David 111;Geo.G. 111;Geo.R.111;Jane 111; Sarah 111;
FRATESI:*219
FREDRICHSEN:Marie 136.
FREEL:*169
FREELAND:Emily 138;F.A.138; T.138;Thos.138.
FREEMAN:Edna 73;Rab.159(w); Sarah 73;*216.
FRENCH:Mrs.S.F.121.
FREY:Willie L.150
FRIEDRICKSEN: *169.
FRIERSON:S.E.155
FRILEY:David:109,41,44,63, 69,75,110,111,114;Hugh 151;*236.
FRUENDT:Adolph 86;Ernst 86; Henry 86;Johana 86;Louise 86;Maria E.86.
FRY:Emory S.109.
FILCHER: *220
FULLER: *220
FULTON:Danl.140
FURNESS: *230

GADDIS:L.46
GAFF:Thos.10;
GALE:Will D.28
GAINEY: *189
GAITHER:E.H.156
GALENOS: *169
GAMBAL: *169
GAMBLE:H.A.161
GAMBUEL:D.60;Emma S.60.
GANIER: *233
GANITH:Chas.H.111
GANOWAY:Kate E.139
GANT:ED 154;Wm.24,25;
GARDNER:E.N.163
GARNER:Henry 67;*199.
GARRETT:O.L.138,140; *218
GARY:Alb.137;
GAY:W.L.104;Caroline 104; *170.
GAYDEN:Louisa 1
GAYLOR:Rev.Geo.138

GAYO:A.152
GAZZELLE: *217
GEISE:Lessie 150;S.R.150;
GENERIS:Louis G.7;
GENSBERGER:Amelia 157;Arthur 157;David 157;Esther 157; Eugenia 157;Helen 135,157; Flora 137,157;Julia 151(w); M.64,71,150,151,157(w); Sarah 135,157;Seymour 157. *179.
GEORGE:Sam B.124;Susie 137;
GERALD:Mrs.Lula 117;*183, 185,216.
GERLICH:Mr.89
GERTITZ:H.86
GIARDINA:*169,172,211.
GIBBS:Carolyn 10;*171,217
GIDDEN:S.W.120;W.B.57,133,136
GIERUTH:J.N.151
GILDART:Robt.E.120;W.K.120;
GILKEY:*200
GILL:N.Rufus 80;*233.
GILLESPIE:Chas.G.137;Chris. 23,24;Mrs.A.A.126;Mrs. Marg.18;*224
GILLIAM:Mary 151(w)
GILLILAND:E.C.135;Mrs.147.
GILMORE:Chas.C.140;W.H.98
GIPSON:Carrie 160;Teresa 160;Violet 160.
GIST:*177
GIVENS:H.C.55;Henry F.26; Robt.25.
GLASGOW:W.164,167;
GLATHERY:Ella W.79;Nannie M.79,148;W.T.79,148.
GLOVER:A.B.14;Eliza 21.
GOETHERT:Emilie 86;Fred W.86
GOFF: *175,176
GOLDEN:R.S.115; *173,185, 227,229,237.
GOLDING:*226
GOLDMAN:Bernard 61,62,136; Bertha 61,62;Henry 61,62; Jac.61;Jul. 61,62,142; *206
GOLDSMITH:Hazel F.122;Leo 110; Rachel 133;Sol 116,122,126;
GOLDSTEIN:Emeline 110;Nathan 89, 101,110,148,149. *181
GOLUCKE:Mrs.101
GOODE:Mrs.L.C.131
GOODEN: *177
GOODMAN:Jonas 119, *170,206.
GOODS:A.D.16
GOODSMAN:W.77
GOODWIN:Wm.98
GORDON:Eug.K.133;Fanny V.145; Sarah S.136.
GORMAN:Addie 122;J.H.122; *217,218

GRACE: *198
GRADDY:Sallie 48
GRADY:E.D.132
GRAINGER:Nellie 119;R.A.119.
GRAHAM: *232
GRANBERRY:J.Dennis 68
GRANTHAM:Jas.63;Mary 63; Silas 63;
GRANVILLE:Jeff 162
GRAVES:Eliza G.58;Thos.45; W.L.58;*211
GRAVITT:Mrs.W.H.118,W.H. 118;*237
GRAVOIS:*200
GRAY:Alice 114;Amanda 114; Annie E.114;Ed.D.155(w); Ellen H.114;Frank 164(w); J.P.114;Louise 114;Maggie 164;Mrs.B.F.127; *174, 180,227,234,237.
GRAYSON:A.26
GREANY:Thos.82,83
GREEN:Belle B.108;Dunc.79; Ellen 103;Ham 95;Isreal 98; Jacob 167;John 103;J.R. 130;Jos.103;J.T.47;Lorenzo 103;Mary 167;Norman 167; Peggy 115;Peter 103;Polly Ann 155(w);Plumber 155; Rich.80;Sarah 157,167(w); Soloman 167;Steph.98;W.H. 118;Wm.98,103,140;Wm.Jr 108;*180,181,183,185, 187,203.
GREENFIELD:Thomp.1,20;
GREENLEE(Y):Dr.12;J.C.124.
GREENWALL:Jake 118
GREENWOOD:Gustave 27
GREGO:Camille 136;Mrs.F.155; F.155;M.155;Mary 155; Vincent 155(w).
GRENSBY:J.C.146
GREW:Peter 140
GREER:*212,213.
GRIFFIN:Clarissa 145(w);Corinne U.158(w);Don C.94,124; Fannie 49(w);Francis 55,94; G.G.94,133;Hellen 94;Isabella 55;J.D.118;J.E.118;Jno.94, 124;Jno.Dry.119;Jno.L.49, 75,119,124,130;Kate 163; Laura 94; Mary 94,155,163; Nellie 155;Sarah 94,124,158; Romy 148;Wm.94,133,155, 156,158,163(w); *171,181, 182,185,228.
GRIFFING:*211
GRIFFITH:Rich.2;Sarah 2;
GRIGSBY:*176,184
GRIMES: *214

*Naturalization,Guardianship,Cemetery   Records - Surname Indexed

GROSS:*175
GUAR:*185
GUCHINGSFELDER:J.T.73;
GUGGENHEIM:M.S.123
GUICE:*179
GUIGNARD:Anna M.60;Benj. 60;Caroline F.60;Emma 60; Jas.S.10,60,104;Jas.Jr. 60;John G.60;Laura 60; Sarah S.60;Susan 60; Wm.60.
GUTELIUS:*224

HABITCH:Jno.70,86,90; Karoline 90;Theo.91.
HAFTER:*201,203,204.
HAIKE:*213
HAILE:Col.101,121;Emily 101;Jno.101;Wm.101.
HAIRE::Len 131;*170.
HALE:*172
HALEWAY:Jane 149.
HALEY:Wm.M.68.
HALL:Fannie 137;Jas.P.131; Jesse 139;Mrs.Jas.131; Laura 141;Henry 141;Ree B.82;W.P.25;*210.
HALLETT:Geo.H.130,136; Harry 136;Laura 136.*180, 181.
HALSEY:Mrs.Ann 6,27,28,82.
HAMER(HAMNER)(HAMMERS): Anna 110;Aaron 110;Eliz.110; J.C.91;J.L.110;Jno.W.104; Loula E.110;Martha G.91;T.R. 110;Willie 110;*193.
HAMIL:*187:
HAMILTON:Jones S.32,33; Susan 168;*219.
HAMLETT:*196
HAMMERS:*193
HAMMETT:J.R.62,63; *202, 213.
HAMMOND(S):Marg.160; *199,228.
HAMPTON:C.F.98;Eloise U. 158; Kate 98;Sampson 74; Viney 74;Wade 31,71,97, 98,129.*181,187.
HANCOCK:Electa F.70;
HANDY:*207
HANNA:84;Jno.H.18;H.18; Mary 18;S.H.B.150;
HANNAH:*227.
HANWAY:A.126;Annie 142; Bart 82,83;Bertha M. 83; Eliz.J.83;Ellen 83;Jno.82, 83,89,90,92,123,140,

142(w); Julia 142;J.V. 126; Mary 83,142;Tim 126,142;
HARBISON:Geo.L.125,137;Hasburg B.96;J.B.133;Jos.125; R.Taylor,Jr.137; *183.
HARDAWAY:Ben 21;
HARDEMAN:Wm.19,24;
HARDY(IE):Amanda 162;Ed B. 132;Jas.W.133; *218,232
HARICHT:*205
HARMON:Charity 163;Mrs. Archer 129,152;*187, 191,192.
HARPER:Alfred 164;Eddie 164; Florence 156;Jerry 164;Lem. 164;Harrison 164;Lucy 164; Mary L.156;Rosa 164;Willis 164(w);
HARRELSON:*221
HARRIS:Allen 82;Bettie C.15;C.E. 137; Rev.David 153;Fanny S.107; Henderson 167; Henry 153(w); J.E.58;J.F.84,153;J.L.29;J.V.67; Lizzie 145;Louis D.140;Mary 15; Martha 35;Matilda 153;R.P.13, 14,15;Sallie B.15;Sam 102,124; *181,182,183,184,200,234.
HARRISELL:Sam.M.168;
HARRISON:Julia 153;Sid.W.136; Wm.H.79,80; *193,225.
HARRINGTON:D.103;
HARROW:Jno.W.54,55;
HARSHE:Annie H.126;Mrs.J.P.125; 126,145(w);M.Neil 126,145; Robt.B.126;
HART:J.H.43;Jos.43,44;W.C.43; *197.
HARTMAN:Bella 118,139;Johanna 86;Lee 118,139;Marcellus 156; M.M.159;Marsy 139;Nancy 139; Nettie 139;Sam 166;*181.
HARTWICK:Flo.159.
HARVEY:Adaline 157;Addie 157; Danl.159(w);D.J.160;Jennie 123; Katie 159;Rose 159;W.R.82,123, 157(w); *199.
HARWELL:*198
HASIE:*190
HAUFF:J.E.98; *194,195
HAVEMEYER:Alice A.144;Amelia 144;Chas.144;Edythe 144; Harriet F.144;Henry 144;Jas. 144;Jno.144;Julia 144;Loomis 144;Sarah A.144;Wm.144(w);
HAWKINS:Lewis 25;Nich.25;Rev. 164;Uncle H.131;*174,192, 236.
HAYDEN:*196

HAYCRAFT:W.A.10,41,54,64, 65,78,104;
HAYS:Mary 80;*172, 182, 215,234.
HAZARD:Eliz.12;
HAZLIP:*197
HEAD:Dan 126,161;*175,196
HEALION:Jos.E.96;Nora O'C.96;
HEALY:*199
HEARD:Mrs.A.A.157,158;Aley 158'Chas.A.100,125;Col.99; Ethel 158;Frank A.157;Geo.P. 157,158;J.C.53,100,103, 104;Jennie S.100;Mabel 158; Nathan A.100;
HEART:Rich.149;
HEATH:Jno.W.40; *205
HEARY:*172
HEBB:Bertha 155;Mr.134;
HEBRON:Jno.L.133;Mrs.J.B.123; Nettie P.118;*174,215
HEDGES:93
HEE:*201
HEFFNER:*210
HEIDINGSFELLOW:J.61
HEIDT:*176
HELMS:C.T.157;J.H.149;W.S. 157;*213,214,215.
HEMPSEY:*173
HENDEL:Ada 113;M.B.113; *172,206.
HENDERSON:Malinda 156;Shelton J.53;W.H.53;W.L.58;W.S.53' *170,175,182,223.
HENDRICKS:Jno.53,58;
HENLEY:Jno.141
HENRY:*195
HENRYDEN:Whit.25
HENSON:A.G.134;
HERITAGE:*234
HERNDON:*179
HERRINGTON:*190
HERRON:Eva 113;R.L.113;WM. 25;
HERTER:Sarah 102;
HESTER:Annie 162;
HEVEY:*172
HEXTER:Amelia 64;Belle 133; Mrs.Lee 124;
HIAH:*182
HICKMAN:Clara 32;David 32; Wm.32;
HICKS:Edith 156;*176,218
HICKSON:W.H.110;
HIDER:A.S.152,167;W.P.167;
HIDES:*172
HIGGINS:Mrs.S.E.130; *171
HIGGS:Louise T.150;*183.

HIGHTOWER:*229
HILL:Amanda 108;Chas.63;
  Mollie 44,67;Ruth 49;
  Wesley 153;Theod.W.44;
  Thos.H.13,14,15,22,41,
  44,67;Thos.H.Jr.44;
  *173,176,179,201,
  214,220,223,224,
  226,232,237.
HILLIARD:*171
HILZIM:Percy T.134
HINDS:(FAMILY)44;Howell
  43,44;Jno.43, 44;Mary A.
  43,44;S.A.133;Thos.43,44,
  72;*174,176,178,205.
HINES:Dolly 138,*170.
HINTON:*181
HIRSCH:Bertha 115,116;
  Hannah 115; Harry 115,116;
  Henrietta 115,116;Jacob 64,
  115,116;Julia 115,116,134;
  Mrs.Jos.131;Leopold 115,
  116,141;Malinda 110;Rosa115,
  116;Saida 115,116;*206
HOAG:69
HOBART:*196
HOBBS:*175
HOBSON:*183
HOFFMAN:Chas.12,13,15;Wm.
  G.15;
HOGDKINS:*170
HOGE:Chas.E.136;Evelyn 136
HOGUE:Belle 77,78;B.Jos.77,
  78;Braswell 77,78; *229
HOGUTT:*222
HOLCOMB:*192
HOLDER:J.K.151
HOLLAND:Adline 153;Eugene
  153;Geo.126;Henry 153(w);
  Linnie 153;*174,218,
  227,234,239.
HOLLEY:*230
HOLLINGSWORTH:H.J.65;
  *177, 229,236.
HOLLINS:Abe 167;Adeline167;
  Gaston 167;Horace167(w);
  Jake 167;Sarah 167.
HOLLIS:David 38;
HOLL(O)MAN: *201,236
HOLLOWELL:*217.
HOLMES:Emma 121;Hinds 123;
  Houston 150(w);Jno.164;(w);
  Lottie 164;Ophelia 164;Thos.
  C.146,150;Zadia 164;*183,
  184,223.
HOLT:A.C.11,12,33;Jane F.111;
  *201

HOOD:Clara H.31,32;Lizzie 31;
  Mary a.31;Mary s.122;M.L.
  146;Thos.H.31,32,122,140;
  W.N.28,31,32; *173,174,
  175,179.
HOOE:*208
HOOKS:*198
HOOTEN:J.C.153;W.W.153;
HOOVER:H.L.45;J.B.16;
HOPKINS:*184,215
HOPPER:J.D.148; *171
HORD:Mary J.29,53;Robt.H.
  29,53; *202
HORN(E):J.Robt.143;Mary R.
  143(w); *232
HORNBICK:G.B.55;
HORTON:*210,213,233.
HOSKINS:*213
HOSSINGER:*176
HOUSE:Baby 151;Mattie 151;
  Mrs. M.E.151;T.P.151(w);
  *226.
HOUSTON:Anna 95;Benton 95;
  Eliz.95;Jonas 95;*189
HOWARD:R.H.5; *171,183.
HOWE:Annie 168;Benj.168;
  Jerry 168;Kath.168;Martha
  168;W.H.168(w); *185
HOWELL:Caesar 60;J.M.60;
HOYT:M.B.114;
HUDDLESTON:*218
HEUSTON:Capt.129
HUFFMAN: *175
HUGGINS:Jennie 141;Matt E.
  141(W);
HUGH(E)S:Amelia 154;Dan,Sr.
  154(w);Dan,Jr.154;Emma
  154;Jennie 154;Junius 25;
  J.J.3;Lelia B.145;Lizzie 154;
  Marg.E.145;M.W.82; Sally
  121;Shep 154;*170,172,
  173,177,179,184,211.
HULL:Mary 139;W.D.55; *232
HUMBER:Chas.H.157;
HUMPHREY:Rufus156;Sarah156
HUNSICKERL:Danl.48
HUNT:Alice C.59;Anna F.150;
  Alex T.150;D.Flournoy 70,
  129;Ed.T.150;Eliz.E.59;Geo.
  B.160;Henry M.150;Jno.150;
  Maria C.126;Mary F.150(w);
  Mary T.150;Prue B.59,126;
  Robt.P. i;Sallie R.150;Thos.H.
  10,11;Virginia 131;W.E.44,50,
  58,59,61,84,89,115,126,129,
  131;Wm. iii,59; *176.

HUNTER:Anderson 56;Anna
  146;Bettie 154;Lewis 56;
  Walter 56;*179,182,238
HUNTINGTON:C.P.74
HURST:*176
HUTCHENS:J.H.148
HUTCHINSON:Eleanor R.149;
  *217,232,235.
HYDE:Emma K.145;

IGO:Bridgett 140;*175
IKERD:Willie Lee 129;
IMMERGLUCK: *206
INGELS:Bert Lee 162;Clarence
  162;Effie 162;Essie 162;
  Ray 162;
INGRAM:Eva K.134;Jno.139;
  *210,213,214.
INMAN:B.W.168
IOOR:Nancy 101
IREYS:Bettie120,121;Evel.153
  Henry 120,131,136,153(w)
  Mary B.135;*173
IRELAND:*213
IRWIN:Annie 41;Betty 18;
ISENBERG:Abe 119;I. 93,109,
  121,124;Mattie 121;Will
  135;*172.
IVY:*210

JACK:E.W.31
JACKSON:Andrew29,54,158,
  164;Ann 79;D.D.6,39,82;Geo.
  75,76;Geo.W.75;Hattie 82;
  Henry 79,82;Jas.B.29,54;
  Jno.C.128;Josie D.137;Lelia
  130,157;Lizzie 29;Lewis 79;
  Mary J.29;Minor 25;N.T.128;
  Stephen 138;Wm.L.56; *170,
  175,177,178,179,183,
  184,185,202,239.
JACOBS:S.135 *184,206,215
JAMES:Benj.106;B.Frank.85,
  90,91;Ed.C.124;Is.I.148(w);
  Mary 94;Nancy 79,106;Nann.
  106; Paul 124;P.R.153;Thos.
  V.149;*188.
JAMISON: *179,234.
JASEY:Mrs.J.E.154
JAYNE:J.M.140,148,152;L.L.
  148.
JEFFERSON:Maria 25;Randel
  25;Simon 25;
JEFFERDS:V.S.51;
JEFFREYS:Sallie 135;*193
JEFFSON: *170

*Naturalization,Guardianship,Cemetery   Records - Surname Indexed.

JENKINS:Caroline 104;Emma G. 104;Estella 104;Jas.104,148; Julia C.C.148;Mary 104;Paul G.60,104;Susan 60,104;
JENKS:Almet 144
JENNINGS: *188,199
JESELNIK:* 169
JETER:Dora 134;Ella 133; Louise 130;Thos.130,134;
JEWELL:Albert 156;Alex M.139; Chauncey A.139,156;Jno.D. 139,141;Jos.141,156;Louisa 156;Mary A.156;Mary J.139; Rebecca C.139;Robt.H.139; Wm.A.139,156(w);
JEWITT: *184
JOBES:C.S.93
JOHL:C.S.93
JOHNS:Jos.C.29;Thos.G.27; Thos.H.29,59;W.E.59
JOHNSON:Alice H.129;Ann 119; Bessie 134;Ben 134;Betsy M. 18;Belle G.54,55;Caroline 95; Chas.119,146,156;Claud M.48, 85,110,112,113,120,129,131, 138;Clinton 146;Edw.P.18,25, 30,54;Edw.P.,Jr.18,54,55;Ellen 35,36;Eliz.J.78,88;Frank 73; Fred M.78;Geo.G.48,106,119, 129,131;Harrow 54,55;Henry J.48,93,119,131;Isabella 116; Jos.78;J.R.114;J.Y.77,88;Junius 18;Laura G.54,55;Lizzie 136;L.R. 55;M.A.164,165;Dr.McWillie 125; Madison W.78,88;Marg.156(w); Marg.A.65;Mary 167;Martha 146 (w);Matt F.24,48;Nancy 73;Nannie 18;Narcissen 119;Nat 145;Nich.B.66, 72,77,78,88;Norvelle 73;R.B.125; Reuben 25;Robt.A.48,119,131;Sallie 48;Sarah F.155;Sol.156;T.D.163; Thos.B.78;WASH.73;Dr.W.C.134;Wm. 156;WM.H.35,36,48,119,120;W.M. 164;W.N.33; *171,171,172,173, 175,178,180,192,205,209, 210,211,213,214,216,223, 224.
JOHNSTON: *192,232
JONES:Chas.98;Emma 120;H.P.135; J.D.152(w);Jno.W.151;J.Rabun 135; Jos.C.27;Madison 79;Martha L.51; Rev.33;Robt.R.46,47;Wm.R.,Jr.147; Willie M.151;*170,175,176,177, 181,183,184,185,195,196, 210,212,217,219,234,237;
JOOR:Jno.S.116,156;
JO(U)RDAN:C.E.134,169;E.M.145;Jno. 97;Lydia 43;Nap.43; *172,182, 190,193,199,233.

JOYCE:Mrs. E.83,Jennie H.123;
JOYES:Clarence 106
JOYNER:J.W.160
JURY:Louis C. 1,29;

KANATZER:Amelia 112,113;Ada 112,113;Cora 112,113,121; Ella J.133; Eva 112,113;Jno. 112,113;Jos.112,113,133; Nellie 112,113;
KAPLAN:Adolph 130;D.130; *180.
KAPPS:Leanne 146;
KARELY :*171
KAZAN:*217
KEARNEY:*223
KEEN:Thorn 116;
KEENAN:Edw.Jr.137;
KEESU(I)CKER:A.P.74; *173
KEIGHER:Kath.155;
KEITH: *228,229,233.
KELLUM:Mary 165;
KELLY:A.D.3,21;L.F.156; Thos.104;Wm.F.21;
KENDALL:J.E.152;Maud E.152; *192.
KENNEDY:Alice 140,146;Byrl 146;Edw.122, 140;Gert.76, 77;Jim 77;Jno.J.127,134, 140,146(w);Kate 8;Liz.77; Lucy 77;Maggie 122,140(w); Marg.140;Saml.H.26;Thos.J. 8,76,77;Tom 77;Wm.140; *172,175.
KENT: *223
KEONE:Eliza 42
KERN:Pricilla 156
KERR:Albert 139;Alice 139; Emma 139;Saml.L.139;Sarah J.139;
KERSHAW:Geo.T.16,17;Jno.P.C. 16,17;Mary J.16,17;Rich C. 16,17;Thos.16,17;
KERSTEIN:Is.110;
KEY(S):JNO.168; *181
KEZER:Alonzo 49;
KHOURY:* 169
KIER:Em.73;
KIKER:* 190
KILLIAN:Mr.122; * 198
KIMBALL:Alberta 137;E.B. 25;W.C.25;
KIMBROUGH:K.71
KINCEAD:Mrs.Peyton 119;
KING:Annie 18;Fred D.139; Jane 150;Jas.A.6;Jno.R.18; Rufus v; *190.
KINNISON:Abner F.168;Helen I.168;*177.

KINSELLA:Jno.96,104; Johanna 96,104
KINTZLER:Amelia 106; Isaac 106;
KIRBY:Sallie 130
KIRK:Ga.142,149;
KIRKLAND:G.H.136; *201, 205.
KIRKSEY:* 170
KITCHENS:* 173
KITTLE: *182,210,211.
KLEIN:Geo.M.35
KLEINSCHMIDT: *199
KLINGER:*206
KLINGMAN:E.E.136; *209
KLYCE:*194
KNIGHT:Em.68; *195,204
KNOX:Geo.W.53;Mattie 122;
KORSTENBROCK:Rev.132, 140,146,152.
KOURY:*218
KRETSCHMAR:Mrs.Kate 117;
KRIGER:H.F.112,113;
KYART:*184

LABENBURG:Nettie 132;
LACEY:Cora 112,113,121; Mary 113;Robt.H.113,121 Rowland B.116;*172,185
LACHS: *189
LACKEY:* 194
LADSDEN:Abr.98;
LAFOE:Edw.157;Jas.157; Ray 157;Sarah 157;T.E. 157;Wm.157; *178
LAKE:* 181
LAMB:Ella 148;Ga.134;Geo. 134;G.H.116,148(w);
LAMHEIR:Edg.B.144;
LAMPMAN:Martha 144;
LAMPTON:Cornella 165; Eddie D.165;Ethel 165; Edw.W.165(w);Pearl 165; LANCASTER:Mrs.G.B.132; *200,210
LANDAU:J.74,78;Marcus 71, 74,138;
LANDON:Clide 162;Ellis 162; Ernest 162;Eugene 162; Jessie 162;L.E. 162;Myrtle 162;Theo.162;
LANDRUM: *231
LANE:Jno.K.94;Rachel 116
LANFORD:Geo.96
LANGER:A.B.126
LANGLEY:Jac.166
LANIER:*214
LASHLEY:Arnold 1;R.M.1;
LATHAM:Harvey 24;Lucy 24

LAUGHLIN:Fla.34;
LAWLER:Jas.L.135;
LAWRENCE:Jas.M.132;Mrs. J.M.121;
LAWS:*193,211;
LAWSON:Annie 153;Eliz.A. 33;Florence 137;Gab.81; Jas.82;J.B.M.33;Jane 82; Lucy 33;Oscar 33;Saml.B. 90;Mrs.S.B.118;'empe 81; Willie 33;*184
LAZERS:*172
LEACH:*220
LEANTHAL:*172
LEARNED:J.L.157;
LEAVENWORTH:J.H.134,146; *171.
LEE:Annie H.130,145;B.M. 17;Cath.68;Clarence P.68, 69,71,72,129;Emma K.68, 71,72;Harry P.68,72,104, 129;Henrietta 95;Jno.M 68,72,89,125,129,130,145; Mrs.Jno.126;Johanna 125; Mary L.68,69,71,72;Nath.68; Sarah 104;Thos.B.1;Wm.H.22, 68,71,72,129;Wm.M.18; *180,182,197,204,211, 212,219;
LEEDOM:*193
LELAND:Frank 98;
LEMLE:D.115,121;*172;
LEMLER:Max 121;Norv.121; *171
LENGSFIELD:B.F.142;Mrs.Eliz. 118;J.71,72;Julius I. 61,62, 66,71,72,74;*171,205.
LENHART:*213
LEONARD:Caroine 34;Frances 140;J.J.132;*179
LESSER:Julius 137;
LEVINGSTON:*181
LEVY:Geo.E.165;Jos.B.165; Julia 105;Maurice 166; *171,183
LEWIS:B.T.165;C.W.46,50, 75;Effie 126;Eug.R.134; Geo.163(w);Geo.B.93;J.M. 126,134;Josh 168;Lawr.H. 165;Ramel 98;Rev.134; Vivian 126;Watt v;*171.
LEYSER:Dave L.141;Dr.D.S. 123;Helen 141;
LIGHT:*189
LIKENS:*187
LILES:Mary 103,104,123;
LINDERMAN:Mary 143;
LIPSCOMB:*173
LISBONY:Arthur 115,116;Fanny 115,116;W.A.115;*173,229

LITTLE:Alf.2;Benj.2; Emily 2;Jno.2;Mont.2; Saml.2;Thos.T.31;Wm. 2,155;*177.
LITTLETON:*232
LIVINGSTON:Walter 154; *184
LLOYD:Caroline R.163; F.A.136.
LOFTON:*174
LOGAN:Danl.P.1,20; H.L.73,74;
LOGGINS:*189
LONE:S.R.16;
LONG:J.A.155;FANNIE *178
LONSDALE:Fitz.18,23;Henry 23,38;Nannie 18;
LONSMAN:*181
LORD:Fred A.150;Stacey 129,150(w);Willie 150; W.L.150;
LOVE:D.A.60,92,93,130; D.Goodloe 154;Jos.T.119 Mary G.154;W.D.130,148; 154;WM.C.154;WM.C.Jr. 154;*223.
LOWE:*227
LOWENBURG:Mrs.128
LOWREY:Mattie B.134; Robt.H.38,134;
LUCAS:Bohlen 50,51
LUCKETT:Beatrice 166; Clinton 166;Lou 166;Sallie 166;*183.
LUMBLEY:*188
LUNG:Lotta 156
LUSBY:J.C.148(w);*175
LUNSFORD:R.S.159;*235
LUTHICOM:Louisa B.102
LYON:G.W.128

MACHER:Jno.37,38;
MACK:Prince 98;*184
MACLOY:Laura A.144;
MAFREDS:*169
MAGIC:Liueser 165;
MAGEE:*211
MAGNUM:*205
MAGRUDER:Jesse K.151(w); L.W.151;Mrs.120;*232
MAHAN:24
MAHONEY:C.A.166;
MAJOR:Simon 153;
MALLET:*183,238.
MALONE:P.H.77;
MANGHAM:*206
MANGIALARDI:*188
MANIFOLD:Jno.78,86,88; Marg.88,126,145(w);

MANIFOLD:(cont.)Sarah 88;
MANLY:Wm.J.78;
MANN:Alb.W.136;Carrie 137;P.L. 145;*180,190,193,226.
MARBLE:*211
MARGHETTI:*190
MARKS:*189,206
MARQUESA: E. 23,24;
MARS:*174
MARSH:*219
MARSHALL:Belle 85;Bertha 164, 166;Chaney 154;E.G.110,118, 139,164(W);Frances 85;Fanny B.156;Lily 85;Mary Belle148; Sarah 85;Wm.85;*180,201
MARTIN:Clarinda G.39;Dwight 39, 83;Frances 167;Geo.39;Henry 39;Howard 39;J.L.8;Jno.39; Mary 39;Robt.74;Thos.H.,Jr.24 *171,201,207;
MASON:*211
MASSEY:O.L.146;*183,184, 189.
MATHIS:*196,213;
MATTHEWS:Ann 16,17;Eddie 165; Jno.165;Martha A.168;Marrie 165;Mrs.R.C.135;Walter 165; W.M.165(w);*221,225.
MAXWELL:Harriet M.146;Jas.A. 146;*176.
MAY:Arthur W.159;
MAYFIELD:W.G.165;
McALLISTER:*207
McALPIN:*231.
McATEE:*171
McBRIDE:*171
McCALEB:Lillie 155;Mary 155; *187,202.
McCammon:*231
McCANE:Jno.25;
McCARTY:*220
McCAULEY:Cath.151
McCAUSLAND:Mary 97
McCAY:143;T.T.157;W.T.157;
McCLAIN:Danl.137;Mrs.Walter 121
McCLEARY:*233
McCLELLAND:Dr.V.S.166;
McCLENNAN:*221
McCLINTOCK:*219
McCONNELL:Susan G.153;
McCOOL:*190,192.
McCOURTNEY:*179
McCOY:Phoebe 163;Will 134;W.T. 146,160;*180
McCUTCHEON:Green 76;J.E.148;Jno. M.107;Mrs.P.M.121;Proctor 137; Wm.25;
McDANIEL(S):Fannie 139;*184
McDILL:Robt.160
McDONALD:Lula P.124;*171,233

*Naturalization,Guardianship,Cemetery   Records-Surname Indexed

McDOWELL:E.P.80;Ham.80; S.R.113,128;
McFARLAND:Alberta 167; Hagger 167;Jas.A.167; Mary 167;N.J.167(w); Susan 167;
McGEE:B.O.127;Mrs.B.O. 127;*185,211,215, 216,227.
McGHEE:*172
McGINNIS:*193
McGINTY:Oscar 3;Robt.F. 3;Z.C.3;
McGOWEN:*211
McGRATH:Alice 120;Cald. 36,108,109,120;
McGRAW:*191,217
McGREW:*187
McGREGOR:Robt.8;
McHATTON:Betty 25;Chas.
McINTYRE:*178
McKAMY:*183
McKEEPY:Mrs.80;
McKEO(W)NE:Pat 65;*206, 212
McKIE:Minnie 128;
McKINNEY:Mrs.C.O.147; Madie 136;*182,230, 231;
McKENZIE:*210
McKEY:*215
McLAUGHLIN:Lula W.139;
McLAUREN:Lucinda 151;
McLEAN:Dan 129;Henry 87;John 87;Phoenix 87; Robt.87;Saml.87;Thos. 87;Wm.F.144;
McLEMORE:Mrs.T.N.118; Thos.118;*191.
McLEON:D.L.152;
McLEROY:*214
McMAHON:R.B.163;*200
McNAMARA:Jno.125;
McNEELY:S.78;
McNILLY:Jno.I. 52
McNEILY:Capt.J.S.120,131; *197
McRAE:Robt.S.131;
McRAVEN:*213.
MEADOW:*235
MEDDER:*172
MEEKER:J.B.16
MEGGETT:Bessie 136;*194
MEISNER:Chas.F.70;Chas.F Jr. 70;Fred L.70;Henry W.70; Jno.N.70;Louisa 70;Mary H. 70;Wm.B.70,143;
MELCHOR:*212
MELLEN:Wm.P.18;
MENDELL:*169

MENDROP:*227
MERCHANT:C.I.34;Henry R.56,64;U. 56,64;
MERRILL:Emma 137;Norv. 57,58;Sarah E.57;Willie S. 57;
MERRIWEATHER:W.M.24;
MESSINGER:Danl.163;Lydia 163;Mary 163;Syb.114;
METCALFE:Clive 151,168; Fred.133,151;Harley 135, 160;Jno.A.132;Jno.M.151; *202,208.
MEYER(S): *169,171,206.
MHOON:J.J.20
MIBLETSCH:*169
MILAM:B.L.120,133; *210, 216.
MILES:Anna 163;Fleming 163; *181
Miller:Allen 154(w);Dr.A.142; Betty 30;Carrie 97;Columsa 154;Electra 97;Harvey 25,30, 124,134;Horace H.26;Dr.J.H. 150,152;Jno.A.10,19,20,119; Jacob 154;Maggie 25,30;Malv. 25,30;Pemb.154;S.G.135;S.H. 97;Shed.98;Sallie 25,30;Sid.S. 134;W.W.140;*180,181,183, 184,185,191;
MILLSAPS:R.W.161;
MIMS:Rev.136
MINISTER:Robt.8;
MINYARD:*199,234.
MITCHELL:Alex.T.35;Ellen 61; Geo.W.61;Jos.D.34,35;Lucy 35;Lydia 52,53;Mary E.34,35; *180,184,237.
MOMMAN: *169
MONASH:E.93
MONROE:Jno.165; *170.
MONTAGUE:Ann D.16,17;
MONTGOMERY:Annie 132,160; Ben T.35;D.C.67,77,107,117, 125;Eliza A.47;Eugene 125; Frances 107;F.P.124,142(w); Heddens 126,135;Isaiah 35; J.M.67,77,117,125;Mrs.J.M. Mary a.c.151;Dr.S.A.137; Sallie 47,142;W.E.107,127, 151(w);Wm.47;Wm.T.35;W.P. 127;*173,174,204,207, 220.
MOON:Jos.84
MOORE:Anita 155;Annie 108; Bacon 155,156;Bettie 155; Benj.F.101;Bowman 156; Chas.A.108;Danl.155,156; Eliz.B.108;Harry 156;Mrs.H.E. 112;Jas.H.155(w);Jas.C.107,

MOORE:(cont)108;Dr.J.H.155;Jno. 107,108,143,150,156;Jos.164 Lawson 155;L.C.128;Mack156; Mary 107,108,155;McB.156; Minnie B.155;Peter 116;Pricilla 151(w);Thos.155;Va.155;Wm.D. 155;*177,182,183,185, 189,210,217,219,232,239
MOORMAN:Geo.31
MORGAN:Alb.C.67,68;C.E.41,74, 83;Emma 52,65,86,87;Lilly 52; Maria L.41,67,68;Mary M.L.67, 68,146(w);Oliver 8,9,10,52,65, 87;Robt.P.68;Thos.S.67,68; *199,224,229.
MORRIS:Anthony 4,5;Chas.H.141; Dave 96;Edwin E.16;E.V.140; Henry H.58;Helen L.140;Jacob 102;Julia 45,102;L.D.58;M.102; W.C.140;Salina 96;Wm.W.47, 140; *195.
MORRISON:C.W.159;
MORRISSEY:Thos.160;
MORSE:Esther 155;
MORSON:J.A.44;Kate B.134; *218,222,227.
MORTIMER:Paul E.26;*181
MOSBY:Carrie 117;Eliza G.21,117 G.S.21,117;Paulina 121;*207
MOSLEY:*173,189,192,211.
MOSS:F.J.41,43,63;Mahala 64;
MOTEN:*171
MOTT:D.W.27;
MOUNT:Annie E.132;Mrs.Edw.130; Thos.132;
MOYSE:Alp.133;Ferd.L.157;Leon 132;*177.
MUFFOLETTA:*169
MUNDELL:Cath. v
MUNDY:Helena 168;Littleton 168 (w);Lucinda 168;
MURDOCK:Robt.84;
MURFF:Martha 116;*222
MULLIN: *172,206
MURPHREE: *237
MURPHY:Emedicus 21;J.W.119; Henry 152(w); *171,184, 224.
MURRAY:Jas.92;
MUSGROVE:Carrie 128;Edgar 134
MYERS:Lily 136;Malinda 136; Will 134;*201,238.

NAIL:*228
NAMED:Julia T.164
NANCE:A.B.143,146;
NASH:Maggie 143;Maria L.143, 144;Mary 143;Rev.O.L.143, 144;Ossie 143;
NASON:J.R.126;Myrtle 126.

*Naturalization,Guardianship,Cemetery   Records - Surname Indexed.

NAST:Bona 146;
NATHAN:*181
NEAL:W.H.124,*170,171, 196.
NEELY:Effie 133;
NEERUM:*170
NEGUS: Carrie B.157;Jas.E. 91,130,142,146,150(w), 157,161; Lou.M.150,151, 157; Susan 150,157;Will E. 146,157;Wade 150,157;
NEIBERT:Wmn.L.161;
NEIDE:REV.135;
NEILSON:Col.Chas.P.120,138; Nannie 120,138;
NELMS:K.H.145;
NELSON:Alice 163;Betty 143; Emmet Y.163;Jesse 143; Jno.H.30,48,58,64,74,86; Robt.163;*195,203.
NEPOTO:*169
NESMITH:*197
NETTLES:*216
NEWHORN:Mrs.J.L.149
NEWMAN:Adolph 137;Burnett 61 J. 92,123;J.A.92,98;Kesiah 77 Louis 61;Martin 77;Mary 92, 123;N.S.145;*171,217.
NEWSOM:Addie 140;Carrie 140. *173,225
NICHOLS:Mrs.S.A.136;*199, 223,232.
NICHOLSON:Mrs.M.83;Roselle 152;*193.
NIXON:Jane C.110,111;Jas. 68;Jno.111;*225,228.
NOEE:G.W.168(w);
NOLAND:Hal T.117;*221.
NORRIS:*188,189.
NORTON:E.E.36;
NOSS:G.W.168(w).
NUGENT:Eleanor 4;Wm.L.4,9, 10,16,18,33,47,51;
NURSE:Harriet 143;Saml.125, 143(w);*169.
NUTT:Jno.K.168;Mary W.149, 168(w).
NYE:N.G. 3;

OAKMAN:*214,217;
O'BANNON:D.B.121,125;Mary 121,125;Sarah 131;
O'BANACK:— 33
O'CONNER:Arthur 96,104; Johanna 96,104;Kennedy 96, 104;Nora 96,104;Tim 96,104;
ODILE:Marie A.23;
OFFUTT:Benj.A.50;Geo.W. v; Maggie 165;Wm.H.50;Z.C.iiii,

OFFUTT:(cont.)50,165;
OGGLESBY:*197
O'HEA:Maj.Rich 118;
OLDHAM:Jno.P.155;
OLANDE:*174
OLIN:A.S.141;*176
OLIVER:Rebecca 137;
ORGLER:Dora 136;*173,206.
O'QUINN:*218
ORR:*178
ORRICK:Mary 30,N.C.30;
OSBORN:*227
OSBURN:Bessie 157;Geo.157;
OURSLER:Belle 133;Ludie 135; Mrs.Mary E.120;
OVERBY:J.A.110;
OVERTON:*210
OWEN(S):*174,175,178, 185,219.

PACE:Rosa J.159(w);*190
PAGE:Comfort 152(w);Rev. 91;Robt.152;*183.
PALMER:A.L.158
PARHAM:J.H.159;
PARISH:H.27;Robt.143;
PARKER:Jno.M.57;Jno.S.144; Sarah R.57;*174,175, 177,217,229.
PARNELL:Emma 121;
PARSON:Frances 62;
PARTEE:Chas.29;
PATLO:Jos.75;
PATRICK:*184,212;
PATTERSON:Eliza 154;Jos.W. 50;*183,209.
PATTISON:*177
PATTON:*181
PAXTON:A.G.11,13,14,117, 148;A.J.30,53,75,147, 148(w);Andrew 12,148; Elisha 148;Hannah M.148; Lucy P.148;Mary N.117; Robt.51;Saml.B.147,148; *174,221,226.
PAYNE:A.G.163;Belle 155; Dr.Wm.148;*192,201, 204.
PEAK:Jas.Ann 108,117;
PEARSON:Mrs.Geo.130; Pat 148;Fr.62;J.R.133.
PECK:Jno.H.144;
PEDRETTI:*187
PEEPLES:*219
PEMBERTON:J.P.P.167;
PENDER:*229
PENNER:Nat 95;
PENNY:Amelia 64,157(w); B.F.64;Caroline 64;Ellen

PENNY:(cont)47,92;Louise 64; S.A.47(w);
PENRICE:Amelia 42;J.S.42,120;
PEPPER:*205,208.
PEPPERMAN:Marx 136
PERCY:Eliz.41;Fanny E.5,120;J. 5,120;Lady 142; L.P.5,6,109, 142;Mrs.Leroy 130;Maria W.5; Nannie 142(w);Walker 142;Wm. A.5,6,64,68,72,78,109,120, 142;Mrs.Wm.A.129;
PERKINS: Allen 164,165;Carol. 93;Danl.93;Lelia 92,93;S.W. 163,164;*172,181,193, 193,199.
PERRIN:Sam V.121;*172.
PERRY:Carrie 86,99;Ellen 86,99 Frank G.86,99;Fred 87;Jas.86, 87,98,99;Mrs.Jas.87;Lou 95; Oliver H.122;Mrs.T.P.87;Thos. P.86,87,98;Sid.L.86,99.*210
PETERS:Bettie 76;Harriet 76, 131;Harry 33;Julia 76;Minnie 76,127;M.L.76,127,131; Mollie 76;*174,175,188, 208,234.
PETITT:Dr.A.119;Czarina F.119; J.J.126;Mrs.J.J.131;Jno.A. 119;*208.
PEYTON:J.J.156(w);Jno.156; Mary 156;Wm.156;*188.
PHARIS:Moses 11
PHELPS:A.J. 7;Mary B. 7;
PHILHOWER:*196
PHILLIPS:Fl.110;J.W.24;Jennie 119;Julius 136;*174,225.
PHILLIPSON:Theo.16;
PHIPPS:*196
PICARD:L. 52
PICKLE:*175
PIERCE:Annie 127;Frank 127; Jonas 7;*173,190,232, 234.
PIGG:*209
PINFIELD:*224
PITT:*213
PIPPIN:*214;
PLANTATIONS:Aldomar 26,119; Arlington 141;Ashland 76; Auburn 204;Ava 18;Belle Aire 142;Belzoni 141,166;Berkley 119;Black Bayou 12, 207; Black Place 155;Blantonia 22; Blue Ridge 148;Boldier's Place 140;Brierfield 35;Brighton 132; Brown Place 19;Buckland 57; Cain 141;Calla Place 83;Carson 206;Clary Place 142;Coldspring 29,202;Daybreak 151;(cont.)

PLANTATIONS:(cont.)Diamond Grove 47;Diamond Place 34; Emma 141;Esperanzo 145; Evergreen 100,102;Ever May 155;Fairy Field ;Fish Lake Place 28;Fisk 166;Florida 165;Forest Home 148;Forest House 151;Forkland 78;Gaddis Place 103;Glen Mary 25;Green Grove 20,21;Hill 141,155; Home Place 81,149;Honey Oak 154;Hopedale 145;Humber 157; Hurricane 34;Isola 36;Joiner Farm 83;Keystone 106,203; Kilarney 32,35,36;Kinlock 221; Lagrange 56;Lake Island 29; Lakeside 145;Lammermoor 202; Linden 76,203;Locust 220; London 29,161;Longwood 155; Loughborough 21,207;Magenta 36,103;Marathon 59,141; Maryland 27;Matilda 142; Montrose 59;Morehead 34; Morgan Place 62;Morsewood 74; Mount Holly 65;Mulberry 220; Neidmore 147;Newstead 202;Oak Grove 91; Oak Hill 43;Oak Ridge 85;Oakwood 148;Onward 78;O' possum Ridge 85,91;Otterburne 60;Percy Place 6,9;Peru 27,29; Peters Place 76;Pt.Chicot 145; Plumridge 44;Puddleduck 46;Ranton Tr.147;Recluse39;Red Leaf 11; Refuge 54,167;Richland 98;River Place 6;Riverside 21,93,94;Robb Place 149;Rose 151;Sally 32,35, 36;Scotland 104;Sligo 11,30,46, 56,226;Smithfield 6;Solona 26; Stella 25;Swisher Place 160; Utopia 50;Valliant 142;Vista 57; Walnut Ridge 98;Wayside 123; Whitehall 161;Wickliffe 142; Wildwood 98,112,207;Willowby 11;Willow Cottage 82;Woodstock 50,116128,153;
PLATT:Chas 73,74;
PLUMBER: *174
POGGEL:A.59;H.A.59.
POHL:Theo.85,105,110,115, 122,162; *175.
POINDEXTER:Ann 23,Geo.23.
POLLARD: *180
POLLOCK:W.A.111,123,141;
POOLE:E.R. 48;
PORTER:Doc 166(w);Jerlean 166; *183,195.
POPE:Wm.H.155
POTEET: *188
POTTS:Jas.H.144;
POUNDS: *183

POWELL:Fanny 106,108; Martha G.85,90,91; Mordecai 51;Mr.50;T.W. 85,90,91,106,108; *189,203.
PRATT: *210
PRESTON:Charley 25; *179, 200.
PRICE:Troy 67; *175.
PRIMROSE:Dr.136;Sarah 136;
PRINCE: *175.
PRITCHARD:Mary E.75;Wm.75
PRYOR:Geo.156;
PSICHALENOPULO: *169.
PSYCHALINOPULOS: *169
PULLEN: Jno.L.86
PULLUM: *182
PURCELL:Saml.H.117;
PUTNAM:Chas.42;Eliz.A.42; 92;H.B.42,59,74;Julia 42;

QUIGLEY:Marian 106,107; Thos.157;
QUILLEN: *234
QUINN:Mrs.122;Wm.122;

RABINOVITZ:M.148;
RABONI:Peter 79
RACHELMAN:Mamie 165;
RAGAN:W.B.116
RAI(Y)FORD:Harry 152, Willie 152;
RAILEY:Jack 35;
RAINEY: *181
RALPH: *171
RAMSEY:Rev.134;
RANDELS:Henry 25;Mrs.87
RANDOLPH:Nannie B.49;Wm. F.26,49,116;
RANSOM:Rich.P.126;Robt. L.127;Wm.A.97; *170
RASBERRY:A.J.167
RATBERRY:A.J.167;
RATHER:IVERY F.63,76; J.T.69; *212,230.
RATLIFF:C.W.166;R.L.135.
RAWLINGS:Wm.C.46,47;
RAY:Saml.L.61; *219,236 239.
READ: *209
REBUHN:Henry 132;Mrs.Henr. 129;Lillie 133;
RED: *175
REDD:Thos.113,163;
REDDEN: *230
REED(REID):Thos.3,4;Whit.H. 136; *171,,177,178, 180,185,194,195.
REESE:Henrietta 19;Jno.W. 19;Laura E.19;Maria L.19;

REESE:(cont.)W.B.19;
REILLY: *210,211
REINHOLD: *209
REUTER:Max 136
REYNOLDS:Danl.H.54,55; *191
RICE:D.M.125;S.A.137
RICHARDSON:Cabell 137;E.54;Eliz 60;Em.133;J.S.116;Miney 75; *170,173.
RICH(IE): *185,200,209,238
RICKETS: *233
RHOMER:Agnes 137
REIDEINGER:Dan 85,86;
RIFE: *177
RIGGS:Frank 135;
RIGNEY:Geo.E.167;
RING:Joe 162,168;Lena 162; *182
RIOS: *191
RIPEE: *212
RITCHIE: *183
RIVERS: *170,212,219
RIVES:Annie 101,116;Jas.101, 116;Jno.101,116;Mary39,101, 116;O.C.39; *222
ROACH:Benj.6,43,121;Marg.43 *172.
ROBARDS:Chas.L.23;
ROBB(S):Anna L.128;E.A.56,73; J.H.34,73;Mrs.J.H.130;Mattie 73; *217.
ROBERTS: *188,212
ROBERTSHAW:Jas.83,140,164; Mary 83; *222
ROBERTSON:F.N.167;Pattie 137
ROBERSON:Geo.153;S.R.152; *232
ROBINSON:Barney 72; Duke 164w; H.B.134,155(w);Henry135;Jane 72;Jona 98;J.S.23,24;J.D.164; Ike 44;Lelia 155;Sallie 79;Willie 67;Wm.W.44,67; *170,173, 174,185,191,197,202,205
ROBISON: *170
ROCHE: *172
ROCHESTER:Olivia 155
ROCHLITZ:Annie 89;Carl 89;Julius 89;Max 89;Robt.89;
ROCKHILL: *170
RODWELL:Wm.E.132
ROGERS:Andrew 39;Ellen 39;Geo. Henrietta 95;Henry 39;Mary 39;Willie 39;Wm.O.39;
ROHELIA: *201
ROHILLIARD: *181
ROMANSKY:Bertha 148;Jos.148; Julius 148;Sarah 148;Sol 128, 148(w);
ROOT:E.E.31
ROSE:A.J.152,159;E.121; *172
ROSEBROUGH:R.L.63,70.

*Naturalization,Guardianship,Cemetery   Records - Surname Indexed

ROSELLA:Jas.122;Mollie 122;
ROSENBERG:Mann 149;Mark 102,129,149(w);Mary 149; Rachel 149;Saml.149;*180
ROSENFIELD:Simon 128;
ROSENSTOCK:Minnie 127; Morris 142,149;*180,208
ROSENTHAL:*180
ROSS:J.Allen 67;*170,171, 225,
ROTCHFORD:Phillip 20;
ROTHSCHILD:Louis 135,151; Yetta 102.
ROUSE:Lawson 27;
ROUSSEAU:Alma b.130;
ROUNSVILLE:Abbe J.111;
ROWLAND:Annie G.154(w); Sallie 163;
ROY:Chas.133;Mrs.Chas. 129,132;
ROYALL:Mrs.E.B.3;T.F.3; *199
ROYSDAN:J.L.97
RUBENSTEIN:*169
RUBRNETREN:*169
RUCKS:Amanda 19,34;Arthur 19,34,35;Benj.N,19;Grant B. 19,34;Henry 19;Jas.4,19, 34,35,94;Jas.T.19,34,117; L.T.19,34;Maria L.19;Mary M.19,34;Mrs.S.B.117;Sallie 19;Saml.T.19;Sarah J.19, 34;Wm.G.146;
RURY:Wm.E.68
RUSHING:Col.51;
RUSS:*170
RUSSELL:Div.136;*182, 230,231.
RUTLAND:Mrs.Wm.C.154;
RYALS:Maria L.147;*230, 231,233,234.
RYAN:Alice 134;Jim 126; Jimmie 126;J.J.132,157; Minnie 157;Thos.131;
RYER:Julian C.159.

SAAD:B*199
SACKSE:*223
SAGE:Mollie 163
SAGER:Agnes 162;Jno.157, 162;*182
SALE:*215
SALMON:*178,206.
SALZIGER:Anna C.150(w);
SAMFIELD:Rev.132;
SAMPSON:Rhos.42;
SAMS:Benj.82;
SAMUEL:Bettie 149;Ed 149; Joel 149;Sally 149;Dr.

SAMUEL:(cont)Wm.W.149.
SANDERS:Jno.H.88;Mary 88; M.R.39;Wm.P.1;*172,212
SANDLING:*237
SATTERFIELD:Earl T.75;Emma 114;Mill M.75,114;Rebecca R. 75,114;W.E.75,77,78,109, 112,114;Vines J.75,114;
SAUNDERS: Charity 80;Rich. 80;Thos.80;W.M.80;
SAWYER:Ed.G.134;
SAYLE:D.B.159;D.M.159(w); Lucy A.159;
SCARBROUGH:Mack 160
SCHLESINGER:Abra.117;Isaac 118;Louis 92,117;
SCHMAHOLZ:Louise 81,152(w); F.X.81;
SCHMIDT:Andrew 157(w);Jno. J.157;Theod.157;
SCHNEIDER:Wm.144;
SCHOFIELD:Fanny 75;
SCHULENBERG:Rud.89;
SCHWAB:A.165;*169.
SCHWARTZ:Simon 164;
SCOTT:Adoline 165;Alice 33; Caroline 57;Ella 153;Esther 165;Fannie 10,104;Hannah 165(w);Harry 108;Hennye 136;Henrietta 165;Henry 102,165;H.63;Isadore 165; Jacob 165; Jake 149;Jas.33; Jno.A.2,10,104;Jno.S.56;Louis 165;Mahala 43;Parm.E.33;Robt. 19,57;Sarah E.10;Solomon 165; Wm.33;*177,182,200,227.
SCUDDER:*188
SCULL:*232,234.
SCURLOCK:W.T.118
SEABROOK:*210
SEALS:*226
SEARCY:*177
SEARLS:T.M.132
SEARS:Claude 143;Fanny A.143; Frances 143;Rev.P.G.143;*205
SEEGER:Julius 136;
SELLERS:Geo.H.168;Lela 134; Rowena C.168;
SELLIGER:*180
SEMMES:Andw.G.30;Jno.R.30,31; Jno.T.31;Lucy 30;Mary 30;
SENN:Thos.J.135;
SENTER:Henry 1;
SESSIONS:Anna M.153;Horace W. 127;Jno.G.153;Maria P.153(w); Rich.153;*177
SHACKLEFORD:C.C.23;J.A.160(w); Jno.W.160,161;*183
SHALL:J.A.138,155;*181.

SHANDANNAIS:Oliver 136;
SHANKEL:*185,223
SHANNAHAN:Ann 43,65,90; Danl.H.43;D.M.45,46,65,90; Fanny E.43,65,90,132;Mary 65;T.B.D.43,65;Tim.43,46, 65,90,120;
SHAPLEY:*220
SHARP(E):J.H.67;Lelia 156; Sallie H.67;
SHAW:Mrs.Chas.119;Truman B. 130;*171,174;
SHEFFIELD:*224
SHEILDS:Fay 135;Sarah 147; Walter 152;*180,195,197 199,220.
SHELBY:Annie 56;Aug.N.56; Bayless P.56,146,147(w); Betty 35,36,56,66;Eliz.123; Kate B.56,120,133;Mary 51; O.L.123;Thos.10,35,36,56,66 *207.
SHELDON:*203
SHELTON:Almedia 154;Amelia 135;Hattie 157;Henry T.16; Inez H.154;W.P.154;*212
SHIPP:Rich.D.26;Wm.26;*195
SHIPMAN:W.W.135;
SHIRLEY:Benj.73
SHIVER:M.O.163
SHORES:Ida 133;
SHOREY:Laura 92;S.O.91,92;
SHORTREED:*214
SHORTRIDGE:Mrs.124;
SHRADER:J.A.77;
SHUTE:Anna E.100,101;Jas.D. 1011;J.O.100;
SHUTT:*192,202
SIENPPENDOEFER:Jennie 102; J.G.102;
SILLERS:Caroline 100;Jas.100 101;Wm.100,101;
SILVERBERG:*206
SIMMONS:Coleman 166;E.P. 153,158,164;*195,197.
SIMMS:*225
SIMPSON:Ceil 161;Denton 162; Ernest 161;Eugene 161,162; Estelle 161;Kern 161;Lawr. 161;M.M.162;Norman 162; Orrin 161;Otho 161;Ruth162; Roxa 161;Stella 161;Ward 161;Wm.162;
SIMS:Chas.11;C.W.74,75;Eliz. A.11;Family 32;F.G.46;G.G. 11,30,56;Jno.H.11;Mary N.F 107;Nancy 11;R.G.11,30,46 Phil 11; Robt.B.11;R.L.11; W.E.11,12;W.R.11,12,32;

*Naturalization, Guardianship,CemeteryRecords - Surname Indexed

SIMS:(cont.)W.H.138; *176, 181,183,235,236.
SINGLETON:Harriet 115; July 115;*189.
SINON:Flor.C.133;
SKALLER:J.69;
SKIDMORE:Lem 144;
SKINNER:Angeline 158;Ancy 158;Ben 158;Caroline 118; Carrie 136;Eliza N.145; Emory 158;Henry 158; Joshua 59,163;Lee 158(w); N.C.61,118,126,145(W); Mrs.N.C.120,145;Oliver 158; *172,214.
SKIPPER:*171
SLATER:*174,200,228,237
SLAUGHTER:J.C.44;
SLAY:Hasty 159
SLEDGER:R.166
SLOAN:S.M.62,63;W.F.138.
SMITH:Abram F.3,4,9;Albert 130;Alfred E.3,4;Andrew 53, 54,69,70;Angela 53,54;Anna 35,130;Anolura 151;Ben 155 (w);B.W.159;Cath.53,54;Chas. H.6,62;Clark 81;Dr.C.P.148; Debey 108;D.L.69;ED.M.89;E. L. 80,81;Evelina 3; Fanny 142, 159;Frances 155;Gracie 159; Geo.M.159;Greenway 136; G.W. 155;Mrs.Harry 121;Irene 155; Isabel 53,54;J.73;Jack 68;Jas. D.34,35,80,81,161;Jas.M.76, 102,138,151;Jos.35, 81;Jno. 108,159(w);J.T.69,77;Kate 54; L.Pink 118,137,145; Lucinda 83; Mamie 165;Marg.53,54;Mary E. 134;Mattie 81;M.Georgie 158(w); Milton 165;Morton J.159; Nancy 159(w);Nanny B.135;Reuben 103; Sarah 68,118;Sidney R.31;S. Myra 3;Wm.81;Wm.F.1,12,19, 20,53,80,81; *170,171,175, 178,181,184,185,187,194, 196,198,205,217,229,230, 233,237,238.
SMITHDALE:Geo.H.135;
SMYTHE:Ella 152;Jas.S.147;Dr.J.D. 120,145,146,147;Jennie 135; Mrs.M.S.120;Roscoe 147;Sadie L. 147;Sallie J.147(w). *174
SNIDER:Aley A.158;Henry 158; Willie P.158;Wm.F.158;
SNOWBERGER:H.M.105; *206
SNOWDEN:*178,239.
SOMMERS:Herr.89,125,129;Ludw. P.137;Maggie 135;*184
SOUTHALL:*221

SPARKS:Jesse 97;S.H.97;
SPEKTER:*169
SPENCE:Mary 87,98;Thos. 87,98; *199
SPENCER:Caesar 98;*198
SPIARS-SPIER:GIB.M.JR.144; Kate 120;R.H.120,133; *176,197,235.
SPINGARN:Sadie P.165(w); Sigmond 165;
SPINKS:Mr.148
SPIVEY:*227,234;
SPRIGGS:*180
SPROTT:*214
SPROULDS:S.E. 16;
SPURGEON:*188
STAFFORD:E.K.86;
STAMPS:Isaac 35.Lucinda 35;
STANDEFER:Rev.133; *215;
STANDARD:S.T.106; *230
STANLEY:Joe 98;
STANTON:Aaron 160;Annie 135;David 160;Fannie M.160, 127;J.M.160;Saml.W.160; *191
STARLING:Annie J.152;Chas. 131,152,154;Lyne 122; Maria H.122;Mary C.131;Wm. 122,128;
STAUT:*172
ST.CLAIR:A.M.62
STEELE:*180,201.
STEIN:Julius 102
STEINER:J.73;
STEINBERG:*206
STELL:*231
STERLING:Chas.164;J.B.82, 96(w)97,102;Jas.S.96; Julia Anna 102,103;Louisa 102;Mary C.82,96,102,103, 134;Penelope 96,102;Sarah Hannah 119;Wm.H.97.
STERN:B.106;Mrs.Fannie 120;
STEVENS:*171,194,201,234.
STEVENSON:*191
STEWART:G.W.62;Jno.63;Steph. 98,Venus 115;*185.
STINSON:J.A.147;Kate 125;W.B. 125; *170,179,182,225, 228,229.
STOCKWELL:*205
STONE:Alf.H.135,156;Alice 134; C.S.36,37,38,80;David L.37; Jas.28,40;Josh.W.37,38;Kate 37;Marg.A.111;Mary W.40; Miss 123;Owen 37;W.W.37; *171,174,200,211;
STOREY:Rev.132
STORM:Edw.130; *200

STOUT:*228
STOVALL:Addie 133;Dr.133; Lyman 91(w); *216
STRAND:*183
STRAUSS:Gerson 124,169;
STRATTON:Caroline M.156;
STRAUGHTER:Albert 166; Lucy 166;Matilda 166; Sandy 166;Susie 166;
STRAUTHER:Jno.W.163; *174.
STREAM:Rebecca S.164(w)
STRICKLAND:Rev.133;
STUART:Willa 134;*234
SUGGS:*174,178
SULKE:Bernard 118
SULLIVAN:*206
SUMMERS:W.J.62,163(w);
SUTTON:Amelia 56;Amy 160; Allen 160(w);Ben H.130; Caroline 57;Emma W.57, 58;Mattie 160;Pete 160; Sarah 57,133;Stephen 57 Thos.58,77;Va.57;Vicky 160;Willie 57;Wm.57,58; *181,207,212.
SWAIN:S.R.118; *182,220
SWAN:Gilbert 25;
SWANNER:*219
SWANSON:J.G.79
SWARTZ:Mrs.Bertha 130; Simon 130;
SWE(E)DEN:Caroline 150; Evey 150;Geo.M.150(w); Geo.151;Jno.151;Harriet 150;Martha 150;Mary 150;Wm.151; *204
SWEENEY:Thos.93;
SWISHER:Annie A.160; Mary 160(w);
SWITZER:JNO.T.48,106; Jno.T.48,106;Nannette 48 85,106,108; *203
SYKES:I.H.133;Lyda 150
SYLVESTER:Mrs.J.A.154

TABOR:*219
TALLEY:Robt.147
TAMPLIN: Eugenia 40;Jno.K 40;Mary Lou 40;Olivia 40;Marg.V.40;Zach.40;
TANN:Bertha A.167;Reub. R.167(w);
TANNER:*214,215,217.
TARPLEY:C.S.138;
TATE:Chaunc.161;Eug.161; Flor.161;Gracie 161;How. 161;Isaac 161;Minnie 162 Sibyl 162;Willie J.161;

TATLEY:Ellen 93;Jno.93;J.S. 93;Lambert 93;
TAYLOR:A.62;D.D.67;D.S.138; Easter 71;Edmund 134;Ed.T. 22;Mrs.E.H.131;Eliz.2;Mrs. G.A.96;Harrison 25;Hinton 127;H.L.159;Hudson A.40, 74;Jane 32;Jessie C.159;Jos. 67;L.L.1;Mary 153;N.C.138; N.S.160;Poldo 71;Reuben 25; Robt.71;Saml.11;Saml.T.21, 22,23,32,36,39;Sanford 25; Susan P.1,121;Wm.H.50;Wm.R. 145;*172,173,176,179, 181,184,198,199,203, 205,239.
TEAMAN *172
TEAT:Mrs.69;
TEE:*169
TEMA:*206
TEMPLE:Lucy E.157;Susan 157;
TENANT:*176,178.
TERNEY:A.J.82;
TERRY:Amelia 57;Wm.H.57
THAMES:*233
THEOBALD:H.B.66,71,119;
THIGPEN:J.M.158;
THOMAS:B.R.35;Britton 81,82; E.H.115;E.N.152;G.W.33,39, 47,48;Imogene 152(w);Jas.W. 47,48;Joe R.152;Lloyd 135; Mary 143,152;Mattie 150,152; Nellie 112;Rev.137;R.W.74,94, 95;S.B.152;S.G.164;*173, 179,180,185,189,204,225;
THOMPSON:Emory B.109;Ermeline 4;Green 25;Jane 163;Jno.B.127; Julius 41;Manluis 25;Mary 4,102, 103,133;Wm.25;*178,198, 207,210,216.
THORNTON:Chas.166;Emma 166(w); *182
THRAIN:Anna M.155;Danl.155;
THREAT:Robt.T.157;Wm.157;
TILLEY:C.B.53,54;Mary V.54;
TILLFORD:Claud.W.128;Gracie 128; Robt.128,131;R.W.145;
TILLMAN:Allie A.158(w);Annie B. 114;Bobbie 158;Hattie 157;J.A. 75,77,114;Jeff.109,112,114; Wm.157(w),158;*229
TILLOTSON:W.W.133,135;
TINKOR:Jos.6;
TINSON:Green 25;
TOAL:*228
TODD:Miller 136;
TOLER:*218.
TOOF:Jno.s.24;
TOOMBS:R.S.112;*184.

TOUCHBERRY:*196
TOY:I.N.117;
TRABUE:Daisey 161;Geo.161; Otto 161;Marian R.161; Maud 161;Rauza F.161;
TRACEY:Rich.149;
TRAMMILL:Hattie 91;Jeff 91;
TREADWAY:*233,234,235.
TRIBBETT:W.H.161(w);
TRIGG:A.B.62,88(w);B.C.167; Ellen 135;Mary 88;M.H.161; Nannie 151;Susan P.88;W.R. 3,16,48,73,88,105,131,163;
TRIM:*212
TRIPLETT:*193;
TRIPP:*178
TRISBON:*183
TSONG:*201
TUCKER:Bev 25;*183,202, 220,234.
TUGGLES:Alice 160;And.160;
TULLEDGE:Fannie C.72;Wm.R. 72;
TUNE:*220
TUPPER:C.H.10;Mrs.Fred 123;
TURNBULL:Andw.17;Chas.R.16, 17;Rose S.16,17;*187, 200,203.
TURNER:A.R.141;Dr.E.R.121; Geo.D.164;Jacob 52;Sadie 164;Sam 167;Squire,Jr. 37,38;Thos.J.B.97;V.H.136; *170,178,182,214.
TUTHILL:A.H.144;
TUTT:W.G.98;
TYREE:E.P.20,21;

UHL:Clara P.118;Jos.146(w);
ULAN:F.Y.66;
ULBRICH:E.A.A.89;Fred.W.89;
UNDERWOOD:Bennie 160;Chas. 160;Sam 160;Violet 160(w);
URGUHART:Alice R.141,154; Chas.T.141;Corinne 133;Mrs. E.C.118;Elise 141,154;Jno.A. M.118;Isabel W.141,154;
UZZELL:*194

VALLIANT:Frank 19,56,79,150; L.B.19,40;Louise 137;Marian 19; Mary 134;Tenie W.108,117,150; *180
VALLARD:*201
VAN ALLEN:Mary A.45;
VANDEVENDER:*197
VANNAMEN:*231
VANNESS:Emily 156;
VAN NORMAN Cyrenus 139;Eliza E. 139;Jas.V.139;Lula W.139;

VAN NORMAN:(cont.)Mary 139;Robt.L.139;Thos. B.139;
VARIEN:Julius 2,26;
VASILICO:*185
VAUGH(A)N:C.A.150;Edith 137;Geo.W.13,36;Sallie 152;*209,220.
VAUGHT:Mary 137;Rosa 152;
VEACH:Louisa V.139,156;
VERNON:Chas.6;
VICK:Annie 7;Geo.7;Henry 7;Mary B.7;
VINCENT:H.G.130;Mary 130;
VORMUS:Alb.105,128,169; Louis 105,145;

WACHSMAN:*169
WADE:Geo.119;Lawr.T.114; Lillian 114;*177,182, 193,222,233.
WADDELL:A.M.116;Edm.147; Geo.C.116;G.M.116;
WAGEMON:Louisa 125;
WAIT(E)S:Jas.135;Kate 135; *214
WAKEFIELD:*200
WALCOTT:Betty C.12,13,14, 15;E.D.163;Jeanette 15; T.G.12,13,14,15,68,75, 78;*232
WALDAUER:Abe 164;Edith 132;Jos.139,166;Lillie 132;Louis 132,139,166; Henry 166(w);
WALKER:Annie 143;Chas.G. Eaddie 165;Geo.D.143;Jas S.37,81,138;J.L.65;M.H. 24;Marc.143;P.M.23,24; Sarah 142;Simon 165(w); *183,191,200,220.
WALLACE:David 36;H.C.163 (w);Jas.36;Jno.P.107; Lillie 163;Marian 106;Pat 106,107;W.M.58,106, 107;*185,198
WALLIS:E.A.4,5;JNO.4,5; Marian 4,5;Wm.A.4,5;
WALSH:Carrie A.121;M.E. 121;Pat 105;*172
WALTERS:Fridonia 4;Harv. W.4;*185
WALTON:Ben 163;
WALUE:G.P.83(w);Maggie 83;Y.J.83;
WARD:Alex 164,167(w); Geo.W.30,59,72,163; J.P.163;Jno.W.78,131; Willie A.167;*173,206

*Naturalization,Guardianship,Cemetery   Records - Surname Indexed

WARE:Eleanor P.68;
WAREFIELD:Alice D.23;Carneal 79;Thos.B.17,23,79,80,131, 154(w);
WARING:*175,176.
WARNER:Laura 163;
WARREN:Agnes 9;Jno.8,9,10; Nelson 12,13,14;Phil 8,9; Sarah 14;Thos.W.81,90;Wm. 8,9,10; *199.
WASHINGTON:Belle 79;Caroline 163(w);FANNY 95;Green 163; Mattie 165;R.L.159;*170,201
WASSON:Ben F.137,149,152, 160,163,168;D.C.121;Mrs. D.C.135;*183
WATERS::Danl. 67;H.124;Jno. H.136;Mrs.N.C.124;
WATDON:W.S.167;
WATKINS:*181
WATSON:Bob 98;H.C.140,142, 143,149,153,157,167;Lamar 152;L.C.152;*175,176, 183,239.
WAYNE:M.28;
WEATHERS:*182,202,208
WEAVER:*169,216,235.
WEBB:J.G.133;*199,222
WEB(B)ER:L.T.33;*237
WEBSTER:Irene 154;
WEDDINGTON:*182
WEED:Maria 73;
WEEKS:*232
WEEMS:Bessie 118;Julia 118; Mrs.Mary B.118;S.B.148; Squire 118;*223
WEILENMAN:*213
WEILER:Wm.N.71
WEIMER:*216
WEINBERG:*169
WEISS:Hannah 110,128;Jake 110;Irena 58,59;L.D.110, M.67,110,134;Soloman 58,59;
WEITZENFIELD:L.63;
WELLER:*196
WELLS:Alice 163;David 163(w); Emma V.165(w);J.A.34;Jno.H. 165;Mamie 165;Mollie 106; Oscar 165;*178.
WERLIEN:R.H.157;
WERNER:*206
WEST:Amelius C.36,40,70,103; Mrs.A.C.33;Carrie 36;Chas.H. 126;E.Winston 40,63,70,103, 121;H.R.39,40,41,70;Jennie D.103;Lizzie 40,70;Mary D. 126;Sallie 46,70;Va.O.41,70; *170,172,190,227,237.
WESTON:---14,15;

WESTBROOK:Jacob 84,85,113; J.W.45,76;Matilda 84,85,113; Saml.84,85,113;Westly 84;
WETHERBEE:D.J.24;Percie 135; *176,177,184,205;
WHALEN:Jennie 165
WHEATLEY:Emma 42;Geo.147,158; Mary146,147,158;Mrs.92;W.B. 42;*173,174,175,180.
WHEELER:Clintha 158;M.158(w); *236
WHILDEN:Mary M.156;
WHITE:Caroline 96;Chas.S.114; Mrs.Chas.92;Frank 163;Geo.96; Ida 114; Dr.S.66,96;S.F.30,79; *177,178,179,191,236.
WHITEANS:*184
WHITEHEAD:Doc 63;
WHITEWAY:Alb.86,87,98,99; Ellen 86,87,99;
WHITFIELD:Benj.2;Lucy 2;
WHITLEY:*184
WHITTLE:*172
WICKLIFFE:Mrs.A.F.119
WICKS:M.R.165;
WIGGINS:*184
WILDER:Geo.G.36;Jos.S.88;
WILE:*175,177
WILHELM:Geo.149
WILKERSON:A.G.37;Eliz.123; Henry B.159;Jeff 123; Louisa 37;*207
WILKES:*194
WILKINS:M.A.141,154(w); *217
WILKINSON:Chas.L.137;G.W.148; *191
WILLIAMS:Amanda 25;Anna 156; Bell 167;Caroline 156;C.H.164; Chas.150(w),156,164;Cora 136;Mrs.C.M.119;Dan 32,33, 129;Emma J.A.71;E.W.164,165; Fanny 156;G.71;Granvil 158; Henry 42,43,166;Irene 156; Jas.141;J.B.42;J.C.43;J.E.164; Jno.71;Kate 156;Lida 133;L.R. 152;Marg.94,95;Mary 156(w); M.A.42;Merritt 156;Nancy 42; Oliver.60;Prince 162(w);Rebecca 127;Ruth 156;R.W.57;Spellinger 158;Thos.42,44,120,166; *171, 174,179,180,184,191,196, 201,218,223,225,230,234.
WILLIAMSON:Betsy 81,82;Char.82; Gab.81,82;Jac.81,82; *212,226.
WILLIFORD:Sam T.92
WILLIS:*207,212
WILLS:Minnie Lee 39,40;Sallie 39,40, 43;Mrs.Wilton 39,40;Wm.S.39,40;
WILMOT:Mans.44; *237

WILSON:Adelia 115;Amelia 115;Annie 73,161Betty 29,73,161;Eugene 115; Floyd 166;Jennie 147; Jeremiah 26;J.H.59;Julia 166(w);Jas.37(w)38;Jno. 115;Louisa 37;Mary 73, 161;N.W.37,38;Ruben166 Saml.147;Sarah 115;S.D. 166;Thomp.37;Thos.29, 73;Wm.B.144;*170, 182,204,211.
WILZIN:L.152;Nath.125;
WILZINSKI:Estella 141;Frank 142;Herman141;Jake 141 Julia 141;Joe 59,83,124, 141(w);Joel 142;L.58; Nathan141;Percy 142; Sadie J.141; *170,171
WINCHESTER: *172
WINDHAM: *227
WINDSOR:David 26;F.R.26.
WINEMAN:Alb.G.153(w);Alb. V.153;Jennie 153;Lawr. 153;Mary 153;Otto 153; Parker 153;Robt.153; Susie 153;*175
WINFORD:A.S.153
WINGFIELD:Anna 46;A.P.46, 148;Bowdrie 46;F.G.46;Frk. 46;J.W.41;Mattie 147;Walt. 46;W.J.46; *226.
WINN:E.S.3,49;Jas.B.49; Louella 49;Martha 0.150; O. 3,39,166;Rich.M.39; Saml.150;*178
WINPEGLER:J.W.45,76;Mary 45;*236.
WINSLOW:C.160
WINSTON:Emma 166;*179
WINTER:B.T.142;C.A.130; Mrs.N.T.129;Wm.S.127; *219.
WINZBERG:Sey.132.
WIRTH:A.A.107;
WISE:*180,190.
WITHERSPOON:*209
WITNEY:Louis A.155;
WITKOWSKI:Flora 109;G.58, 109,110;Lula 109,110; Clarence 110;Sadie 110;
WITT:Clar.110;Flora 110; Lula 136;Sadie 110;
WITTE:*220
WOLF(E):Bella137;C.W.59, 65;Gust.102;Jas.E.47; Katie 137;
WOODBURN:Jno.R.25;
WOODRUFF:Paul 82,95;

*Naturalization,Guardianship,Cemetery   Records - Surname Indexed

WOODFORK:Walter 167;Willie 167;W.W.164;
WOOD(S):Benson 78;Emile P. 136;Houston D.134;Mrs. Houston 126;S.H.114;Virgil 78;Wm.114,148; *171, 173,181,182,185,210, 216,225,236.
WOODSON;Jno.A.38;
WORD: *185
WORDEN:Geo.42;Julia R.42;
WORSHAM:O.A.159;
WORTHAM:Mrs.E.R.124;
WORTHINGTON:Amanda 11,40, 149;Ann 108,149;Arlense 149;Ben T.94,108,117;Carrie 133;Chas.T.84,98,113,149, 168;Edna 149;Edw.T.8,129, 149(w),168;Elley 94;Flournoy 149;Frances M.133;Geo.133; Isaac M.108,117;Jas.Ann 108; Lillie 149;Mary 11;Saml.10,11, 40,55,56,85,101,168;Thos. 108,117,149;Wm.117;Wm.M. 10,11,123;Wm.W.8,40,149, 168;Mrs.w.W.119; *176,180
WRIGHT:A.L.142;Cald.117;Flor.E. 142;G.G.142;J.Price 117,124; J.W.142;Maggie 149;R.L.142(w); T.W.166;*177,178,180,181, 182,184,236.
WREN: *219
WULF:Henry F.132;
WYATT:Eliz.D.108;
WYCHE:Dev.137;Mrs.Julia D.125;
WYNN:J.H.132,150,160,161,163, 166,168'; *195.

YAGER:Geo.A.129;Lula 127; Mary 127;
YARBROUGH: *223
YATES:A.D.166
YERGER:Alex 19,94;Carrie 134; Eliz.B.19;Hal 124,126;Harry 25;Henrietta 19;Jas.Allen 119, 147;Jas.R.119; Jennie 146,147, 158;Jimmie 146;J.S.4,126;Malv. 19; Mary 24;Mary H.104,119; Mary L.24,146,147;Rebecca 112; Sallie 25,124;W.4,112,128,142; Wm.17,19,23,34;Wm.G.(Shrf.)2,17, 104,109,112,119,124,126,127, 146(w)147;Wm.G Jr.146;Wm.N.146, 147,158(w);Wm.S.19; *185,204.
YEARMANS:Alb.139
YORK: *219
YOUNG:Anna 62;Caroline C.67;C.R. 145;Danl.E.94;D.L.122;Fannie 145;Jane 166;J.H.67;Louisa N. 12;Mary 122;Mattie A.94;Paul 145;Viola 145; *174,178, 198,205.
YOUNGBLOOD: *193,195.

ZADEK:I. 137
ZEIGLER: *183,210.

*Naturalization,Guardianship,Cemetery   Records - Surname Indexed

www.ingramcontent.com/pod-product-compliance
Lightning Source LLC
Chambersburg PA
CBHW030546080526
44585CB00012B/281